# MOTHERLESS

# MOTHERLESS

FROM BESTSELLING CATHOLIC AUTHOR OF "FATHERLESS"

## BRIAN J. GAIL

Visit Human Life International on the Web at:
www.hli.org
or call 800-549-5433
to order copies of *Motherless*.

Printed in the United States of America

ISBN 978-1-55922-063-7


Gail, Brian J.
  Motherless / Brian J. Gail.

*To my wife, Joan, my partner in all things
and the greatest mother I've ever known.*

# 1

---

John Sweeney hung up the phone and jumped to his feet, knees creaking in protest. He was running late. *Relax*, he told himself, *Mom isn't going anywhere.*

It was almost 5:30 p.m. and the sun was already in for the night. He grabbed a Philadelphia Eagles windbreaker, a gift from an assistant coach and parishioner, and headed out the door. A light snow was falling. For an instant he thought about going back for a hat. *Forget it. You're late. Keep your feet moving.*

He bounded down the rectory steps and in moments crossed Windsor Avenue. He eyed the Narbrook movie marquee ... and shuddered. *Ah yes ... Sunday's sermon.* He stopped at the light at Haverford and waved to Lance Clemons across the street who was returning from the city and a day's work as a chemical engineer. They'd played semi-pro baseball together in their youth. "If I don't see you at the 10:15 this Sunday, I'm knocking on your door, lefty."

Clemons ducked his head and gently beat his breast in a pantomimed mea culpa, then looked up and smiled.

"Father, are you going to do anything about that movie? It's been two weeks now!" demanded Anne Marie Pavoni, head of St. Martha's Sodality, as she rushed out of the corner pharmacy and was now almost on top of him. "I'm on it, Anne Marie," he said, tight lipped. He made a mental note to be gentle with her husband, George, the next time he saw him in the confessional.

He crossed the bridge covering the railroad tracks and turned onto Winchester road. He noted he was breathing heavily. *Not taking care of yourself, padre; gotta get off your butt and do something … anything.* He climbed the three steps leading to the porch and, to his surprise, found the front door slightly ajar. He entered a home both dark and cold. A single light in the kitchen allowed him to see his breath. In the center of the living room was his mother's bed; she lay in it as though entombed.

"Mom! Where's Eileen?"

"I'm cold."

John approached and took his mother's hand, a multi-fingered ice pop. "Mom, where is Eileen?" he repeated, slowly and loudly. Vacant eyes stared back.

He found a light, then another, then the thermostat in the dining room which he jacked up as high as it would go. He went upstairs and found one of his sister's sweaters and an old house coat and returned to his mother's bedside. He lifted her twice, gently, to wrap her in the clothing. He found two blankets in the hall closet and bundled them around her.

"Who are you?"

"It's John, Mother."

"Are you the one who was killed?"

"No, Mother, that was Peter."

"Why doesn't he ever come to see me?"

"Because he's in heaven and they have very strict rules about visitations."

"Oh well, what are you going to do, shoot the swans, those loverlies?"

"It'll be warm in a few minutes, Mother."

"Where's your father?"

"He's in heaven too."

"I always told him, 'If you die first, I'll kill you,'" she laughed.

"You scared him to death."

"Now, your father's alive and I'm dead, right?"

"Yes, that's right, Mom."

"Why doesn't anybody come visit me?"

"Barry and Kevin and Brendan were all just in a few weeks ago for Christmas; brought their families too."

"I must have been away."

"As soon as they showed up, you headed out of town with a younger man."

She laughed. "When are you going to find a younger man for Eileen?"

"Whenever I find Eileen."

John heard the front door open and shut, and from the hallway, "Why is it so cold in here?" It was his sister, Eileen. She approached the bed. "Oh, Mom! You're shivering." She looked at John accusingly.

"I just got here. The front door was open." *Thank you, Lord, for a celibate priesthood.*

"Oh My God ... it must have blown open when I left."

Softly, "Why did you leave, Eileen?"

"Mrs. Owsik fell. She broke her hip. I waited with her till the ambulance arrived."

*Another 30 minutes and the driver could have saved himself a trip back.* "Well, we were lucky Mom wasn't dancing around with her clothes off like she usually does before dinner."

Laughter rose from the slight figure in the bed. "Where's your father?"

"Dunno. He came in, turned the lights and thermostat off, opened the windows and doors, and took off. Didn't say where he was going."

"John!" Eileen admonished, then patiently: "Dad's in heaven, Mom, waiting for you."

"When am I going?"

"When hell freezes over, Mom. In about another 15 minutes."

"Oh, don't listen to him, Mother. Those sons of yours! As you always said … together they're the one wit."

"Who are my sons?"

"John and Barry and Kevin and Brendan; Peter's in heaven with Dad."

"What happened to Peter?"

"Some bad men flew a plane into his building in New York and he died."

"Maybe they were lost, I don't know."

"They *were* lost, Mom," John said quietly.

"Where's John?"

"I'm right here, Mom."

"Are you the liberal?"

"No, that's Kevin; he's in Portland."

"What about Barry?"

"He's in California."

"I always said Barry was born in California."

"Who's the other one?"

"Brendan, Mom; he's in Texas."

"I don't remember him."

"We don't either."

"John!" Eileen screeched. "Brendan's with the FBI, Mom. He has two little girls. He's a wonderful son."

"I'm going to slit my wrists."

"Mother, don't talk like that! John and I are right here — and always will be."

"That's why she wants to slit her wrists," John interjected.

"What's the matter with me?"

"Nothing, Mother," Eileen said tenderly. "You just… forget things sometimes."

"Oh there's nothing wrong with my memory. John, Peter, Barry, Kevin, Brendan, Rosemary, and Eileen. See!"

"Yeah, but what about our SAT scores?"

"What?"

"Don't pay any attention to him, Mom. I'm going to go get dinner ready. Just ignore everything John says."

She laughed. "John was my first born. Whatever happened to him?"

John cleared his throat and leaned close to his mother and whispered, "No woman would have him … so he became a priest."

"That's a shame. What do you suppose was wrong with him?"

"He was a mama's boy."

"Oh. I wonder who his mother was."

"She was a saint."

"Is she in heaven?"

"Not yet. Soon."

"Will I go to heaven?"

"It's an absolute certainty."

"You don't know."

"Of course I do. I know everything."

The shrunken figure in the bed waved a semi-frost bitten hand dismissively. "Where is the knight in shining armor you promised Eileen?"

"He's on his way."

"That's what you always say."

"I speak only truth. Remember, I'm a priest."

"You're a priest!?"

"Yes, but don't tell the others."

She laughed, "I won't. They wouldn't believe me."

"What's the matter with me?"

"The matter!? You're the most beautiful woman in the world. The paparazzi hound you; the press follows you wherever you go; fans are constantly coming to your front door demanding autographs. Who wouldn't feel a little … confused … now and then …"

She laughed. "You make me laugh. I always said: 'laughter is the best medicine.'"

"Well, Pop always liked to laugh too. Know why?"

"Why?"

"Because it was free; he was cheap."

She laughed. "I wonder what he did with all that money he saved."

"He took it with him."

She laughed. "Don't be silly. You don't need money in heaven."

"Nobody told him."

"I told him! Time and again I told him."

"Yeah, well, apparently he was convinced there'd be a cover charge for Happy Hour."

Silence.

"Why don't my rotten kids ever visit? I want to slit my wrists."

"They do, Mom. They call. They send flowers. They visit. They're very good to you."

"Is someone writing all that down?"

"No, Mom. None of us can write."

She laughed. "I told you to study. You never obeyed."

"It was all a misunderstanding."

Eyes vacant, staring.

"You preached faith, family, education; we thought you said faith, family, *recreation*."

Nothing.

John bent over and kissed his mother on the forehead. "Gotta run, Mom. See you tomorrow."

"Tomorrow?"

"Yes, Mom."

"You come every day?"

"Yes, Mom."

"Oh good! If you didn't I would slit my wrists?"

"Oh no you wouldn't."

"I wouldn't?"

"No, by the time you found a razor … you'd forget why you wanted it …"

She laughed. "I love you."

"Love you too, Mom."

John turned and saw Eileen observing from the hallway. Tears were spilling down her cheeks. "I'm so sorry, John. I'll never leave her again. Ever."

"'Ever' is probably about six months, Weenie."

"What are we going to do?"

"Nothing. We just wait – and pray."

"John, we can't extend this suffering. It's horrific."

"We're getting ahead of ourselves. I'll make sure we're properly advised when the time comes."

"The Church won't make us stick tubes in her and have her live like a vegetable, will they?"

"No." *Please God!* John Sweeney hugged his sister and left; outside, he bundled up, descended the porch steps and headed back to St. Martha's rectory in the falling snow.

His tears ran warm on cold cheeks.

# 2

The large auditorium was filled beyond capacity. The sense of anticipation, building slowly over the past hour, was now palpable. Nervously, Maggie Kealey entered the room from its rear and began making her way through the crowd; at the sight of her, the applause started. Hands reached out to touch her; several men stooped to hug her. Others shouted encouragement. As the cacophony grew, she climbed the steps to the stage and headed toward the podium; the cheers swelled. She felt goose bumps running up and down her arms, back and spine. She laid her notes on the riser and adjusted the microphone. The room was now pulsing with sound and motion. *My lord, so this is what a revival feels like.*

Twice she tried to begin only to stand by helplessly as the clamor rose to new plateaus. She leaned into the microphone a third time, determined: "Thank you. Thank you. Thank you very much."

The room grew quiet in stages. Maggie waited. From the back, a voice: "We love you, Maggie!"

Pandemonium.

She motioned emphatically with both hands to restore order. "I love you too, all of you. But if we don't get some work done we'll have to take this party to a soup line."

Silence.

"I'm profoundly humbled to be your new CEO. This institution, our Regina Hospital, is one of Philadelphia's most prized and enduring community treasures. Five generations of South Philadelphians have entered these doors in search of healing for all manner of illnesses and maladies. They came, many of them, without the ability to pay, trusting that the good sisters would find a way to love them back to health. That we're all here today, standing on the stooped shoulders of hundreds of those nuns and thousands of their dedicated doctors and nurses and administrators, is a tribute to how deeply they loved and how well they healed."

She paused and allowed her eyes to sweep the crowd.

"Now it's our turn. We face a daunting task. The world of patient care has changed ... forever. We are confronted with challenges none of our predecessors could have imagined. Over 90 percent of our patients are on Medicaid. Government reimbursements account for less than half our costs. We are forecast to lose over $20 million this year. The Order of the Regina has told me they will continue to provide subsidies for as long as they can. But we all know those subsidies depend on cash transfers from our sister subsidiary, Catholic Health Insurance Corp. We are now in the beginnings of a political season. There is talk of significant health care reform. Those transfers, our subsidies, may well be threatened by legislated reform." Pause. "None of us can know how all of that is going to play out.

"We can't control the unknown. So we will waste no energy trying. What we can control is the level of care we provide each and every day ... to each and every patient who walks through our doors. And, every bit as importantly, we can control the way we organize ourselves to provide that care."

She paused again and modulated her voice.

"Twenty years ago, as many of you know, I was a patient in this hospital. I came to Regina Hospital, the least convenient of all my options, because there was an extraordinary young doctor on staff by the name of ... Jim Gillespie; Dr. Gillespie, at the time, was in the early stages of developing a national reputation for treating women with breast cancer. I was sick and I was frightened. I couldn't contemplate dying and leaving five young children, particularly as a single mother."

Maggie paused and smiled. "And, truth be known, I didn't much like the idea of living the rest of my life with ... ah ... less of me than I walked in this hospital with."

Raucous laughter.

"When you gonna marry that man!?" said a voice from the middle of the auditorium.

The room exploded.

Maggie waited for the din to die down, smiled coyly and said: "As you know it is official Hospital policy *not* to comment on ... potential mergers."

More bedlam.

Off in a corner, a distinguished looking physician in an immaculate white smock turned beet red.

*Get control. Now.* "Over these past 20 years Regina Hospital doctors and nurses have arrested the spread of breast cancer in over a thousand women from all over the city and beyond. I was just lucky to be one of them. It is my intention to build on that legacy and to expand it. Today, on my first day as Regina's new CEO, I'm happy to announce the opening, this fall, of The Regina Women's Clinic." Pause. "Think of it as a kind of hospital within a hospital. RWC will focus exclusively on women's health issues. We will become a premiere destination for women suffering from breast and cervical and ovarian cancer, diabetes and heart disease related to obesity, drug and alcohol addictions, and physical and emotional abuse."

Long, sustained applause.

"This will do two important things for Regina Hospital: *one,* it will permit us to reflect the changing needs of this community; these problems are now all but pandemic in this part of the city and no one is adequately addressing them. *Second*, it will permit us to change our payer mix. It will allow us to attract customers who carry health insurance from large third party payer networks. This will mean we will be able to do something we haven't been able to do in this hospital for a very long time: to charge patients what it actually costs to heal them."

Perfunctory applause.

"I'm also delighted to announce that Dr. James Gillespie will oversee The Regina Women's Clinic ..." Tentative applause. "... and Beatrice Masterson will replace me as Head of Nursing." Bedlam. One of their own had broken through a granite ceiling. An elderly maintenance man in the middle of the room held a boom box high over his head and the crowd began to dance to Sister Sledge's *We Are Family*.

Maggie looked over to the corner where Jim Gillespie was standing. Next to him was a woman in a plain white blouse and dark blue skirt. It was Kathleen Sullivan, the head of the Order of the Regina. Her eyes were wide and expressionless.

Maggie motioned the crowd quiet. If there were any dissenters among staff or the Order itself upon hearing of her promotion ... they were not in evidence this morning. "On behalf of Jim and Bea, I ask for your help. Regina Hospital and The Women's Clinic cannot ... *will not* ... succeed unless each of you does three things in the coming year."

Total silence.

"One, treat every patient who walks through our doors as family."

Heads nod in unison. "Yeah baby. We gonna do that ..." a man in the back yelled.

"Two, treat each other as you treat patients."

Uneasy silence. Another voice from the back: "Now y'all gone too far ..." Loud, raucous laughter. "Too far. She gone too far ..."

Maggie smiled and waited for the laughter to exhaust itself.

"And three ..." Pause. "Evangelize the mission! Tell your family and your neighbors about our new Women's Clinic. Tell them to talk it up to the people they work with ... and for ... especially those professional women with the fancy shoes in center city and the suburbs who are paying those expensive health insurance premiums!"

Spontaneous combustion – equal parts laughter, song, dance, and several head–bobbing choruses of 'Amens.'

Maggie searched for Kathleen Sullivan. Jim Gillespie had a large arm around her slender shoulders. The nun's eyes met Maggie's. They revealed ... nothing. Maggie smiled tightly. *You didn't think I had this in me, did you? You wanted a man. A doctor. An outsider ... whose hiring, when it was announced, would project an entirely new image beyond these walls, and revitalize this place from the inside, all in a single PR release. Well, let me tell you something, Sister, just wait till you see what I do with your hospital.*

She leaned into the microphone and silenced the crowd one last time. "All right!" she bellowed. "Everybody back to work ... while you still have a job!"

The crowd, over 400 strong, turned and began filing out bearing the sweet elixir of hope.

Maggie stepped away from the podium and turned to welcome the nursing staff, now rushing the stage.

# 3

___

arol Burns spoke first. "What would we do with all that
money?"

Michael eyed his wife from across the table at a tony
French restaurant in Old City. They were celebrating. "You'll do
what you do best ... spend as much of it as you can as fast as you
can ... establishing a new land record for total stores and dollars in
a contiguous three-day period. Whatever's left, I'll give the first
ten percent, maybe twenty percent, to charity ... and hope there's
enough left for me to ... who knows ... buy a new set of golf clubs."

Out of the dimness of soft dinner lighting came ... what ...
"*Une baguette*!?" It landed on the right pocket of Michael's suit
jacket. It was buttered.

"—or not," he added thoughtfully.

"How much did you say it was again?"

"Somewhere between 25 to 30 million dollars."

"How do people come up with such numbers?"

Michael waved a waiter over. "Seems Mrs. Burns needs
another drink. She's starting to talk business." The waiter, a man

who looked to be in his early fifties, smiled, nodded in Carol Burns' direction, and departed.

"Multiples."

"What are multiples?"

"They're value ranges. Every industry pretty much has their own. In the Advertising business, when times are good, as they are now, the average multiple is somewhere between six to eight times earnings. Pretax earnings."

"And what are—"

Michael quickly interrupted. "Pretax earnings are what the owners of a business are left with after they pay all their bills: salaries and health insurance, rent and utilities, computers and software, creative materials and free lancers, travel and entertainment, etc."

Carol's eyes squinted then began to glaze over. Michael loved the pure innocence. "Is it a done deal?" she asked.

"Pretty much."

"You signed!?"

"No. But I did agree in principle to a multiple of 7.5 ... contingent upon due diligence." Then quickly: "That means we sign after they review the books ... to make sure everything is as we represented it."

"They don't trust you!? Don't they know who you are?"

Michael nodded in affirmation. "Trust but verify. It's good business policy too."

"So, when do we get the money?"

"We'll get half up front, immediately upon signing; we'll take it in either cash or UltraCom stock; do you have a preference? The rest is what they call an 'earn out.' In our case, that'll be four years."

"What does that mean!?"

The waiter arrived with fresh drinks – a gin and tonic for Michael, a glass of Chablis for Mrs. Burns. Michael sipped and paused. "It means I'll have to continue working, and producing, for four more years ... if we want the other half."

"Well ... you're not ready to retire anyway."

"For better or worse ... but not for lunch?"

Carol Burns smiled coyly. "Something like that."

Dinner arrived, under brass cover, with two attentive escorts pausing ever so dramatically. Then, voila! A warm, dead fish looking none too happy about it … and something equally lifeless apparently removed from the 'center' of a steer. Michael looked up and smiled. "Hey, where's my pizza?" The young men looked at each other uncertainly … and headed back to the kitchen.

"Nobody gets your humor."

"You do."

"You're just like your father. Neither of you is funny."

"Well, he's dead. That's pretty funny given he thought he'd live forever."

Carol laughed despite herself. "Actually, he *did* make me laugh."

"And *I'm* going to make you absolutely giddy when I hand you a portfolio statement with another 12 to 15 million in it."

Carol Burns suddenly stared at her husband: "Why did this happen to us, Michael …?"

Silence.

Again. "I mean, why us? There's so many people who … who … work so hard and can't even get by. Why do some people get so … much?"

Michael cleared his throat. "It's a test. Like everything else in life. We'll have to account for every dollar. That's why I propose we start by giving the first 20%, after taxes, to charity. Maybe start a foundation. Who knows? Maybe that'll buy us some wiggle room with God if we get a bit carried away somewhere down the line …"

"Well, first, shouldn't we pay off our debts?"

"We don't have any debts."

"We have children … who have debts."

"My father always said, 'you don't do your kids any favor by spoiling them.'"

Carol Burns sniffed: "That's why he never tried?"

"That's one reason; the other is because he was cheap."

"Well, I'm not talking about paying off mortgages; just help-ing out with credit cards."

Michael felt his blood beginning to boil. "Been there, done that. *Before* they were married. Remember?"

Carol eased into her role as advocate for the profligate. "Everything is *sooo* expensive today. Who can afford anything? I don't know how the children are doing it ..."

"Apparently they're not." Pause. "And why am I hearing about this now?"

"I always have to wait until you're in a good mood."

"My ... mood ... is the issue!?"

"Michael, hush. People at the other tables are looking at us."

In a loud hushed voice: "What's the number?"

"What do you mean ... the number?"

"I mean what's the number? What's the total number in that beautiful head of yours? The number you brought with you into this restaurant?"

"Well I don't know ... I didn't add it all up ..."

Michael moaned softly. "Oh great. We need a calculator."

"It's not funny Michael. And I don't think you should be mak-ing fun of our children."

Exasperated. "Sweetheart, *I* can't always be the issue. Let's spread the joy around ... just for fun." Pause. "We've given those three girls as much private education as they could handle. We paid off their credit card debt so we could marry them off. Big numbers, remember? We paid for big, expensive weddings to pay for exotic honeymoons. We put big, expensive down payments on their first homes so they wouldn't have to, God forbid, rent flats. We even helped them furnish their homes, as I recall. Remember my den furniture? You gave away to Kate ... because her husband happened to like it!?" Pause. "Love, when does it end? Humor me. Please. Tell me there *is* an end!"

Brief silence. Then: "You should be glad the twins don't ask for anything."

"Honey, they're still home! Living with us. What in God's

name would they ask for ... a better menu? Better laundry service? Better ... what ... rents? *Free* is ... too much?" Pause. "Of course the boys aren't asking for anything ... yet. They haven't been seduced by expensive women ... yet."

Silence. Then, out of the silence ... not to mention the darkness ... this dart aimed at an unprotected carotid artery: "How can you talk about selling your company for $25 million one minute ... and quibble over $70,000 in credit card bills for your own daughters in the next?"

The next sound heard from the Burns' table seemed to surprise the other patrons. It was the sound of a man's head banging the table in cadenced sequence. The sound was unusually loud because the table was made of a high end imported cherry hardwood from the Amazon rain forest.

# 4

----

It sat in a mid-rise just off Route 30 about 20 miles west of the city; from the outside it looked like an oversized glass bird cage. Inside, it was 60,000 square feet of iron-pumping, bag thumping, cycle spinning, treadmill climbing, lap swimming, sauna sweltering, carbo burning, muscle toning madness. On work days, it filled at lunch time with all manner of body types from the executive suites above and below it. They came in search of the big heart pump and, perhaps, a hook up for a smaller heart pump on the weekend.

Off in a corner, so as not to disturb the concentration, if not the sensibilities, of its clientele stood a boxing ring. And in that boxing ring, stood the implausible figure of Joe Delgado. He was clothed in a sleeveless muscle shirt that accentuated his girth and a pair of oversized gym shorts. His back lay against the ropes and he was fidgety.

"Time!"

On cue, Delgado moved crab like to the center of the ring. His round shoulders hunched, chin tucked, and his large 12-ounce gloves gave every appearance of being a natural extension of his ample jowls. He tried to move his head as he had been taught, to no avail. His mind was elsewhere.

In a nanosecond he was jolted back to the here and now as a stinging left jab bounced off his forehead. "C'mon Mr. D. ... you gotta be here," Clarence Cribbs yelled, voice muffled through a black mouth guard. Cribbs danced away on surprisingly light feet, forcing his student to follow. Delgado, aroused, picked up the trail. Slightly wounded, he followed his prey into a corner where the instructor covered up; Delgado let fly with both hands. Grunting loudly, he pounded away, blows raining down on Cribbs' shoulders, arms, and mostly, gloves. Too late he realized his vulnerability. Feet wide apart in a flat horizontal stance, he offered his victim no point of resistance. Eyeing his student's feet from a crouch, Cribbs uncoiled a left hook which thumped against Delgado's chest, thrusting him backwards and, ultimately, onto the seat of his shorts.

Cribbs walked over and extended a gloved hand. Delgado reached for it. "How many times I gotta tell you, Mr. D. ... you can't stand that way. Anybody hit you when you like that, you fall. Never come out of your stance. Never. Okay?"

Delgado took in air quickly and said: "Remind me again. How much am I paying you to inflict this pain on me?"

Cribbs laughed and motioned Delgado to put his gloves up. Attention arrested, Delgado began throwing left jabs into Cribbs' headgear, even as the younger man retreated at alternate right and left angles. "Double up, double up," the instructor shouted. Delgado complied ... throwing two, three jabs at a time at his rapidly moving target.

Following his instructor out of a corner, Delgado saw an opening and threw a straight right at the left side of his instructor's head. Cribbs slipped it deftly and tapped Delgado smartly on his exposed chin. For several seconds, he was disoriented. Cribbs stopped. Another lecture. "Mr. D., how many times I gotta tell you ... you can't leave your chin exposed. It's where all the circuits are. Take a good one there, all the lights go out. If you throwin' that right, you got two choices: either it comes back real quick like this," Cribbs shifted his weight subtly, shot a short right from his shoulder and brought it back to guard position with astonishing suddenness. "Or … you gotta get that left hand, fast, to the right side of your chin, like this." The instructor threw his right and, seamlessly and simultaneously, covered his exposed chin with his left glove to protect against the counter.

"You see?"

"Si … CC."

Cribbs motioned Delgado's gloves up again and resumed the sparring at a slightly accelerated pace. A muffled horn went off at the three minute mark and Delgado went back to his corner and plopped himself down on a stool. His lungs immediately signaled him he had miscalculated. The early round flurry had required too much energy. He was now borrowing oxygen that would not be available in later rounds.

From across the ring he heard, "breathe deep: long, slow and deep."

Delgado nodded.

"You got three in ya today?"

Delgado nodded again. Sound required too much energy.

"Want me to give you an extra .30?"

Delgado shook his head emphatically.

"Whoo wheee … I got myself a warrior," Cribbs' grin was ear to ear.

Delgado gained control of his breathing and was surprised that the slight burning sensation in his lungs started to vanish.

"Tanks and jets, Mr. D.! We were a couple of tanks in there … first round; second round … I'm a be a jet. I be buzzin' all around you … makin' you move those feet."

Delgado groaned. His instructor's hands were so preternaturally quick, he couldn't pick up movement … until they had struck and were back in guard position. Clarence Cribbs was a little over six-feet tall and weighed 212 pounds. His body fat was said to be in the 7% range. He was 24-years-old. Fatigue, like quite a few other words, was not in his lexicon.

"Time!"

Delgado got up stiffly, wincing as he did, and moved to the center of the ring. True to his word, CC was immediately on his toes and darting in and out at angles - tapping Joe with piston-like lefts on the way in, straight rights on the way out. Delgado knew better than to chase; he stood in the center of the ring and waited. Occasionally, he'd flick a jab at the moving figure in front, beside and behind him, seldom making contact. Then, about two and a half minutes into the round, as Cribbs neared again, Delgado decided to time the first left hand that came toward him. It came quickly, but this time with his eyes on his instructor's chest, he picked up motion. He lacked the reflexes to slip the punch but saw an opportunity to counter it. At the moment of impact, he shifted his weight quickly and let fly with a straight right from his cheek over Cribbs' left before it could recoil. The punch caught Cribbs flush on the jaw as he was coming in. His headgear flew sideways, half off his head, and his legs buckled. Delgado clutched him quickly as he headed for the floor.

"Whoo whee! Whoo whee! I got myself a thumper!" Cribbs yelled from a sitting position. A dozen or so others on treadmills and stationary bikes stopped to behold the improbable sight of a student standing over his instructor. "Wow, just let me sit for a spell. Whoo whee! You can thump man!"

Delgado sat back down on his stool. He felt good. Not good enough, however, to answer a bell for round three within 60 seconds. He was breathing heavily. "How you doin' over there CC?"

Big sheepish grin. "Comin' atcha in a minute big boy. Just gotta dial down the ringin'."

Delgado, oxygen depleted, hoped that ringing continued, unabated, for at least … *oh the next 10 minutes*. But no sooner had he eased his sore back against the sagging ring ropes, it seemed, than his instructor was back on his feet yelling: "Time."

Delgado leapt off his stool to demonstrate a freshness both

men knew he did not possess. This prompted trash talking. "Uh oh. I'm in deep doo doo now. My thumper got his second wind. He comin' for ma *heaaad*." They traded jabs back and forth and CC was suddenly all angles and edges, flashing here and there, punches coming from anywhere and nowhere. The pace was suffocating and Joe started feeling a burning sensation in his lungs. At the two minute mark, he dropped his hands in exhaustion. Three quick, light jabs peppered his face. Back up went the gloves. With .30 seconds to go, he hit a wall. He couldn't go on. "Don't stop now, Mr. D! ... you almost home," CC yelled, popping him twice on the chest. Joe dug deep for one more flurry ... but came up empty. There was no oxygen left to borrow. He pitched forward in sections using his gloves to cushion the fall. He lay on the canvas prostrate, breathing heavily.

Clarence Cribbs threw his head and shoulders back and laughed; then he pulled his gloves off and slumped down beside his student. "You almost made it, Mr. D. Missed by ... oh, maybe 'bout .15 seconds."

Joe Delgado moaned softly. He'd set himself a goal and trained for three months; he wanted to go the distance ... a full three, three-minute rounds. The last several nights he'd lain in bed wondering if he could, would, make it. 'Making it' had suddenly become very important in his life. Slowly, he rolled over and held his gloves up. CC yanked them off. "Thank you, CC ..." he rasped.

"You changed colors, Mr. D. Nobody I know went from what you were ... to what you are now."

Joe grunted in appreciation. The words soothed his weary bones.

"What you at now?"

"226."

"Ha. In your dreams; don't you be messin' with me now. What you weigh, for real?"

"240 ..."

"... and some change! Real change. I'm talkin' heavy silver," CC laughed the laugh of the innocent. "Don't you worry, we gonna get you down. I'm thinking 210. What you think?"

"In *your* dreams!" Joe laughed.

"Hey, they told me I gotta get down to 205 to roll Light-Heavy." Pause. "It's gonna be harder for me to lose seven pounds than for you to lose 27 pounds!"

"I'd pop you … if I could get back up."

Silence. In the distance they could hear iron weights clanking on and off their stands.

"How long it been Mr. D.?"

"A year ago last March."

"You were on a plane?"

"Yep."

"You a lucky man."

"I was in First Class because it was a transcontinental flight. There was a cardiologist across the aisle. He quickly stabilized me. An ambulance was there to greet us when we landed. I was on an operating table at University of Pennsylvania hospital within 30 minutes." Pause. "Otherwise …"

"You got them grandkids, right?"

"Five."

"Reason to live?"

"Reason to live."

"This is good for you Mr. D. I tell all the young guys too: 'you're better off thumpin' than pumpin'." Pause. "But I discovered pumpers ain't thumpers."

Ever so slowly, Joe Delgado pulled himself into a sitting position. "This, my friend, is better than sex." Pause. "Of course, I speak from memory."

Cribbs threw his head back and laughed, a deep rich resonant sound that seemed proprietary to barrel-chested black men. "You a warrior, man. You bring it … every time."

Delgado smiled. "Boxing is life. We come into this world fighting for air … and go out the same way."

"Yeah … and in between … we always fightin' somebody … for somethin'."

Delgado nodded. "Sometimes you win… but the decision goes the other way. You don't get the job or the promotion … or whatever. But you move on. In life, you can be dazed and bleeding; it doesn't matter. You gotta keep swinging."

Clarence Cribbs nodded appreciatively in silence. He decided to change the subject: "You in health care, right?"

Joe laughed gently, "No, I'm in need of health care."

"What you do, Mr. D?"

"I'm what they call a 'bean counter.' I count the money at Pittman Labs upstairs."

"Bet there's a whole lot of that up there."

"There is indeed."

"You 55?"

"58."

"You a smart guy, Mr. D... how come you not the boss?"

Joe sorted three possible answers in nanoseconds, looked at his young instructor and said, "Conscience."

# 5

---

John Sweeney, clerically collared, entered the Narbrook Deli and immediately encountered a small sea of arched eyebrows. In the back, in a corner, sat Dr. Stanley Koblinski, President of the U.S. Catholic Bioethics Network. He raised a cup of coffee to signal his guest. John saw him and headed toward the back, nodding as he did so to several patrons who happened to be parishioners. Not a particularly warm welcome. *Okay; we can take our hands off our wallets*; *I'm not going to be taking up a collection … this morning.*

Like much of the rest of the American landscape, Narbrook had undergone something of a makeover over the past 20 years. Generations of mom and pop retailers of fringe household items had given way, reluctantly, to niche clothing boutiques, organic health food outlets, and European style cafes. The borough's three bars, however, remained largely immune to gentrification. Inside, hard-core "Narbs" nursed their grievances behind shots and beer and lamented the vanishing buffalo.

Sweeney shared their sense of loss. The borough had been

discovered. The Main Line affluent, seduced by its charm and authenticity, bought homes and shops in Narbrook – for their children. Once settled, the newly entitled reached for the levers of power, such as they were. Pitched battles, cultural at their core, were fought in borough council meetings over everything from police budgets to bicycle paths, speed limits to playground equipment, bar ordinances to gay and lesbian housing rights. Gradually, the inevitable arbiter, the marketplace, took stock of these developments ... and spoke. Housing prices soared. The children of multi-generational "Narbs" were slowly priced out, severing family settlements that went as far back as the late 19th century. The tone and character of the borough began to change ever so slowly. Dug in, the old guard braked its pace ... but not its arrival.

Sweeney pulled a chair from a narrow table and eased himself into it. "Thanks for making time, Doctor."

"Pleasure, Father." Koblinski took stock of his friend from point blank range. The table was so small their foreheads almost touched when each leaned forward. "How you been?"

Sweeney waved his hand dismissively. "Good, good." Then, reflectively, "I'm worried about Mom."

Koblinski nodded sympathetically. "The time is fast approaching when she won't know who you are."

Sweeney smiled tightly. "... And that, as they say, will be the good news."

The proprietor, a pleasant and energetic older woman in a coffee stained apron, approached. "What can we get you, Father?"

"What would you bring me if I were your son?"

The woman smiled and said, "Nothing; I'd send you to the kitchen to cook for me."

Sweeney laughed and said: "To get even, I might just go."

"How 'bout a ham and cheese omelet, Father. I'll see if I can do it without breaking any eggs."

Sweeney hooted. "Not on my account; I never worried about breaking a few eggs."

Koblinski saw an opening. When the waitress had mentally

filed the order, turned back toward the kitchen and was safely out of earshot, he asked: "How is love, Father, the second time around?"

Sweeney studied the other man's eyes. He shrugged. "Too soon to tell."

What's it been ... 20 years?"

"17."

"You didn't want to come back did you?"

Sweeney paused. "No. But I also didn't want to be driving an hour and a half round trip every day."

Koblinski reflected on that. "You look in on her, everyday?"

"Everyday."

"Must be painful."

Sweeney laughed. "Coming back or seeing Mom?"

"Both!"

Hot coffee arrived. John took it in his hands before it hit the table, a welcome distraction. "I'm grateful to the Cardinal Archbishop. He didn't have to do what he did."

"Yes he did."

Koblinski's tone startled John. "Well ... it's all in the past, Stan."

"You never should have been removed."

Sweeney shrugged. "... ah, transferred ...; and it was probably best for all concerned ... at the time."

"Grogan should have put his foot down. Extremely disappointing." Pause, then: "When a few parishioners can get a faithful priest removed ... for preaching what the church holds to be true ... something has gone radically wrong in our church."

Sweeney smiled ruefully. "It was more than a few ..."

"... Not many more. Most of the people were with you."

Sweeney shrugged. It hurt to think about it. "Let's talk about something cheerful ... like Alzheimer's."

Koblinski smiled and sipped his coffee. "Well, good news and bad news. Which do you want first?"

"I only want the good news."

Koblinski smiled. "The good news is ... the Good News.

Your mother's heading down the final straightaway; eternity is in sight. And every step of the way, she'll be accompanied by a priest. A good priest. We all should be so blessed, John."

Sweeney nodded. "... And the bad news?"

Koblinski paused. "Think of a house filled with lights. One at a time, the lights blink off. In the end ... only darkness."

John Sweeney felt a lance pierce his heart. A kaleidoscope of images raced across a screen in his mind. His mother as a little girl, a school girl, on her wedding day, the day of his arrival, the births of the other children, the holidays and vacations ... then his father's death and the slow motion, slightly surreal funeral. His mother in her nurse's uniform ... leaving the house after all the children had been put to bed. The graduations, the marriages, the grandchildren. The phone call that brought the news that Peter was in Tower One. Then ... nothing. He suddenly realized it was that single phone call that had stopped time. It was the moment his mother stopped smiling. A tipping point. Life had finally exhausted her seemingly limitless reservoir of joy. Looking back, he understood that event was the spark that set fire to his mother's short term memory. *How much of it was volitional?*

"How does it end, Doctor?"

"The system breaks down. Everything stops working."

"What does that look like ...?"

"Your mom will be unable to swallow. Swallowing is a fairly complex neurological operation. Without food and water, she dehydrates, and ... dies." Koblinski all but swallowed the word.

John sat bolt upright. "Well ... we're not going to let that happen!"

Koblinski, gently: "John, you can have a tube inserted and provide hydration at the very end ... if it is in fact the very end ... but the church doesn't require it."

"I don't understand that. How can the church not insist ...?"

"She insists only ordinary measures be provided; when a loved one's system is no longer working, she does not insist that her children be forced to use what then, in that circumstance, become extraordinary measures."

"When does food and water, or at least water, become an extraordinary measure?"

Koblinski nodded: "Under two conditions; when the procedure itself becomes invasive ... burdensome to the patient herself ... and/or when a doctor certifies a system failure is imminent ... and the extraordinary measures would provide no benefit ..."

The food arrived. When the waitress left, John pushed it away. *Holy Mother of God! I'm to watch my mother starve to death!? How will I explain that to my brothers?*

"Doctor, what happens if we insert the tube and keep Mom hydrated ... until the end?"

Koblinski nodded again. "You should do that. But sometimes families have a tube put in at what is clearly the end ... only to find the procedure itself causes ... additional, if not unforeseen, complications; and these, on occasion, actually contribute to cause of death."

Sweeney smiled tightly. "I take it you don't recommend it."

"John, when it gets down to the bitter end, I don't recommend, period. That decision is for the family to make. The Church, in her love for her children, wishes only to remove ... obstacles ... that can cause additional anguish at a most difficult time ..."

John Sweeney stared at the table, head in hands. *This is going to be too hard.* He thought of his younger brothers and sisters. He saw them as small children looking to him, wide eyed, for guidance. Looking to a big brother who would step up and be what a big brother was supposed to be in moments like this.

"Doctor, could we do a teleconference? I'd like to get everybody on board with this ... whatever we decide. I don't want to make this decision alone. I have ... three now ... younger brothers and, of course, my sisters, Rosemary and Eileen. I want everyone to weigh in."

Koblinski smiled. "Of course, Father. Just book a time that works for all of you with my assistant."

Sweeney felt only dead weight around his back and shoulders.

He looked at his omelet; suddenly he didn't feel hungry. He thought about asking the maternal proprietor to warm it up, but thought better of it. "Gotta run, Doctor. Thank you."

Koblinski stood, surprised, his paper napkin falling to the floor. He extended his hand, glasses slightly askew. "Father, I'll get the check."

John Sweeney shook the extended hand, nodded and said with mock sincerity: "Thanks. I didn't bring any money. I usually just bolt."

He left smiling.

# 6

---

Jim Gillespie opened the door of the blue Porsche Carrera.
Maggie Kealey, soon to celebrate her 58th birthday, hiked up
her formal evening gown and bent low to ease her way into
the passenger side. "My word, Jim! I'd rather ride in a pickup
truck."

Gillespie reached over to kiss his date discretely on the cheek
and said, "Well ... we can't very well have Philadelphia's newest
CEO arriving at the Philo ball in a pickup truck ... can we now?"

"What if you can't get me out? Can you wheel this toy into
an elevator?

Jim Gillespie thumbed a button on the steering wheel and the
Grateful Dead entered the tight confines. He reached inside his tux
pocket and pulled out a cigar. This drew the expected response:
"Oh, no you don't. I don't care if you stink yourself up ... but you're
not stinking me up too. We'll end up sitting alone. Give me that
dreadful thing."

Gillespie waved the cigar dismissively as he approached the
light at Haverford road: "Just a prop, Dearest. No intention of

lighting it." Pause. "That part about being alone, though, I want to hear more about that."

"Oh God, Jim. You're not in one of your frisky moods, are you?"

"Anytime I'm in the vicinity of a CEO, my heart quickens."

Maggie Kealey laughed and put a gloved hand on the back of her escort's neck; she patted it gently. Abruptly, she pulled her hand back and placed it on her lap.

Gillespie eyed the cramped quarters and said somewhat philosophically: "Oh well ... it wouldn't have worked out anyway; I should have brought the pick up."

Maggie laughed again and Jim Gillespie glanced at her silhouette highlighted by shimmering street lights. He marveled at her natural beauty and effortless charm. *She is irresistible. Tonight, she will be, as she always is, the most beautiful woman in the room. Oh Lord ... if I only could take her home with me ...*

"Who's going to be there again?" Maggie inquired, oblivious to the struggle going on beside her.

Gillespie cleared his throat. "Ah ... the crème de la crème of Philadelphia's Catholic Society."

Maggie looked at him warily. "Who might *that* include?"

"Well, the Cardinal Archbishop for one." Pause. "Wait till you see him break dance."

The imagined sight of the roly-poly prelate gyrating on the floor to rap music set Maggie off again. She convulsed in laughter. "You'll burn for that one; I'm not sitting anywhere near you." Then: "Who else?"

"The pro-life crowd, the Main Line cliques, the upper level archdiocesan bureaucrats ... usual suspects."

"Will Father John be there?"

"Sweeney? I believe so. Dr. Koblinski's bringing him. Talk about an odd couple ..."

"Hush! Fr. John is a living saint."

Gillespie hesitated, then nodded: "Must be. Lord knows he's suffered."

"Will the Burnses be there?"

"Better be. He's being honored."

"Whatever for?"

"Dunno. Must have given the archdiocese a bundle when he sold his company."

Maggie grew silent. Gillespie stole a glance and wondered if she were on a walkabout – those moments when she fled somewhere remote, well beyond his reach. *What planet does she visit; is there life on it?*

She turned toward him and said: "Remind me to talk to Michael about the Women's Clinic."

"Another pro bono?"

"No; he's got too much overhead."

"That's no way to refer to his children."

Sharp jab to an exposed right arm. "I was referring to his staff; he's got a couple hundred people working for him. Most of them have families –"

"Yes ... and more than a few have domestic partnerships ..."

"Now, now. We don't go there, remember?"

"Yes, yes, my lovely. We love all God's children. Even those who call down sulfur upon our heads."

"You're incorrigible."

"If that's a synonym for 'eligible,' I am indeed."

Maggie shook her head in the darkness. She loved Jim Gillespie; he had saved her life in every way a man can save a woman's life after her husband walked out on her and their family. But, as she told him every time he asked, she would not marry him. Not as long as Bill Kealey was still alive. A covenant was a covenant. She did believe in annulments ... for others; but she couldn't comprehend how her marriage to Bill Kealey could be declared annulled. In her mind their marriage was valid in every way a marriage could be valid. Bill had remarried in a civil ceremony. If he resented her unwillingness to participate in the annulment process, it wasn't evident in their many interactions at family events. He was always cordial, as was Jane Sammons, his former secretary and second wife.

The children seemed to accept, if not welcome, her decision to live alone and the girls in particular had long since given up trying to encourage her to marry Dr. Gillespie.

They arrived at the Bellevue parking garage and a white-uniformed attendant came out to greet them. "Hello, Doctor. Who's that beautiful woman ... and what is she doing with you!?"

Gillespie feigned irritation. "Already working me for a tip, huh Jason?"

The attendant opened the small passenger door and said: "Hello Mrs. –?"

"— Kealey."

He bowed deeply. "Welcome to the Bellevue, Mrs. Kealey! We're honored to have you with us for the evening."

Gillespie extended his arm and Maggie nestled her left arm within it. They entered the hotel and headed for the elevator bank just off the main lobby. There, waiting for an elevator to the second floor mezzanine and ballroom, were the Delgados. "Fran, Joe ... hi," Maggie said seeing them first. She was genuinely happy to see friends before strangers.

Fran Delgado, dressed in an expensive Versace evening gown, turned immediately and lit up at the sight of her friend. "Maggie!" She stepped closer and extended her left cheek for a cursory buss. "I was hoping you'd be here. I am so thrilled about the news ..."

Maggie blushed reflexively and said, "Thank you, Fran." She turned to Joe and inquired, "Joe, how are you?"

"Good, Maggie. You look lovely, as always." He turned to Jim and smiled. "Didn't you get the memo, Gillespie? You can't date the boss. The good sisters won't approve."

"Just one more thing to confess," Gillespie retorted.

The two couples rode up to the ballroom exchanging light banter. The door opened to a grand sight: a majestic ballroom, a full orchestra, and several hundred formally dressed patrons laughing, drinking and moving from one small field of energy to another. Jim and Maggie followed Joe and Fran to the welcome table for sign in and table designation. Four animated young women sat behind the table accommodating patrons. One, a college student from LaSalle University, saw Maggie and exclaimed: "Mrs. Kealey! We were just talking about you in class the other day." Others in line turned their heads to take in the minor celebrity in their midst.

"And what class was that?" Maggie asked politely.

"Women's studies."

Jim Gillespie fired first. "On the whole, I approve of women studying."

Maggie shot him an eye dart. "What year of study are you in … Tricia, is it?"

"Yes, Mrs. Kealey, Tricia. I'm a junior."

"What do you want to do when you graduate?"

"I want to go into health care." Pause. "Does Regina Hospital have internships?"

"Why, yes, we do."

"May I send you my resume?"

"Yes, of course," Maggie said, sorting through her hand bag for a card. "I'll be looking for it." Something about the young lady reminded her of a lost daughter.

"Here's your table number, Mrs. Kealey," Tricia said, extending a small card with the number seven on it. "Looks like this is your lucky night."

Gillespie took the card. "I doubt she'll get lucky tonight. I already have a headache."

The carefully coiffed heads behind the table swiveled from the beautiful woman to her tuxedoed escort. It wasn't until Maggie turned away from her date and looked at them, smiling ruefully, that they exhaled and began giggling.

When they were out of earshot, Maggie pulled Jim closer and whispered in his ear: "Behave!"

Jim Gillespie dropped his arm from Maggie's waist and lightly pinched her satin covered posterior: "Promise."

She dug a sharp elbow into Dr. Gillespie's rib cage, drawing a quick expulsion of air.

Fran Delgado was waiting for Maggie several yards from the table. "Maggie, where are you sitting?"

"Table seven."

"Oh … we're at 24."

"Promise you'll visit," Gillespie interjected.

Maggie ignored him. "Joe looks good; how's he been?"

"Oh, He's fine," Fran Delgado answered dismissively. "Tell me about your promotion. I am so proud of you!"

Maggie was somewhat put off by her friend's indifference to her own husband's heart attack. She was quite fond of Joe. "Just time in grade," she shrugged. "You hang around long enough and … there's really nothing else to do with you than kick you upstairs," Maggie said without a hint of false modesty.

Fran Delgado's eyes widened and she fairly gushed, "Oh Maggie, you are great. Just great."

Gillespie couldn't restrain himself. "Yes, but as they say, 'behind every great woman … is an even greater man.'"

Fran Delgado laughed so hard her mascara started to run; her husband arrived with their drinks and politely handed his wife something darkly mixed. He turned to Gillespie. "Where you sitting, Jim?"

"We're at seven."

"We're 24."

Gillespie eyed Fran Delgado, whose girth was still reverberating slightly from laughter, and said, "Yeah well, something tells me you guys are going to have more fun …"

Delgado smiled grimly and escorted his wife away.

"Oh Jim, you offended him." Maggie was crestfallen.

Gillespie nodded. "Perhaps. Certainly not like me —"

"— He's such a dear man. And he always looks so sad. My heart just breaks for him."

Gillespie throttled back slightly. "I'll apologize later."

"I don't know … maybe you shouldn't say anything more."

"How 'bout I promise to dance with his wife until she falls

down ... either drunk or exhausted or both; would that make it up to him?"

Maggie didn't dignify the remark.

They arrived at their table to find Father John Sweeney and Dr. Stanley Koblinski seated. "Oh Father John!" Maggie exclaimed. "What an absolutely delightful surprise." She circled to greet him and kissed him lightly on the cheek. He responded with a light and proper hug.

"Maggie, do you know Dr. Stanley Koblinski of the Catholic Bioethics Network here in town?"

"Oh I most certainly do ... though I doubt he knows me. Doctor, I'm a great admirer of your work," she said, extending her hand.

Stanley Koblinski stood abruptly and a bit awkwardly and took the proffered hand and shook it vigorously. "Oh, I do know of you, Mrs. Kealey. Congratulations on your promotion. Are you aware you are the first woman to be named CEO of a hospital in this city's history?"

Maggie did not respond.

Koblinski added: "This is significant, both as a personal achievement and an institutional statement."

Maggie blushed. "No, quite honestly I was not aware of that; maybe that will give the Church's critics pause, Doctor."

Gillespie cleared his throat. "Yes, well, I'm one of the Church's critics and nothing gives me pause ... when the bar is open. Dear, what would you like?"

"A glass of white wine would be wonderful, Jim, thank you."

Gillespie turned to the men. "Father, Doctor, can I get either of you anything?"

Two heads shook simultaneously. Father John smiled and said, "I'd say we're good, but, at least in my case, I'd be exaggerating."

Gillespie laughed. He liked this priest. He struck him as the kind of guy you could have a drink or two with.

The lights dimmed on and off and the orchestra began playing; the crowd slowly filed to their tables. Maggie, Doctor Koblinski and Father Sweeney took their chairs. Three couples Maggie did not know arrived and introduced themselves. She did not catch any of the names. Momentarily, Jim arrived back with the drinks. "What'd I miss?"

Maggie leaned in and whispered, "Nothing. With the orchestra playing, I didn't hear a one of their names."

Gillespie surveyed the table, theatrically bolted out of his chair, eyes darting and feigning apprehension, and said, "My name is Jim ...... and I'm an alcoholic." He sat down to the kind of silence that generally greets nature being eased, inappropriately. The only sound was the laughter of the priest.

A master of ceremonies approached the podium, leaned into the microphone, and introduced himself. An unrelated gale of laughter from a distant table split the abating sound and generated a measure of sympathy for the speaker; he quickly exhausted it however by droning on and on about the history and mission of the hosting institution. Well before he had finished, the room had returned to its original decibel level.

When the gentleman finished, the Cardinal Archbishop was observed making his way to the podium for the invocation. A respectful silence slowly descended upon the room. Cardinal O'Hallaran adjusted the microphone, down, and intoned an extemporaneous prayer that gave evidence of a deep prayer life. When he finished, the master of ceremonies returned to the podium ... the noise in the room building with his every step. Maggie Kealey looked two seats over to John Sweeney for an explanation of what was being said; the priest merely shrugged. Dr. Koblinski, despite Maggie's fervent wish otherwise, sat between them. He reached for his glass of room temperature Chablis and said, "Well, Mrs. Kealey, you certainly have your work cut out for you in your new assignment."

The comment caught her cold. She gulped merlot from the glass in her right hand and turned to the Doctor and said somewhat defensively, "If you're referring to my being both a mother *and a*

CEO ... my children are all grown. Only two are at home, and they're both working."

Koblinski smiled and sipped. "I assure you Mrs. Kealey ... I have acquired at least a minimal level of political correctness. *That is none of my business.* I was referring to your on-staff docs."

"What about them?"

"Are you aware four of them have affiliations with fertility clinics?"

Maggie blanched. There had been whispers of course; as a nurse, she simply was not in a position to know ... and had no desire to find out. Now, hearing this, from this man, in this setting ... she immediately grasped the significance. She had just been notified an IED had been placed under her desk. The consequences of both action, and inaction, would be monumental. She eyed Koblinski coolly and asked, "Do you have ... definitive proof?"

"Of course. Would you like to see what we have?"

"Oh no! I mean... yes." *Holy Mother of God. Why this? Why now?*

"I could send it, or I could bring it in person. Do you have a preference?"

Maggie was deeply disturbed. *I don't need this; I don't want this. Please Lord, let this cup pass ...* "May I ask how you came by such ... definitive ... information, Dr. Koblinski?"

Koblinski smiled the slightly peculiar smile of the very bright. "I had my staff at the Center dig it out of the ground."

"How?"

"We checked the physician roster of every fertility and reproductive clinic in the Greater Philadelphia area and crossed checked it against every Catholic hospital in the area. Believe me when I tell you ... Regina Hospital is not alone in this."

Maggie winced. There would be no evasion. *I'll be John Kennedy with all those oversized photographs of Cuban missiles sitting right there in their silos ... spread out on my own desk for all to see. Then the eyes of my world will be upon me ... watching and waiting. Please God! Why did I take this job? Pride. Pure vanity. Why!? It's Bill. Almost 18 years later ... and it's still about him. Proving him wrong. Now ... whatever I do ... I'll end up proving him right.* Maggie turned to Jim and asked, "Honey, may I please have another glass of wine?"

Koblinski noted the distress. "Mrs. Kealey, I repeat. You are not alone."

Maggie suddenly felt very much alone.

Dinner arrived and the mood at the table gradually grew more subdued. Jim Gillespie, sensing a measure of reticence in the others, was center stage holding forth on the personalities at the head table. The wine began to flow and laughter was its sound. "Look at O'Hallaran sitting there next to Burns trying to get his hand into his *other* pocket. Now ... see Carol Burns slapping it away ..."

Presently, the master of ceremonies returned to the podium to introduce the man who would introduce the man who would introduce the evening's honored guest ... Michael Burns. More wine. By the time Michael Burns made his way to the podium, a third of the room was either in a restroom or trying to find a large plant. Burns opened quickly as was his wont and within minutes was mid stride in a rant about something or other. Gillespie noted the prelate's discomfort and guessed, correctly, that Burns had taken dead aim on Episcopal timidity in the culture wars. The sight of an actual train wreck left him in a state of euphoria. "This is the Cardinal's note come due," he fairly shouted to the others. "Burnsie bought the mic; it's a kamikaze run. He is a rarest strain of the species ... absolutely unique and totally out of his mind!"

When Michael Burns finished, the audience sat stunned, not knowing whether to applaud or to run to the bar for another drink. They did both. Immediately the orchestra began playing a Viennese Waltz. Gillespie announced another bar run and asked Maggie if she wanted anything. She pointed to a nearly empty glass and nodded. She turned to look for John Sweeney and found him talking to Michael Burns, who had wasted no time in pursuing a gut check from his confessor. Maggie observed Sweeney awkwardly trying to find a middle ground between distancing himself, in plain view of his superior, and affirming his friend's outing, however anonymously, the content of their many private conversations.

Maggie stood to move her seat nearer to the two men. She was surprised to feel herself floating a bit and immediately sat down. She attempted the move again and this time her struggle attracted the men's attention. Michael Burns grabbed the chair and pulled it next to his own which was facing John Sweeney's. He returned to gather Maggie and escorted her to the chair. As he eased her into her chair, he smiled and said: "Maggie, Father John is hearing my confession; you're next."

Sweeney turned to Maggie and said with mock seriousness, "I keep trying to explain ... I don't have the authority to hear *his* confession." Maggie turned to Burns and said, "Michael, I'm going to need help with a few things at the hospital. Could you call me this week?"

Burns smiled broadly. "Okay, but I'm not delivering any more babies. Been there, done that."

Maggie responded with feigned irritation. "Well just forget it then."

Gillespie returned with drinks and put a half shoulder bump on Burns. "I saw the Cardinal in line at the bar; he's ordered a urine test for you. What day this week works best?"

Burns convulsed and tried to give Gillespie some variant of a high five ... but missed. "Yeah ... well ... it's their fault. They should have known better than to give me an open mic."

Sweeney laughed and said, "They convinced themselves you wouldn't dare. This was one time they might have consulted me."

Maggie laughed with the others. "Michael Burns, Sister Veronica was right; you are a bold, brazen article."

"I actually thought about having that tattooed on my butt when we were in New York, but Carol didn't much care for the idea."

Sweeney looked down at his feet; Gillespie looked up and let out a loud guffaw. He stood and said to Maggie, "I believe they're playing our song."

Maggie looked up, puzzled. "Jim, what is it they're playing? I didn't know we had a song."

Gillespie whisked her in the direction of the dance floor. Watching them, John Sweeney turned to Michael Burns and said, "It is so very good to see her happy. I thank God everyday for what's happening in her life."

"Think she'll ever marry him?"

Sweeny paused. "I don't know. I've encouraged her to get an annulment. I believe the Church would grant one. She's been … unresponsive." Pause. "I just think she gave her heart to Bill Kealey when she was 17, and she's never taken it back."

"Think Gillespie gets it?"

"No doubt. Jim's a savvy guy. Still, it must be painful."

"Lots of cold showers," Burns said, laughing.

Sweeney nodded and turned his attention back to the elegant single mother. "Yes … through all the suffering she has somehow managed to retain her beauty."

Burns gave his friend a hug and said, "Gotta cut, Father. I'll call you this week."

John Sweeney smiled and jabbed, "Thanks for the heads up."

Sweeney headed back to his table and ran into Jim Gillespie who was just leaving the dance floor. He handed him a card key. "Don't take her outside, she could slip and fall. And don't leave her alone, if she heaves she could choke. Use my suite upstairs. It's got a rollout couch in the living room."

Jim Gillespie just stared, for once speechless. *Lord, this isn't the kind of prayer you usually answer!*

When the dance floor was full again, Jim Gillespie gently took Maggie Kealey by the arm and said, "Come with me."

"Where are we going?" she asked with a slight hint of a slur.

"Someplace where you can lie down and rest a bit."

"Oh good. I'm not feeling so well, Jim."

All but unnoticed, Jim led her out the back of the ballroom to the Hotel's main elevator bank. He pushed the button for the penthouse. In moments the elevator picked them up and shot for the moon. When it stopped, a light on the front panel flashed. Jim slid the card key into the slot. The elevator door opened directly into the white marbled hallway of a large and professionally designed three-bedroom suite. He entered the living room with Maggie on his arm and glanced across the room at the large bay windows beneath which lay the city glittering in its evening dress.

As he entered the master bedroom, Maggie suddenly became a dead weight on his arm. Her head slumped onto his shoulder; he realized she was now in a state of semi-consciousness. He tugged her, feet dragging a bit, to the bed and laid her gently on her back. She rolled over on her side and moaned. He removed her shoes and placed them on the floor beside the bed. He looked upon the still figure, now beginning to snore ever so lightly, her face that of an angel at rest. He looked at her body enveloped in luminescent white satin and thought of the hauntingly beautiful rock anthem … "Knights in White Satin." How he longed for just one night in white satin. He took a long, deep breath. *How many nights have I dreamt this dream?* He stared at the other side of the large bed. *Why not? Who knows … maybe she'll wake up in the middle of the night, frightened, calling for me.*

He stood there several more moments. Then, Jim Gillespie eased the love of his life under the covers, turned off the light, and headed for the pull-out couch in the living room.

# 7

eter Feeney, both hands on a sheaf of papers, breezed past executive secretary Maria Esposito to peek inside the large opaque window of the corner office door. He turned back to the secretary and said, "Who's in there with him?"

Without looking up from her computer screen, Esposito answered, "He's alone." Pause. "How 'bout we leave him alone. It's Monday."

Feeney feigned a silent shudder. Everyone who worked at Burns Advertising knew better than to schedule meetings with the boss on a Monday. Some suggested he arrived hung over from weekend binges; others that he was simply a manic depressive and didn't much care for the start of another work week with all its attendant challenges and difficulties.

Feeney, some 20 years Burns' junior, regarded his boss as both model and mentor. Five years earlier, at the age of 34, he had been promoted to Chief Financial Officer and awarded a 10% share in the company's private stock. He tended to see more good in Burns than most of the company's other 215 employees did.

From inside the office came the sound of a raised, unintelligible, voice. The decibel level rose and fell with an almost lyrical Irish symmetry. Maria smiled grimly. "I'd say he's just about ready for you. Should I buzz you in?"

Peter gulped and offered her his arm full of papers. "Your turn."

Maria's gaze returned to the computer screen. "Only if we trade paychecks."

Presently, a silence seemed to descend upon the corner office. Immediately, Maria buzzed and, without waiting for a response, said, "Michael, Peter's here. May I send him in?"

"Sure, why not. The day's already ruined."

Maria smiled and, with her left hand, pantomimed a 'he's all yours.'

Peter opened the door and found the boss behind his desk. He immediately went to the far side of the room and the formal sitting area and eased into a large leather couch. From behind his desk, Michael Burns, fully comprehending, smiled. He got up and came around the large desk, crossed the room and joined Feeney, sitting on a matching leather easy chair. "Coffee, Peter?"

"No thanks, Mike. I'm good."

Burns eyed him, somewhat bemused. "You sure?"

"Well ... I could be making more money."

Burns laughed and Feeney hoped the sound in and of itself might presage a change in room temperature. "Good weekend, Michael?"

"Yes. You?"

"Terrific. Mary Ellen and I watched young Peter play two games on Saturday. He was 6 for 8 with two home runs and two doubles."

Burns bit. Some 10 minutes later he was still talking about his own coaching days with his Little League sons. Feeney didn't have to search for the laughter button. Burns' stories were, mostly always, borderline outrageous, simply because they tended to be, mostly always, about him. Feeney knew, however, the clock was ticking. He needed two requisition approvals and then he'd be ever so content to tip toe out. He glanced at his watch to send a quick, silent signal. Burns read it immediately and said, "Well, I digress."

Feeney cleared his throat and plunged. "Michael, just a couple of things this morning. First, Beth Larkin in accounting just found out she has ovarian cancer. She begins radiation therapy in two weeks." Feeney knew to always begin Monday report outs with the personal plight of an employee. Predictably, the coldness immediately drained from Burns' eyes and a watery softness appeared in its place. "My Lord! How far along is she?"

"Not far. There is some hope they caught it in time. She's asked, specifically, for *your* prayers."

Burns leapt to his feet and was at the door in four strides. "Maria, please come in!" Maria Esposito appeared in the doorway in nanoseconds, concern etched into her delicate features. "What's the matter, Michael?" She searched Peter's eyes for an answer that was not forthcoming.

The staccato sounds that followed were like rounds from an AK 47. "Beth Larkin just learned she's got ovarian cancer. Get her on the phone immediately. Send flowers to her home immediately. Get Father John on the phone immediately. Find out where she is going for treatment and when, exactly, it's scheduled to begin. Put her on my agenda for today; I'll visit her on the way home. Remind me to tell her we'll pick up any and all expenses the company insurance doesn't cover. Now, what about her children? Who's going to care for them? I think one's a junior in high school, but the other is in seventh grade? Maria, look into child care options, today. Remind me to call her husband. Did we find him a job yet? Who's working on that, Peter?"

"Ah, one of our board directors, Jim Cassidy."

"Get him on the phone, Maria. I don't care where the hell he is. I want Beth's husband working in two weeks."

Maria fled the room. Peter stood awkwardly. Michael started to pray out loud. "Lord, please heal this good woman. Her husband needs her. Her children need her. We need her. You can do all things, Lord. You've proven that over and over and over again. Please, grant this faithful child of God long life. Her children's children, Lord, please ..."

Maria appeared in the doorway. "Father John on 81."

Michael rushed to the phone and picked up. "Father, one of our employees, a woman in her late 30's, was just told by her doctors she's got ovarian cancer. Could you please remember her and her family in your Masses this week?"

Pause, then: "Beth Larkin." Another pause. "She starts in two weeks." Michael exhaled audibly. "Thank you, Father. Thank you. God love you. Yes, yes. I'll call." Click.

Maria: "Beth on 82."

Michael Burns looked at the ground and paused; he then took a deep breath. Peter noticed his lips moving. Then, another click: "Beth," calmly. "Thank you so much for taking my call. Peter Feeney just told me the news. I'm so very sorry. How are you feeling?" Long pause. "Well ... Beth ... I just want you to concentrate on getting well. We'll take care of everything else, including the prayers. We're going to storm heaven. I'm going to ask my wife to offer up some of her suffering." Pause. "Me!" Laughter on both ends of the phone. "Beth, are you able to see visitors?" Pause. "May I stop by tonight, just for a few minutes?" Then, "Good. Thank you. See you then." Click.

Peter was back in the sofa feeling a bit guilty. Burns returned to his easy chair with his game face on. "Get a memo out and ask our people to pray ... and I don't give a damn who that offends ... we are going to storm heaven for that good woman and her family. This black plague is unsparing, is it not Peter? It is certainly no respecter of virtue."

Burns looked at the floor and slowly shook his head. "Okay, what else you got?"

"Well, a bit of bad news on the revenue front. There's a little softness in Dick Weber's third and fourth quarter forecast."

"The softness is all in Weber's spine! You tell that lazy SOB he either delivers original forecast or he's history. Do you want me to tell him?"

"No, no, no. I'll take care of it."

"Good. No wiggle room for that limp biscuit. If he misses by a dollar, I'll pack him up myself."

"Understood, Michael."

"What else?"

"Well, another little problem upstairs in Creative. They didn't respond well to, ah, your challenge last week. Someone punched a hole in one of the walls. It's actually pretty large. Want me to just have maintenance patch it and paint it?" Feeney closed his eyes and counted to five ... and waited. When he opened his eyes, Burns was at the door telling Maria to get Mobley. Ed Mobley was the award-winning Creative Director for Burns Advertising ... and resident anarchist.

Burns returned to his seat behind his desk. "Peter, take off. I don't want you looking like a snitch ..."

Feeney, relieved, fled the room. Momentarily, Mobley was at the door. "You wanted to see me?" he asked with studied nonchalance.

Burns eyed him coldly. He pointed to a seat on the other side of his desk and said, "And close the door."

Mobley sauntered toward the seat, casually removing his sun glasses. Before he reached his destination, Burns was around the desk and standing in his way, arms folded. Mobley stood about two inches taller than Burns, at six feet three, and was eight years his junior. He was said to have been an amateur boxer in New York City. He stopped two feet in front of Burns. "What's goin' on ...?"

Burns looked through him. "Me. I'm goin' on. And that is not good news for you and your home boys up on 15."

Mobley feigned ignorance. "You gotta problem?"

Burns smiled. "No. *You* gotta problem. Here's the way this is going down. You have the idiot who punched that hole in the wall upstairs, in *your* department, fix it ... himself ... today."

Mobley, slyly. "And if no one claims responsibility?"

"Then I hold *you* responsible." Pause. "And *you'll* fix it. Today." Pause. "We clear?"

Mobley shifted his weight and smiled coyly. "And if we can't get our hands on the plaster and a matching paint?"

"Then I start taking hostages."

Mobley blinked. "Come again?"

"You heard me."

"What the hell does that mean?"

"It means I start laying people off in Creative; one a day … until the hole is fixed."

Mobley stared incredulously. "Are you crazy, man? We're backed up two, three weeks with work. We need to be hiring people, not firing them."

"Then why you standin' here?" Burns replied, postured for action.

Mobley deeply resented being 'schooled' by a suit, any suit. He started to the door, paused, turned and said, pointedly, "You oughta know, everyone in the entire Creative Department has their reel on the street."

Burns immediately started toward him and Mobley stiffened. Burns leaned slightly into the taller man's space and said, "Glad to know that. Whoever's still here in six months will be fired. I refuse to be the only adman in town dumb enough to be signing their checks."

Mobley's eyes widened. He shook his head, slowly and dramatically, and left.

"Maria, get Feeney back in here."

Feeney, who was waiting in the screening room on the other side of a small adjoining conference room, appeared immediately. "How'd that go, with Mobley?" he asked, eyes wide.

Burns looked preoccupied. "Huh? Oh, fine. Ed'll take care of that hole, or whatever the problem is up there."

Feeney marveled at the man's ability to compartmentalize. "Just a couple more things, quickly."

Burns motioned Peter to sit, this time on the other side of his desk. "Okay. Whatcha got?"

Feeney reached across the table and put two requisitions on the desk in front of Burns. "These are for those entry level account management positions on the Hudson Bank and the Pennsylvania Tourism accounts."

"Hold 'em."

Feeney only half expected this. He had come over early the previous Friday afternoon to get Burns' signature, which was always slam dunk certain on a getaway day. But Burns had already left for his vacation home at the South Jersey shore. He'd promised Frank Russo, the Group Management Director, he'd get the signature, on both requisitions, before the week was out. A 'no' on a Monday usually meant at least a two week wait. "Uh, Mike, we've got revenue starting up on both accounts in about ten days."

Burns smiled. "Good. Come back and see me then." He picked up the papers and gently tossed them over the desk to his CFO. He looked at his watch. "Anything else?"

Feeney dealt the good news first. "I got a call from UltraCom's outside accountants early this morning."

Burns stiffened. "And?"

Feeney paused a bit theatrically. Then he crossed and positioned his arms at waist level like an umpire calling a base runner 'safe'. Smiling, he said, "Everything checked out. They're good to go."

Burns sat back in his chair and allowed himself a small smile. "Good, Peter. Very, very good."

Feeney then inched closer to what he knew would be a black abyss. "One slight problem."

Burns eyes clouded. "What!?"

"Before we sign, they want to meet one more time, to talk about "build out" opportunities."

Burns' eyes were uncomprehending. "As I recall, that was my idea."

"Yeah, well, they want to monetize them, and include them in next year's forecast."

Burns shrugged. "Well, that *is* a little aggressive, but I'd probably do the same thing if I was the buyer."

"Just one wrinkle."

Burns just stared.

"They see their national client, Proper Parenthood, as a major growth account; and they see PP's local affiliate here in Philadelphia, Women's Right, as a major build out opportunity for us. They expect us to book over a million dollars in new revenue from them next year."

Michael Burns sat back in his chair and closed his eyes. Several minutes later, when they had still not reopened, Peter Feeney quietly rose from his chair and tip toed out.

# 8

Theresa Delgado Simpson opened the door to greet the delivery man. He was a dark, delicate man with a crimson dot in the middle of his forehead. His dialect was clipped and precise. She guessed him a British-educated PhD candidate, perhaps at the University of Pennsylvania. "Chicken Caesar, for Mr. Delgado?"

"Yes, thank you," Terry nodded.

"Mr. Delgado not get tired of same same?" he chirped.

Terry smiled. The man's good cheer shamed her. *Here he is, an educated man, working for tips in an alien land and culture ... and he's happy!*

"No, no. Mr. Delgado's on a diet. As soon as he loses the weight, he'll go back to his high carb menu."

The delivery man laughed and lifted a dark tee shirt to reveal his abs. "Tell him *rice*! But don't tell owner I said it." He extended a small chit for her signature. Terry added a generous gratuity and signed it, returning it with a smile. "What's your name?"

"Anil," he answered with a smile of his own, momentarily

brightening the early evening darkness. "I see you again, soon. Tell Mr. Delgado, two more orders and we rename: Delgado Chicken Caesar."

Terry laughed and watched him get into a small car of indeterminate origin and ease himself out of the large circular driveway. He was smiling.

Terry returned to the kitchen and placed the transparent plastic container in the refrigerator next to a bottle of Evian water. She opened the door to the freezer and pulled out three frozen dinners, unwrapped them and placed each in a large microwave. Dinner preparations were over. She went into the family room to quiet two small children engaged in a life or death confrontation over a toy truck. "Pop Pop's on his way. He won't want to hear you fighting!" On cue, the fighting escalated. "Joseph, I said stop it now," she yelled to the older of her sons. The boy yanked the truck from the hands of his younger brother and tossed it in the direction of his mother. Terry ducked the flying missile and stormed over to wreak vengeance. She grabbed the boy's hand and spanked it harshly. His younger brother appeared startled, but not displeased, at the immediacy of justice served. The chastised son immediately fell to the floor writhing and wailing. The younger boy got up on unsteady legs and went to reclaim his treasure. The sight of paradise lost only caused the older son to wail all the louder. Terry picked up the two-year old and put him on her hip, and returned to the kitchen. A phone rang. She reached for it with her free hand. "Hello?"

"Kitten, I'm in the car; I'll be home in five minutes."

"Okay, Dad; your dinner arrived."

"Good, good. Everything okay?"

"Yes. Everything's under control here."

"Okay." Click.

Terry Delgado Simpson hung up the phone and walked into her father's den. She hoisted the toddler on her hip and half fell into a deep couch. *I can't do this.* The sound of crying from the family room subsided. She found the quiet even more unnerving. She willed herself to her feet and approached the family room.

There she beheld her first born, poker stick in hand, lashing the furniture. Two bright, matching arm chairs were stained black. A cherry wood end table had a gash at its base the size of a half dollar. She watched in horror as the microterrorist bearing her DNA took dead aim on an ornate lamp, her mother's favorite, sitting on an end table. He struck before she could reach him. The lamp skidded, tottered, and fell. The sound itself discouraged closer inspection. Terry managed to shift the toddler from one hip to the other and grab the poker stick with her right hand. Her grip was immediately compromised by soot; her hand loosened and the stick fell to her side. The unmasked assailant grabbed it and fled the room in search of cover. His mother gave chase. She cornered him in the library, only to see him slither away, poker still in hand. He raced upstairs and into a bedroom. She gave dogged pursuit. She caught him by the collar in his younger brother's room, hiding under the crib, and dragged him into the hallway, intent on homicide. As she sorted her lethal options, she heard the front door open.

"Where's my little guys!?"

Joseph fled the collar and bounded down the steps and into his Pop Pop's arms. "Mommy's being bad, Pop Pop." Joe Delgado looked up to see his daughter coming down the circular staircase with his second grandson on her hip. Her hair was disheveled, her face streaked with what looked like patches of blackface, and her blouse appeared to be torn. "Tommy, come to Pop Pop," he said, extending his arms. Terry quickly yielded the dead weight and looked for a place to sit down. She chose the bottom step.

"Everything okay, Kitten?" Joe Delgado inquired, studiously avoiding his daughter's eyes.

"Joseph is just … incorrigible," she answered, eyes watery.

"Joseph, you being good for Mommy?" The little one at his feet instinctively comprehended the best defense was a good offense and flung himself, arms wide, at his grandfather's midsection. Joe Delgado, one in his arms, one now literally on his feet, looked at his daughter and smiled painfully. She started to cry. "I can't do this, Dad. It's too much. He's taken me over the edge with him."

Delgado made a move to comfort his daughter but discovered he couldn't move without dislodging the junior-level Al Qaeda operative on his feet. He was hot, he was tired, and he was hungry. And all this made him, in this instant, an irritable landlord to his daughter's unruly house pets. "Kitten, if you could just give me a few minutes, I need to get something cool in my hand."

Wounded and guilt ridden, Terry Delgado got up to retrieve her sons. "I'll try to get them to bed. Then I'll get your dinner ready."

Joe Delgado shook his head. "No need. If it's in the fridge, I'll get it myself." Momentarily liberated, he turned abruptly and escaped into what used to be his kitchen. He opened the refrigerator and grabbed the plastic container with his dinner inside, and the plastic bottle of water next to it, and thought of Dustin Hoffman in *The Graduate*. Amid the sound of a symphonic wailing and gnashing of teeth coming from somewhere overhead, he pulled out a counter stool at the granite island in the middle of the kitchen and sat down. It felt good. He flipped the cap off the water bottle and quickly drained it. He took three quick steps and retrieved another from the refrigerator door. He sat down and opened dinner. *You say you don't know how much longer you can do that. I don't know how much longer I can do this.* He searched for a fork; none to be found. Then he spotted a plastic fork under a white paper napkin inside the container. He looked at the plastic fork and thought of his wife. At this moment she was no doubt sleeping soundly in a private berth of either a ship or a train somewhere in the heart of Old Europe. She would be surrounded by three of her college classmates whom she had enticed to join her, at his expense. Each of her guests was divorced. They would have enjoyed a white tablecloth dinner at a scenic table overlooking the Blue Danube or the Alps ... perhaps both. *How was the Roast Duck, honey? Tender? And the wine? Good. Anything else, Dearest? No? Well then how 'bout I tuck you and the girls in for the evening ...*

Joe Delgado stuck a plastic fork into a cold, brittle piece of chicken and tried to forget the dog whistle sounds coming from upstairs and the flashing images of *Murder on the Orient Express*. What was it his mother was so fond of saying? Oh, yes. Life is unfair. He bit into something that was neither chicken nor lettuce; he suddenly realized he was holding half a fork. He flung it at the sink and, having not the foggiest idea where the silverware drawer was, decided to eat the rest of his dinner with his hands. His daughter arrived before he finished, looking more hopeful than triumphal, took one look at him and exclaimed, "Daddy!"

"Where do you and your mother keep the damn forks," he said sullenly and not a little defensively.

Terry went to a drawer and removed a silver knife and fork and wordlessly placed them on either side of her father's open plastic container. She returned to the refrigerator and withdrew another plastic bottle of water. She removed the cap and set it before her father, removing two empty bottles and depositing them in the recycle bin. "Sorry, Dad," she said quietly.

Joe looked at his daughter. "Life is unfair, Kitten."

Terry pulled a counter stool around to the other side of the island and sat down opposite her father. "Dad, I need to get a job."

"You have a job," he answered without looking up.

"I mean a real job."

"You have a real job," he answered looking up.

"You don't understand."

"I do understand."

This engendered a characteristic mixture of petulance and resolve. "Mom said I could."

"I'm sure she did."

"Then why won't you support me?"

*Not enough to eat a steady diet of this at work; gotta swallow it at home, too.* "Oh, I dunno. Maybe it has something to do with those two little ones upstairs."

"I'll put them in daycare."

"The hell you will!" His own vehemence startled him; his daughter seemed to expect it.

"I'll pay."

"Then why work?"

"I need to get out of the house."

"Three months ago you begged to get *into* this house."

"The kids are driving you and Mom crazy; I can tell."

"No, they're not," he lied.

"That's easy for you to say; you're at work all day."

Ah, sweet tipping point. "Easy!!!" he erupted. "Easy??? I'm at work all day doing the unthinkable; I come home to the unspeakable. And *I* have it easy!? You and your mother live in a bubble. You have no clue, neither one of you. No sense of responsibility. No comprehension of, of reality. It's only and always about you! It's time to grow up, Theresa Mary Delgado Simpson! Time to grow the hell up!"

Her tears were immediate and abundant and unceasing. She laid her head on the counter and wailed, not unlike, he thought, her first born. He sat there helpless and ever so slightly guilt ridden. *These women of mine are geniuses. Evil geniuses. They transfer their moral lapses, and the guilt they come pre-packaged in, to me … and somehow I end up wearing it. All of it. How? Why?* He was determined not to cross the line of enablement, having spent a near lifetime on the wrong side of it. As the sound of the wailing downstairs began to ebb, he was able to detect the sound of wailing upstairs. He slid off the stool to seek relief among the more rational of his bloodline. He made his way up the center hall stair case and followed the sound into Joseph's bedroom. He was sitting up in his bed sobbing, apparently frightened by the sound of adult despair coming from below. In the adjoining room, Thomas was standing in his crib, head back in a full-throated roar in an attempt to command first attention. For an instant, Joe thought of climbing into the crib, curling into a fetal position, sticking a thumb in his mouth and joining the chorus.

He was startled by movement rushing past him. It was Theresa. She reached for Thomas and hefted him out of the crib. She walked into the adjoining room and sat on Joseph's bed and placed a wet palm on his wet forehead. Immediately, the cacophony abated. Joe tip toed out and down the stairs. He headed into the garage looking for one of his wife's Michelob Lights. On this night he would come crashing off the wagon. He found a stash in a drawer at the bottom of the garage refrigerator, pulled two bottles out, brought them back into the house and headed for the library. He plopped into a thick leather easy chair and twisted the cap off his first beer in over a year. He looked at it longingly. *What is that lyric? "In this world of over-rated treasures and under-rated pleasures … I'm glad there is you …"* He emptied its contents in a single breath, then belched. He sat back, contented. *Lord, thank you for under-rated pleasures … for quiet and solitude, for cool air and cold beer, for a wife on another continent and grandchildren that are incontinent …*

The library door opened. His daughter entered tentatively. He suppressed something primal, a hybrid of a human scream and an animal growl.

"Dad," softly.

"Yes, Kitten."

"I'm sorry."

He felt his heart begin to thaw and was powerless to stop it. "That's alright, Honey. It's alright. Nothing to worry about."

"I feel so guilty. I'm a terrible mother."

"Not at all. You're a good mother."

"I wish I could be more like Mom."

He choked on a short swig. "Ah, Kitten. You're on your way to being every bit as good a mother as … ah … your mother was … is!"

She sat down heavily. An awkward silence ensued. Then, "Dad? What did you mean by unthinkable?"

He stared uncomprehending. She repeated the question: "Earlier, when you said you spend your day doing the unthinkable?"

He felt his stomach tighten and his peace departing. "Oh … nothing, actually. Just me whining about nothing as your mother likes to say."

"They're asking you to do something wrong again, aren't they?"

He hesitated, not wanting to compound a big, black evil with a small, white lie. "Well, right and wrong has become quite a debatable proposition today."

"But *you* know it is wrong, what they're asking you to do. Don't you?"

Put that way, he couldn't, wouldn't, deny truth. "Yes," he said, simply.

"What is it, Dad?"

He smiled, intending to disarm. "It's confidential, Kitten; if I told you, I'd have to kill you ... as they say."

She knew him well enough to know that would be the final word on the subject. Being her mother's daughter, however, she decided to make one more pass. "They're making you buy something Pittman Labs shouldn't be buying, aren't they, Dad?"

He was genuinely surprised by her prescience. Unlike her mother, she pursued matters from her heart, not head. Her concern caught him flat footed. He looked at her for a long moment and said, "Actually it's the opposite, Kitten. But it's strictly confidential and I'm not at liberty to discuss it with anyone. Sorry, but that's all I can really say right now."

"I understand," she said, getting up to leave.

"And Kitten, would you mind shutting off the light on the way out?"

She took her leave, complying with his wishes. From the doorway she glanced back at the large figure now sitting in almost total darkness. She thought she saw movement, a slight quivering; she couldn't tell if her father was laughing or crying.

# 9

John Sweeney entered the darkened church from the covered second floor walkway which connected church and rectory. It was late, slightly after 11:00 p.m. He slid noisily into the first pew opposite the statue of the Blessed Virgin Mary. He was tired, distracted, and in no mood to pray. His mind was filled with the day's events – the mundane, the tedious, the contentious. Then there was his mother, a 24/7 burden. With effort, he lifted his gaze in search of the statue of his heavenly Mother; in the darkness he couldn't see her, so he summoned her. "Help me, Immaculate Mother. Help me be faithful in my prayer life."

Years ago, while in Rome, he had come upon the prostrate figure of Pope John Paul II deep in prayer before the Blessed Sacrament in his private chapel. It was maybe 5:00 a.m. and that chapel, too, was cloaked in darkness. What he saw and heard and felt in that moment changed his priesthood forever, and he resolved then and there to keep a daily "one hour watch," as he referred to it, before this Living Presence. It was, he liked to tell others, something of a spiritual tanning salon. That single hour, if faithfully practiced, yielded a measure of peace not otherwise attained; a peace, he had discovered, that produced "good soil" for the practice of virtue.

Most days, he came at night. In the beginning, he got up one hour before Mass, but found himself dozing off in minutes. He then tried middle of the day. That, too, proved problematic; the demands on a priest serving 245 families seemed to peak with the mid-day sun. Gradually, he ended up coming at night, after dinner, after parish meetings, after return calls to friends and parishioners. Even that proved no panacea. Many nights he was tired and irritable and unable to concentrate. One hour became 45 minutes, became 30 minutes, and some nights, no more than 20 minutes. He came to realize compromise bore a cost. Inevitably, after a mini visit, he'd discover, on the following day, a heightened inclination to assert self rather than deny self. Peace would take flight, and with it, fragments of virtue painstakingly knitted together over time. He'd retire for the evening dejected and defeated, confidence eroded. This ultimately brought fresh resolve. In the middle of one of these "slumps," as he referred to them, he'd pledge yet again to be faithful in answering his Master's Gethsemane question.

Tonight would be another short night. He desperately craved sleep. He struggled to keep his eyes open in the darkness. For an instant he thought of lying down in the pew, but quickly and vigorously fought off that temptation. He thought of several of his parishioners and their difficulties, and immediately flushed those images from his consciousness. He thought of his mother and her staged and accelerating deterioration, and forced the anxiety of it from both heart and mind. He was aware he was in a pitched battle and losing ground. Suddenly, he bellowed into the nothingness, "Abba, Abba, Abba!"

Nothing.

Then came a slight, familiar stirring in his heart. "Abba," he moaned, all but inaudibly.

Stillness. "Well Lord, if you're not going to talk to me, I'll talk to myself."

"*My stout heart, I am not deaf to your pleas.*"

"Lord, I bring you your sheep. You see they are hungry; I have not fed them well."

"*You have confused their hunger with thirst.*"

"Lord, what are you saying to me?"

Silence. Then, *"They thirst … for your thirst."*

"Lord, please. I'm a simple man?"

*"They want to know Him for whom they thirst."*

"Lord, show me how to reveal You for whom they thirst."

*"Show me your thirst for me, and I will show you my thirst for them."*

"Lord, are you displeased with me?"

Silence.

"Lord?" Nothing. The line was dead. He felt chastised. His head fell to his chest and he felt pain in some remote region of his heart.

Then, *"Why do you come to me for affirmation? Why can you not come with affirmation?"*

He brightened. A landline restored. "Yes, Lord. I can … and I will." Pause. "Forgive me, Lord."

*"I asked you to 'come and follow me.' You said, 'yes.' Are you now unwilling to follow me into the abyss?"*

He stiffened. "No, Lord … I will follow you. But I am a weak and sinful man. I am frightened when you ask such questions of me."

*"Do you not trust Me?"*

"Lord, I don't trust me!"

*"But I trust you, John."*

Suddenly, his chest burned and his eyes watered. He made no attempt to fight the sensation welling up within him. Instead, recognizing it for precisely what, Who, it was, he threw his head back and let his lungs fill slowly with this Spirit's power. In moments, he was borne aloft, floating somewhere outside his body. All was now transcendent peace. He half yelled, "I love you, Lord! I love your church, Lord. I love your people, Lord!" He broke into tongues, unintelligible save for their power to give expression to the deepest yearnings of his heart. Gradually, the intensity of what he was experiencing began to ebb. He sat back down. He was aware of an acute consciousness. Into the silence, he bellowed, "Here I am, Lord. I come to do your will."

Immediately, he felt, rather than heard, *"My will for my priests is self immolation."*

He felt an instant anxiety in the pit of his stomach. His mind darted about with astonishing alacrity, sketching scenarios, probable and improbable, for such immolation. Oddly, he remembered the last line of Bernanos' *Diary of a Country Priest*: "All is grace." He felt a sudden surge of this mystical substance and heard himself say aloud, "Yes, Lord!"

*"It is in your immolated self where you will find Me. If you truly wish to reveal Me to others, we must meet at the appointed destination ... which is always in the wounded heart. Will you meet me there for the sake of those for whom I thirst, my stout heart?"*

He immediately thought of Peter. "Yes, Lord. With your help, I will follow you there. But you *will* remember, won't you, that I am a weak and sinful man?"

*"How could I not? Did I not create you? Did I not come to earth to redeem you? Have I not called you* here *to sanctify you?"*

He felt himself on the verge of crying. "Yes, Lord. I just wanted to make sure you wouldn't, you know, forget."

*"Love doesn't forget, John."*

He fell to his knees and said, out loud, the prayer his mother taught him and his brothers and sisters to say at the end of every rosary. "St. Michael the Archangel, protect us in the battle. Be our protection against the wickedness and snares of the Devil. Restrain him, O God, we humbly beseech thee, and do thou, O prince of the heavenly hosts, by the power of God cast into hell, Satan, and all the evil spirits who prowl through the world seeking the ruin and destruction of souls."

He stood, left the pew and walked up three steps to the sanctuary. He held his arms outstretched in front of the tabernacle and bowed his head in silent prayer. Then he blessed himself, left the altar, and went back to the rectory through the covered walkway.

Tonight, he would sleep.

# 10

"Surely you could not have been unaware of this."
Maggie Kealey steeled herself and fought to suppress molecular impulses that had their origin in a distant people and land. "Doctor, if I may suggest, this will work much better if I'm not put on the defensive."

Dr. Stanley Koblinski smiled. She was, as reported, a most formidable woman. "Yes, I understand, Mrs. Kealey."

In the brief awkward silence, Koblinski's secretary, Cara Rivello, entered the office and announced, "Bishop Munson's on the phone, Doctor."

"See if I can call him back, Cara." Pause. "And get a number and time."

The small dark beauty eyed Maggie without circumspection, nodded and left.

"Mrs. Kealey —"

"Maggie."

"Maggie, thank you for coming. I understand why you may not have wanted me to come to you."

Maggie nodded, unsmiling.

Koblinski shifted weight in his walnut swivel chair, which squawked in protest. "How can I be helpful to you?"

"You can tell me what you know, and what it means."

"Means?"

"What's at issue, morally?"

"Yes, yes. I can, and will, do that."

"First, tell me again how you came to know these Regina Hospital doctors are also on staff at local fertility clinics."

"Well, as I said, we crossed checked your directory with those of fertility and reproductive services clinics in the area. And there they were."

"Do you have their names?"

"I do."

"May I see them?"

"Of course." He handed a manila folder across the desk; in the folder was a print-out which identified 36 Regina staff physicians by name, phone number, area of specialization, affiliated health organizations, town, and a brief commentary on the ERD watch.

Maggie looked up. "ERD's?"

"Ah, yes. The ERD watch is a recent invention of the USCCB, the Catholic Bishops Conference in Washington, D.C. The acronym stands for Ethical and Religious Directives; the intent is to provide moral guidelines for Catholic Health organizations across the country."

Koblinski had no difficulties with the ERD's – either in principle or in their intended application. To him they simply reflected the Vatican's seriousness about the so-called "life issues." It was his task to explain them to others, particularly the presidents of Catholic universities and hospitals. This was not a part of the job he especially liked. "Generally," he would tell hospital administrators, often referring to his own written talking points, "these things track long-standing church teachings on matters like contraception, abortion and euthanasia." When that produced the expected yawn, he would add, "More recently, Pope John Paul II updated church teaching to reflect modern technological advancements in medicine, particularly In Vitro Fertilization and embryonic stem cell testing." And finally, "And his successor, Benedict XVI, has recently issued a papal encyclical, Dignitas Personae, which, in effect, codifies the entirety of the church's teaching in this area, and calls for normative standards for all Catholic hospitals." Heads would slowly nod and bodies would swiftly file out. The issue, as Doctor Koblinski was quick to point out privately to friends, was of course *enforcement*, which was largely hit or miss. Mostly miss, as he somewhat reluctantly conceded.

"Tell me about Roberts," Maggie Kealey asked about the first doctor identified to be affiliated with a fertility clinic.

"Well, according to your own web page, he's a partner in the first fertility clinic to, and I quote, 'cryopreserve an embryo pregnancy … in America.'" He observed his guest wince and immediately regretted the reference to the hospital's web site. *Didn't need to go there, did we?*

He paid a price in her icy silence. Then the clouds seem to pass and she asked, "What's the story with Gutelius?"

"Gutelius is a partner in a firm that claims to have, and again I quote, 'the highest success rates of any IVF practice in the Philadelphia region.' Pause. "His firm is quick to add that its success is due to their 'best-in-class embryologists who are able to determine which embryos have the best possible chance of success.'" Long pause. "Of course I don't see any reference to what happens to the embryos their 'best-in-class embryologists' decide might *not* make it."

Maggie felt a sharp pain in her heart. *This is worse than I thought. Mother of God, help me!* "And the other doctors?" she asked, clearly signaling she did not want to hear more.

Koblinski throttled back. Point made. "Maggie, I'm here to help."

"How?" she asked, unable to avoid the drip of cynicism.

"That's up to you."

She looked at him and smiled wryly. "Switch jobs?"

"If you want to appoint an ethicist to your board, I'll volunteer."

"Oh, no!" Maggie immediately saw her board of 18 assembled in the hospital's recently renovated conference room. She saw herself standing at the head of the table and introducing, *'Dr. Stanley Koblinski, our new CCO, that's Chief Conscience Officer.'* She made an attempt to recover. "What I mean, doctor, is that's something that might very well be helpful somewhere down the road."

Koblinski laughed. "I think I understand." He decided to shift tactics. "You're familiar with the specifics of the USCCB's EDR's?"

"No."

Koblinski sat up, elbows on the desk, hands arched at the top of his head. "Maggie, these directives are there to protect people like you."

"From whom? From what?"

"From yourself. From serious errors."

Maggie didn't want to hear any more. The pressure to perform had become an enormous burden which robbed her of sleep and energy, and joy. The Order was telling her they wanted a 'more robust' outreach to the poor in the neighborhood. Her Chief Financial Officer was telling her she had to change the 'payer mix' to more patients with insurance, if they hoped to keep the doors open. Her department chairs were telling her she had to recruit more 'and better' doctors if she wanted to upgrade the institution's image and draw more patients: doctors, they promised, who would bring patients with them to the hospital, patients who were privately injured.

She looked at the list of staff physicians in her hand. Chase them away, chase insured patients away. Chase insured patients away, chase revenue away. Chase revenue away, close the doors. *What good does it do to be in the business, no the mission, of doing good, of healing a community's mind and heart and body, if you can't do the things you need to do to keep your doors open?*

"Doctor, tell me how this patient referral thing actually works."

He nodded, understanding. "A young Catholic couple goes to see a Catholic doctor who is on staff at a Catholic hospital. The meeting may or may not actually take place in the hospital. But, make no mistake, all subsequent blood tests, ultra sounds, MRI's and so on, will. The couple has a problem. They can't conceive a child. Your doctor doesn't believe he can help them; he refers them to another doc who, he says, can help them. They make an appointment to see this doctor in his "fertility clinic" in the next suite, or down the street, it really doesn't matter. When they arrive, they are told how the IVF process works, what its typical rates of success and failure are, and what it will cost. The couple, desperate for a child, signs the papers, writes the check, and begins." Pause. "I don't need to tell you how the process works?"

Maggie shook her head. Her mind formed a mental image of a Petrie dish of sperm, captured with the aid of 'stimulative' material, from a man who was at this moment probably trying to sell someone a credit swap derivative, and a dozen or so eggs successfully oscillated from a woman who was, at this same moment, probably driving her children to soccer practice.

Maggie saw the dish lying on a lab table with a white-coated technician standing over it. He appeared to be waiting for ... what? She fast-forwarded to the newly created embryos, whom she knew to now be living human beings, lying in the dish. One was selected. The others were placed in tubes and inserted in a freezer at the far end of the room, their fate momentarily postponed. She shuddered involuntarily. She looked at Koblinski and said, "Stan, what ... exposure ... do I personally have in something like this?"

*Good.* "Let me break it down for you. In matters like these, matters involving 'grave evil,' the Church distinguishes between 'material' and 'formal' co-operation." Maggie Kealey leaned forward in her chair. *Even better.* "'Material cooperation' is when you know what's going down and do nothing. 'Formal cooperation' is when you're an active part of what's going down." He paused several beats and added, "'Material cooperation' with evil is bad; 'formal cooperation' is ..." he let his voice trail off.

Maggie's eyes widened. "How bad!?"

Koblinski modulated his voice. *Easy does it now. Don't overstate it. Just give her the facts. Trust it'll settle the way it should.* "Ultimately, the Church leaves that to penitent and confessor. There may always be subjective issues in play that might lessen ... culpability." He paused again for effect. "But, objectively, and where public scandal may be given ..." he lowered his eyes and slowly shook his head.

Maggie felt her blood quicken. "What would the Church have me do? If I speak out, I'll lose *all* my docs and half my nurses. The nuns will fire me. The hospital will shut its doors. How is that going to do anybody any good? Doesn't the Church take any of *that* into account!?"

Koblinski knew when to say nothing. Ultimately, Maggie's eruption ebbed, then began anew. "Where's the Bishop in all this!? Where is *he!?* I haven't heard a word coming out of his mouth or his office." She paused and took a breath. Then, softly but pointedly said, "Am I supposed to be more Catholic than my Bishop, doctor?"

He didn't want to go there. *Smart. She's deftly cornered me and left me with no out, save truth.* "O'Hallaran is afraid, Maggie."

"Of what!?" She was incredulous.

"The same fear you just gave voice to."

Her face clouded and she grew impatient. "I'm not getting it. Spell it out."

He felt the full force of her will. "He's afraid he'll lose what in effect are his docs: his priests."

The cloud began to lift in stages. "But why would he lose them if the Church teaches that In Vitro Fertilization is a grave evil?"

Koblinski nodded. "Because the people have spoken."

"You're talking about the rank and file, the Catholic in the pew?"

"Yes."

"And they don't think this is wrong?"

"Why would they? They've never been told."

"But those papal encyclicals, and pastoral letters ..."

"Who reads them?"

"So, they never really hear any of it."

"That would be correct."

"Then it's really just a matter of ignorance?"

Koblinski raised his hands and pantomimed quotation marks. "Invincible ignorance."

Clouds return. "What does *that* mean?"

Koblinski patiently: "It means 'let's not unduly arouse and unsettle the people of God.' People ... at this point, we simply no longer know how to catechize. It would only cause mass hysteria, a run on the bank, so to speak, and that is the worst of all evils."

Maggie pulled her head back in shock. "*That* certainly doesn't sound right."

Koblinski shrugged. "It *isn't* right."

She paused and looked directly at Koblinski. "So, what you're telling me is, I'm not going to get any help from downtown ..."

He felt her vulnerability in that moment. "I'm suggesting ... you shouldn't count on it."

For several minutes neither of them spoke. Maggie studied her feet; he studied her face. Then, "Doctor, what does the 'right thing' look like in this hellhole of a moral dilemma?"

He locked in on her eyes. They were as unblinking as his. "Let's leave that for another day, Maggie. Call me when your head is clear. I'll have some ideas for you." He stood and extended his hand. She was a bit taken aback at his abruptness and did not move at first. In moments, she gathered herself slowly and stood, reaching a bit awkwardly for his hand across the desk. She yanked on it and said, "Good. I'm going to hold you to it."

With that, Maggie Kealey turned and went back to work.

# 11

Michael Burns slowly made his way through the late afternoon shadows and the melting snow. He climbed the rectory steps and knocked on the front door. He heard footsteps and braced himself. He was uncharacteristically nervous. The door opened. Behind it stood his friend and confessor of some 30 years. Neither man said anything until both were inside, the front door was shut and the male shoulder hug ritual was completed. John Sweeney spoke first. "Come on in and tell me about it."

Burns followed him into a small parlor off the center hall. He watched as his pastor shut the double doors and motioned to a matching sofa and arm chair in the corner by the window. Burns chose the sofa. He sat heavily, reflecting the weight of conscience stirred. "How you doing, Father?"

Sweeney sat stiffly in the arm chair and shrugged. "Useless servant," he said with a smile.

Burns laughed and said: "I figure I'm about half that."

"How 'bout a beer?"

"No, no. You'd never get me out of here."

A brief awkward silence. Michael cleared his throat and leapt. "Got me another Class A dilemma, Father."

Sweeney merely nodded.

"I've reached an agreement with Ultra Com to sell Burns Advertising, for close to $30 million." He paused to see if the sum registered. No indication. "I'm due to sign next week." He looked at his friend intently. No signals. "There is a problem." Still no reaction. "I'm going to be asked to do something you're going to advise me not to do." Eyes widened.

"Oh? And what might that be?"

"Proper Parenthood is one of Ultra Com's national clients. Their local affiliate is Women's Right." Sweeney nodded in recognition. "They will expect me to work with Women's Right to build their reputation and their business in the Mid-Atlantic region. The fees will be, uh, significant." He paused, not wanting to go where he was about to go. "Those fees are part of a payout which has already been calculated and agreed to."

Sweeney smiled. "A worm in every apple."

Burns exhaled. "Precisely."

"Sure you don't want that beer?"

Burns laughed. "Got anything stronger?"

Sweeney let the walls absorb the laughter. "Michael, what do *you* think you should do?"

Burns hunched forward. "Well, way I see it, I've got three options. I can sign and work it; I can sign and ignore it; or ... I can *not* sign and tell 'em to go stick it."

Sweeney smiled. "The Michael Burns I once knew would have only seen one option."

Burns fidgeted. "Father, I want to sign."

"And what?"

"Ignore it."

Sweeney recollected himself. "Think that's honest?"

Burns paused and shook his head.

"What do you think would happen if you ignored it?"

"They'd force the issue."

"And?"

Burns shrugged. "Dunno. Maybe if everything else is going well, they won't make a big deal out of it."

"What's the likelihood of that?"

After what appeared to be first reflection, Burns conceded, "Probably not too good."

Sweeney allowed the realization to settle. "Well, I do see a couple of problems with that option."

Burns' eyes narrowed and his forehead creased in neat folds, but he said nothing.

"First, signing itself is an assent, a commitment to promote, at least in part, the evil of surgical abortion. It sends a signal to your employees, your clients, your industry, and the general public that you intend to co-operate in this evil. Second, signing and ignoring your assent breaches honesty; and although clearly not as serious, it is still nevertheless wrong."

Burns drooped in resignation. "Father, it's an awful lot of money to walk away from."

"How much was it again?"

"About 30 million dollars."

Sweeney grimaced. "30 pieces of silver?"

Burns smiled mischievously. "Inflation."

Sweeney's laughter changed the room tone. Burns eased back in the sofa. "Michael, the problem with signing that agreement is it binds you morally to a third condition to avoid culpability, a condition that will prove problematic, to say the least."

"And what's that, Father?"

"To avoid what the Church regards as 'material cooperation' in evil, it's not enough to avoid involvement and withhold assent." He paused for effect. "You're also obligated to speak out against it." Momentary silence. "Could you see yourself doing that?"

Burns half snorted. "Been there, done that, Father."

A long silence fell. "Michael, there must be other buyers out there."

"Oh, there are, Father. Just not at this multiple." He noted the priest's incomprehension. "That's shorthand for … money, Father."

Sweeney nodded. "So, there are other buyers, but they wouldn't pay you as much."

Burns' hands flew up in explanation. "Ultra Com is what's called a 'strategic buyer.' Their assets – their people, their core competencies, and above all their clients – compliment ours, and ours compliment theirs. The anticipated synergy is what pumped the multiple." He paused and shook his head. "Not so much with other prospective buyers."

Sweeney thought he understood at least enough not to probe. "So, you'd have to settle for what, a few million less?"

Burns shrugged. "Could be as much as five to seven…"

Sweeney's turn to shrug. "Like you said, it's a Class A problem. I suppose there are other guys in your position who would be grateful to have those options?"

Burns nodded glumly.

Sweeney saw an opening. "Michael, let's pray."

Burns brightened momentarily but remained silent.

Sweeney pulled the arm chair closer to the sofa and extended his left hand. Burns took it and bowed his head. For several moments neither man said anything. Then, Sweeney began, "Lord Jesus, you promised wherever two or more were gathered in your name, there you would also be. We come to you, Lord, for your guidance. This good man has been faithful to your eternal word, and he intends to continue to be faithful. Please continue to guide him in his business matters. Show him how to glorify you in all he does. Give him peace of mind and strength of heart that he may know and follow your will in all things." Father Sweeney paused briefly before concluding: "And we ask this Lord, as indeed we ask all things, through the intercession of your immaculate mother. Amen."

He pumped Burns' hand which was enclosed within his; it appeared to revive his sagging spirit. He stood up and said, "Thank you, Father. I needed that!"

Sweeney smiled and said, "Michael, go home and read Mark 10:17, with Carol. Then pray and discern. Together, make your decision. And when you make it, don't look back." He struggled to his feet on knees that were perpetually cranky. Michael narrowed the distance between them. He wrapped his confessor in an expansive bear hug. Together, they headed for the door. Michael squeezed his friend's arm and said, "Why do I think I'm going to be re-introduced to that rich young man?"

Sweeney smiled. "Michael, whatever you do, just don't go away sad."

# 12

"How ya comin', Joe?"

Joe Delgado looked over his computer screen and grunted an acknowledgment to Harold Fairfax. "Should have something for you by end of day, Hal."

Fairfax surprised him by walking over to his computer and taking a peek at the screen. The violation of his space did not sit well with Delgado. "Or tomorrow, depending on how many interruptions I get today."

Fairfax laughed and moved around to the other side of the desk. "Big time heat on me about now, Joe." Delgado merely nodded without looking up. *So you're going to dump all of it, here and now, on me? No you ain't. Get the hell back to your own office and do something productive.* Fairfax pivoted and began pacing back and forth nervously. "I've got the Board pounding on me every day; some days I get two, three calls from Willis. Apparently he's in contact with the other side."

Delgado stopped working, pushed his screen to the side and

looked at his boss. "What does that mean, 'in contact with the other side'?

Fairfax fidgeted. He was 11 years younger than Delgado and their relationship had never settled. He was told by the Board when he accepted the CEO position at Pittman Labs that he was "inheriting a two edged sword" in his Chief Financial Officer. And indeed while he had discovered he couldn't operate the business without him, he had also discovered Joe Delgado was very much his own man. Not outright insubordination, of course: never that. Just a virtuoso passive resistance that could effectively erode a business' most precious asset: time to market.

He paused before answering. "The Chairman has friends on the HM Board. Apparently, they want this done as bad as our guys do. They see a window for the stock. They're telling him they can't check off the due diligence box until they get the numbers from 'that financial guy of yours'" Pause. "Uh, that would be *you,* Joe."

Delgado sat forward in his chair. He fought to suppress his anger. "Hal," he began evenly. "I told you to tell the Board, over a month ago, that this is a six week project. I've been working day and night to finish early. The numbers I'm getting from the field are riddled with inconsistencies." He felt a sharp pain in his chest and his blood began to run hot. "I could have given you projections two weeks ago, Hal. I presumed you wanted numbers that would hold."

Fairfax picked the shrapnel out of his face and measured his words. "Of course I expect good numbers, Joe. I also expect a sense of urgency." Pause. "I just haven't seen that."

Delgado exploded. "We've got 26 commercial products in distribution, in 16 countries; those 26 products now have 12 generic threats either in distribution or FDA approved; in addition, we've got another three Pittman Lab products, and seven competitive products, in late stage development. Add another four of our own products, and 16 competitive products, currently in clinical trials; and you want all that rolled up and verified and packaged into bite sized, one, three and five year projections, within stipulated ranges of confidence … overnight! All with the help of just one kid, barely out of college, who doesn't know his butt from first base!" He stopped to catch his breath, which was now shallow and belabored. "Are you out of your mind?"

Fairfax struggled to compose himself. Delgado's voiced had carried well beyond the office and into the other offices in the corporate suite. He tried to recall who was actually in those offices at this moment. He was not looking forward to a lonely retreat across the common area. "No, Joe. Not yet anyway," he said calmly. "But I will be if I don't get those numbers by end of day." He lingered to let the threat settle and quietly turned and took his leave.

He was no sooner out the door than Paula Gomez entered. "Joe, are you alright?"

He looked at his secretary and rasped, "They're nuts, all of them!"

Paula Gomez was an attractive woman in her early 40's; her husband, a marine colonel, was on government disability from Iraq War wounds. They had three children, two of whom were in college. At $62,500 with a $7,500 bonus, her job was important to her family. She feared her boss had just jeopardized it. "Joe, Hal looked pretty upset when he left."

"Good!"

She sat down. "What aren't they getting?" she asked calmly, wanting to dial down his angst.

He shook his head. "I mean, have they no idea of the, the thought that has to go into every number on one of those projections, and how much is at stake?" His eyes widened. "If *they* were the ones who were responsible for the accuracy of this stuff, they'd be begging for time." Deep breath. "Do they forget I have a fully vested equity stake in this sale? Do they think I want to see this deal blow up in due diligence because our revenue projections are all, all hoped up?" He seethed quietly.

She searched for a drop of solace. "He doesn't know you very well, Joe." *Of course you've never let him in, have you? The mere sight of him in that chair, your chair, the one you earned, is simply too much to bear, isn't it?*

He looked up without expression. "No, I suppose he doesn't."

"Think somebody poisoned the well?"

He thought of Helen Hurd, his former secretary, whom he had fired years ago for compromising him on another highly confidential matter. It was said Hurd moved in some of the same cultural circles as Fairfax and his wife. "Perhaps."

She knew he had to get the bile out of his system or it would retard his progress the rest of the day. That would do neither of them any good. "If it weren't for the 'cash out' opportunity for you, I just wish this whole sale to HM would go away, Joe."

His eyes widened with concern. "Paula, please. We're all sworn to secrecy on this thing. We shouldn't even be discussing it."

She got up and shut the door and returned to her chair. She fixed him with a look of resolve. "But we are, Joe. We are. There's something about the whole thing that's bothering you. I want to know what it is."

He blinked. He had not breathed a word about the sale to anyone. He had learned the value of secrecy in war. In Vietnam, where he had served as an Army Captain, it was, at times, a matter of life and death. In the corporate world, the blood spilled belonged to the people who held jobs in what was called 'the back office' – accounting, finance, law, human resources, communications, and information technology. It was *their* salaries and benefits and bonuses that helped justify, and ultimately helped pay for, an acquisition. He had seen deals blow up because they were leaked prematurely to the press, usually by a disgruntled insider in a back office somewhere. True, he was disgruntled. But he didn't want to be fingered as the guy who blew up the sale of Pittman Labs to one of the world's leading conglomerates.

"No," he said softly. "I don't like it, Paula."

"Why?" she all but whispered.

For several interminable minutes he said nothing; she was content to sit and wait in the silence. *She has proven worthy of my trust. And besides, if she leaks any of this, she'd be right out the door with me.* He shot her a quick glance then began with a matter of fact tone that surprised her. "HM has always said it had no interest in the therapeutic research industry. It wasn't a strategic fit, they said publicly. Turns out they've been planning to get into our business for some time."

"Why not just come out and say it?"

He brightened: "Because they wanted to grease the skids for a grand entrance, a big, very wet splash, at just the right moment to pump the stock big time." He paused. "It's always about the stock. That's where the real money is for these optioned-up guys."

She nodded wordlessly, knowing the next sound she heard would be the sound of a dam bursting.

He leaned forward in his chair and declaimed, "Just connect the dots! They know the demographics better than anyone in the world! They know the West is aging at an accelerating rate! So, they know they have to get into the healthcare industry sooner rather than later. But how? How about through a back door? First, let's get a toe in the water through the diagnostic industry, with our imaging equipment, the MRI technology. Then, let's fund new discovery, to see if new chemical compounds, once injected in imaging dyes, will permit our equipment to identify more disease with even greater precision. Well, well, what do you know? Hey, they do! What now? How about we buy Chemnex, that big chemical company in the U.K. that produces the chemicals for the dyes; that'll get us critical mass quickly and erect a barrier to potential competitors in the imaging industry. Okay, done. Now what? Oh, you say we have to get FDA approval for those new magic imaging compounds because they're injected into human bodies? No problem! We'll just tip toe across that diagnostic industry line and find us a therapeutic research house, one of those big pharmaceutical companies. This shouldn't be too hard; there's lots of 'em here and in Europe. Those guys know all about that FDA stuff, the whole clinical trial thing. Let's see now: how about that Pittman Labs? It's just a short train ride away. And those fellows were pioneers in the life sciences revolution way back when. About a quarter of their business is still in oral contraceptives. They'd be a perfect funnel for what's next!"

She stared, confused. "Next?"

He fiddled with his tie. Then quietly, "It's true we're being sold to HM. But that's only part of the story."

"What's the rest of it?"

He looked at her with a gravity she could almost feel. "We're only the first piece of HM's rollup. I have it on good authority, and Fairfax doesn't know I know, that HM is currently in discussions with another major pharmaceutical house here in the east and several biotech firms on the west coast."

"But, why would they buy another pharmaceutical company?"

"Because the pharmaceutical company they are going to buy is the only one in the industry that has said, publicly, it will research the utility of embryonic stem cells for the treatment of Alzheimer's."

She inhaled audibly.

He turned in his chair and looked out the window at the heavy spring rain pelting employees in the parking lot as they exited their cars for another day's work. He lifted his jaw and spoke as if he were addressing them. "HM is preparing to enter the life sciences industry in a way which will first change its trajectory, then its destination; and Pittman Labs will be yoked to that mission like a plow horse, whether we like it or not."

She coughed nervously. "How do you see it playing out, Joe?" *Will I still have a job?*

He turned away from the window and looked at her for a long moment. "HM buys Rossiter and Pittman. They merge us into one entity. They buy several cutting-edge bio-tech companies on the west coast, firms that are well down the road in researching embryonic stem cells. They tuck those firms under the merged pharmaceutical company, probably under the Rossiter brand name, and announce a new turnkey capability in the life sciences industry, with both boxes checked: diagnostic and therapeutic. All of it focused on narrowly-targeted therapeutic categories that deal with aging. The new HM healthcare division will have a new strategic intent: to harvest huge profits from the cells and tissues of human embryos. Cells and tissues, they will claim, that will heal chronic and incurable disease among aging boomers. And, yes, if you're wondering, most if not all of that clinical work will pass through what was once known as Pittman Labs."

He stood and flexed his knees and grimaced. "And do I think that's a bad thing? Yes, Paula, I most certainly do."

This struck a very deep fear in Paula Gomez' heart. She had entered his office bringing, and seeking, solace. She was leaving with a bad case of heartburn. "Joe, I won't betray this confidence."

He smiled and said: "Oh, I know you won't. You and I just entered what the U.S. and the Soviets used to refer to as the 'MAD Zone.' MAD for: Mutually Assured Destruction." He paused and added pointedly, "We both need our jobs, yes?"

Paula Gomez nodded painfully and went back to her workstation.

# 13

Bill Fregosi and John Wallingford were waiting in the rectory kitchen when John Sweeney entered, distracted and preoccupied. John went to the refrigerator and removed a bottle of water and chugged half its contents. He returned the bottle to its rightful place and turned to see his two young charges sitting patiently at the small table in the corner. "Oh, you again!" he said behind a wide smile and arched eyebrows. "Can't get rid of you, can we?"

Fregosi was the first to answer. "Not easily, and certainly not around dinnertime."

He motioned the pair into the dining room and pointed to place settings on the opposite side of his at the head of the table. The young men went to their places and waited for the priest to arrive at his. Once in place, he blessed himself and offered a small prayer for the food they were about to eat, and the woman who had prepared it. He concluded with a prayer for the men and their church. They sat as one.

Carmella Francone appeared as if on cue carrying a large platter of homemade lasagna and placed it in the center of the table. She slid a large serving utensil onto the edge of the platter and quickly smacked John's hand when he reached for it. "Guests first!" she hissed, fixing him with a maternal glare. The young men threw their heads back and emptied their lungs. John feigned offense. "Whatever happened to the male dominated church?" Carmella returned with an oversized loaf of freshly baked bread on an oak carving board and set it in the middle of the two young men, well out of Sweeney's reach. She left without saying a word, chin thrust slightly upward. This set the men off again.

"Now, aren't you glad you're not married, Father?" Wallingford needled.

Sweeney's mind raced into a distant forest of memories. *You'll never know how close I came. And how I still occasionally think of that woman.* "Yes," he smiled upon his return. "God is good."

"Somewhere there is a woman who is living proof God is all merciful!" Fregosi chortled. "However bad you think you have it now, Ma'am, just know this: it could have been a lot worse."

John fielded their laughter cleanly and replied, "Yeah, she could have had you two as sons."

He loved these men. They were laser smart and effortlessly mystical. They had met as Philosophy majors at Catholic University in Washington, D.C. Each was in his mid-20's and was what social scientists called a "white collar professional." Fregosi was an electrical engineer with a major chemical company headquartered in center city Philadelphia. Wallingford worked for a hedge fund down in Delaware, about an hour outside the city.

They knocked on his door one spring evening over a year ago, wanting to talk about, of all things, the priesthood. Their discussion, the first of what would become bi-weekly sessions, lasted until well past midnight, when he finally threw them out. His approach was always the same: listen patiently to whatever they wanted to talk about, answer their questions honestly, and witness, always, to the inner joy of an authentically consecrated heart.

Gradually, over the past 10 years or so, John Sweeney had developed a reputation for helping young men discern vocations. It had not escaped the notice of the episcopacy that of the six to eight men who were routinely ordained from the archdiocesan seminary each year, there were always one or two men among them who had come to John Sweeney for discernment before entering.

Tonight, it was soon clear, the men wanted to talk only about the state of the church. Over several helpings of steaming lasagna and a chilled bottle of red wine, they discoursed on the various challenges confronting what Sweeney was fond of calling 'the Bride of Christ'. Never content with supposition, they stalked the root causes of her decline, and, more insistently, the instruments of her renewal.

"Pope Benedict once said, when he was Cardinal Prefect for Doctrine, that the church of the future would be smaller and holier," Fregosi posited at one point.

Sweeney nodded. "Yes, indeed he did."

"Do you see that too, Father?" John Wallingford asked.

"I do."

"A purification?" Fregosi wanted to know.

"No doubt."

"A re-start?" Fregosi followed up.

"Yes, something along those lines."

There ensued something of a silence; it was broken by Fregosi: "Will it be a stronger church?"

"Yes," Sweeney responded, unblinking. "Meeker because she will be poorer; more prophetic because she will be stripped of her social prestige; more transcendent because she will more closely image her groom."

"And what will draw men to her?" Wallingford asked.

Sweeney smiled broadly. "Men like you. Men prepared to give themselves away, to bear any burden, to guide a soul to its eternal destiny."

Wallingford felt a stirring in his heart. "Truly counter cultural."

Sweeney affirmed. "Salt …"

The men reflected in silence. "Where was it lost, the battle, not the war?" Fregosi asked.

Sweeney shrugged. "Ideas have consequences."

"Too much bad philosophy," Wallingford suggested.

Sweeney nodded. "There was a 19th century French philosopher who suggested there has been something of an evolution in the thought of man through the millennia. Early on, he suggests, we see man's thought dominated by a search for God. He called that the *theological* phase, the biblical narrative. The middle stage of Man's development was dominated by the *metaphysical*, man's search for a sense of self and meaning. In our latter period, we have man's thought dominated by the *scientific* disciplines, man subjecting *all* thought to the empirical process of the natural sciences in his search for dominion over matter." He paused and added pointedly, "This has caused a few complications."

Fregosi nodded: "If you can't prove it, it doesn't exist."

Sweeney smiled. "The problem arrives when our theologians wander into the tar pit. In their intellectual hubris, they attempt to explain the unexplainable. As a German philosopher once said, "Whoever wants to prove the Faith ... has already betrayed it.""

"Hasn't stopped them, has it?" Wallingford smiled.

"No, no. They're still at it," John replied. "The problem they have, but don't see, is what the Irish poet Yeats said over a century ago: 'the center has not held ...' The Enlightenment, ironically, marked the end of Philosophy; now we have philosoph*ies*. And who's to say mine is better than yours? So faith, in our time, has lost its coordinates as a consequence. Man has made subjective what God made objective: *truth*; and he has made an object of what God has made a subject: *man*."

Silence momentarily descended upon the table.

"For most of man's history," John Sweeney continued, "philosophy was a Ming vase for the living water of theology. It held the vision of what man beheld from within, and therefore most treasured. It also provided a bridge to the physical sciences, a kind of intellectual half-way house that served faith on one hand and reason on the other."

"The vase cracked," Fregosi affirmed.

"Had to," Sweeney replied quickly. "Man was holding it too tightly. Once you start trying to codify and verify the metaphysical as though it were a natural science, it begins to fragment. The vase cracks, as you say. And what was in it spills out. In this case, it was the living faith of man."

"'And yet it moves,' as Galileo once famously said of the earth's movement around the sun," Wallingford interjected. "Even modern man cannot live without his search for meaning – existential meaning well beyond anything the natural sciences can ever hope to provide."

Sweeney nodded. "Man is perpetually lonely. Augustine once said: 'Thou hast created us for thyself, O' Lord and our hearts are restless until they rest in thee.' The more man centralizes his governance, the lonelier Man becomes. It is in this solitude that he cries out for meaning. A meaning he can only find in the unseen, but nonetheless very real, person of Jesus Christ."

Wallingford: "Do you foresee a movement toward a grand, dare I say a global, centralization of man's planning designs?"

Sweeney smiled. "Do you?"

Wallingford nodded, quickly.

Sweeney confirmed, "God is a unity. His creation is a unity, *was* a unity before the Fall. His intent is to help his fallen creature create a City of Man on earth, built in the reflected image of the City of God in heaven. But in turning his back on this "unverifiable" Supreme Being, man sets out to build his City without God." He paused and added, "Man's history suggests this doesn't work out too well."

Fregosi, with palpable intensity, interrupted. "This centralization, the great gathering of all God's children under one umbrella, so to speak, it's not of God?"

Sweeney looked at him with paternal affection. "Bill, where is the finger of God in any of it? Clearly, it is man's wish to be free of this God, once and for all, in our time. After 400 years of hard labor, he believes he has finally killed him. Yet, his heart still longs for him. So, not understanding the source of his restlessness, he proceeds to build a dependence on self, and, in the process, renders that self impotent.

The men sat in uneasy silence. Then, Wallingford said, "We are slowly being suffocated by our own thought; is that what's happening to our generation, Father?"

Sweeney reflected. "Well, yes. From one age to the next there has always been a continuity in the thought of man, particularly as relates to identity and purpose. Modern man has severed this metaphysical umbilical cord. He now creates his own truth. As Benedict XVI once said: '… from being the measure of man, truth now becomes his creature …'"

Fregosi: "But maybe this second and decisive Fall of man is necessary."

Sweeney smiled and nodded. "Ah, yes — the power of man on his knees. Absent a future, man in his despair will inevitably be driven to his knees. It is this cri de'coeur that his creator answers; and it is then, through his encounter with the Lord of all, that man rediscovers hope. And it is this hope that allows him to create his future, a future worthy of himself."

Wallingford's face brightened. "And that is what it means to be a priest."

Sweeney's eyes misted up. He looked upon the faces of the two men at his table and saw pure light. In a flash he saw them laboring in the vineyard under a broiling noonday sun. Then he saw them in a deep, dark trench with no sound save the distant wailing of men. "Yes, John," he whispered, eyes averted. "We must shout our lungs hoarse and when our cries go unheeded, we must follow man into the abyss. And when he turns to us, and he will, we must be there at the ready, to point the way to Jesus Christ, who alone is his hope and his destiny."

He redirected his watery gaze toward the two young men; they rose and closed the distance, arms outstretched. Returning their embrace, he felt their tears on his neck. Slowly, he withdrew. They would have to let themselves out. He had one more stop to make before calling it a night.

# 14

---

Maggie Kealey counted the houses from the corner and steered her late model, egg-white Acura into an open spot midway down the block. The neighborhood rested on the top of a hill overlooking the river on the western ridge of the city. The two-story twin homes were immaculately and, at first glance, all but uniformly maintained; the American yard flags large and small suggested, if not quite openly declared, the deeply held traditional values of the small borough's residents. Maggie scanned the mailboxes hanging on the red brick exteriors looking for her destination. Finding it, she opened the waist-high door of a white picket fence that enclosed a small, tidy lot. She stopped briefly to look at the newly installed swing set in the rear of the yard. *My God, where have the years gone? Thank you, Lord, for allowing me to conceive and nurture life. Thank you for the gift of motherhood. You have been so good to me, so merciful. Forgive me, Lord, for taking that demonic pill and closing myself off to new life.* She climbed the two steps leading to the front door and knocked once; immediately the door opened and a woman stepped from behind the door. She appeared to be in her mid-30's and was holding an infant in her arms. She smiled warmly and beckoned Maggie inside. "Mrs. Kealey, I've so been looking forward to meeting you."

It was early spring and the chill in the mid-morning air made the warmth inside welcoming. Maggie quickly shed her coat and laid it casually across the back of a red upholstered arm chair just inside the door. "Thank you, Liz, for seeing me," she said, reaching for the infant. The younger woman smiled and offered the small bundle in her arms to the older woman. Maggie quickly hugged the infant and held him to her neck, patting him gently on his back. "And what's this little treasure's name?"

"Jude."

"Jude? Is there a message in there somewhere?"

The younger woman smiled broadly. "He is the answer to prayer, desperate, pull-out-all-the-stops, don't-take-no-for-an-answer, prayer."

Maggie held the infant less than a foot from her face and said, "Do you hear that Jude Posner? You're a living, breathing miracle! You will be a sign of hope for many in the time to come." She kissed the child on the forehead and began to rock him gently.

Hearing this seemed to greatly delight the child's mother, whose eyes quickly welled with tears. "Oh, Mrs. Kealey!"

"Maggie."

"Maggie, God is so good!"

Maggie nodded: "He *is* that."

The woman nodded her head toward the kitchen which sat off the dining room in the rear of the house. "C'mon out, I have a pot of coffee brewing."

Maggie followed the woman out of the living room and through a small dining room into an even smaller kitchen. There was a table for two next to the refrigerator, and on the table were two white porcelain cups and saucers. Two small matching pieces of china bearing cream and sugar had been placed in the middle of the table. Maggie promptly sat, cradling the infant. The younger woman went to a coffee maker next to the sink and withdrew a pot of steaming black coffee. She returned and wordlessly poured two cups before returning the pot to its holder. She reached for the infant before she seated herself, to allow Maggie to prepare her coffee. She looked at Maggie and smiled. "Maggie, I just love your daughter. She has been a godsend, literally."

"How long have you known Grace?"

The question momentarily caused a contortion in the young woman's face. Maggie was surprised at the depth and severity of the lines etched below her eyes. *My God, this one has suffered!* "I think it's been … I don't know … maybe two years now?"

Maggie nodded. *Where to begin?* "Grace is very fond of you, Liz. She says you've been an inspiration to her." She smiled. "Believe me, that's high praise from that one."

The young woman's eyes instantly welled with tears and Maggie quickly understood this would not be an easy conversation for either of them. To ease her host's self consciousness, she sipped the hot coffee and said, "Oh, Liz, how I needed this!"

Liz wiped her eyes with her open hand and laughed. "My God, you must think I'm a basket case."

Maggie replied, "All I know is Grace said *she* would have been a basket case if she had gone through half of what you've been through."

"She is such an amazing woman, Mrs. Kealey – Maggie. My husband and I just love her."

Maggie regarded Grace as the crowning achievement of her life. When her oldest daughter had taken her own life, and her husband had abandoned her and their six young children for another woman, it was Grace who convinced her mother that she would persevere in faith and come through the dark night stronger and better able to minister to the absence of hope in others. She'd often wondered what God had planned for this special child; the answer had come in recent years from a growing number of women like the one now sitting adjacent to her, caressing new life.

"She is indeed, Liz."

There was a brief silence. Then Maggie tip toed into the breach. "Liz, are you okay to talk about this?"

The younger woman smiled bravely and nodded, but her eyes revealed a lingering apprehension. "Oh, sure. I'm just hoping this will help other women ..." her voice trailed off.

Maggie said gently, "Why don't we just start from the beginning. I'd like to understand as much of this thing as I can."

She nodded and began. "My husband and I married in 2002. It took me two years to get pregnant. I lost the baby in the third month. We tried again and again over the next two years without success. Finally, I went to my Gynecologist. He put me on Clomid, a fertility drug. The only thing that did was cause excruciating pain. Eventually, I just told him, 'hey, no more; I'm through with this thing.'"

The infant started to cough and his mother lifted him to her shoulder. "Anyway, my Gynecologist sent me to a Reproductive Endocrinologist at Regina Hospital, a Doctor Samuel. He suggested IUI; are you familiar with that?"

Maggie nodded. "Intrauterine Insemination."

"Yes." She paused before resuming. "So my husband, Tom, and I prayed about it and decided to do it. Tom insisted we use his sperm. So the doctor put me on all these ovulation stimulants. Cost us about $5,000. I had to inject myself three times a day. The drugs were supposed to help my body produce enough follicles to create eggs. Then the eggs drop down to catch the sperm." She shrugged. "We did, like, three cycles over the next six months."

Maggie interrupted. "What's the nature of the, uh, process for capturing the sperm?"

Without a trace of self consciousness, the younger woman answered. "Oh, they made my husband come in one half hour before the procedure. They put him in a room with movies and magazines." She smiled. "Then they wash the sperm to make sure there are no, you know, contaminants that might infect the uterus."

Maggie stiffened slightly. "What did the procedure itself cost?"

"Oh, around $4,000."

*Holy Mother of God! What a racket!* "And nothing?"

She shook her head. "Nothing."

Maggie winced. "Then what?"

"Doctor Samuel recommended IVF: In Vitro Fertilization."

"At this point, Liz, you're thinking what?"

"I'm thinking, God, you better come through now because this is it, our last shot." She laughed nervously.

"Okay, take me through what happened."

"Well, first they bring you in and explain the process – the meds, the transplant, the surgery, the whole thing; they also tell you about the side effects because they can really create a strain on the marriage, to put it mildly." Another small smile. "This time they put me on six meds! When I was ready they brought me in to harvest the eggs. They called my husband, to do his thing" Smile. "Then they mix the eggs and the sperm in the Petrie dish, add water or whatever, stir, and voila!" She shrugged innocently.

"How long does it take for the fertilized eggs to become embryos?"

"About three days."

"And where does that happen?"

"In the fertility clinic."

"And where's that?"

"Next door to the hospital."

*Next to the hospital. My hospital!* "Liz, how many eggs were involved?"

"Twenty-four," she smiled proudly, adding, "They said normal is, like, 6 to 8."

"Did any of this cause pain?"

"Oh, it was awful! Terrible pain. My ovaries and uterus were so bloated and cramped I couldn't stand upright for days on end. I had to quit my job; I was an orthodontic assistant. Plus, the mood swings! My God, I was a wretched bitch, just a horrible person. I'm surprised my husband didn't leave me. He's a saint, he really is.

Ask Grace. Anyway, he said later, I became a different person; so he prayed God would make me *me* again."

Maggie shuddered involuntarily. "So what happened to the 24 eggs?"

"When they thawed them, six were lost," her eyes fell. "I insisted they insert three; usually they only do one or two."

"What did they do with the other 15?"

"They froze them."

"In the hospital!?"

"No, in a big freezer in the fertility clinic next door."

"How does that work?"

"Well, they put the embryos in a tiny tube and put the tube in a small plastic container and put the container in a big freezer."

"My word!" Maggie blushed and collected herself. "Liz, how many, of the three embryos they inserted, attached?"

"Only one," eyes averted.

"Didn't hold?"

The younger woman shook her head. "Didn't hold."

Maggie whispered, "Liz, may I ask what that whole ordeal cost you and your husband?"

"About $15,000, not counting the fees for cryopreservation."

"And how much were they?"

"About another $1,000."

"And that bought you, what, storage?"

Liz nodded. "For one year."

"Then?"

"Then, if you don't use them, they, uh, dispose of them."

"How, Liz?"

"I don't know."

Maggie halted. "May I use the bathroom?"

"Sure. It's upstairs at the end of the hallway."

She quickly exited the small kitchen and exhaled; as she ascended the stairs she was breathing deeply. She didn't need the bathroom; she needed out of the kitchen. *Lord, forgive us; we know not what we do.* She repeated this short prayer. Once inside the bathroom, she splashed cold water on her face and stared into the mirror. *Lord, give me the strength, please. The strength you had when you chased the money changers out of the temple. I can't do this without you, Lord.* She reached for a towel and dried her face. She re-folded and hung the towel and retraced her steps downstairs to the kitchen. As she neared the bottom steps, however, she noticed that Liz and the infant were now on a love seat in the living room. She took a seat opposite them on a small couch. Liz spoke first. "It's all so hard to take, I know."

Maggie's transparency embarrassed her. "I am just over-whelmed by what you've been through; I don't know how you did it, I really don't."

"Looking back, neither do I," the younger woman answered with an unselfconscious laugh.

"So, please excuse me; you were saying?"

She nodded. "Well, only one of the three embryos they inserted actually attached; it didn't hold."

Maggie grimaced. "So, what are you and your husband think-ing at this point?"

"We're thinking, 'in for a penny, in for a pound,'" she smiled.

*Oh no!* "So what did you do?"

"We went for a frozen round, at half the cost."

Maggie blinked. "Say again?"

"A frozen cycle is when they just thaw the embryos you're storing in the freezer, and insert the ones they think will have the best chance of surviving."

"How many did they thaw?"

"Ten, but only four survived."

"Liz, did you ever get a look at these tiny little embryos?"

"Yes. They showed them to me on a kind of close circuit TV monitor. I saw them all. Each one was numbered."

"Numbered!" Maggie exclaimed.

The younger woman's eyes fell at the sound of stridency.

Maggie immediately felt self conscious. "I'm sorry, Liz. The idea of numbering the embryos just caught me off guard. Sorry."

Liz just shrugged. "Well, it's not like I named them. Guess they didn't have much choice."

"Of course, of course." *You pompous hypocrite! How dare you make anyone feel guilt about anything!* She rushed to recapture the low ground. "So, they inserted the four, all four?"

The younger woman's eyes were clear and forgiving. "Yeah. Probably not too smart on my part, but, again, I was pretty desperate."

"How long did you have to wait this time?"

"Ten days. They sent me back to Regina Hospital for the blood test." Pause. "I wasn't pregnant." At this, her eyes started to moisten. "That was really a low point for us; the $7500 cleaned us out. We had run though our entire life's savings."

An awkward, painful silence. Then, softly: "Can I get you another cup of coffee, Maggie?"

"No dear. I'm fine. I just — I just feel so badly for you; my heart is broken. God love you for all you've been through."

"Well, I wish I could tell you that was the end of it; it wasn't."

Maggie's eyes widened but she said nothing.

"My husband and I went to the bank for a home equity loan; we went back to the clinic and did two more rounds; one fresh, one frozen."

*Why?* Maggie struggled to get the tone of her question properly calibrated. "Uh, what was driving that, Liz?"

"My husband's a policeman. The township force is very close. We have a lot of events and things. You know, picnics and barbeques and swim parties in the summer; and a lot of winter things, too" Her eyes began to water. "We would go and see all the children, and it just broke our hearts. We couldn't bear to look at each other. We felt defective, like we had somehow let the other down. It was horrible. Oh Lord, just the memory of it ..." she began to sob. Maggie moved quickly to the love seat to comfort her. She wrapped the younger woman in her arms and pulled her and the infant to her bosom. Gradually, the sobbing abated. Maggie reached for the cloth diaper on the woman's shoulder and handed it to her; she wiped, then dabbed her eyes. "I felt so bad for my husband. Then, I got even more desperate! The next round, we created 21 new embryos; I had four inserted. I got pregnant. We were so happy! We praised and thanked God! We just knew, you know sometimes how you just know? We knew this was the moment. God had blessed us, finally! Then ..." her voice quivered and trailed off. Maggie held her tighter.

She wiped her eyes and nose with the end of the diaper and shifted the infant to her far shoulder. Her eyes remained downcast as she continued in a subdued voice. "After that, I just thawed everything, all 24 of them. Eighteen didn't make it. I told the doctors to insert all six. I didn't care. They told me some of them might split. I said, 'I don't care; insert 'em all!'" she began to cry softly.

*Job's daughter. How else to see her? Please, don't ask any more questions, okay? Just don't!* "Liz, can I get you anything?" She felt the younger woman's whole body shaking.

She sat up abruptly. "You know, Tom and I both fell into depression. That's what nine miscarriages will do to you. Not to mention another $25,000 in debt, just before the housing bubble burst!" She paused, breathing audibly. "We separated from our friends, almost from each other. We were like walking zombies. And I was having acute pain, the worst of my life. Finally, I went back to my gynecologist at Regina Hospital. He recommended a surgeon. They opened me up. Said it was the worst case of endometriosis they had ever seen: just a bright green fungus all over everything. It was like a small pond in late summer." She laughed. "They removed it: all of it. They told me I'd be able to carry; so believe it or not, we tried again. Just ourselves this time. We were out of money." She laughed and Maggie glimpsed her youth for the first time. "I did get pregnant. This time I made it to the 10-week mark. They rushed me to the hospital and gave me a full blood transfusion." She shook her head. "Didn't help."

Maggie reached for the infant to allow the mother to collect herself. He began to cry softly at the sudden transfer but there was no movement from his mother to reclaim him. Maggie asked the question she wanted to ask since she first set foot in the home. "Liz, how did Jude find his way to your front door?"

The younger woman turned to Maggie on the sofa and said, "Grace."

Maggie nodded. "Grace never told me the circumstances."

"We became friends through St. Mark's, our parish, when Grace and Scott moved in a couple of years ago. She heard what Tom and I had been through and approached us. She'd just started with this NFP program, the Natural Family Planning thing. She was so vibrant and positive. Like everyone else, we were just, you know, very much taken with her. We became friends very quickly. Anyway, one day she was at the hospital with one of her, I don't know what you would call them – customers, I guess. It was just before noon. I'll never forget it. The phone rings. It's Grace. She says a woman just gave birth to a perfectly healthy baby boy and wanted to give him up for adoption. I didn't ask any questions. None! I just screamed and hung up. I called Tom and he came home and picked me up. We were at the hospital in, like, half an hour!"

Maggie's heart reflexively tracked suffering. "Did you ever find out about the other woman?"

Liz nodded. "She was, is, Catholic. Twenty-eight years old, I believe. Her husband threatened to leave her because she wouldn't abort the child. So she asked if anyone on duty knew a good home for the child. Grace heard, she was on the floor at the time. She went to the woman's room and told her about us. The woman started to cry and said, 'I want that couple to have my child. They'll be good parents.' Grace called us immediately."

The woman's joy was so boundless it was contagious. Maggie started to sing to the child. She held him up and began to dance slowly in rhythm to the Beatles' eponymous standard. The infant started to coo. This delighted Maggie. "Look, he's a ladies man already. He's making eyes at me!" She laughed and looked at Liz, who was still sitting on the couch taking it all in. "Oh, Liz. I am so happy for you and Tom. God is so good, so very good. He never abandons us. Never. And now, look! Jude! Jude the Possible. Because all things are indeed possible with God."

Liz looked soberly at Maggie for a moment and said, "May I tell you something?"

Maggie promptly sat, cradling the infant. "Of course, Liz. Anything."

"A little over a month before that phone call, Grace told me to name the nine children we lost; then to go to St. Mark's and light a candle for each of them. She said to kneel in front of the Blessed Mother and ask her to prepare me to be a mother, and then to go home and start a 40-day rosary novena. So I did. All of it. On the 41st day, the phone rang. It was Grace."

Maggie's eyes welled up. "Oh my. Oh my …" there were no more words.

The younger woman felt a need to continue. "I've always been, you know, a good Catholic. Tom, too. We never missed Mass on Sunday, even when we were at rock bottom. Do you think, maybe, that's why God blessed us in the end?"

Maggie answered her indirectly. "I think God loves you and Tom so much, and his own heart was broken. I think He was just looking for the right moment to give you what you asked for." She paused, unable to suppress her curiosity. "Liz, did you ever talk to your pastor about any of this?"

"Not really. I mean I would confess it, you know, the things we were doing … but we never really talked about it."

"You confessed it!?"

The younger woman opened her palms in explanation. "Yeah. I knew what I was doing was wrong. I did."

"Did your pastor agree?"

"I don't know. He never said anything."

"Never said *anything*?"

She shook her head. "No, he'd just listen, give me a light penance, and then absolution."

"That's all?"

"Yeah."

"And this is over, what, four years?"

The younger woman shrugged her shoulders. "About that, I guess." She paused reflectively, then added, "I have an aunt who's a nun. When I told her what Tom and I were doing she just said, 'well, you have to do what you have to do.' I don't know. I don't think either of them thought it was wrong. But I knew it was wrong. I did. That's why I confessed it."

Maggie felt a sharp pain in her heart. She wondered how many other young women had similar stories. *Lord, where are our bishops? Where are our priests? The flock is being scattered among the wolves. Who will find them and bring them back? Lord, please, I beg you. Send us shepherds, Lord! We need shepherds.* "Liz, I'm just so sorry you didn't meet my Grace earlier."

A pained expression crossed, then seemed to fill, the younger woman's features. "So am I."

Maggie cradled the infant and returned him to his mother. She went to retrieve her coat. She flung it over her shoulders absentmindedly. They stood awkwardly for several moments by the door. Maggie gently stroked the infant's back. She looked at the young mother and smiled. "How about we pray for each other, Liz?"

"That works for me!" she responded. Then, as an aside to Jude she said, "Honey, I think mommy got the better end of that deal."

Maggie laughed and opened the door to leave. Before descending to the first step, she half turned and said, "You know, Liz, I really am counting on those prayers."

"I'll start tonight, Maggie: one rosary a day for 40 days."

Maggie nodded and smiled; she descended the steps carefully and in moments was back in her car.

# 15

—————

Aaron McKenna entered the foyer from the office of his center city townhouse and immediately did a double take. "Lord Burns himself! To what do I owe the honor?"

Burns smiled and said, "Just making the rounds of all my remote outposts; making sure my subjects are content."

McKenna didn't let the opportunity pass. "Well, if you come bearing largesse, your Excellency, you'll not find me ungrateful."

Burns laughed and feigned condescension. "Gratitude becomes you, McKenna; it's why I find it so easy to be generous toward you."

McKenna led his visitor into a museum of an office. It was large and dark and richly appointed with expensive ceiling to floor crimson drapes and built-in bookcases which were filled with ornately bound classics. On the walls hung an eclectic assortment of art treasures from French Impressionists to Post Modernists. On end tables there were elaborately framed photographs of the proprietor with a wide assortment of athletes, entertainers and politicians.

Even in a large room with a 12-foot ceiling, however, it was the executive desk that dominated the office. It sat in the middle of the room, a small, exceedingly well polished oval with nothing on it save a bound executive calendar, and no chair behind any portion of it. In one corner, adjoining one of two sitting areas, there was a hand-carved nook that housed a small but well stocked bar.

Burns Advertising had been doing business with McKenna Communications for 12 years. Michael was first among his competitors to comprehend that lucrative state advertising contracts were more effectively bid when bid in tandem with minority proprietors. He'd recruited McKenna out of a local university where he had been a basketball star, and, after a two-year stint with Burns Advertising, set him up on his own. Together, they bid Pennsylvania's tourism, lottery and development business. Together, they'd run the table. Burns Advertising created the "umbrella campaigns" for mass markets, within which McKenna Communications created the segmented adaptations for minorities. This had proven exceedingly lucrative for McKenna since it relieved him of having to invest in expensive market strategists and high-powered creative teams. Burns also did all the media planning and buying, which meant all Aaron McKenna had to do was hire a secretary and find some free lancers to create ethnic variations of the print campaigns. The arrangement had catapulted McKenna into the city's upper echelon of movers and shakers, and rendered him so grateful that he took to calling Burns 'Dad,' which the older man had done nothing to discourage.

Burns trailed McKenna to one of the two sitting areas, and without waiting for his host to point to a sofa, commandeered the large leather-bound armchair facing the door: the power perch in the room. McKenna smiled to himself and dropped into one of the adjoining sofas. "So, Dad, am I still in the will?"

"Pole position," Burns responded with a slight nod.

McKenna pantomimed a sitting, waste up version of a break dance. "Then what the hell am I working for?"

"So you can start a family and have ten kids; that's the only way I can arrange to get you into the Catholic Church."

The younger man laughed. "And I thought the Union League was difficult."

Burns smiled and said, "Actually, the Church is even more desperate for minorities."

"Why? It's got you Irish Catholics. Haven't you gotten the memo? You're now, officially, a minority."

Burns laughed and nodded. "Soon enough, Mick, soon enough."

A brief silence followed, then McKenna asked, "Hey, let me get you something cold."

Burns waved him off. "No, no. Don't tempt me. I'm good, I'm good."

Another silence. This one created a measure of surprise in the younger man. Hesitation, however momentary, was most uncharacteristic of his mentor. He had modeled his own high-purpose, high-energy approach to business on Burns' soaring trajectory, and he found this sputtering a bit unsettling. He decided, however, he would not throw himself into the breach, but would instead simply wait for the older man to speak.

In time, he did. " I come with a proposition, Mick."

"I figured," McKenna smiled.

Burns' eyebrows arched. He immediately wondered what his protégé knew. The Philadelphia Advertising community was so closely knit that it was not at all unusual for a causal breakfast conversation between two executives to make the rounds by mid morning. Incessant rumors of acquisitions, new business solicitations, and new hires and layoffs kept the rumor mill's machinery properly lubricated and stunningly efficient.

"Heard something, Mick?" he asked with feigned nonchalance.

"No, nothing," McKenna responded quickly, trusting no chemical emission would compromise his small prevarication.

Burns stared for several uncomfortable moments, and then

continued. "What I have to say must, I repeat, must, be kept in strict confidence, Mick." Brief pause. "Are we good on that?"

McKenna nodded tightly. "We are, Michael."

Burns nodded and paused again. "Mick, I've entered into an agreement with Ultra Com to sell Burns Advertising." He stopped to appraise his protégé's reaction.

The younger man immediately ginned up the kind of performance he had long ago mastered to seduce referees into calling offensive fouls on his opponents. His body gyrated this way and that in his seat, he made a train chugging and whistling sound and motion, then he leapt from his seat to high five Burns, who remained sitting and ostensibly nonplussed.

"When's the signing?" McKenna asked breathlessly, having bounced back to the sofa.

"The end of the month," Burns replied evenly. "And I want to make sure we're synched up when we make the call to the Governor and our clients out in Harrisburg."

"When will that be?"

"Depends ..." Burns responded with a trace of a grimace.

"On?"

"On when it's clear we're about to lose control of the story," Burns answered pointedly.

*In that case, should I call him now? I've got him on speed dial.* "Why would we lose control of the story, Michael?"

Burns sniffed artifice and answered disingenuously, "Oh, I don't know; sometimes stuff leaks."

"Not from here! Not from here it won't." The younger man was adamant.

Burns had learned to trust his well-honed instincts in New York, the world of advertising's largest shark tank. Instincts were *the* indispensible survival mechanism; you either developed them quickly, or you were devoured quickly. He was not without his suspicions regarding McKenna's ultimate ambitions and loyalties. To head off the kind of rupture that would leave his large state contracts vulnerable to competitors, he had invested a significant amount of time in making sure the interests of Burns Advertising and McKenna Communications were properly aligned.

"No, I'm certain of that," he said a bit opaquely. "Of course, you and I do have competitors who would love to have that information about now, as we both know."

The younger man nodded vigorously. "Right!" He paused and added earnestly, "Michael, I will keep my ear to the ground. I promise you. If I hear anything, I mean anything, I will call you and I will make sure I get through."

Burns nodded reassuringly, while summarily dismissing the pledge. He had something more binding in his gift basket today. "Mick, I think this sale could be a bonanza for you, in a couple of different ways."

McKenna bounced off the sofa again and toward the bar. He opened the small refrigerator and removed a pair of green Heinekens, removed their tops and handed one to Michael. "Well, if we can't celebrate you, we sure as hell can celebrate *me*!"

Michael laughed and drained half the bottle with his initial slug, apparently oblivious to the signal it sent his protégé. He exhaled audibly. "Well, as the man said, it's 5:00 somewhere."

Aaron McKenna leaned forward in the sofa and rubbed his hands together. "So, Dad, tell me, how we gonna get rich together?"

Burns looked at him with mock reproach. "What you mean '*we*,' Kemosabe?"

"Hey, we're blood!" McKenna half shouted with feigned outrage.

Burns drained the rest of the bottle and fixed the younger man with a hard stare. "Okay, let me tell you how that's going to happen." He got up and walked to the bar and placed the empty bottle on its surface with one hand, while opening the door to the refrigerator and withdrawing another bottle with the other. He removed the cap and returned to his seat. To heighten his host's anticipation he sipped the brew slowly and deliberately, eyes fixed on its contents. Then, abruptly, he lifted his gaze and settled it on his host. "Okay," he began with studied deliberation. "Here's how this is gonna go down. First, Ultra Com has what they call 'affiliate companies' on every continent. Burns Advertising will be one of those companies. There are three others here in America. None of its affiliated companies has so far figured out how to do official business with their host states or countries, most of which now have tourism and lottery budgets. The guys who run Ultra Com intend to change that." He paused to gauge the younger man's reaction. "That's where *we* come in. We're going to form a separate consulting arm, you and I: just the two of us. And we are going to hire out, at very large per diems, to show the Ultra Com affiliates how to tap those government spigots."

McKenna was very nearly off his seat. "Hey boss, can we start in Sweden?"

Burns shuddered. "Remind me to have a leash made for you: a very short leash."

"How much you thinking?"

Burns shrugged. "I don't know. Maybe $5,000 a day for me, and $3,000 for you."

McKenna's eyes widened. "Would they pay that?"

Burns smiled. "The ones who are struggling will be encouraged to do so by the guys who run Ultra Com. And if we're successful with them, the others will fall like ripened fruit."

Burns watched McKenna's mind do a quick computation. *He probably just booked 25 days of revenue for next year and double that for the following year.* Michael had a strong hunch the likelihood of this "found money" would keep his young charge on the reservation. *But just in case* … "And Mick, there's something else."

The younger man blinked. *If this is what I think it is, I hope his number matches mine.*

"Mick, I'm going to buy your company."

McKenna just stared, poker-faced.

Burns smiled. "How's two million dollars sound?"

The younger man tried to suppress his euphoria. Burns' number was almost twice his own number. *How to respond!?* "Michael,

I'm floored. I don't know what to say. I'm just, just ..." he shrugged his shoulders, waved his hands and allowed his voice to trail off. He immediately pictured himself in a new Bentley. *Man, this is gonna be one fat ride.*

Burns quickly brought him back to earth. "You're going to get the same deal from me that I'm getting from Ultra Com; half up front at signing, the balance paid on a four-year earn out." He eyed his young partner carefully. "Any problems with that?"

McKenna shook his head. "That means the first million in profits, anytime over the next four years, are mine, right?"

Burns nodded.

"And you and I are going to work together to make sure those profits happen, right?"

Burns smiled. "Oh, I'm going to do more than that, Mick." He paused for effect. "I'm going to guarantee them."

The younger man was stunned. One of the first things practitioners in the advertising business learned was that there were no guarantees in the advertising business. Ever. He looked at his mentor with incredulity. "How?"

Michael Burns stood up and walked to the bar; he leaned his backside against the slab of marble and folded his arms. "Ultra Com has a potential build-out opportunity for me; a local, uh, service organization loosely affiliated with one of their national clients. They want me to help this outfit expand their business beyond Philadelphia." He paused. "I think it's a better fit for McKenna Communications."

Aaron McKenna's pupils looked as though they had been dilated. "Why?"

Burns didn't hesitate. "They're younger and hipper than my folks. We won't match up well. You're a much better fit."

"How big?"

Michael smiled. "Let's just say, the annual fees from this single new client will more than guarantee your earn out, in less than two years."

The younger man was speechless. *Man, I got to find me a church.* "What can you tell me about this new client?"

Burns shook his head. "Nothing now, but soon."

In the silence, Michael watched the younger man struggle to get his head around his extraordinary good fortune. *This will keep him, and my state contracts, in harness for at least the next couple of years; it will also solve my other problem.*

McKenna broke the silence. "Michael, what are our next steps?"

"Have your lawyer draw up an agreement of sale, then immediately kill him." Small smile. "Call me on my personal line when you're ready, and I'll have my attorney come over here and review it."

McKenna jumped off the sofa and, in three long strides, reached Burns. He hugged him tightly and said, "You've been real good to me, man. I will never be able to repay you. You do know that, don't you?"

Burns gently withdrew from the embrace and laid his hands on the younger man's shoulders. "All I ask, Mick, is that someday you do for someone else what I've done for you."

The young man nodded earnestly. "I will, I swear I will, Michael."

Michael Burns nodded, squeezed both shoulders tightly and departed.

# 16

The sound of the doorbell startled the Delgados at late dinner. Mother and daughter looked at each other with 'were you expecting someone?' expressions; Joe Delgado did not bother to look up. For several moments no one at the table moved. The doorbell rang again. Fran Delgado looked at her daughter and said, "Would you be good enough to get that Honey, looks like your father has the night off."

Joe Delgado stifled an obscenity and fixed his wife with a hard stare. Some years ago they had agreed on boundaries, but his wife tended to regard all established boundaries as negotiable. Privately, he called her 'Arafat,' and often visualized her with the former Palestinian's trademark headdress wrapped around her head. The agreement, which Joe referred to as "The Delgado Peace Accord," stipulated that he was entitled to respect in front of the children. That's all: just a Rodney Dangerfield level of respect. In return, she was entitled to burn through credit cards, bank accounts, and her own stock portfolio like Sherman rampaging through Georgia. In addition, there would be seasonal vacations for her and friends of her choosing: 'seasonal' ultimately defined as one every winter, spring, summer and fall. Those had been his idea. When he and his wife were forced to appear in public together for a business or social event, she was to maintain at least a modicum of sobriety. And there was one last stipulation: there was to be no sex. Absolutely, positively none. When she had insisted on this stipulation, he had attempted to feign resistance, but he weakened quickly and found himself reduced to a paroxysm of laughter. At the sight of her storming off, her level of contempt suitably elevated, he had clutched his side and dropped to all fours in tears.

Their marriage had ultimately settled into a cold war of attrition, each content in the knowledge they would outlive the other. Joe liked to say he could 'live' with either alternative. He was adamant, however, that she show him respect in front of his own children, and on those occasions when Fran Delgado was in default, he was capable of calling her on it in the most fearsome manner.

The sound of Theresa's voice brought them each to a fixed gaze upon the other. "It's Father Sweeney," she announced from the marble entrance way to the formal dining room.

"Oh, not that dreadful nuisance. Honey, just tell him we're not home."

"Uh, Mother, why don't *you* tell him."

Fran Delgado half turned in her high backed, well-upholstered chair and did a quick double take at the sight of the priest following her daughter into the room. "Oh my God! Father!"

"Father, take no offense. She was only speaking her mind," Joe Delgado chirped happily.

"I'd say she's onto me," John Sweeney said with a broad smile. He went to Fran first and hugged her warmly, then circled the large mahogany table to give Joe a man-sized shoulder hug. "I was next door at the Delaney's and thought I'd drop in. Sorry to interrupt family dinner. I'll come back another time."

Cries of "no" all but echoed through the large room. "Father, come sit next to me," Joe said, pointing to an open seat. "As you can see I'm outnumbered."

The priest feigned hesitation. "I don't know, I always kind of liked piling on."

Red faced, Fran Delgado made a half motion to rise. "Father, let me get you a warm plate."

"No, no. Please," he said, waving his arms emphatically. "I've eaten. I just wanted to see how you all were doing."

One by one they sat. There was an awkward silence. Theresa broke it. "Well, as you can see, Father, we're just one, small, happy family!"

"Terry!" her mother scolded.

"Your mother's right, honey. You mustn't exaggerate," her father added wryly.

"Sounds kinda like my own family," the priest laughed to ease the tension.

More silence.

Finally, Joe Delgado stood and said, "Father, I'm going into the garage and I'm coming back with two Michelobs." The priest started to protest, but Delgado simply waved him off. He looked across the table at the two women and shrugged. No one spoke. *What in God's name was I thinking, wandering into this morgue?* "Well, Theresa, how long are you in town?"

The daughter looked at her mother with the face of a dependent child. Fran Delgado put her wine glass down and said with transparently synthetic gravity, "Terry is here with her children, Father. Her husband is away for awhile."

The implication was clear: the husband had some sort of problem. *Wonder what lured him over the edge?* "Oh well, it's good to have you with us again, Terry."

More silence. *Hey Joe … forget the beer. Got any Jack Daniels out there?* "And how about you, Fran? Did I hear you were in Europe this spring?"

This released an unexpected torrent of words, many quite unintelligible. John had no idea what the woman was saying but it was clear she was delighted to have at a fresh set of ears. Mercifully, Joe returned bearing cold relief. He thrust a Michelob in John's hands and sat down heavily next to him and winked. "Fran, I'm sure Father would like to see the pictures. Where are they?"

Sweeney choked most of his first swallow back into the bottle. The look of alarm on his face delighted Delgado. "Or, perhaps not," he added, thoroughly bemused.

Sweeney attempted escape, "I've really got to be going." He immediately felt Joe Delgado's strong hand on his right shoulder. Pointing to his wife, he said, "You aren't going anywhere. Think Kathy Bates in Steven King's *Misery* ..." John did and shuddered.

Joe Delgado's return meant an end to the silence. "So, to what do we owe the honor of your presence, Father?"

John looked at him directly and said, "Haven't seen you in awhile. Just wanted to make sure everyone's alright."

Joe took a long swig and decided to avoid the question. He settled his gaze on his daughter. "Well, Terry here has had a bit of a setback, Father." He paused and added, "Her husband left her for another woman."

John immediately looked at Fran Delgado who stared back with a peculiar smile. She said nothing.

John looked at the daughter and felt her pain. His own impossibly long dark night had opened his heart to the suffering of others. He immediately wanted to minister to the pain but did not know how to do so in the present setting. *If I ask her to come see me, will the mother discourage it? If I dive in now, will the father permit it?* "Terry, I'm seeing so much of that now. Just know you'll be in my prayers, and if there's anything the Church can do, please, don't hesitate ..."

Something in the sincerity of his voice appeared to loosen the bonds of her reserve. She started to cry, softly at first, then quite openly. Her mother rushed to embrace her. Her father seemed to retreat into a shell.

Presently, she stopped crying and looked at the priest across the table. He read her eyes. "Our Dear Lord has a tender love for children, particularly children who have young children themselves and no one to help them."

Her eyes filled again but her voice was strong and sure. "Thank you, Father; I needed to hear that."

"These men: they're treacherous today." It was the mother and she was fast out of the gate on what John thought might be a most inopportune rant. He wanted to head that off, *but how?* Just then he received some unexpected help. "Oh Mother, please stop with that." Fran Delgado stared across the table at her daughter, then back to John, and said, "We didn't see this coming; we thought Clark Halverson came from good 'stock.'" She hugged her daughter protectively. "Why did this have to happen? It's not like they didn't know each other. They've been friends since college."

John made a decision. "Well, sometimes in life there are surprises."

The mother stared. "What's that supposed to mean?"

John felt Joe Delgado's eyes upon him. "Love dies and we know not why," he said, attempting to make poetic what he knew to be anything but.

Theresa looked at him, eyes pleading. "Father, why?"

John quickly scanned the faces of the father and the mother; then turned to the daughter. "Sometimes we do things, inadvertently, that cause love to die, Theresa." He steeled himself for cold fury from either or both parents, and was greatly surprised when it was not forthcoming.

"What kind of things, Father?" the daughter asked.

"We violate mystical laws, laws we don't even know exist."

"Laws?"

John chose indirection. "Your mother said you and your husband knew each other for quite a while?"

Theresa Delgado nodded. "Over ten years."

"How long were you together?"

She looked off into a distant past. "Together married, or together?"

"Both."

"Well, we lived together in London for two years before we

were married, and we were married for almost four years ..." her voice trailed off.

"May I speak plainly?"

"No sermons, father!" the mother rebuked him.

"Hush, mother!" the daughter rebuked the mother.

John saw the tension and prepared a hasty exit. *Not here. Not tonight. Not with this crew. Bad idea.* "Your mother is quite right, Theresa; this is no time for sermons."

"It's my life!" she shrieked. "I've had enough of you managing it for me, mother!"

"Here, here!" Joe Delgado interjected, raising a bottle to salute his daughter.

She turned back to the priest. "Father, I want to hear what you have to say. Will you tell me, with or without my mother's permission?"

He looked at her and said, "Yes, I will. But perhaps another time and place would be better."

"No!" she exclaimed more loudly than John knew she intended. "This time and this place, please, Father."

He set his all but untouched beer aside and leaned forward, elbows on the table, chin resting on folded hands. "Alright, Theresa. I feel your thirst." He paused, then tip toed into the pain. "Allow me to oversimplify." Slight pause. "Suffering is always a signal. When it's physical, it's our body telling us something's not working properly. When it's emotional, it's our mind telling us we have unmet needs; and when it's spiritual, it's our heart calling us closer to God."

Theresa Delgado leaned forward in rapt attention.

"Theresa, what I say now is by no means a judgment of any kind, okay? Are we clear on that?"

She stared quizzically.

He leapt into the shallow end of the pool. "When couples decide to cohabitate, they are ultimately deciding to contracept too. And because they contracept, they also abort, though most don't realize it. Hormonal contraceptives are abortifacients." He paused to make sure she was following. "And because they cohabitate and contracept and abort, everything seems to change. They begin to see each other not as partners on a great adventure together, but as strangers who somehow ended up shipwrecked together. Somewhere along the line, the love does indeed die, so even if they do marry, as many indeed do, the vast majority of them, roughly three in four, end up divorcing."

Theresa Delgado gasped. "My God, I never knew any of that! Why am I hearing this for the first time? Oh my God!" She turned to her mother who stared back vacantly.

"The pain in the hearts of so many of our young people is telling them something basic." He paused. "It's saying, none of us can cohabitate and contracept, abort and sterilize, fornicate and prevaricate, marry and divorce, without consequence."

Theresa Delgado shrieked, "Father, Clark was sterilized!"

The priest nodded ever so gently, his prescience not lost on her parents. "Nothing drives a man *away* from a woman faster, precisely because it drives a man *toward* other women faster."

Theresa started to sob. John pulled back. They all sat in silence for several moments. John felt a surge of warm energy which he tended to associate with the Holy Spirit. "The gift to create life, for all eternity, is a primordial gift. What else do we do that even approaches its significance, its transcendence?"

He felt them listening: all of them. "It stands to reason the Creator, if indeed He is a loving Father, might want to establish a few guidelines for something so important, knowing how man can sometimes get a bit confused." Small smile. "He does this to help us. He *created* man, so He has a pretty good idea of what works for him, and what doesn't, for mind and body, heart and soul."

*Keep it simple. Don't lose anybody. Right down the middle of the fairway.* "Let's call these guidelines the divinely established order, what I referred to earlier as 'mystical laws.' Can't see them, but they exist, much like the laws of physics. And the laws are quite simple, even if they're not always as clear in a particular age."

*Slowly.* "So when it comes to the most important things of all, love and life, it's now pretty clear what the Creator had in mind: sex is for love. Love is for marriage. Marriage is for families. Families are for society. Societies are for civilization. Civilization is for creation. Creation is for man, a gift from God."

He paused. "When we traverse that divine order, it's not unlike doing something that's ruinous to our physical health; the only difference is, in the spiritual realm the stakes are so much higher." Slight pause. "Because the immortal soul is involved, and almost always, the souls of others."

Theresa Delgado began to sob. It was the only sound in the oversized dining room. This time her mother made no move to comfort her. It seemed to John that the mother herself was paralyzed by the raw, prophetic nature of what she was hearing. He did not turn to see Joe Delgado's reaction. His audible breathing told him all he needed to hear.

"Okay," he said as he stood, "enough sermonizing for one night." His abrupt conclusion appeared to catch all of them by surprise. Theresa began to remonstrate, "Father, not yet, please."

Over the years, John had developed a feel for the rhythm of his work, the sowing and the planting, the reaping and the replenishing of souls. It was time to go. He turned to shoulder hug Joe who jumped up and hugged the priest tightly. "Thanks for coming, Father. I need to come see you," he said in a loud whisper.

John simply nodded. "You know where to find me."

He circled the table and shook hands at a respectful distance with mother and daughter. Theresa looked at him and said, "Father, may I come to see you too?"

"I would like that very much, Theresa."

"Then I will," she smiled.

John smiled discretely at the mother and departed.

# 17

———

John Sweeney was reading his breviary in a small sitting room next to his office when the phone rang. He glanced at the clock on the freshly painted wood mantle; it read 3:12 p.m. He heard his secretary, Cathy Donegan, pick up the phone in the office. "Yes, yes …" Laughter. "Oh, he's not that bad …" More laughter. "Yes, I'll get him, Monsignor."

"Father John, it's Monsignor McManus."

"What's he want, another loan?" John replied, launching his opening salvo into the receiver.

"When are you going to stop paying the help with indulgences?" McManus needled.

"The day they make you a bishop!" John roared back, laughing.

Silence on the other end. John stared into the receiver. Had he lost the connection? "Joe … Joe? You still on?"

"Starting tomorrow, you're paying Cathy in cash."

John blinked uncomprehendingly. The wheels started grinding but they weren't getting any traction. He simply had no idea what his friend was saying. "Say what?" he slipped into street slang.

"John, I just got a phone call."

"Me too."

"John, I'm being serious."

The synapses in John Sweeney's mind began firing. Suddenly, the right wire found the right socket. "Oh my God, Joe! Oh my God!" Pause. "Joe, I've got goose bumps running up and down my arms!"

Momentary silence. Then, McManus haltingly prayed, "O Lord, I am not worthy …"

John's eyes began to fill. "God, I wish I was there to give you a big hug."

McManus spoke through his tears. "Yeah, well, I'm glad you're not; I don't need my ribs crushed."

"Joe, when? Where?" his eagerness was palpable.

"The call came, oh, seven minutes ago: at exactly 3:05. It was the Apostolic Nuncio, Stephan Wittig. He was very cordial. He asked about my dad, my brothers and sisters, Cardinal O'Hallaran. I had no idea where he was going. Then, suddenly, bam! He just said straight away, 'His Holiness, Benedict XVI, has asked me to inform you that he has appointed you to the apostolic role of Archbishop, and is assigning you to the archdiocese of Cincinnati, Ohio.'"

Silence.

McManus continued softly. "I couldn't feel my legs. I had to sit down. I just mumbled something about being overwhelmed, and promised my filial obedience to the Vicar of Christ." He paused and added, "When I hung up, I just put my head down on the desk and cried."

John was dumbstruck. They had been classmates, close friends, and verbal sparring partners for going on 30 years. Even in their seminary days, it was clear to both men they had very different ideas of how best to accomplish the Church's apostolic mission. But they'd never let their differences strain their friendship. The turning point in their relationship came when they returned home from their tenth anniversary trip to Rome with their five classmates. John returned imbued with the spirit of the New Evangelization preached so eloquently by John Paul II. He had tried channeling the iconic pope's message in his home parish of St. Martha's in Narbrook, only to have several small but vocal groups of parishioners complain to the pastor.

They regarded certain "moral truths" as "fallibly held" and, in any case, subordinate to the Church's "social justice" imperative. Those truths were also, they argued, an artifact of a pre-Conciliar church and, therefore, simply out of step with the *vox populi*. They demanded change, either change in message or change in the messenger. The bishop acceded to their wishes and re-assigned John to a tiny, black parish in a remote corner of the archdiocese.

All but alone, cut off from family and friends and former parishioners, he began to wither on a desiccated vine. It was Joe McManus who had saved him from severe depression. He came every week, a solitary figure in black, from the most distant point in the archdiocese. They had dinner together. They prayed together. And they took long walks together, until they realized it was unsafe. McManus also called at least once during the week for a "mood check." It was John's singular lifeline in those early years after their Roman holiday. John was determined never to forget his friend's extraordinary kindness. When a new Cardinal Archbishop had re-assigned John to his old parish, this time as its pastor, in order that he might be close to his failing mother, it was McManus who was the first to call, the first to send a prayer card, the first to arrange a celebration with their classmates.

"John, I'm scared," McManus confessed.

"Thank God! If you weren't, *I'd* be scared," John replied.

"No, I mean it. It's starting to hit me right now. I can't do this."

"Who else knows?"

"No one else."

John felt warm inside. He was 'first call.' "Joe," he said softly, "I just wish your mom was alive."

"I know. Believe it or not, that was *my* first thought," McManus conceded.

"What she would have given to see this day. Speaking of which: when is it?" John inquired.

"June 24th, at the Cathedral."

"The feast of Saint John the Baptist."

"You had to mention that …"

John fell silent at the symbolism. "How about the actual installation in Cincinnati?"

"Two days later."

"My God, Joe! That's three weeks from Friday!"

"I know." Pause. "John, I'm not ready."

*How can I help my friend, Lord?* "Any idea of what you're walking into?"

"Think O'Malley in Boston …"

John moaned. He had heard the stories of the Cardinal Archbishop being overwhelmed at the depth of the depravity he inherited. It was said he begged God on his knees every night to take his life before dawn. John's heart sank at the prospect of his friend being hundreds of miles away from home, for the first time in his life, and very much alone.

"What kind of help will you have?"

"Want a job?"

John laughed. "Well, that would be one way to get sent home."

"I don't know. What I've heard isn't good," McManus disclosed.

"What've you heard?"

"Polarization …"

"How bad?"

"Bad."

John fell silent, then brightened. "Joe, if anyone can bring a spirit of unity, it's you. I'm guessing that's exactly why the Papal Nuncio made the recommendation to his Holiness."

"It wasn't the Papal Nuncio."

"Then who?"

"I think it was O'Hallaran."

"He's got that kind of clout?"

"He does; he's on some important committees in Rome, and I'm told he has the Pope's ear."

"Well, I'll bet he's proud to see one of his own get an archdiocese."

"Maybe."

John was taken aback by his friend's sudden change in tone. Gone were the excitement and the tears and the joy. "I don't know if I'm reading you, Joe."

"I have it on pretty good authority that he'd be happy to pack me up himself."

"Good God, why?"

"According to my source, and I believe it's unimpeachable, O'Hallaran doesn't like the good press I get around the archdiocese. 'Too much praise,' he told someone. Apparently, he thinks that means I'm not doing the job."

John was stunned. "My God, they transfer me because they get complaints; and they transfer you because they get compliments. What is it with …" he immediately cut himself off, realizing he was now talking to one of *these guys.*

"Yeah well, 'uneasy lies the head,' as they say."

John thought about that. He had once been quick to criticize bishops: no longer. O'Hallaran's personal kindness to his dying mother had struck a chord deep within him. He may not always understand some of the things he saw and heard, or did *not* see or hear, but these days he tended toward extending the benefit of the doubt. He simply accepted certain decisions as the prudential judgments of imperfect men doing the best they could under what had become dire circumstances, and thanked God he would forever be spared that responsibility. "Joe, none of that matters now. We move forward and trust the Holy Spirit."

"Amen, my brother."

"Joe, I'll give you the afternoon to call the others. Then, in the morning I'll be on the horn. We're going to celebrate: big time!"

"Applebee's?"

John laughed. "Not if I have to start paying the help in cash!"

"So, take out?"

"We'll see. No promises. First, I'll have to convince the others this isn't a prank."

"Love you, John."

"Love you too, Bishop."

John Sweeney hung up and immediately left for the church; he wanted to say a rosary for a friend.

# 18

———

"Okay, he's waiting for you," Jim Gillespie said from the entrance to Maggie Kealey's spacious office.

"What did you tell him?"

Gillespie adjusted his glasses so they would hide the lower portion of his eyes. "What we agreed: a spot- check colorectal exam by the new CEO; new policy, everybody gets one, starting with the docs."

She glanced up from her paper work and shook her head in mock disapproval. "Tell him to come in; and make sure he has his pants on."

Dr. Frank Ciancini was ushered into her office by her secretary, Lori Needham. He waited for Maggie to point to either the chairs on the other side of her desk or the formal sitting area on the other side of the room. She stood and extended her hand across the desk, and gently guided the young man to the sitting area. Frank Ciancini was in his late 30's, small and wiry, extremely fit and stunningly bright. He was Catholic school educated K–12, and won an academic scholarship to the University of Pennsylvania, where he finished at the top of his class and earned a seat in Philadelphia's prestigious Thomas Jefferson Medical School. He had been trained as an obstetrician, and joined Regina Hospital in his late twenties. He was quite popular with staff and patients, but clashed often with administrators over seemingly minor issues. Maggie was wary of him in her new role.

"Thank you for making time, Frank" she opened politely.

Ciancini merely nodded.

She discovered the value of bluntness early in her career as a nurse; it earned her wide respect, even grudgingly from doctors. "So, tell me about our Fertility Services practice."

"What do you want to know?" he asked, more mouse than cat.

*Ah, a tractor pull; maybe Jim was onto something.* "Everything."

She observed him recoil slightly. "Well, where to begin?"

"Is that a question for you or me?"

He offered a small, wry smile. "We've got eight of us on staff and on site; four are partners in the Mid-Atlantic Reproductive Services Group; they have a clinic next door."

Maggie nodded. "Okay, let's begin with the four of you *not* directly involved with the clinic."

He shrugged. "What do you want to know?"

"I want to know what you do," she enunciated each word.

He laughed. *She won't make it: wrong approach, totally clueless.* "We help women give birth to children," he answered with thinly disguised disdain.

"Do you prescribe oral contraceptives?"

He was stunned. He opened his mouth to speak, twice, but a lifetime of Spartan-like self discipline would not permit it.

She smiled and opened her palms. *Next word is yours, Frank.*

He avoided her level gaze and looked, in the peculiar habit of the very bright, just slightly off her bow. "Sometimes, yes."

"How often?"

"Oh, I don't know," he answered, his level of exasperation rising.

"Every other patient? Two out of every three patients? Nine out of ten?"

He looked at her icily. "I'd have to check the files."

"No need. Just trying to get a feel for how you help women give birth to children," she replied acidly. She thought he looked like he needed water, or air. "Can Lori get you anything, Frank?"

"Some water would be good."

She called his order in through the open door, and presently, Lori Needham entered with two plastic bottles of cold water and handed one to Frank Ciancini first. He took it without as much as a nod. This did not sit well with Regina Hospital's new CEO. "Thank you, Lori," she said with a slightly elevated decibel level. "We're sorry to have interrupted your work."

The young secretary blinked and replied in the idiom of her generation, "No problem."

Ciancini opened his bottle quickly and took a long slug. Maggie held hers in both hands and watched him carefully. "Frank, I may have gotten us off track in focusing on couples who *don't* want to have children."

He eyed her coolly and interrupted, "Quite often, Mrs. Kealey, it's a case of those couples simply wanting to wait a few years before they have children."

She nodded and smiled. "Well, hmm, am I to understand that it's mostly newlyweds who come to you for the contraceptives?"

"I didn't say that, Mrs. Kealey."

"Of course not, Frank. You merely implied it, correct?"

He was unable to hold her gaze. Again, he looked away in silence.

"Okay, let's get back on track. Talk to me about what you do with the couples who come to us because they want to have children, but can't."

He stared at her for several moments before answering. "We begin by gathering information."

She nodded. "What do we ask them?"

"We ask them how long they've been married; what they've

done to try to conceive; what specialists they may have consulted; what tests, if any, have been conducted; if they know of any reason they might not be able to conceive: it's pretty pro forma."

For some unfathomable reason, she thought of Jim Gillespie conducting those interviews with infertile couples and felt a volcanic eruption in the pit of her stomach. She suppressed it only with great difficulty. "What do you usually hear?"

"It varies."

"Really?" she responded with transparent disingenuousness.

This did not please her young ob/gyn. "Some have tried pretty much everything when they come to us," he said flatly.

"What are they expecting from us at that point?"

"Expecting?" he pounced. "They're not *expecting* anything; they're *hoping* – often against hope itself – that we can, somehow, open a door to their dream."

She immediately thought of Liz Posner. She probed his eyes to see if he was a true believer or merely an artful poseur. She couldn't tell. "So, what do you tell them?"

"Obviously it would depend on what they've told us."

She nodded, patiently. She made a mental note of the pawns and rooks she had already collected and moved with all due deliberation in the direction of his king. "Do we provide references to Mid-Atlantic?"

"Of course," he answered, folding his hands neatly on his lap.

"Tell me about the process?"

He shrugged. "After it's clear we can't help them, we send them next door to make an appointment."

"Do we ever see them again?"

"Of course, for basic gynecological services: lab work, MRI's, ultrasounds."

"Who bills whom?"

He looked at her with a puzzled expression. "We both bill the insurance companies."

"And what kind of services do they purchase next door?"

He hesitated slightly, which did not escape her attention. "IVF, most commonly."

"Does that work take place in the hospital?"

"Absolutely not," he answered eyes widened, voice elevated.

She stifled a smile. *Of course not! That would be, what, oh yes, immoral?* "Where is that work done?"

"At their clinic, next door," he answered, too quickly.

"Let me see if I'm clear. The patient comes to us; we send her to Mid-Atlantic Repro in the next suite; *they* send her to their own clinic, which is next door, to get them, ah, started; then they send her back to *us* for 'basic gynecological services'; finally, the business is concluded in *their* clinic … in a petrie dish." She paused. "Do I have that right?"

"Almost," he smiled. "The business is concluded in the woman's womb, with the implantation of the embryo."

She leapt. "But that supposes that all the embryos have been inserted, which is generally not the case, correct?"

He froze.

"Actually only a small number of the embryos are inserted, correct?"

"Yes," he said simply, in the manner of a man who wished he were elsewhere.

"And the embryos which are not inserted, what happens to them?"

"They are discarded or frozen."

"And if they are frozen, who pays?"

"The patient."

"And what's that generally cost, ballpark?"

"About $100 an embryo."

"For how long?"

"One year."

"So, ten embryos … $1,000; twenty embryos … $2,000. What, no volume discount?"

No reaction.

"Okay, fast forward one year; Then what?"

"The patient decides if she wants to continue to pay … to have them stored for another year."

"And if not?"

"They are discarded or sold."

"Sold? To whom?"

The color drained from his face. "I don't know," he stammered. "I know nothing about that. Nothing." He clenched and unclenched his jaw causing his right cheek to bulge.

She waited patiently for him to collect himself. "Well, Frank, let's review the bidding. We recruit these fellows because we want our community to think we're a full service health care operation, right?"

Small nod.

"And the idea is, if we offer more services, particularly for women, more people, particularly women, will come to *our* hospital, and not another community hospital, for those services?"

Another small nod.

"So, we're really happy to have these fellows. We charge them nominal rent, advertise their services on our web site and in our registry, and provide them with a steady stream of referrals, correct?"

Frozen faced nod.

"Then they send *our* patients to *their* clinic next door, where *they* do things *we* know to be wrong, right?"

No reaction.

"And they charge *our* patients, couples *we* directed to them, tens of thousands of dollars for services that, by their own admission, often produce nothing." She paused for effect. "Nothing, except dozens of tiny human beings who end up discarded, frozen, or sold." She paused and said pointedly, "And out of all that we get, what, a few hundred dollars of lab work?"

Long silence.

"Dr. Ciancini, we both know I'm just a simple nurse who's in way over her head, but help me here. This arrangement with Mid-Atlantic doesn't seem to make even business sense."

His agile mind, having recognized sealed exits, warned him to say nothing. He simply shrugged.

She studied him for a long moment. *This is second tier talent. Forget the shameless absence of morals. Intellectually, he can't even get out of the box he's put himself in. He's not our future. I'm going to have to find another hospital and encourage them to steal him from us.* She brightened, suddenly, and said, "Well, Dr. Ciancini, this has been most help-ful. Thank you for making time from your busy schedule to share your knowledge and insights with me." She stood bolt upright and extended her hand.

He stood and looked at her hand, then grasped it a bit too firmly. He turned and walked out in silence.

# 19

———

Peter Feeney approached Maria Esposito's work station warily. It was a drop dead gorgeous early Friday morning in mid August. "Did he leave yet?"

"No, no. At least not physically. Where his mind is, God only knows." She eyed Feeney suspiciously. "You're not going to make it rain, are you?"

He grimaced. "I just got a phone call from Ultra Com's head of mergers and acquisitions. There's a storm brewing."

She looked at him with alarm. "Will it hit land today?"

He shrugged. "Depends on how he reacts to what I have to tell him."

She glanced at her phone, saw a light disappear, looked up and pleaded, "He's off. Just give me ten minutes to evacuate the area."

Peter Feeney took a deep breath and opened the door to Michael Burns' office. His boss was seated behind his desk signing requisitions with abandon. He wished he'd asked Maria to slide a dozen blank ones into the bottom of the pile.

"Ah, Father Feeney, do come in and hear my confession," he said, not a cloud in sight.

"Hey, Boss, got a big weekend planned down the shore?"

"All the kids and grandkids are comin' down," he answered quickly, looking for all the world like a man who had just been given a stiff dose of anesthesia. "I'm thinking at least two divorces and one homicide..."

"Just hope you and Carol don't end up in any of that," Peter suggested, trying to mirror his boss' mood.

Burns shot him a hard glare, then softened a bit and said, "Hell, after 40 years, who else'd have us?" He looked at Peter's empty hands and said, "This a social visit?"

"No, Boss, it isn't. I just got a call from Ackerman in New York."

Michael Burns' eyes narrowed. "What'd he want?"

"He's raising questions about the McKenna acquisition."

"What kinds of questions?" Burns responded intemperately.

Feeney did not like this side of Michael Burns. *Power does indeed corrupt; and wealth anticipates power. How can this guy sell the hammer— for $30 million— and think he still owns it? What world is he living in?* He sat down opposite Michael Burns, a signal his boss did not welcome. "They want to know why they weren't tipped off before you signed the letter of agreement."

Burns sat back in his chair and looked coolly at Peter. "And what did you tell him?

"What we agreed: McKenna's wired to the governor and neither of them wanted this thing leaking," he replied evenly. He resented being put in these positions which he found to be compromising. He'd worked hard to establish a reputation as a straight shooter in an industry suspicious of such men and did not take kindly to being deployed as a spinmeister. He'd cautioned his boss about the McKenna deal and suggested he wait until their own deal with Ultra Com had settled. Six months, he'd advised. Burns nodded and plowed ahead, as was his wont. Now Feeney found himself heading up the shovel brigade. He had another, far more preferred, use for the shovel.

Burns stared off to his left and through a floor to ceiling door which opened out onto a small balcony overlooking center city. Presently, his gaze returned to Peter. "What's their problem? Don't they get this deal is in all our best interests?"

"They don't understand it, and they sure as hell aren't happy with the timing of it," he answered in a monotone. He prepared himself for a burst of pure irrationality. He was not disappointed.

"Don't understand it! He's our insurance policy on 20% of our revenue base, through his, his, uh," right hand rotating furiously, "his relationships in Harrisburg. Why the hell not get him wrapped up at the same time we get in bed with Ultra Com? What's so damn hard to understand? Plus, as part of the Ultra Com network he's incented to help the other companies develop business with their host countries." Pause only for a breath. "And he'll be a much better fit for those Women's Right lesbians that Ultra Com's gonna foist on us. I mean the guy's in his mid–30's and he's still single. Who knows what the hell's up with that, know what I mean?" suggestive look under arched eyebrows.

Peter's stomach began to churn. "You know corporate types, Michael. They hate surprises." This seemed to blunt the charge, momentarily. He knew no one hated surprises more than his boss.

"So, what are they saying?" he asked quietly. "Are they saying the deal is off?"

He looked so forlorn, Peter almost felt sorry for him. Almost. "No, but they do want an explanation. They asked us to come up next week."

"Oh, that's not good ..." he said quietly. This part of the Michael Burns character continually surprised Peter. For all his gifts, and they were many, his boss was a bred–in–the–bone pessimist. He always saw danger lurking around the corner, even if there was no corner. Every silver cloud had a dark lining and Michael Burns could find it even before the cloud formed.

"I didn't commit to a date, Michael. I wanted to give you time over the weekend to think about how you want to approach this," he said, trying to tamp down the anxiety he observed building in his boss's darkening features. "I told Ackerman I'd call Monday morning. He said he's busy, but he'd make time."

"Why? Because it's a make or break issue for them?" Burns was in full paranoia mode.

"No, because they want to get it straightened out quickly, so they can settle with us before Labor Day."

Burns nodded. He liked hearing that. He didn't want this McKenna thing squirreling the deal, but he also didn't want to come back from New York next week wearing the Women's Right account, as of Labor Day. He'd already had far too many sleepless nights worrying about the fallout from that one. *What would Carol say? Would his own children ever take him seriously again? What would the Catholic community in Philadelphia think? Would he be asked to resign the boards and committees he chaired? Would the archdiocese return all the money he'd given them? Would the city's newspapers pillory him for being a hypocrite? Would he be excommunicated, denied a Catholic burial?*

"You have any thoughts on that?" he asked Peter, trying, unsuccessfully, to hide his vulnerability.

*Yes, as a matter of fact I do. How about you just level with them. Not a bad way to do business. Builds trust and all that other good stuff. They're about to give you $30 million; how about telling them you took leave of your senses, and that it won't be the last time, so get used to it. And hey, how 'bout we all have a beer and forget this thing ever happened.* "No, but I'll think about it."

Not good enough for Michael Burns. "What if I brought McKenna with us; let 'em see how impressive he is. They fall in love with him, the whole thing goes away?"

Peter coughed politely. *By the 'whole thing' do you mean our $30 million deal? One look at Puff Daddy and Ackerman will see his whole corporate life pass before his eyes. On balance, not a particularly good idea. Of course, I'm a bit biased. You know, with the three kids and all, college tuition, that kind of thing. Not to mention a wife who thinks having credit* *cards mean you don't really have to pay for stuff.* "Might work. Why don't we both think about it?"

"You don't like it, do you?" Burns asked, eyeing him carefully.

*What was the tip off? My puking on your desk?* "Well, I worry that maybe three's a crowd, that kind of thing."

Burns grew reflective. "Yeah, you're probably right. Maybe next time we go up we bring him."

"Probably be better ..." *Not to mention the added advantage of giving me time to find another job.*

Long, painful silence. "Think they'll go for it?"

Peter was momentarily confused. He also was in acute discomfort. For several minutes he had been suppressing a call from nature. He was on the verge of crossing his legs in front of his boss, which he knew would provide Burns with sufficient material for his subsequent public introductions until either his death or retirement, assuming they were not concurrent events. "Why not?" he asked innocently.

"I dunno. I'm just worried about this Women's Right thing. I don't want that work going through our shop."

Eureka! All dots were now connected. This was indeed a quandary. He did not see the Ultra Com folks, who were nothing if not New York savvy, getting down with a sloppy baton toss. Especially to Aaron McKenna. They regarded Proper Parenthood as a major growth account for the entire syndicate; they would expect Michael Burns to put his considerable marketing acumen at their service. "I understand your reservations, Michael. I really do. But do you think McKenna Communications, which is really just McKenna, is up to the assignment?"

"Why not?"

"Well, he's not staffed for it." *And of course the real women at Women's Right would de-pants him out of his empty suit before he made it through the door.*

Burns shot him a 'give me a break' look. "We'll provide the people, Peter. That's not a problem."

"We will? How would that work?"

"We just assign a team and transfer them to his payroll."

"Who, uh, do you think might want to sign up for that duty?"

"I dunno. I'll let Mobley figure it out. He's not doing much else up there, except getting plastered and plastering holes in walls."

Peter envisioned a run on the bank: the whole house of cards just toppling. He could not foresee a good outcome, under any scenario. In his mind, Michael Burns was about to self destruct, at just the wrong moment. He was not sure whether to mention any of this to his wife, reasoning it might only accelerate the household spending in the fear that she might be odd woman out on a really big end of world sale. "Yeah, you're right. Ed'll come up with something good. He always – usually – *occasionally* – does."

Burns shot up from his seat as though electrocuted. "Well if he doesn't, you and I will. Right, Feeney? He gave Peter a solid clap on the back. Peter panicked, fearing the jolt caused a premature— emission. At the moment, other than looking, there was no way of knowing. He smiled at his boss and said, "Have a great weekend with the kids, Michael. Lord knows you sure do deserve it."

And with that he left, hastily, in search of a bathroom.

# 20

Joe Delgado entered the Pittman Labs executive conference room for a final check on his power point presentation. It was just after 7:00 a.m. and the coffee bar wasn't set up yet. This momentarily depressed him; he ran on morning java. His slides were as he had left them after his final midnight run. He spun through them again, quickly, more out of nervousness than anything else. All was in order. He'd discovered early in his career that he had something of a photographic memory. If he stared at a page or a slide long enough he could pretty much commit it to memory. This allowed him to concentrate solely on his audience. Over time, he'd developed a mastery in this important art that had separated him from his peers. It helped explain his meteoric rise in a Fortune 500 corporation filled with many other bright men and women. It also helped that he outworked his competition, often remaining at his desk well into evening. It was widely held that he had an unfair advantage being married to such an understanding wife.

He had two agenda points on this postcard day in early

September. He wanted to position himself as the go-to guy at Pittman Labs for the HM Healthcare Division senior executives. This meant using the revenue projections on the screen as a pretext for unveiling his encyclopedic knowledge of the therapeutic research industry, commonly known as Big Pharma. And secondly, he wanted to connect with his counterpart, HM's Chief Financial Officer, Chad Henley. He had important plans for this relationship.

He decided to forgo his wait for coffee and to return to his office. He entered and shut the door behind him. He went over to the dark blue couch under the large window in the corner and lay down for a brief rest. He merely wanted to relax and reflect, not nap. He'd learned the hard way that a small cat nap prior to important presentations left him groggy, which was never a good idea when trying to answer pinpoint questions from senior corporate executives about supporting data for major business recommendations.

Despite his best intentions he did doze off. He all but immediately found himself in what he took to be some kind of mortuary; he stood alone amidst a sea of tiny children without faces. They were all looking in his direction as though they could see him. He had the sense they were waiting for him to say something to them, but he didn't have anything to say, and, therefore, said nothing. He wondered what they were all doing there, indeed what he himself was doing there. In this room with an all-pervasive smell of death there were only questions, no answers. He heard a sound. Someone was calling his name. He tried to yell but no sound came out of his mouth. He grew restless and anxious, and awoke to Paula Gomez standing a respectful distance from the couch, telling him the HM executives had arrived and were waiting for him in the conference room.

He leapt off the couch and looked at his watch. It was 7:50. He was due to present at 8:00. He looked around for his suit jacket but could not find it. Then he saw Paula holding it in her right hand, and a cup of coffee in her left. He took the coffee first, afraid he might otherwise put the coat on backwards. The hot, rich, dark taste awakened and delighted him, clearing his head and getting his blood circulating. He returned the large earthen mug and reached for his coat. "Thank you, Paula," he said a bit sheepishly.

"Give 'em hell, Joe. I'll be praying for you."

He grunted acknowledgement and was off. The executive conference room was at the far end of the hall. It was elaborately furnished and equipped. Upon entering he was surprised to see the video conferencing equipment set up. Hal Fairfax spotted him and excused himself from the small group of HM execs and made his way over with a look of concern on his face.

"Hankinson's gonna join us by video; I just found out." Phil Hankinson was HM's rising star and head of HM's Healthcare Division. If Joe Delgado's suppositions about HM's plans proved correct, Hankinson was about to become arguably the most important health care executive in the world. "Not to worry; we're ready," he smiled, hoping to relax his CEO.

But Fairfax did not relax. "I'm not worried about your presentation, Joe. It's the questions he might ask." Hankinson was a tall, elegant black man in his early 40's. He had an undergraduate degree from Stanford University and an MBA from the University of Chicago. He was a former All Pac 10 basketball star and a top tier marathoner who competed in New York and Boston every year. His brilliance and ambition were assiduously masked behind a charismatic personality. He had a reputation for being able to ferret out middle and even senior management "wannabes" with astonishing suddenness and precision. HM execs did not like making presentations to him.

"Which one is Henley?" he asked Fairfax.

"The one with the tire around his middle. He's a Brit. C'mon over, I'll introduce you."

Subconsciously he grabbed what remained of his own threadworn tire and followed Fairfax to the far end of the conference room.

"Fellows, meet our CFO, Joe Delgado. Joe, this is Chad Henley, HM's Healthcare Division CFO; Bill Siegel, head of HM's Acquisitions and Mergers Division; Jim Barret, HM's General

Counsel; and Ted Kazanski, the Chief Operating Officer for HM's Healthcare Division."

Joe shook every hand extended and memorized names and titles. This was not an easy task for him; he was much better with numbers than people. But, in an effort to further separate himself from his peers, he had worked at it assiduously, eventually developing somewhat of a proficiency. It would be put to the test this morning.

Chad Henley leaned in Joe's direction and said, "And then there is Hankinson, whom you will meet momentarily. Delightful chap ..." This induced immediate laughter from the others.

Jim Barret was quick to add, "Delightful in the manner of, let's say, a colonoscopy ..." More laughter.

Joe observed that Kazanski's laughter was thinner and more forced than the others. It signaled that as the division's number two, he may well be a Petrie dish creation of Hankinson's: there to watch and report the interpersonal dynamic among the men near to his dear leader. Joe's internal Geiger counter began buzzing caution.

Out of the corner of his eye he saw movement on the large screen to his right. He immediately knew it was Hankinson. Tall and composed, he had entered a conference room at HM's Headquarters building in New York with a small posse; he was quickly outfitted for a small personal microphone, despite one sitting in plain view on the conference table in front of his seat. There was no small talk. When he sat down, the posse left and he signaled his readiness to begin. "Okay, let's get started," he said into the small camera on the far side of his conference table.

The men in the Pittman Labs conference room scrambled to their seats; none faster, Joe noted, than Ted Kazanski. Joe walked slowly to his seat and awaited introductions. As the senior man in the room, Chad Henley introduced Joe and Hal Fairfax, in reverse order. Joe noted Henley was as tight now as he had been loose moments ago. He felt a knot in his stomach begin to form.

"Okay, let's get on with it," was all Hankinson said when Henley finished. Joe stood up so Hankinson could better see him, and as he did so he observed that his power point presentation lay on the desk in front of Hankinson and appeared to have a fair number of red markings on the first several pages. He began tentatively, which is not at all how he wanted to begin. Everything in his DNA told him to present to the people in the room with him, after all there were five of them. But the force of will coming through the video screen challenged that, and caused him to half turn his body away from the audience in the room and present to the immobile figure behind the microphone. He immediately thought of the Wizard of Oz. Not a good "swing thought" on which to begin the most important presentation of his life, he told himself.

He began as he always did by summarizing the data with clean, concise conclusions, carefully linking them to what he knew would be the central business concerns of the men in the room. *This is what Pittman Labs will generate from our existing portfolio over the next one, three, and five years, and you can take it to the bank because you'll see I've taken every reasonable factor into consideration and weighted them in an algorithm I created myself. In Game Theory it's called "centering," and it has permitted me to be right about these matters to such a degree that, I dare say, no one even challenges me anymore. So, fire a way at your own risk.* Hankinson immediately understood the dynamic and challenged him, but in a manner that Joe regarded as more pro forma than substantive. This permitted him to respond in a manner more substantive than defensive.

As the presentation proceeded, Hankinson's questions were fewer and more conceptual; by its completion it had become largely an in-depth conversation between two men about the future of various therapeutic categories. As he sat down, Joe mentally checked off the first of his two boxes for the meeting. The conversation, he was happy to see, continued and now involved the other men. It was bounded on all sides by the markers he had established in his presentation. This was good, very good, he told himself.

Suddenly, Hankinson rose and nodded and, in the manner of the business world's alpha males, departed without a word to anyone in the Pittman Labs conference room. The others waited until the audio visual man arrived to shut down the system before saying anything further. The silence was a bit surreal, and Joe, coming off a "speaker high", was tempted to leaven the moment with an irreverent comment or two, but something in the look on the other men's faces suggested it might place them in danger.

Hal Fairfax was the first to speak. "We have a reservation for lunch at a small bistro in Wayne; the cars are waiting down stairs. Why don't you fellows go wash up and meet us in the lobby?"

Chad Henley held his hand up, silently calling for attention. When he had it, he said, "Joe, that performance was masterful." The others quickly nodded and began to offer their own congratulations. Henley, however, had not relinquished the floor. "I've sat in on far too many of these things and I can tell you, I've never seen anyone yet who could hold his own with Hankinson," he looked at the others for affirmation, "until today." All heads nodded in unison, save one. "Jolly good go!" he said with a wave of an empty coffee mug.

As the men filed out of the room in search of the executive lavatory, Joe noted that Hal Fairfax was not smiling.

They arrived at the small, tony Bistro and were ushered into a private room in the back. Joe waited to see which chair Henley would choose before attempting to position himself next to him. Henley appeared to be waiting for Kazanski to seat himself, and when he did near the head of the table, walked to the far end of the table. Joe immediately skirted Fairfax's flank and grabbed the chair next to Henley at a right angle. The others filled in, Fairfax at the head, carrying on small talk.

After drinks, light by corporate standards, the conversation turned to the acquisition and its development potential for both organizations. As in most business conversations, a fair amount of helium was pumped into the ether gradually inducing a harmless, purposeless euphoria among the men at the table. Joe attributed it, in part, to each man's sense of relief that Hankinson had not inflicted pain. He thought he might be the unlikely beneficiary of an extra measure of good will as a consequence.

When the others were in full flight, Joe made his move. He noted that Henley was more spectator than participant in the discussion and he leaned forward and said to him, quietly, "Well, I guess we can retire."

Henley laughed and said, "I'm thinking British Virgin Islands to your U.S. Virgin Islands, but we'll visit each other, by boat, for a round of golf now and again."

Joe grinned broadly and noted a mischievous twinkle in the Brit's eyes. *This is good. Privately, he's a rogue, like me. We ought to be able to get a lot done together.* Joe instantly abandoned caution. "How's the Rossiter acquisition coming?"

Henley's eyes widened and his lips appeared to tighten. For a moment, Joe thought he had miscalculated, badly. Then the twinkle returned. "Should be all buttoned up by year's end."

Joe nodded with feigned indifference. "Watching a big company begin to move, once it sets its sights, is something to behold."

Henley smiled. "You're very clever, Joe." Joe immediately probed his eyes for a that's-all-you're-going-to-get signal. He saw something else. "Of course, you made that quite clear this morning."

Joe knew better than to feign humility. "Staff people usually get long vacations after they're acquired. I actually prefer to work."

Henley laughed. "I'm going to arrange to have you summoned to New York, on some pretext or another; we'll have a pint or two."

Joe did not like hearing this. He had a visceral need to walk away from this lunch with his HM roll-up scenario confirmed. "Chad, let me run something by you; you don't have to say yes or no. I read body language—"

"I have no doubt," Henley retorted, clearly amused.

Joe scanned the table. The others were deep in conversation. A waitress had arrived and was taking orders, mostly salads and light fish entrées. When she finished, the conversation resumed. Joe waited several minutes, then turned to Henley and said, "I see a major play. HM targets the aging boomer therapeutic classes— principally Alzheimer's and Diabetes— buys two, maybe three biotech pioneers in Silicon Valley, and merges them for scale; then buys Rossiter and Pittman and merges them for functional utility. Pittman is for the back end clinical process, getting the products to market; Rossiter for the front end marketing muscle once they arrive."

Henley smiled. Joe couldn't read it. Clearly, he reassured himself, this man had not risen to the top of the global corporate world without mastering the art of the opaque non-signal business signal. But then a strange thing happened. Henley leaned forward and spoke in the direction of Joe's right ear. What he said would excite Joe's imagination to such a degree that he would endure many a sleepless night in the ensuing months.

"You're about half right," he said enigmatically. "You've got the middle part pretty close to figured out. But there is a front end and a back end, and their sheer scope and scale will take your breath away."

Joe stared, mouth open, speechless.

Seeing his reaction, Henley couldn't resist stoking it. "Think global, geo-political, industry transformation."

Joe's heart began to quicken. *What have these men planned? Will there be a role for me in it? Will I want a role for me in it?*

Henley was not finished. One last tidbit was tossed on Joe Delgado's plate before his salad arrived. "HM will have a horse in next year's presidential election here in the U.S., and a world class jockey to ride him into the winner's circle."

His lunch arrived at the same time his mind rocketed into the stratosphere. He couldn't eat. He couldn't think. He wasn't even sure he could speak.

Chad Henley took note of all this and leaned into Joe's shoulder one final time. "C'mon up, we'll talk more ..."

Joe heard his name being called. He turned and saw Hal Fairfax waving to him. "Earth to Delgado!" The others were smiling. Having secured Joe's attention, Fairfax proceeded to ask a question of utmost banality. It signaled to Joe that he was deeply concerned at the sight of him and Henley carrying on a private conversation at the far end of the table. *He'll think I was submarining him. The hell with him. I'll just feed his paranoia by stonewalling him.* He asked for the question to be repeated. Fairfax, a bit impatient, repeated the question. Joe took a sip of iced tea, nodded his understanding, and said, "I have absolutely no idea." For a moment, no one at the table spoke. Then Henley laughed and the others followed in turn. The table erupted as though he had dropped a witticism worthy of American humorist Mark Twain. Sensing the joke was on him, even Fairfax laughed to demonstrate he was a good sport.

Joe turned his attention to his Cobb salad. He made a mental note to have Paula book him on a metro to New York before the end of the month.

# 21

---

He loved the rain. Soft or hard, warm or cold, vertical or horizontal, it did not matter. When he was young he wanted to be in it; now that he was older, just months shy of his 57th birthday, he was more than content just to be near it.

Tonight it was a warm, steady, soaking rain, and the sound of it pelting the worn, dark green awning that provided cover for the rectory porch greatly pleased him. As he sat rocking gently in his Adirondack, he fingered the beads in his right hand. Moments earlier he had been in the church making his evening visit, but at the sound of rain on the old church's slate roof he begged his heavenly mother's indulgence and raced to the rectory porch to continue his prayer.

It was providential. Without warning a dark Cadillac Escalade turned too quickly into the driveway between the rectory and the Grotto and came to an abrupt stop. Out jumped— who?— covered in a yellow rain slick and running in the direction of the rectory porch.

It was only when the figure reached the top step that the matter of identity was resolved. "Oh Father, I hope I didn't startle you."

John Sweeney smiled and reached for the wet slick. "Theresa, I've been expecting you. I didn't know what day, month or year, but I knew you'd come."

He laid the slick open-out on a small wood table between the rockers, turned and said, "Let me get you a towel so your mother doesn't accuse me of making you sick, though I'm not sure that will be a sufficient defense." Before she could register protest he was inside and, moments later, reappeared with an oversized, white terrycloth towel. He tossed it onto her head and laughed. "Now, just bow to Mecca and all will be forgiven."

She took the towel, dabbed her hair and forehead and eyes, and with a hint of uncertainty made her way to an unoccupied rocking chair. As she sat, he looked at her silhouette in the backglow of a street light and saw a surprising degree of fragility in her eyes and slender form. He guessed her to be in her mid-30's, but on this night she looked much younger. He observed in her the bearing of a child of privilege encountering the harsh realities of life for the first time: absent the coping mechanisms many of her peers had been forced to develop much earlier in their lives.

In silence, they listened to the rain together. He longed to simply close his eyes and escape into the mystery of existence, but his ministry was an 'on call' covenant to the People of God and it required he keep his eyes and ears open and, often, his mouth closed.

"Father, is this a bad time?"

"Terry, it is a perfect time."

He felt, rather than saw, her groping for a way to begin and decided to help. "Ever heard of Scott Peck?"

The question appeared to catch her deep in thought. She looked at him with a blank expression, offering nothing in return.

"He was a popular psychiatrist and author who died two years ago, in 2005. His most famous work was a book entitled *The Road Less Traveled*, a reference to the Robert Frost poem. Anyway, the first sentence in the book reads: 'Life is difficult'." He paused. "My guess is you now know that to be true."

She started to cry, softly at first, then in audible sobs that seemed to arise from the depths of her small frame. He watched, perplexed. He knew he didn't dare move to comfort her, lest he give scandal to a happenstance passerby, but he certainly wasn't comfortable with the callousness of remote observation. She solved the problem for him with a question. "Father," she asked when the pain ebbed, "think I chased God out of my life?"

His smile lit the darkness. "Terry, you don't know how many times I've asked myself the same question."

This seemed to greatly surprise her. "You sometimes think that too?"

"I wish it were only sometimes."

"My Lord, I had no idea."

"My Lord, how often I've had no idea."

This induced a brief silence accompanied by the blissful sound of rain. She broke it with a question. "Why is it we think the way we think about God, Father?"

He stared at her in surprise. "That's a mighty heavy question, young lady."

He thought he was tracking her but suddenly she veered off. "I think, in my life, he just took off. I used to be able to, you know, feel his presence. Now …" she shrugged, gaze directed into the evening's watery darkness.

He nodded quietly. "I've been there." His mind drifted back to a searing 'dark night' of purgation some 20 years earlier, when he had contemplated leaving the priesthood. He had given some young couples very questionable counsel in matters of life and love and work, and they had made the mistake of following it, causing no small amount of pain in their lives, families and careers. Some hadn't survived intact, yet inexplicably, his God had given him a second chance. *Why are you so good to me, Lord? Why wasn't I the one who paid the price for my failure? You should have discarded me on the scrap heap of 'useless servants' right then and there, Lord. Why didn't you?* He turned to her and said, "I suspect we all end up there at one point or another in our lives."

Then, abruptly: "Father, I've done terrible things."

He let that confession hang suspended between them for a moment. "Terry, we all have."

"No, Father, I mean really terrible things," she was emphatic.

He looked at her and saw, with the aid of a light coming from the rectory parlor, an all too familiar mixture of pain and fear and guilt in her eyes. He was seeing this same look in the eyes of too many young people. He thought he knew what he was about to hear.

"Father, I had two abortions."

He braced himself. "I'm so very, very, sorry Terry," he whispered.

She began to cry. "I didn't want to have them, I was told I had to." A dam suddenly burst. The sound of her pain silenced even the rain. He made no attempt to console her, understanding the uniquely purifying power of tears from firsthand experience. Gradually, the blessed sound of rain returned. "Father, do you think God knows I didn't really want either of those abortions?"

"I'm certain he does."

"Does it matter? I mean my babies are still dead, and I killed them." The wail that followed sounded, he thought, not unlike the Narbrook Firehouse alarm when it sounded during the dead of night. *Mother Immaculate, I can't imagine this pain. Please ask your son to flood this poor child with his mercy. Please.*

He turned his chair toward hers and moved the small wood table between them out of the way toward the porch railing. He was now sitting within two feet of her. He straightened her chair, with her sitting in it, by a quick thrust of his powerful right arm so she was facing him. "Terry, listen to me. Forgiving is what our God does best. The only hard part is learning to forgive ourselves."

"But there is a hell, isn't there Father?"

"Yes, Terry, there is a Hell. But the people who go there are what we call 'unrepentant sinners.' They steadfastly refuse God's mercy, even at the end of their lives."

"But I knew it was wrong and I did it anyway. Not once, but twice. Oh Father, I'm so ashamed."

"I know, I know," he soothed. "But more importantly, your God knows. And if you're feeling any sense of peace in all of this pain, it's a sign of his very presence within you. He hasn't left your soul, and he never will."

Slowly, she raised her head. In the sliver of light between them he saw what he thought were years receding from the outer edges of her eyes. "Father," she began, voice now fully modulated, "I need to talk about this. May I?"

He nodded, and it was as if a NASCAR flag had dropped. Her mother had started her on the Pill when she was a junior in high school. She confronted her daughter after school one day with evidence from her laundry that she was having sex. She demanded to know who the boy was so she could call his mother. Terry had refused to 'out' the boy who was a senior at a local Catholic prep school. The mother threatened to go to the principal at the convent school to demand an investigation. Still, she refused to identify the young man. It wasn't the act of fornication itself that her mother found so abhorrent; it was the potential disruption to her plan for her daughter's life. There would be college, possibly graduate school, a career, and then, at the right moment, there would be the right marriage to the right man from the right family. An unwanted child posed an ominous threat to all that and therefore would not be permitted.

They worked out a compromise. Rather than submit to house arrest for the rest of her junior year, Terry would go on the Pill. There were complications immediately. She gained weight and required a new wardrobe, which her mother dutifully provided. She grew irritable around the house and bickered constantly with her sisters and her mother. She did not go out for the varsity basketball team despite having been a promising junior varsity player in her sophomore year. She resigned from the school paper and even stopped attending a number of school events which normally attracted her enthusiastic participation.

This greatly concerned her father who was unable to get a satisfactory answer from either his daughter or her mother to explain the marked mood swing. He even proposed seeking professional help and found it perplexing that his wife seemed relatively unconcerned.

Then tragedy struck. The summer before her freshman year in college, the roulette wheel stopped on 'go': the Pill malfunctioned and she conceived. When she told her mother, the wheels came off. For over a week she thought her mother might be having a nervous breakdown. Then, without warning, she entered Terry's bedroom late one afternoon and announced she had a very simple solution to 'the problem.' Terry would have an abortion. Immediately.

Greatly frightened, she did not resist. In the dark of night, however, she remembered crying out to God to spare her child. She even attempted to barter her life instead. But early one hot summer morning in her 17th year, she found herself being driven by her mother to Lankenau Hospital for "the procedure." As she lay on the operating table, she recalled thinking, *This can't be happening. Why am I allowing this? What will they do with my baby when they remove it?*

She was in and out in under three hours. Not a word was said on the drive home. She entered the house and went straight to her room. It would be three days before she came out. When she did, she knew she was, and would forever be, a different person.

He listened in silence, trying hard not to form judgments about her mother. He didn't entirely succeed. In these instances he'd learned it was best to say nothing. And so he did.

She talked of her college years and of her infatuation with a young lacrosse star from Boston College. They met at an off campus party and had taken a long walk along the Charles River on a silvery autumn evening in her sophomore year. By the time they arrived at his apartment, she knew he was the one. She spent what was left of the night in his bed, and when she awoke in the morning she remembered feeling happy. Her happiness lingered through a long week, right up until she saw him walking the same path with another woman the following weekend. She was sitting on a bench near the spot they had first kissed, hoping he'd return. He walked past so deep in conversation he did not appear to even notice her. She said that, too, was a transformative experience. She became guarded after that, rarely letting men get close to her even in casual friendships.

That is, until she met Clark Halverson. They'd re-acquainted in New York after graduation. Mutual friends at Boston College had introduced them at a foreign policy lecture given by an angry Jesuit from Central America. There were no sparks and they lost touch effortlessly. It was with deep and mutual surprise that they encountered each other in Central Park on a brisk Saturday morning in early spring. They were running in opposite directions and passed each other with a perfunctory nod. He was the first to stop and call after her. She turned, still jogging in place to keep her heart rate elevated, and squinted into an early morning sun. He came closer, repeating her name. From ten feet away she recognized him and half shouted his name. There was a brief awkward silence, neither wanting to disrupt anything as important as a scheduled run. They semi-jogged in place while they caught up, exchanged cards, and promised to "do lunch."

She had not given their chance meeting another thought until several weeks later, when her cell phone rang one afternoon while she was working in her cubicle at a mid-town public relations firm. It was Clark and he was ready to do lunch. They met at a west side pub and ended up talking too much of the afternoon away. He was a trader on the derivatives desk at JP Morgan. They were living in the same Upper East Side neighborhood and were even members of the same gym, though neither could remember having seen the other during their thrice weekly visits.

They began seeing quite a bit of each other in the months that followed: dinners, shows, museums, ball games, long Sunday afternoon walks along the East river. In time, they even began running together early Saturday morning, which was a bit awkward at first when she would spend the night at his apartment and they would have to go back to hers for a change of clothes.

She felt herself slowly relaxing her guard; in time she opened her heart and took him into her confidence. He did the same with her. Each had been wounded and each struggled with trust issues as a consequence. In time they each came to see the other as a kindred soul with whom one might share at least a portion of their damaged heart.

The news of his promotion to the London office came as a bit of a shock. Not that he hadn't spoken of it; he most certainly did, and often. But it had always seemed out of reach: something the firm's senior managers, all of whom were Ivy Leaguers, saw as their own private turbo track to the top and not something to be shared with lesser lights, no matter how productive they were. But Clark Halverson had managed to distinguish himself in his first four years at Morgan. He'd demonstrated a genius for innovation in the complex area of securitization, particularly in the relatively new categories of mortgage-backed securities and asset-backed securities. Indeed, several of his product concepts had taken off in the past two years and were already generating fees in the tens of millions of dollars for the firm. Afraid of losing him to a rival like Bear Sterns or Goldman Sachs, Morgan's senior management had little choice but to put him on the fast track. And that meant the London desk.

He asked her to meet him for dinner at a tony, upper east side restaurant just before Christmas. The snow was falling gently as he entered the restaurant nearly one hour late due to a celebration at the office, in which his accomplishments, and promotion, had been celebrated in the time-honored tradition of Wall Street. He immediately noted she was not particularly thrilled at having to endure the wait alone. But already in his young life, Clark Halverson was learning how to anticipate and solve problems before they festered and corroded relationships.

He strode proudly to her table in the back corner of the room and kissed her lightly on an unturned cheek. Seeing her stiffen and sensing the eyes of others now observing their operatic improv, he reached into his pocket and fell to one knee in the same motion. She turned to him in astonishment. Now at eye level, he placed a small, very familiar light blue box on her plate and told her he loved her and that they were going to London. She opened it to discover a 14-carat, heart shaped diamond ring and a small note which read: 'you own my heart forever.'

She hugged and kissed him and heard the small intimate room break into raucous applause, during which a tuxedoed waiter arrived with a bottle of imported champagne, that she later learned cost over $200. In the excitement which followed, the subject of his tardiness did not come up.

Despite her father's strong misgivings, her mother approved and with her support Terry moved to London with Clark Halverson. The firm arranged a small flat overlooking the upper Thames, within walking distance of theatre district. She had no problem finding work as an account executive with the London office of Ogilvy Public Affairs, and began almost immediately, although at a somewhat reduced pay grade, which at first she found both surprising and disconcerting.

They lived alone in London for three years, very much enjoying its many cultural treasures and traveling the continent during winter and summer work holidays. It was the stuff of dreams, as she told her mother in their weekly phone calls— most of which lasted well over an hour, raising the ire of two men on opposite sides of the Atlantic.

During this time, there was the occasional talk of marriage, but they agreed, a bit reluctantly on her part, that it would be best to wait for a transfer back to the States, where the schools were believed to be more advanced. Though each set of parents inquired about "a date" from time to time, neither of them had any serious difficulty spinning the questions into discussions of a triumphal return from Europe and a family life of high privilege in the States, most likely in Southern Connecticut.

The tectonic plates began moving early in the fourth winter of their London years. Suffering from lingering and inexplicable flu-like symptoms, Terry visited her doctor, who ordered tests. Rather than report results over the phone as he often did, he asked them to come to his office, assuring them it was in no way a "life threatening matter." There, rather unceremoniously, he delivered the shocking news that she was with child. They were each so stunned they took no notice of the other's response. Her first thought was of her mother and how she would react. His first thought, he was to say much later, was of a marriage he wasn't at all certain he wanted.

An uneasy silence accompanied them on the ride back to their flat. He thought of his career and of a new commitment he feared might be a "derailer." She thought of the arduous task of finding a second bedroom in a green section of the city, then packing and moving in her seventh month, during what would no doubt be the middle of another severe continental heat wave. Neither of them appeared to regard the "surprise" as welcome.

Perhaps the greatest shock, however, was what came next. After two weeks of uncharacteristic moodiness, he announced at yet another silent dinner that she would have to "dispose of the fetus." The sheer callousness of his manner tripped wires she thought had been safely buried. She sobbed uncontrollably, so much so that he took his leave only to return early the next morning without the sobriety with which he had departed.

Much to his surprise, she was waiting for him. Her eyes were so red and her cough so deep that it roused a sense of pity in him, and quickly visited a degree of clarity upon him that appeared to surprise them both. What came next was the only fight they had ever had, and ever would have. She told him she was keeping the baby. He told her it would mean the end of their relationship. She said she would leave in the morning. He pointed out it was already morning. She began to cry again and took to cursing him for the louse he had revealed himself to be. He defended himself and said he didn't want to raise a child "in the streets of London." He begged for more time, promising to marry her upon his next promotion, which he believed would occur sometime within the next year. With the promotion, he said, would come a commanding raise that would permit them to find a two bedroom flat in a secure section of the city, and allow him to begin job prospecting back in the States from a greatly strengthened career position.

She blinked back a fury that frightened them both, its origin uncertain and its ultimate destination equally so. She reminded him she had arrived at this crossroads once before in her life and had taken a wrong turn. She vowed then, as she was vowing now, she would not make the same mistake twice.

Some ten days later, on a night of freezing rain and black ice, her second child was aborted. Something in her died that evening in a hospital in the Chelsea section of London. She left the hospital the way she had entered, a convicted criminal going to her own execution. For months afterward, they didn't speak. They passed their time together much as two boarders struggling to maintain a civility which each knew was not sustainable.

His promotion came as scheduled. Just before the following Christmas, he was named senior manager of Morgan's Asian Hedge Fund. It would require, he fully understood, much travel and he was reminded, lest he have other ideas, it was much easier to fly into world markets from the Continent than it was from the States. He immediately arranged for a week on the Mediterranean in a luxurious villa just north of Nice. Once there, he apologized for the "difficult personal decisions" he had forced her to make for his career, and promised to make it up to her. He suggested they marry in the spring and offered to fly her entire family over for the wedding, which would be held in a Devonshire palace owned by the firm. She reminded him her father was quite wealthy, and her family did not need to be "subsidized."

The marriage was a glittering affair that merited several column-inches of coverage in the London Times. One of the pictures captured her father singing into an open mic with an improbably high, very black, universally familiar, genuine fur hat "borrowed" from one of the Queen's own men. There was also a picture of a very proud groom and a bride whose countenance was shadowed by an enigmatic smile.

JP Morgan subsidized the lease of a four-story townhouse

on a small square in an exclusive section of the City. Four homes bordered a small park with play space for young children. The night they moved in, she flushed her oral contraceptives down the toilet and advised her husband they were going to have two children "as quickly as God permits." God required four years. The arrival of her children elevated her mood considerably. She even began attending some of her husband's business functions on the Continent and traveling with him once to the States, where she proudly showcased her first born to his new grandparents in Philadelphia.

Gradually she began to repair her fractious relationship with her husband. Though she was uncertain as to whether she could ever fully forgive him for what she regarded as *her* sin, the delight he took in his children was clear and his gentle solicitousness toward her equally so. It wasn't the mad, rapturous love she had sought, but she was, nonetheless, mostly happy, or, as she often reminded herself, at least as happy as she could be living over three thousand miles from home. But that too would change, he had promised, when the second child arrived. There in the hospital, as she lay on her back nurturing new life, he vowed both of their sons would be "educated in the States."

It was a promise he did not keep. One night in late summer he returned from an extended business trip to Asian capital markets and announced he was leaving her. It was late and the children had been put to bed. There was a single candle on the dining room table, and a roasted pheasant, seasoned by their personal chef and presented under glass. The wine had been poured in anticipation. It did not go to waste.

Though he had packed and left in less than an hour, it took her months to extricate herself and her children from him, the marriage, and the country. She learned during the process that he'd met a young doe-eyed Asian beauty on Morgan's Hong Kong desk, and began sharing her apartment when he was in town. Soon his business excursions to the Pacific Rim increased in both length and frequency. Ultimately, he'd persuaded Morgan's executive management team in London that it would be in everyone's best interests to allow him to operate out of Hong Kong. It was not immediately clear to his superiors that 'everyone' would not include his wife and two young sons.

She arrived home with a divorce, a generous monthly stipend and custody of the children. Her mother had insisted she move back home because the large house was empty too much of the time, with her father still traveling a good bit. With some reluctance, and no good alternatives, she accepted and took up residence in the bedroom of her childhood. She placed her sons in an adjoining bedroom. It was not a sustainable arrangement. For one thing, she was shocked to learn her mother and father not only didn't sleep in the same room, but barely talked to each other. She immediately became the medium of exchange between them. That only added to a misery that knew no depth.

She finished her informal confession, hands folded neatly on her lap. Her hair had dried and was matted in sections to her forehead, giving her the appearance of a small child. Father John was tempted to comb it back with his fingers but did not dare. Instead he offered her a glass of iced tea, which she readily accepted. In his kitchen, he glanced at the clock and saw it was already past 11:00. He dipped his head into the sink and splashed cold water on his face. He had no idea where this conversation was headed next. He removed a pitcher of iced tea and poured two tall glasses. He returned the pitcher to its place on the first shelf in the refrigerator. On the way out of the kitchen, he stopped at a small icon of the Blessed Virgin on a pedestal above the narrow table. There, with his hands full, he prayed the *Memorare,* a powerful prayer of petition to the Mother of God.

Upon his return to the rectory's front porch, he noted she had straightened her wrinkled blouse and skirt and combed her hair. He also noted the rain had all but exhausted itself and fell now as a gentle Irish mist. He handed her the glass and she took it eagerly. Without waiting for him to sit down she proceeded to empty half its contents. He momentarily debated whether to go back inside for the pitcher, before opting to sit down. He, too, was thirsty.

They sat in silence for several minutes. He simply didn't know where to begin. He didn't have to; she teed him up with a question. "Father, where did it all begin to go wrong?"

His mind did a quick scan of several alternative responses, rejecting each as quickly as it surfaced. "Eve," he deadpanned.

She burst into laughter, and other than the shockingly high decibel level of the sound itself and the particular lateness of the hour, he was delighted to see her face transform into that of a teenager. His answer apparently spoke to something deep in her heart; the place where one's own conception of humanity was lodged, the veritable storehouse of largely confirming information accumulated through years of observation and lonely nights filled with suffering.

"You don't think I'm going to hell, do you?" she asked with a smile both tentative and plaintive.

"I'd bet against it," he answered matter of factly.

"Why?"

He looked at her with great patience and said, "Remember your grade school catechism?"

Her face crinkled. "God created us to know, love and serve him, and to be happy with him in Heaven?"

"Yes, yes. There is that. But we also learned there are three conditions which are required for mortal, or deadly, sin. Do you remember what they are?"

"No, Father. I'm sorry." She hung her head.

"Well, don't feel bad," he said brightly. "Virtually no one else your age does either."

She laughed again, self consciously. "What are they, Father?"

He raised a single finger. "First, the act itself has to be seriously sinful. Again, serious as in a terrible moral assault on the dignity of the other, or even self." He held up another finger. "Second, you yourself have to *know* the act is seriously sinful. You are *not* in doubt." He lifted a third finger. "And finally, you have to fully consent: what's called full *consent* of the will." He paused for effect. "The third condition has always been the tricky one for confessors in every age. But in *this* age, among young people *your* age, both the second and the third conditions are very much in play."

She fell silent. "Father, I knew the abortions were wrong, seriously wrong. *Both* of them."

He nodded. "Indeed they were. The question is whether you gave full consent of the will in each case; and that is a matter that is strictly between you and your confessor."

"Father, I don't have a confessor."

"When was the last time you went to what the Church now calls the Sacrament of Reconciliation?"

"Oh, Father, I don't even know!"

He bit his lip. "When was the last time you received Holy Eucharist?"

"Oh, a couple of weeks ago. I try to get there most Sundays, now that I'm home."

This pained him greatly. John Sweeney believed unworthy reception of Holy Communion was the singular cause of the demise of the Catholic Church in America. But the hour was indeed quite late. "Would you like to confess now?"

"Can I? Right here, like this?"

"Of course, unless you feel uncomfortable confessing sins to a lowly parish priest," he said with a disarming smile.

"Father, will you help me? I don't even remember how to begin."

In her later years, Theresa Halverson Delgado would tell people that her re-entry into the Church of her birth was a lot less painful than her exit. She'd remark that her first confession in over 15 years had required over one hour of patient probing and careful explanation about the Church's teachings on life and love by her parish priest, in what seemed more a continuation of an extraordinarily healing discussion than "a church thing." But when it was finished, well past midnight, she felt the otherworldly sensation of grace awash in her spirit and soul.

Terry Delgado took her leave in the early morning drizzle not knowing what she would do with the rest of her life; she only knew that whatever she did, it would involve an active engagement in the life of the Spirit.

# 22

---

platonic relationship with Philadelphia's most eligible single woman would not have been Dr. Jim Gillespie's first preference. He was madly in love with Maggie Kealey in every way a man could love a woman. He arose each day in anticipation of seeing her, and he went to bed each night thinking only of her. He'd taken to accessing his e-mail from home, at dawn, knowing she was a night owl and would send out a torrent of instructions, questions and requests for information to her direct reports after midnight. The very sight of her name above his on a computer screen spiked his heart. His screen saver was a photograph of the two of them in formal wear at a center city charity event – the occasion of their first "date," though she had insisted "it was no such thing." On days he was scheduled to meet with her, he always made sure he showered, shaved and brushed his teeth, and refrained from smoking his beloved Cuban cigars the evening before.

He had never married. It was the source of ongoing tension between him and his mother. She was 84 and lived alone, 22 years widowed. He was an only child and she believed she deserved, if not a priest, at the very least a grandchild. He had failed her, she reminded him on his weekly visits. There had even been a time when she would humiliate him by suggesting that her neighbors questioned his sexuality. Initially, it was not clear to him what she was implying. She kept repeating the phrase, 'they think you're, you know, funny.' From childhood, he'd been told he was funny so it didn't register. Ultimately she was forced to be more graphic. 'Funny,' she would say, 'in a way men who don't like women are funny.' His response was always measured and forever consistent. He just hadn't met the right woman yet, he'd tell her— and others who would inquire, often no less graciously.

He awoke early one autumn weekday morning to see he had a correspondence from her. It was sent at 1:46 a.m. It asked him to see her "first thing, about something important." First thing for him meant 6:30 a.m.; for her it could mean 5:00 depending on the matter at hand. He glanced at the time in the lower right-hand corner of the screen. It was already 5:37. He immediately shut the computer down and headed for the shower.

At 6:27, he opened the door to his office and found a note on his desk. It read: "I'm in, Slacker." It was initialed as customary. He sniffed the card to see if he could pick up her scent. He could not; he consoled himself that it was far better he not be able to detect her early morning smell than she detect his. He placed the card in his pocket, dropped his shoulder bag on his chair and headed for the corner office. She was sitting behind her desk, reading a report and sipping coffee. At the sight of him, she jumped up and went to the coffee pot and poured him a cup, adding cream and four small packets of sugar. "Need you wide awake this morning, Dr. Gillespie," she said brightly.

"Any chance we could just sit on the couch and hold hands instead of drinking coffee?" he suggested. She had developed a facility for tuning him out on virtually all matters save those medical or operational. She handed him his coffee, pointed to the formal sitting area, and said, "I think I may have something of strategic significance." He waited for her to sit on one of two facing couches and then took his seat opposite her, deciding against attempting to sit next to her, which would, he knew from experience, only cause her to slap his wrist, which would in turn mean coffee stains on an otherwise immaculate throw rug.

"Hmm, strategic significance! Let me guess: all docs will now report to nurses?"

She looked at him coyly and said in an affected southern dialect, "Why, Dr. Gillespie, they already do!"

He winced and nodded, and decided he needed more coffee.

"My conversation with Dr. Ciancini was not particularly productive, we can each so stipulate?" she asked, a small smile playing at the corners of her mouth.

"Oh, I don't know," he responded. "It kept the ER busy all night. And the severe case of hemorrhoids, which only lasted about a week, actually improved his disposition, according to his clinic partners."

What Maggie Kealey said next would be among the last things Jim Gillespie would remember deep into old age. "Well," she began philosophically, "if you can't give an occasional case of hemorrhoids to a well deserving doctor like this, what's the sense in even having the job?"

His cup of coffee seemed suspended in air for longer than the few seconds it took to follow the laws of gravity onto the immaculate white throw rug connecting their feet. His doubled-up body followed. The sounds of his convulsive laughter muted the sound of cup and contents meeting two inch thick carpeting. An untimely small splash, however, left stains on his white physician's coat, which would be embarrassing to explain to colleagues and patients. She seemed only mildly annoyed at his clumsiness and said, with a perfectly straight face, "You're getting the next cup yourself."

He did, while she introduced him to Dr. Henry Seelaus from a report she had been reading when he entered. She covered his resume and filled in some gaps anecdotally. "Hank" Seelaus was a gynecologist with a "conversion story." In his early 40's, with a wife and five children, he'd transitioned from a highly successful family practice in partnership with four other physicians, built around the prescription of oral contraceptives, to a marginal practice built on the principles of Natural Family Planning. Reportedly, at one point, he almost had to give up his practice in order to support his family, so precipitous was his all but immediate decline in fees.

"Jim, I'd like you to pay a visit to Dr. Seelaus," she suggested.

"And to what would I attribute my interest, should it occur to him to ask?"

"Oh, I don't know," she said with mild annoyance. "Just size him up. Find out if he's a franchise player, the kind of doc we can build a 'culture of life' fertility practice around."

He was too stunned to reply. His mind raced to connect the dots she had plotted with that single sentence on an otherwise blank whiteboard in his mind. She was thinking the unthinkable. She was intending to overhaul their entire Ob/Gyn offering, which was currently the cornerstone of their Women's Health platform. He knew she had 'chutzpah,' but this was beyond audacity. "He, by chance, isn't expecting my call, perhaps?"

"Of course not," she said dismissively. "Must I tee everything up for you, Jim?"

There was the occasional moment, he realized, when platonic was more than sufficient. He chirped a cheerful goodbye and happily took his leave.


Hank Seelaus was curious enough to agree to a meeting, as long as it would be held in his home, after office hours. He'd never met Jim Gillespie, but he'd heard only good things about his professional competence, his prodigious charitable work, and of course, his "companionship" with the iconic Margaret Ann Kealey. He attempted several times to ascertain the purpose of their meeting during the initial phone call, without success. He hung up with the uneasy feeling that Gillespie was no less certain than he. Nevertheless, when the last couple left his office on a blustery

March evening, he updated their folder, turned off the lights and headed upstairs to the family living quarters. It was a little past 10:00 p.m., and his wife's laughter intercepted him at the top of the stairs. It surprised him, given her practiced reticence, that she'd stay up to entertain a perfect stranger, and a guest of his, in their living room at such a late hour. When he opened the Dutch doors leading from the hallway into a step down living room, he understood why. His first sight was of his wife doubled over in laughter, and his guest, the inestimable Dr. James Gillespie, standing in a suspended state of pantomime.

"Straighten up, Clare, the principal has arrived," Jim Gillespie said in a hoarse whisper quickly followed by a staccato burst of coughing.

Hank Seelaus laughed in spite of himself. "I'd send you two to your rooms immediately, but I'm not sure that would end the mischief," he said as he walked over to Jim Gillespie and extended his hand. "Why do I suddenly feel like Richard Dreyfus in *What about Bob?*"

"I'm *not* a slacker, Dr. Marvin," Gillespie replied with mock indignation. Clare Seelaus went off again and, hand over her mouth, nervous glance at her husband, left the room.

"Sit down, Bob. And you can call me Leo," Hank Seelaus said, easing himself into his own easy chair next to an empty marble fireplace. When they were both seated, he inquired of his guest, "So, tell me again. What could possibly bring such a distinguished physician to the home of a lowly Ob/Gyn, particularly all the way up in Warminster on a night like this?"

They spoke for over two hours, and when the conversation ended, each man had that peculiar sense, all but unique among believing Christians, that their destinies were somehow inextricably linked. One hour into their discussion, Hank Seelaus shared his conversion story. He'd been in a practice with four other Catholic physicians for over 20 years. Most of their patients came from local parishes. Each of the physicians prescribed oral contraceptives routinely, and referred infertile couples to neighborhood fertility clinics where they underwent IVF procedures, the great majority of which were unsuccessful.

He and his wife were coaxed by friends into making a Marriage Encounter weekend; he felt a stirring in his heart. Nothing more. He began reading the Bible at night after his wife and children were in bed for the evening. He felt challenged by what he was reading. He called a priest. Ultimately, the priest confronted him about his practice. 'How can you reconcile what you're doing with your confession of faith?' he'd asked him. He didn't have an answer. It took almost a year for him to get up the nerve to tell his wife what he felt led to do. She was supportive, without reservation. That made the next step in the process both possible and inevitable. He told his partners he was leaving the practice, and why. Several responded as if he had taken leave of his senses. One actually became defensive and accused him of being judgmental.

He set up a practice in his house and watched his income drop by half in the first year. He was paying late fees every month on both his car and home mortgage loans. He asked the local Catholic elementary school to grant him tuition relief for three of his children. His wife went to work as a receptionist for a dentist who happened to be a neighbor. It was a harrowing experience, he told Jim Gillespie, something he never would have permitted his family to go through, had he known in advance the fear it would induce in his wife and the utter helplessness it had induced in him. But they survived. His practice, which was built around the Creighton Method of Natural Family Planning, was now running 30% ahead of his best years with the group. Far more importantly, he was now helping young couples have children who had previously been unable to have children; and young couples who'd been blessed with a natural fertility to space children without having to resort to relationship-sundering, and generally less effective, artificial methods. He was happy, and at peace, he told Jim Gillespie. And he had no intention of disrupting that, for any reason.

Nonetheless, he'd surprised Jim, and in at least one instance shocked him, with his intimate knowledge of Regina Hospital's

Ob/Gyn offering, particularly the symbiotic relationship between the Ciancini in-house group and its next door neighbor, Mid-Atlantic Fertility Services. Their discussion veered off track several times, once onto the subject of a hypothetical black market for unused frozen embryos among Silicon Valley bio engineering firms, major U.S. state universities, and the big pharmaceutical houses headquartered in the Northeast. Though the U.S. market for freezing and storing fertilized eggs in the nation's 250 to 300 fertility clinics was relatively small – an estimated $50 million annually, or $100 a piece for an estimated 500,000 embryos – Hank Seelaus believed the going rate for a "premium live embryo," one with thoroughbred lineage, on the U.S. black market was currently approaching $10,000, which made *that* market, almost five billion dollars annually, considerably more significant. He also believed there was a highly developed global market where premium embryos were being sold for up to three to five times that amount. But he professed not to know how the market was structured and who its main operatives were. He was dealing only in hearsay, he cautioned.

Jim Gillespie had heard enough. Hank Seelaus, he would tell his CEO, was indeed a franchise player, whatever that meant in the context of Regina Hospital's future plans. They agreed to stay in touch. Jim looked at the clock on his dashboard when he got in his blue Porsche Carrera 911. It was 12:50 a.m. He had a long drive home and an early call in the morning: early in the sense that his boss would be waiting in his office, whenever he arrived, in anticipation of a full report.

· · ·

"What time did you get home last night? I left messages for you at midnight and a little after 1:00 a.m." Maggie Kealey was working at her secretary's desk in the common area in order to pounce upon seeing the reds of Jim Gillespie's eyes. It was 6:12 a.m.

"About 1:40. I thought about calling you, but I didn't want to interrupt your cardio workout," he replied.

She nodded vacantly and pointed to the coffee. "How 'bout we try to drink it today rather than wear it?"

Unperturbed, he opened the door to his office, flicked on the lights, and turned to her and said, "the usual: extra sugar."

Moments later she entered and handed him his coffee. She sat down in one of two chairs opposite his cluttered desk. "What is all that crap?" she asked, eyeing all the files and folders and correspondence.

"Oh, nothing much, just my deportation papers and some correspondence to the Immigration Board from my attorney."

She ignored him without difficulty. "Well?"

"He thinks Ciancini may be on the take," he said offhandedly, while emptying the contents of his shoulder bag. He took great delight in outracing her to "nub issues." He looked up and much to his pleasure, her mouth was agape. In fact, he saw she was speechless.

He continued matter of factly, "Mid Atlantic is offering his young referrals, our Catholic women patients in their 20's, about $5000 a shot for their eggs, which they then freeze and sell to women in their 40's whose own eggs tend to have low success rates. The buzz in the tiny NFP community is Ciancini is getting a 10% 'finder's fee' on all referrals. That may help explain that new addition he's been building on his home in Penn Valley."

"That greedy bastard. I'll fire him this morning!"

"You'll do no such thing, of course," he said, now sitting.

She backtracked self consciously. "I didn't mean this morning as in *this* morning."

"No, no, of course not. You merely meant sometime today, right?" he smiled at her discomfort.

"Oh, Jim, you know well what I meant. We can't have this. Every day he conducts this kind of business in this hospital we're, you and me, we're in the business of aiding and abetting murder. How do we confirm it? How do we lawyer it up, and how do we confront him?"

He nodded soberly. "Well, I guess you're not going to like the part about the sperm banks then." He paused for effect before detonating another bombshell. "He's doing the same thing with our young Catholic husbands. But hey, at least he's cutting us in on some of the business. We get the ultrasound revenue from the female patients who use the stuff, and don't forget the $500 in staff dues we collect every year from Ciancini's docs and those fun guys in the next office working for Mid Atlantic."

Her face registered her horror. "My word, Jim. How far down does this stuff go?"

He made sure he had her in the crosshairs, then slowly squeezed the trigger: "To hear Hank tell it, the question in the pro life community is how far *up* does it go?" The moment he saw her head drop, he felt a tsunami of guilt. *What is it with me? Why do I do this to her? Am I attacking her because she won't marry me? Lord, please help me— am I venal or merely deranged?*

She lifted her head slowly, and he was shocked at how much she appeared to age in but a moment. He had an immediate image of Tom Hardy rounding third base and heading for home in *Damn Yankees*. What was most troubling, however, was what no longer was in her eyes. They were empty of the fire and determination that set her apart. She seemed listless and fearful. He prepared himself for the worst – her tears – but they did not come. Instead what he heard was a gentle summons. "Jim, I need help. I can't do all this alone. I'm not strong enough. I'm working day and night, and barely making a dent." She paused, then added morosely, "Maybe this wasn't God's plan for me." He immediately had an unsettling image of her at her father's dinner table, hunched over a plate and under the weight of lofty expectations; then a second image of her going into her bedroom alone after her husband told her he was leaving her for his secretary.

Her plaintive cry for help was the sound track for the images and it split his heart open. He wanted to rush to her and hug her and tell her how wonderful she was and how dependent they all were on her drive and talent and sheer goodness, but he did not trust himself. Because somewhere in that grand colloquy, he knew, he would slip slide off platform and tell her how much he loved her and how he longed to live and die with her. So he sat, saying nothing, bleeding from her wound: a wound he himself had willfully inflicted on the woman he loved.

She got up to leave and he stood abruptly and said, "Please, Maggie, sit down." He struggled to find a way onto another conversational trajectory. "The meeting with Seelaus was a good one. He's our kind of guy. Could we get him to headquarter his practice at Regina Hospital, if that's your plan?" he paused reflectively. "I think it's doubtful, but—" he smiled and flashed his high wattage charm, "—I would never say never; you are, after all, a most persuasive woman."

He watched the color come back into her lovely face and noted a hint of sparkle returning to her stunning blue eyes. It delighted him. *How true it must be that young girls so desperately need the affirmation of their fathers. Absent it, they spend the rest of their lives pursuing self esteem from men in other relationships that are unable to provide it.* He wanted to say something, anything, but again could not find quite the right words.

"Don't worry about that, Jim," She said with an electric smile. "He'll come. And he'll be happier practicing medicine here than he ever imagined he could be."

He nodded and smiled. "Poor sap. Never had a chance." He immediately thought of Irish playwright George Bernard Shaw's famous theatrical line that 'Reasonable men were men who adapted themselves unto the world; unreasonable men were men who adapted the world unto themselves. Therefore,' he suggested, 'all progress depended upon unreasonable men.' *To which I would respectfully add: and women, Mr. Shaw.*

She asked him about Hank Seelaus' family and his practice, the state of the NFP movement in Philadelphia, his view of the

Catholic Church's current role in the decision-making process of its young families, and whether Seelaus thought there was a role for a Catholic hospital in the future of "fertility services." Long ago he'd given up trying to sate her curiosity and had learned to discipline himself to answer specific questions in a highly specific manner; and, above all, to be careful to avoid the kind of editorializing that would only incite another full volley of questions. He was never entirely successful; nor was he in this instance. Just when he thought he had whacked the last mole, up popped one more: "How do we get a handle on the money trail, Jim?" she asked, a half mask of perplexity shadowing her features.

He glanced at his watch. It was only 6:53 and already he was exhausted. It would be a long day. "I don't know, Maggie. Let me think about that for awhile." Then he remembered something Seelaus had said, something he found troubling, and added, "He did say that all of Ciancini's docs were prescribing contraceptives, even the Morning After Pill, from their offices downstairs. He reminded me that all their billing goes through our hospital billing system. And that our billing department is billing the insurance companies for both the visits and the pills.

Neither of them said anything for several long moments. Then, Maggie asked him the one question he did not want her to ask him. "Jim, do you think Sister Kathleen and the Order know any of this?" Her eyes were wide with expectancy. It was clear she wanted, needed, to hear 'no.'

"Yes," he answered.

Slowly, quietly, Maggie Kealey took her leave. She had another long and difficult day ahead of her.

# 23

Peter Feeney stood on track platform 16 waiting for Amtrak train #118 to New York. It was 6:26 a.m. The train was due to arrive at Philadelphia's 30th Street Station from its stop in Wilmington at 6:36, and arrive at Penn Station in Manhattan at 7:37. He stood with dozens of others in small clusters where the doors would open when the train arrived. His black leather shoulder bag was filled with various "pocket" documents that may or may not be required for the scheduled 8:00 meeting with Clifford Ackerman, Hanley Siliezar's right hand man and Ultra Com's Chief Operating Officer.

He heard the train before he saw it. Nervously he looked through the platform's windowed doors to the bank of escalators, hoping to see Michael Burns descending. No Michael Burns among the scurrying crowd of late arrivals. He folded his Wall Street Journal in quarters then doubled it over to prepare for his entrance to the café car, where he hoped to commandeer a table that he and his boss could use to spread out and have a light breakfast.

The train arrived and the doors opened; Peter was among

the first to step on and the first to stake out a table in the café car. He dropped his bag heavily on the opposite side of the table to signal the imminent arrival of a companion. He removed his coat, folded it, and laid it next to him on the seat. As he did so he caught sight of his boss bulling his way through the bottleneck at the café car's entrance. He arrived at the table breathing heavily, and Peter guessed he had raced from the underground parking garage up to the station's main floor, only to race across it and down the escalator to the train platform. He smiled as he watched him unload clothing and materials. *Well, like God himself, seldom early, never late.*

Burns sat down heavily and said, "Let's wait till the crowd at the counter clears before we get some breakfast."

Peter turned around to see the size of the crowd at the counter. There were three people in line.

"Ackerman say if Siliezar was going to sit in?"

Peter saw if not fear then certainly apprehension in his boss' eyes. He truly hoped Michael Burns wouldn't have one of his patented meltdowns in a mid-town Manhattan boardroom. *On the other hand, it would be pure gift for my memoir.* "No, didn't say."

"Don't like this one, Petey. These guys may be using this McKenna thing as an excuse to re-negotiate, or back out of the deal entirely."

"Extremely doubtful," Peter replied.

"What makes you say that?"

"I don't know. It's just not Siliezar's style."

Hanley Siliezar was a Madison Avenue icon. One of 12 children born into poverty in the hills surrounding Buenos Aires, his keen intellect and white hot ambition caught the attention of the Immaculate Heart of Mary sisters from the States, who nurtured his relentless curiosity and fast tracked him through their convent schools. He entered Harvard at age 16 on a U.S. government grant, and graduated Summa Cum Laude four years later with a degree in international business. He caused a bit of a stir just before graduation when he challenged his class ranking: he'd finished second, less than a tenth of a point behind the son of a fabled industrial scion, and demanded the administration investigate what he characterized as "certain irregularities." The administration denied his request and suggested he get over it. He never entirely did. He entered the University of Chicago that autumn on a full scholarship, and earned an MBA in international finance one year later. He finished first in his class with a perfect 4.0: two full tenths of a point ahead of his nearest rival.

It was his intention to return to his beloved Argentina upon graduation and run for political office to address grave and systemic societal imbalances. He took a job as an assistant plant manager for an HM manufacturing facility 20 miles outside Buenos Aires. Very quickly he discovered that virtually all of the country's political class, from the mayors of small municipalities to the president and his cabinet, were handpicked by wealthy landowners and industrialists. He came to believe the only truly leveragable power on earth was to be found in great wealth. He befriended a middle-aged man, Jorge Valdivia, who was a close personal friend of his plant manager. Valdivia owned a small advertising firm; his wife, who was educated in the States, wrote the copy and selected print design from among a small coterie of free lance artists. The proprietor handled the business functions: buying space and placing the ads and pursuing new clients. Hanley noted the man was much more accomplished dealing with the media than he was in soliciting and acquiring new clients. So, he convinced the man to let him run the new business development function on a commission-only basis. The first six months he nearly starved. Then he discovered he was pitching the wrong people. He began going over the heads of the marketing functionaries in town, and pitching the business owners themselves, many of whom lived in other parts of the country behind gated walls. He quickly learned how to get inside those compounds and ingratiate himself to the men who owned a highly disproportionate share of the country's wealth. His U.S. educational pedigree, his charismatic presence, and his ingenious ideas on how his clients could multiply their wealth, allowed him to penetrate social circles he had not known existed.

Within three years he had quintupled the small firm's bill-ings, and he approached the proprietor one morning in early spring with a buyout offer. The man resisted. He and his wife were quite happy with the present arrangement, he told Hanley. Indeed, they had finally been able to pay off their debts, purchase a suite on the top floor of an exclusive apartment tower overlooking the city and coast, and begin putting money aside for their two children's educa-tion in America. Jorge Valdivia did not want to lose his new busi-ness thoroughbred, however, and countered – offering to double Siliezar's commission rate to 10 points on all new revenues and 5 points on recurring revenues for a period of up to three years. Siliezar rejected the counter offer out of hand. He was no longer interested in being a hired hand. He now wanted to create his own wealth and use it to pursue his own larger interests.

As it happened, the mayor of Buenos Aires went to see Jorge Valdivia the following evening as he was leaving his office. It was never clear what was said – or by whom – but the following morn-ing, Hanley Siliezar received the joyful news in a telephone call from the mayor himself that the Valdivia's had reconsidered his offer.

Within 20 years Hanley Siliezar built the largest advertis-ing network in all of South America. He owned 24 offices and employed over 2,000 men and women in 12 countries. So great was his reputation, that men all over the world sought his counsel for the marketing of their automobiles and soft drinks, wrist watches and software, publishing ventures and financial innovations. None of this was lost on the men who ran the largest advertising con-glomerates in the United States, Europe and Asia; they took to boarding planes for what became an annual pilgrimage to Buenos Aires, always in winter, in vain attempts to buy Hanley Siliezar's advertising network.

Sol Katz watched the comings and goings from his suite of offices overlooking Central Park. He was the Chairman of Ultra Com and its Chief Executive Officer. He took special delight in the futility of his competitors. One winter morning he penned a simple note to Hanley Siliezar in his own hand. It read: *I have something you want. Come see me next time you're in New York.*

Two months to the day, he received a phone call as he was leaving his office for his home in Saddlebrook, New Jersey. It was Hanley Siliezar; he suggested it might be a good time for he and Katz to have a drink. They agreed to meet at a small Italian restaurant in Hoboken, lest they be seen together in Manhattan and provoke no end of media speculation. That night, Sol Katz offered Hanley Siliezar the one thing he wanted most in all the world: the top job at the world's leading advertising conglomerate. The cashless transaction called for Katz to buy Siliezar Advertising with Ultra Com stock for 8 times earnings; Katz, after 14 years at the helm, would move upstairs and become Chairman of the Board. Siliezar would be named Ultra Com's new Chief Executive Officer, and become its largest single stockholder, on the day the transaction closed. The combined revenues of the two networks would establish Ultra Com as the largest advertising conglomerate in the world, and, more importantly, the only network with a substantial and strategic position on every continent. The deal took all of one hour to complete and was ratified by a simple hand shake. Both men left without ordering dinner.

Hanley Siliezar had spent the last nine years building Ultra Com into the most powerful and pervasive media force on the globe. The corporation had acquired newspapers in Europe, broadcast networks in South America and parts of Asia, and powerful think tanks in the U.S. with strategic links to major governments throughout the world. He was reputed to have no peer in leveraging personal wealth to amass influence in the power capitals of sovereign nations, and was the subject of endless speculation about his ultimate "end game," as the press routinely referred to it.

"Hope you're right, Petey," Michael Burns said as he exhaled loudly. "Frankly, I don't care if I ever meet that guy."

This surprised Feeney greatly. *If someone was buying my company for $30 million, not only would I want to meet the guy, I'd at least want to buy him a Chase Utley jersey.*

The rest of the ride to Penn Station was quiet, which delighted Peter Feeney, who had work to do. He noted Michael Burns borrowed his Wall Street Journal before reading his own New York Times. The train arrived two minutes late, and Burns and Feeney emerged from the underground on 7th avenue at 7:44 to hail a cab uptown. They arrived at Ultra Com's World Headquarters on the top three floors of a 48 floor office tower on the south western corner of Central Park. Feeney paid the cabbie; Burns rarely carried cash. They made a beeline for the farthest elevator bank, which offered an express ride to the 48th floor. They arrived at 8:01 and were met by a dark haired, slow-eyed South American enchantress who introduced herself as "Ediana Rodriquez, Mr. Siliezar's assistant."

Press reports frequently linked Hanley Siliezar to various international beauties, but none, Michael Burns believed, could be any more stunning than the woman standing before him. Siliezar's wife, a former Miss Argentina, was said to have died alone in the bedroom of their private suite 11 years ago, in circumstances some in the media found suspicious. When he accepted the Ultra Com position, he'd moved to New York with his only child, a daughter who was currently studying architecture at Yale University. His name had been conspicuously absent in the society pages over the past year, and Michael presumed the reason was now leading Feeney down a corridor, with him trailing, to a small private conference room off Hanley Siliezar's magisterial office suite, complete with its own bar, screening room and private bath.

Burns dallied momentarily to peek inside the office itself, which was currently unoccupied. He found it breathtaking. The floor to ceiling windows overlooking the park gave the illusion that the picture-perfect small blue lake at the park's southern entrance was but a step, and a 48-floor fall, away. Burns was overwhelmed by the selection of early and late Renaissance originals hanging on walls of deep mahogany. He noted a select number of engraved lithographs of magazine covers and articles bearing Siliezar's likeness. He also found himself admiring elegantly matted and framed photographs of Siliezar and world leaders. One in particular caught his attention: it featured him flanked by Vladimir Putin and Stefan Boros in an outdoor setting with Lake Geneva as a backdrop.

"It is quite enthralling, Mr. Burns, yes?" Ediana asked gently, from just behind him, all but startling him in the process.

Michael recovered quickly and recognized she was ever so graciously coaxing him into the conference room so she could get back to work. He nodded and replied, "Aye, 'Tis …" in pitch perfect country dialect to deflect his defensiveness.

He followed her into the conference room, and immediately encountered the outstretched hand of Clifford Ackerman. "Good to see you again, Michael," he said behind a small, tight smile, which only added to Michael's apprehension. Across the small round table Peter Feeney unloaded his bag and smiled. Michael spotted a decanter of what appeared to be fresh-squeezed orange juice, among various fruits and pastries on a portable cart in the corner. He headed over and felt the decanter; it was cold. He reached for a slender glass, eschewed the ice in the silver bucket, and poured himself a full glass, which he downed in several breathless swallows. He poured another and downed it almost as quickly. He poured a third and heard Feeney say, "Understand Cliff, Burns will do this until lunch if we let him." Ackerman let loose a loud, undisciplined cackle that suggested he may well have been the one who led his fraternity's beer runs.

Michael headed for the conference table with his third glass of orange juice, and noted for the first time a folder sitting on the table in front of an empty, fourth chair. He understood instantly. Hanley Siliezar would be joining them this morning, and his "talking points" had been prepared by Ackerman to quickly focus his attention on the salient issue. Michael had little doubt as to what that issue was. His blood pressure was suddenly and suitably elevated.

He sat down and waved toward the empty chair with his glass. "Hanley joining us?"

Ackerman cleared his throat and replied, "Yes. When he returns from his breakfast meeting downtown."

"Well, I'm anxious to finally meet him," Michael prevaricated.

"Oh, he's anxious to meet you too, Michael," Ackerman said. "Of course he's met Peter, and he's quite familiar with your company."

A nervous, silent tension quickly filled the room, which Cliff Ackerman wouldn't, or couldn't, ease with a throwaway line, a small joke or a funny story; it reminded Michael why number two men were number two men. He looked at Ackerman and decided to throw the first pitch. "So, you're wondering why I bought McKenna advertising?"

"Actually, that question is of lesser significance, Michael," Ackerman answered. "The question we're asking ourselves at headquarters is, 'What kind of partner goes out and buys a company without telling you?'"

Burns felt scalded. He did not anticipate the question to be put to him in quite that way. Suddenly his Adam's apple seemed lodged in his throat.

Ackerman waited patiently for an answer that Michael Burns simply could not find in any of the files his mind zip-sorted through in milliseconds. In his desolation he was shocked to hear the voice of Peter Feeney. "That's my fault, Cliff," he offered. Burns looked at him with incredulity. "We were so busy getting that thing nailed down, and keeping it a secret, that I never got around to calling you like Michael asked me to."

Ackerman appeared stunned. He looked from Feeney to Burns, then back to Feeney again. He'd been caught off guard. He and Feeney had had at least one, often two, telephone conversations a day for the past month. They'd even met three times in New York. Yet in no single one of their meetings or telephone conversations had Feeney ever let on something was afoot. This was beyond odd. His Madison Avenue-trained mind immediately probed for motive, but he was unable to come to grips with why Feeney would take the hit for his boss, diminishing Burns' stature in the process. Was Feeney angling for Burns' job?

"Well," Ackerman said a bit hesitantly, "why in hell *would* you guys go out and buy a tiny little nothing of a company two weeks before we're due to close?"

Sensing tentativeness, Michael pounced. "It's a strategic acquisition, Cliff. For one thing, Aaron McKenna is a minority and very tight with the Governor. The state's lottery, corporate relocation, and tourism accounts combine for about 20% of our business. McKenna's status as a high-quality, minority subcontractor has helped us hold that business through the last four bidding cycles. He was feeling a little disaffected, a little left out, when he heard about *our* deal," Michael said, nodding toward Feeney.

Peter smiled at the thought of McKenna's strategic significance. *That's right, Cliff. That's why we had to buy him off. No, not because he would have been out shopping his sub contract to our competitors for a better deal the minute he heard about our deal; but because he is a great strategic marketing weapon. And now, believe it or not, you're gonna have access to this genius too.*

"He's also going to help us cast Women's Right, Cliff." Michael Burns was on one of his patented runs. "This guy is a stud: Former D-1 basketball star at LaSalle University. Early 30's, successful, handsome, charismatic, single. That crowd over at 11th and Walnut will fall down and worship him when I introduce him as the head of the account."

Burns thought Ackerman was looking at him oddly. "What's the matter?" he asked.

Ackerman made no attempt to hide his discomfort at Burns' ignorance. "You do know, of course, they're all lesbians over there, right?"

Peter Feeney convulsed onto the floor. He rose with tears in his eyes, only to go down again. It was at that moment that Hanley Siliezar entered the room. He took one look at Peter Feeney struggling to rise again to his feet, looked at Ackerman who was laughing at the sight of Feeney on rubbery legs and said, "Perhaps we overpaid."

Michael Burns felt limp. He looked for a window from which to jump, but there were of course no windows. He wondered if perhaps he should excuse himself, find a men's room and hang himself from one of the stalls.

But he underestimated, yet again, Peter Feeney. "Hanley," he said laughing. "You have just acquired the firm of the funniest man in the entire advertising world, and believe me when I say this: you're gonna be callin' him on dark days for a lift. Everybody does. Michael, tell Hanley that story— oh never mind. Cliff will tell him later."

Hanley Siliezar, slim and silvery and elegant, took it all in without blinking. He went to his chair and sat down, and immediately Ediana Rodriquez entered the room and set fresh-brewed coffee in a white porcelain cup and saucer next to his folder. As he opened the folder in front of him and scanned the first page, Michael took stock of his new employer. He was impeccably groomed in his dark Armani suit, sparkling blue French cuffs, trim pencil mustache and fastidious razor cut, which looked like it had been completed within the hour. He nodded abruptly at what must have been the memo's summary comments, and, with a quick, reflexive glance at Ackerman, closed the folder, setting if off to one side. He leapt to his feet and walked over to Michael's chair and half lifted him out of it. Michael was shocked at the man's upper body strength.

"Maahkill, Maahkill, please excuse my poor manners." He was holding Michael's upper arms in his two strong hands and sizing him up with what appeared to be genuine affection. "Thees ees the first time we meet."

Burns stared, transfixed.

"How much I have looked forward to this moment," Siliezar said, smiling benignly. "You are indeed just what I imagined you to be, youthful and handsome and ... sturdy," He added, "Ours will be a grand partnership, Maahkill."

"Maahkill" was more than relieved to hear this; his mind immediately abandoned thoughts of a deal scuttled and took a soaring flight of fancy. He treated himself to an image of his own regal presence on the bridge of a 60-foot yacht he had long coveted. His family and friends were cavorting on the deck below. Tuxedoed waiters were serving hors d'oeurves. He momentarily relaxed and submitted to the sweet sensation. He was slapped back into reality by Siliezar, who clapped him firmly on his left shoulder and cradled his head in his left hand, planting a kiss on the left cheek before returning to his own seat. Michael, somewhat dazed, dropped back into his own seat, and reflexively turned it toward the alpha male in the room.

Siliezar took a small sip of his Jamaican blend coffee and set the cup down with two fingers, ever so delicately. He fixed Michael with a beguiling smile. "Maahkill, I am going to take you into my confidence this morning." He paused for effect. "You and I have much work ahead of us, and it is important work." Longer pause. "Important for Burns Advertising, important for Ultra Com, important for America, important for the peoples of the world, but most of all, Maahkill, important work for future generations."

On Madison Avenue, it was referred to sardonically as "The Spell." It was equal parts vision, gravitas and charm – each nuanced and blended and delivered organically, without a trace of artifice. It had mesmerized brilliant men in virtually all the world capitals, and succeeded in moving tens of billions of their advertising dollars from rival firms to Siliezar's over the past decade. Michael was well aware of "the legend of The Spell," indeed he had mocked it, along with countless colleagues and competitors in the industry. Now, however, he found himself being drawn ineluctably into its radioactive field of energy.

"Maahkill, you and I weel make heestory."

Michael nodded mutely.

"Our world cannot long continue in its present state," he said with elaborate sobriety. "There is far too much poverty, disease and illiteracy: what I call The Unholy Trinity of injustice." He paused and smiled at his own cleverness. "Mankind has reached a point of no return. We must either address this great civilizational failure in our generation, or we will perish in our children's. Half the world lives on less than one dollar a day. One dollar, Maahkill!" Siliezar's eyes blazed and a righteous forefinger stabbed the air.

"I fear the clash of civilizations is imminent. The world's poor will soon have access to weapons of mass destruction." He paused dramatically. "Maahkill, what will they have to lose? They have nothing. Nothing!" he half shouted, arms outstretched, palms up.

"We who prize reason must *do* something, wouldn't you agree, Maahkill?"

Michael nodded reflexively.

"We cannot simply stand by and allow the species to bomb itself into extinction. We have come too far. Surely this is not what our God expects from us. We must exercise the gifts of intellect and will through which we image his own likeness, his own creative powers." Slight pause. "Man must come together. We must reason together. We must create a new vision, a new reality, for all God's children." Hanley Siliezar's voice now appeared to settle into something resembling a velvet fog. "And we will, Maahkill; we will."

He stood erect behind his chair and rested his arms on its back. "I have spent the last five years of my life pursuing this vision, Maahkill. As Clifford will tell you, I have lived on an airplane." He nodded to Ackerman for confirmation and, on cue, received it. "I have spoken to the world's leading industrialists, politicians, military men, investors, scientists, intellectuals, and NGO's. And, Maahkill, I am happy to report, they all agree." Pause for dramatic effect. "Something must be done, and soon."

He began to pace, head bowed. "So *I* have done this ... something." He stopped and fixed Michael with a hard stare. "I have created a vision, and the outline of a plan, for the Fourth Great Revolution – The Life Sciences Revolution – and it will do what the industrial, cultural and technological revolutions all failed to do." He paused. "This revolution, Maahkill, will be *inclusive*. There will no longer be haves and have not's. All men, not merely the privileged, will have access to the fruits of the Life Sciences Revolution. And it is precisely *this* social justice which will provide a lasting peace for a world that has grown all too weary of incessant war ..." He let his voice trail off and took his seat.

Michael looked at him in disbelief. *What in God's name does this have to do with me?*

Siliezar held Michael's gaze until he was certain he had absorbed what he intended as context for their discussion. "Now, you are no doubt saying, 'why is Hanley telling me all this? What does this have to do with Burns Advertising?'"

Michael nodded, involuntarily.

"Well, let me tell you the rest of the plan," Siliezar said, relaxed and smiling again. "Let me begin by saying just as I am the plan's architect, Ultra Com will become its gatekeeper. We will plan new markets, Maahkill, around new technologies. These new technologies will offer man new solutions for his most intractable problems, beginning with disease and death and including poverty and illiteracy. These markets must be planned not in the sense governments plan markets, and fail. No, no." Purposeful wagging of the righteous forefinger. "They must be planned conceptually, so businessmen can determine self interest and invest accordingly; because it is only through their activities that free markets will discover their rightful form and purpose." Pause. "Now for this to happen there must be an end to the restrictive barriers inherent in the legal codes of all sovereign nations; a temporary halt to the geo-political maneuverings of nations, which forever ups the ante and raises the anxiety levels of peoples everywhere; and an end to the isolation and the nationalization of discovery in our laboratories, both private and public."

Michael found this stimulating and recalled the story of the little boy on Christmas Day who was led by his parents to a barn filled with horse manure; he immediately cried out in happiness, certain there was a pony in there somewhere.

"Maahkill, do you know why I buy Burns Advertising, and pay nearly eight times multiple?"

Michael sat bolt upright in his chair. If he remembered nothing else from this day, he was sure as hell going to remember what he was about to hear. "I buy you, Maahkill," Siliezar said with a wry smile. "I buy your marketing acumen. I know many men of great wealth who see what I see. But these men at the end of the day must also see returns. So I need you to conceptualize for me what is possible by way of new markets. This will let us begin a massive reallocation of the world's private capital, harness great public and private energies, and harvest the technologies which have already been created in laboratories all over the world."

Michael understood this was *not* a Q&A, but still … "How can I help you conceive new markets if I don't know the products and services you hope to conceive?"

Siliezar smiled broadly. "Interesting choice of terms. And quite apt, Maahkill. You are indeed a clever fellow."

Michael fell silent.

Hanley Siliezar took the measure of the man and nodded graciously. "You want to know more, do you not?"

Michael nodded wordlessly.

"You are asking yourself, 'what kind of future does Hanley Siliezar envision? What is it that will drive this Life Sciences Revolution so that it touches the lives of people all over the world?" He leaned forward in his chair and rested his elbows on the conference table. "Let me say only this for now. We are determined to unleash the creative forces within man. He must no longer be restricted by confessions and ideologies, borders and tariffs. He must be allowed to learn the secrets of the human genome and apply them to his own survival. Only then can he breed out his ever-increasing mutations and pathogens and replace them, within the molecular structure itself, with life correcting, life extending, DNA." He paused for effect. "We must begin a forced march through disease – beginning with the villainous strains of Malaria and HIV which kill millions every year, and not stop until we have arrested the runaway pace of the cancers and brought them under our control. And when we have conquered disease we must turn our energies toward literacy, which virtually alone pre-determines a nation's ability to create wealth. Information itself, the lifeblood of innovation, must be made available to all, for all. There can be no closed "on ramps" to the information highway. And just as all must have equal access to information, all must also have equal access to capital, even the poor. It is only in this way that a field is leveled for the kind of global competition that drives new discovery."

Siliezar sat back in his chair and studied Michael Burns. He found his silence compelling. *This one is not yet sold. This is good. He is a true believer. The force of his conversion will be combustible.* He decided to cut the tutorial short. "Maahkill, you will have many questions. This I know. But we must leave it there for now. We will have much time, you and I, when Burns Advertising is officially part of the Ultra Com family. And, I must assure you, all your questions will be answered at that time. For now though, I must request your permission to ask *you* a question." He waited intently for Michael's approval which came by way of a wary nod of his head.

"Maahkill, will you permit me to make you a man of enormous wealth? A man of great influence in all the world's major capitals? Will you permit me to help you create a legacy that will outlive your children's children?"

Michael's eyes widened. He counted three questions but he didn't think it was a good time to nitpick. *The influence thing sounds pretty cool … and that legacy thing is something I'd like to hear more about sometime, but tell me again about the wealth part. What's your definition of enormous?* And with that he was off again on the high seas. He was standing on the flying bridge of, this time, a 110 foot yacht, a mirror image of Tiger Woods' *Privacy,* which was docked at a mega marina in Palm Beach. His children intermingled with celebrities from the worlds of cinema and literature, politics and industry. There were two bands playing on the two decks below. Black tuxedoed white men and white tuxedoed black men were serving elegant trays of the day's catch. His grandchildren were climbing the stainless steel circular ladder to the bridge, to be closer to him.

"Ah, yes. Sure." He nodded agreeably making him appear, in Peter Feeney's estimation, like something akin to a bobble head doll. "Hey, works for me," he replied with a rather expansive smile, provoking coarse laughter from Clifford Ackerman.

"Good," Hanley Siliezar replied with a firm smile. He then surprised Michael by rolling his chair back from the table and rolling it over next to his in order to ask one very final, and very personal, question. He drew to within two feet of Michael and stopped. "Maahkill, this McKenna thing, is it important to you?"

Michael's heart began to race. *Hey, not in the grand scheme of things. Right about now I don't see him on deck below if that's what you're asking.* He didn't trust his voice so he merely shook his head.

Hanley Siliezar jumped from his chair and pulled Michael from his in a clamp-down bear hug. "This is good, Maahkill. I did not think so. You are too wise a man," he whispered into his ear. Then he pulled back and held Michael's upper arms within his strong hands and said, "We do not need distractions right now, do we?"

Michael shook his head again.

"You will make this go away then, yes?"

Michael nodded lamely.

"You will personally head up our work for Women's Right, yes?"

Michael nodded in slow motion.

"This is very, very good, Maahkill." Siliezar was smiling beatifically. "This will help us enormously with Proper Parenthood; and Proper Parenthood will help us enormously with the World Health Organization. So you see, this is very important to me."

Michael stared blankly.

Siliezar embraced him again and kissed him on both cheeks. Then he turned to Ackerman and said, "Did I not tell you, Clifford, this Maahkill Burns is the one I must have?" His head rotated from one man to the other. "Did I not say 'take good care of him?'" Ackerman nodded. "Did I not say, 'give him whatever he wants, I want him happy?'"

Ackerman replied, "Yes, Hanley. You did."

Siliezar turned back to Michael. "And are you happy, Maahkill?"

"Yes, I'm quite happy, Hanley. You've been most generous."
He quickly glanced at Peter Feeney, who rolled his eyes.

"Then we are *all* happy." Siliezar shot his arms into the air
above him, and smiled grandly in a rare display of exuberance.
"And that is how it should be for men who live in the United States
of America, the greatest country in all the world."

And with that, he was gone.

Michael immediately felt the room decompress. He sat dazed
and confused. He looked to Feeney, who was smiling as he loaded
his bag with unused materials, including a power point presentation identifying the merits of Burns Advertising's acquisition of
McKenna Marketing.

Michael was extremely interested in Feeney's take on what had
just transpired. He waited for Ackerman to depart, but Ackerman
showed no signs of leaving. "I think you fellows did very well," he
said looking at Michael behind a tight smile. The smile was of a
slightly ominous nature, which suggested it was critical that Hanley
Siliezar had heard what he heard. Had he not, the implication hung
heavy in the air, it was not clear how the two companies would
have proceeded.

Ediana Rodriquez entered the small room with information.
"I've got a town car downstairs waiting to take you gentlemen to
Penn Station." She was smiling, which immediately elevated the
room's temperature.

"Thank you, E-Rod," Michael replied, eliciting a loud groan
from Peter Feeney.

Cliff Ackerman walked around the table and extended his
hand to Michael. "See you in two weeks, Michael." He paused and
added, "I'll bet you're counting down the hours."

Michael did not like the implication or the tone in which it
was sheathed. "No, not really, Cliff. But I do intend to do a lot of
counting on the day itself," he replied with an aggressive smile.

Ackerman waved a goodbye to Feeney and said, "You've got
some paperwork coming my way, right?"

"Sure do," Feeney replied without looking up.

Ackerman halted at the door, awkwardly. Waiting for an adios, a goodbye, a thank you, something, anything. When it was apparent there was to be none forthcoming, he turned somewhat sullenly and departed.

Michael Burns slung his bag over his right shoulder and followed Peter Feeney to the elevator down to the lobby.

It wouldn't be until the two men were safely ensconced in Amtrak train #112's café car that Michael Burns would learn what Peter Feeney thought about their meeting with the famous Hanley Siliezar.

# 24

Joe Delgado did not like to travel. He was a creature of habit and took comfort in his early morning routine, particularly his 12 minute commute which included a stop at Starbucks. He looked forward to his thrice weekly sparring sessions with CC instead of lunch, and to his microwaved frozen entrée dinners alone in front of the television at night. His tastes were simple, he liked to remind himself. He didn't need much. He merely wanted to be left alone to do his work and live his life the way it was.

His marriage had descended into something resembling the film *The War of the Roses*, starring Michael Douglas and Kathleen Turner. He and his wife were currently engaged in a cold, silent battle – a protracted life and death war of attrition – each determined to outlive the other. He took no small satisfaction in the fact that he was now reversing his aging process, while his portly wife seemed intent on accelerating hers.

The great difficulty with bad marriages, he'd discovered, was not so much the festering wounds that leeched into other relationships, but the side effects of the palliatives required to subdue the pain. He had developed an addiction to alcohol which threatened both his career and life. One night over dinner his two closest friends, John Sweeney and Michael Burns, quietly informed him he was the subject of an intervention. This was no good cop, bad cop routine. Both men were unsparing in their criticism and challenge. The message had its intended effect. He left the small restaurant in Narbrook that evening determined to rescue his life from a certain abyss which lay only steps away.

As the car pulled up in front of 30th Street Station in Philadelphia, he mused over the irony of his current schedule requiring him to commute to New York two to three days a week. Earlier in his career he was offered a job in New York, strangely enough with Rossiter Pharmaceuticals, in their accounting department. The money was significantly better and the advancement certainly quicker. So, over dinner, he'd consulted his beloved wife. Fran Delgado was very clear. She had no interest in moving her life to Southern Connecticut or, God forbid, North Jersey, so he'd politely declined. In truth, he hadn't wanted to move, either, rationalizing that life was far more civilized on Philadelphia's storied main line than it was in the nerve center for world trade.

He handed the driver a credit card which he swiped for payment. Joe deposited the chit in his wallet along with the card and made his way into the terminal. He glanced at his watch. It was 3:23 p.m. The Amtrak Metro Liner #137 was scheduled to arrive on Track 12 and depart for New York's Penn Station at 3:36. Joe bought a *New York Times*, drawn by a lead article on HM Inc, with speculation that it might be preparing for a "major foray" into the world of healthcare. Joe quickly noted that no corporate sources were quoted, at least for the record.

The train arrived six minutes late; Joe quickly boarded and settled into his reserved seat in the Club Car. A white-coated waiter arrived promptly to take a drink order. He requested a Diet Coke. He placed the newspaper on top of the travel bag next to him and settled back in his seat; he replayed the phone call he'd received earlier in the day from Chad Henley, his counterpart at HMH, HM Inc's healthcare unit. It was the call he'd been waiting over a month for: a follow up to their discussion at lunch in the Bistro after his closed circuit presentation to Phil Hankinson. It was 11:47 a.m. when his secretary, Maria Gomez, buzzed him that Henley was on the line. He'd surprised Joe by coming right to the point. "Do you have plans for dinner?" Joe fought off the impulse to say something about having to check with his wife and answered, simply, "no."

Despite having already spent two successive long days commuting to and from Manhattan earlier in the week, Joe hung up and immediately asked Maria to book him on a mid-afternoon Metro. He and Henley were scheduled to meet at 6:00 p.m. at a small French restaurant on the Upper East Side called Bondu's. Henley made a point of telling Joe the restaurant had been open only two weeks but had already created something of a buzz among Manhattan's artistic community.

The train arrived on schedule at 4:48 p.m. and Joe disembarked, following a portion of the herd through the underground labyrinth to the Madison Square Garden entrance on 7th Avenue; he emerged into a brilliant, mid autumn, late afternoon. The azure sky was cloudless, and the winds swirling off the Hudson and East Rivers gave warning that winter was approaching. With extra time on his hands, he decided to walk to the shops on 5th Avenue and buy a new tie. He crossed the Avenue of the Americas at 48th and was drawn to a small storefront just off 5th. He saw a red power tie made of Paisley silk in the window. He entered and bought it. He found a floor length mirror and untied his Penn rep tie and knotted the new one into a tight Windsor. He sized himself up and down and smiled approvingly. Diet and exercise had trimmed a good 25 pounds from his rumpled suit of a body. He estimated that in another two months he'd drop another 15 pounds and be down to his college playing weight of 215. He saw a Hermes light blue print hanging from a rack in the corner and bought it. He folded it along with his old school tie and stuffed both into his shoulder bag. He walked outside and glanced at his watch. It was 5:22. He still had a few minutes to kill before heading uptown. In a matter of moments, he found himself standing before the great cathedral at 50th and 5th. He decided to make a short visit. He entered, found the holy water font in the back of the church, dipped his hand, and blessed himself. He slid into a back pew and bowed his head. *Lord, heaven knows I don't deserve your blessing, but I'm asking for it just the same. I don't want to lose my work. I don't know what I'd do if I did. I need to keep busy. I need to do something useful. Please show these people who are buying our company that I can be helpful to them in some important way. Please open their eyes to my abilities and my desire to help them succeed. Lord, please, don't let them take my work away.*

He blessed himself and left, unhappy with both the tone and content of his prayer. *God, I'm sorry. I hate it when I whine and beg; I can only imagine what you think. Sorry, Lord. I should know better. Your will be done. Still, if it's not out of the question…*

He decided to walk over to 6th and hail a cab uptown. The cabbie, a slender man from Rwanda, had not heard of the restaurant and Henley's address proved to be incorrect. The man did not speak English particularly well, and Joe was unable to persuade him to ask his dispatcher for help. At 78th and 2nd, Joe motioned for the driver to stop, and he got out and flagged a passerby for directions. The elderly gentleman happened to be a European, Joe guessed Portuguese, who spoke intelligible English, and though he was unsure of where Bondu's was located, he'd heard there was a restaurant which had just opened on 2nd Avenue: he thought, perhaps, somewhere in the mid 80's. Joe thanked him and glanced at his watch. It was 5:56 and he would no doubt be late. This was inexcusable. In a panic, he jumped back into the cab and told the driver what the elderly gentleman had said. He nodded and, hearing the urgency in Joe's voice, gunned it up 78th and turned onto 2nd. The cabbie began weaving in and out of lanes like a NASCAR driver. As they passed 86th doing roughly 50 miles an hour, Joe thought he saw a tri-color canopy about four doors in. He asked the driver to pull over. He leapt from the cab and ran back some 30 yards. The canopy had a single word written across its top:

Bondu's. Joe glanced at his watch; it was 6:08. He started walking back to the cab, fumbling for an excuse that would not put his host on the defensive. After all, he told himself, Henley just might end up being his boss.

Joe handed the cabbie two $20 bills for what turned out to be a $16.45 ride. He thanked the man and told him to keep the change. The man's dark expressive face broke into a broad smile and he said, "Tank ooh, tank ooh." Joe made his way back down 2nd Avenue to the restaurant. He entered to discover it was empty, save for a swarthy, barrel-chested bartender and two men sitting at a small table just off the bar, who looked like artists or lovers or both. Joe took a seat at the bar, and the bartender, looking a bit put out, slowly walked over to where Joe was sitting. He did not ask Joe what he wanted, but rather looked into his eyes with a blank expression, waiting for his instructions. Joe ordered a Diet Coke and the corners of the man's mouth turned up slightly in what Joe took to be a sneer. *He thinks I'm going to stiff him. Well, well. Let's have a little fun with Frenchie.*

"So, Francois, what do you think of our President?" Joe asked, as the man poured a glass from the tap.

The bartender looked over and rasped, "He ees a menace."

Joe smiled. "Yeah, but he's done a good job of keeping us Americans safe, right?"

The man's face reddened instantly. "At what cost? He wants to war with everyone, he does not care who he fights with. He wants the whole world to war."

Joe nodded. "Yeah, but don't you think a lot of that is just him being a prankster; you know, what with his being a big frat boy in college and all?"

The bartender's features morphed into those of a gargoyle. His carotid artery bulged within his thick neck. "Pranks! You speak of pranks," he spewed. "What kind of man plays such pranks on women and children? Bombing them from the sky! Shooting them with rifles while they wet nurse their cheeldren! I ask you, who plays such pranks on the innocent?"

Joe shrugged, "Yeah, but it's not like they're French women and children."

The man shrieked as though he were cattle prodded. "They are human beings! What deeferance does it make where they are from? It is human life this cretin is destroying, and the world hates you for it!"

"So, a third term is out of the question?" Joe asked matter of factly, probing for a detonation button.

It was a direct hit. The implosion began in slow motion. The man, cursing violently in French, slowly untied his white apron, rolled it up in a ball, and threw it in the direction of several shelves of expensive liqueurs behind the bar. It struck two bottles on their labels, one of which teetered momentarily before slipping its mooring and crashing to the floor, secreting its contents into the elegant hardwood. He stared at Joe with undisguised disdain as he ripped off his bow tie and threw it in the direction of the cash register. Then he bolted around the counter so quickly that Joe, for a moment, thought there might be a physical confrontation. He prepared himself to unload quickly, but the man ran past, eyes ablaze, in the direction of the front door.

At the door he collided with a patron, who, at that unfortunate moment, was just entering. The man's bowler hat went flying off his head and onto the restaurant floor some five feet or so away. The man himself was knocked off stride and almost off his feet. He clutched the door handle and steadied himself. When he turned, coat and tie askew, Joe saw that it was Chad Henley.

He leapt off the bar stool and retrieved his host's hat; he grabbed Henley's right arm to steady him and handed him his hat. "You okay, Chad?" he inquired solicitously.

"What in God's name got into that one?" Henley asked, wide eyed.

"Don't know," Joe replied. "Hope it wasn't the food."

Henley looked at him dumbstruck. "Don't be ridiculous; Clarissa and I had dinner here Saturday night. The food is excellent."

Joe shrugged. "Maybe it's the prices. Are they especially high?"

Henley laughed despite himself. "C'mon, follow me. I need a drink." He headed to a secure table in the back. It was a table for four that granted each man a commanding view of the room and an opportunity to sit with his back to a different wall. "Here," Henley gestured, dropping his hat onto an empty seat. "We'll be well positioned here with very little distraction or interference."

Joe was only too delighted to hear this. Henley, it was rumored, had spent the last 11 days in London, and it was Joe's fervent hope that he'd returned to the States with the complete HM Inc game plan. In Joe's mind, that made the sole objective of this evening's dinner a massive data transfer.

From the back came a small, wiry man in a black tuxedo. He was fumbling with his bow tie as his feet scurried across the floor. It reminded Joe of a cocker spaniel the family once owned, who used to race across the linoleum kitchen floor in the morning in search of his bowl.

"Gentlemen, gentlemen, my apologies," he said bowing from the hip. "I am late to my post. Please excuse me. May I get you each a complimentary drink?"

Henley smiled an all-is-now-forgiven smile and replied, "Martini, extra dry."

The maître d's eyes turned to Joe. "Monsieur?"

"Diet Coke works for me."

The man nodded and turned to the bar. "I wonder where ees our 'Enri tonight?"

"He said something about having a date with an East European track star," Joe deadpanned, causing Henley to chortle.

The maitre d' looked at Joe with a blank expression and departed.

"I know what you're thinking, my friend," Henley said when the man was out of earshot. "Has old Henley flipped his bowler? But I assure you, you will not be disappointed in the wine *or* the food."

Joe nodded. "So, you brought your wife here, Saturday night was it?"

"I did," Henley replied. "And we had an absolutely delightful evening. So I am quite surprised at the rudeness we just experienced. I do not know how to account for it."

Joe smiled brightly and said, "Forget it. I have."

"You are most gracious, Joe," Henley said appreciatively. "And you will be well rewarded tonight. I have much to tell you."

Joe let the comment pass but he could barely contain his excitement. "So, they just opened this place, did they?"

"Two weeks ago, Saturday," Henley answered. "You know how these things go. The artists arrive first creating a buzz. The business class picks up the buzz, chasing the artists away. Then the tourists get wind of it and chase the Philistines away. The menu rarely survives such an assault."

Joe laughed and saw the waiter approaching out of the corner of his eye. He arrived and placed the drinks on the table. Henley immediately picked his up and drained half of the small glass. Several more hurried swallows and he was finished.

"Monsieur, would you like another?"

Henley lifted his head and fixed the waiter with a stare. "Yes. And this time, make it extra dry, as I requested.

The waiter nodded wordlessly and departed.

"I could tell you didn't like that one," Joe said behind a small smile.

"Ah, Delgado, I see you are a trouble maker," Henley laughed. "Ours will be a grand partnership."

Joe held up his glass and tipped it toward Henley in response. Henley picked up his all but empty glass and tapped Joe's gently. "I'd like that very much, Chad," Joe said gently.

Henley set his glass down and opened his menu. Joe did the same. He was blindsided by the prices. The appetizers were priced as entrées, and the entrées priced as off-the-rack suits at Barney's in the Bowery. "Are we buying or just window shopping?" Joe asked his host.

Henley smiled. "It is a bit pricey, but then so was Pittman Labs."

"I hope the food is as good a value," Joe fired back immediately, forcing an engaging smile, and reply, from Henley. "Well, if it isn't, wait till you try the wine."

The waiter arrived with Henley's second martini and a recitation of the chef's special dishes for the evening. Henley listened carefully and when the man finished said, "My guest and I will split the chateaubriand, and we'll have a bottle of Cabernet from the Norman Vineyard in the South of France." Henley looked at Joe and added, "Clarissa and I had the chateaubriand Saturday evening and it was superb. The portions are very generous."

The waiter looked at Joe as if he were a potted plant, turned back to Henley, bowed slightly and departed.

Henley immediately stood to remove his coat; he laid it over the back of the chair that was serving as a hat rack for his bowler. He sat down and smiled at Joe as he loosened his tie and rolled up his shirt sleeves, well past his forearms in a manner unique to Europeans.

This delighted Joe, signaling as it did a night of informality and candor. "Uh oh," he deadpanned. "Am I about to receive my first formal review?"

Henley chortled. "Let me tell you something, chap. You scored an A+ in your first test with Hankinson." He paused. "Know how I know?"

Joe shook his head.

"He never said a word!" Henley laughed. "Believe me, that is high praise from that one. He tears everybody apart, especially after a presentation, which he considers his proprietary area of expertise."

Joe nodded. He did not particularly care what Hankinson *thought;* he was much more interested in what Hankinson planned to *do.*

"So, you're telling me I might have a job?" Joe inquired, concealing his nervousness.

"Oh, you will have much more than a job, Delgado. I'm bringing you up to New York to work with me after this transaction closes."

Joe immediately felt conflicted. He was stunned, and greatly relieved, to learn his most imperfect prayer had been answered so quickly; on the other hand, he detested the thought of coming home to an empty apartment four nights a week somewhere in this unforgiving city. *What if those towel-heads dirty bomb it while I'm in a cab stuck in traffic?* "Thank you, Chad. That would be a great opportunity for me to learn, under a master."

Henley snorted. "Modesty becomes you not, lad. It's your cocksureness about the future of our business we're interested in."

Joe struggled to recover from his amateurish sop. "Do you have a particular role in mind?"

Henley shook his head as he sipped his martini, audibly. "We haven't sat down and figured any of that out yet."

"Who's 'we'?" Joe quickly inquired.

Henley didn't blink. "Me and Hankinson, Joe. You'll find we call the shots for HMH. Just as Benton and Shillingford call the shots at Corporate."

Joe nodded. The reference to Geoff Benton, HM's charismatic chairman and chief executive officer, and his chief financial officer, Thomas Shillingford, was revealing. He immediately plotted the co-ordinates for future reference. He debated whether to make the next move. His heart began to beat quickly in anticipation. Suddenly he was having difficulty quieting his nerves. Since the Hankinson presentation he'd thought of little else other than "The Plan." *Was I right about HMH's strategic intent, the reason for the bio-engineering and big pharma rollups? What's the missing piece, or pieces, that Henley hinted at over lunch at the Bistro? Will he level with me tonight? Will he hold back until the deal is done?*

His anxiety was quickly put to rest.

"Joe, I'm going to take you into my confidence," Henley intoned solemnly, after carefully surveying the room and each of its recent arrivals. "When we're finished this evening you will know what I know." He engaged Joe directly with a purposeful stare. "We are about to enter what you Yanks like to call a MAD zone?" Joe sat stoned faced, forcing Henley to elaborate quickly. "Mutually Assured Destruction," he added. "If anything we discuss tonight leaks, anywhere, at any time, for any reason, it will serve to blow *two* careers to kingdom come." He paused and asked again, "are we clear?"

Joe nodded instantly. "Yes, Chad, we are clear. I spent six years in Army Intelligence during the Viet Nam War. I understand the deadly cost of secrets not kept."

Henley surprised Joe by maintaining his fixed gaze for what seemed like an eternity. Joe almost challenged him on it but as he was debating whether to do so, Henley relaxed and smiled, and said, "Good, Joe. I didn't think we'd have a problem in that regard."

The waiter arrived with appetizers. Joe looked at his small plate and tried to fathom what in hell was laying on it. He put a fork in the middle of it to make sure it wasn't alive. "Mussels," he heard Henley say. "They're excellent."

Joe toyed with them to divert his host's attention. It appeared to work.

"Joe, let me lay this thing out for you best I can."

Joe smiled and nodded.

"The cost of healthcare has become a global problem. In five to ten years, healthcare entitlements for aging populations alone will collapse governments. This will invite, if not guarantee, anarchy. All sorts of advanced weaponry will be loosed from the control of these governments. They will fall into the hands of the undeveloped world, which has had grievances with the developed world dating back to the first millennium, for heaven's sake. This sad state of affairs has caught the attention of the men who run our governments, as well as the men who control much of the world's public and private wealth, through NGO's and the major investment banks here and offshore.

"In a word, they are all quite 'anxious.' The government leaders don't want any of this happening on their watch; and the men who control great wealth do not much like the idea of hiding in their underground bunkers until the doomsday scenario has played itself out. My God, what would they do without their planes and yachts?"

He paused and looked at Joe with great solemnity. "Now, let me be clear: there is no collective "who." No single group or coalition of groups that meets to talk about such things. But there are men who are working very hard to focus some of the best minds in science, commerce, technology, finance and government on the problem. And something like a rough working consensus seems to be emerging as to how to attack it. Let me quickly add, you will be quite happy to learn that if the consensus holds it will keep you and me working for as long as we want to work."

Joe's eyes widened. He wasn't much for mussels but he was devouring every clipped and precise word coming from the proper man sitting at a right angle from him.

"So, let me outline my take on the working consensus for the "Big Fix," as I call it. By the way, full disclosure: Benton, Shillingford and Hankinson hate the name. They refer to it as: "US," code for "Ultimate Solution," which, as I keep telling them, sounds too much like Hitler's "Final Solution." They don't find that very amusing.

"Anyway, this thing will all go down in stages. Right now there are three. First, we've got to free the labs. There are scientists all over the world developing what we call first generation solutions under the shadow of the Human Genome Project. We're talking about genetic screening and, ultimately, genetic therapy, about stem cell research that isolates the very genes in fetuses and infants that cost societies mountains of money they simply no longer have. Money that societies would be far better served using strategically, using stem cell discovery from frozen embryos and aborted fetuses to build replacement kits for their most productive members. Right now the labs are constrained by political considerations, particularly in the West, where most of the discovery is taking place."

"Political considerations?" Joe interrupted.

Henley stopped abruptly at the interruption and regrouped. "Yes. Politicians the world over are fearful of getting out in front on this embryonic stem cell issue. Right now they feel constrained by so-called ethical concerns raised by a very vocal minority in almost every developed country.

"Anyway, we'll target the diseases people ultimately fall victim to as they age: diabetes, breast and prostate cancer, Alzheimer's, those sorts of things. The idea is to have the replacement parts "catalogued in inventory" as they say, and to have them implanted and working before the original cellular structures break down. This will not only save trillions in healthcare costs throughout the developed world, it will also create many jobs, quite a number of which will be spread into the undeveloped world. This will allow us to introduce The Life Sciences Revolution as the first revolution that will truly touch every man, woman and child on the planet. Lord knows the industrial, cultural and technology revolutions all failed to do that, which is precisely why the world remains so hopelessly divided and endlessly roiled."

Joe was troubled. "Excuse me, Chad. I'm sorry to keep interrupting while you're on a roll, but I'm unclear about something you said. What did you mean by societies' "most productive members?""

Henley blinked. "The ones who are working, contributing something."

"And those who aren't: the aged and handicapped?"

"Joe, I started this discussion talking about global cost constraints for a reason. You're not going to start citing scripture on me, are you?"

Joe felt a chill race up and down his spine. He feared Henley would call a halt to the data transfer he so desperately needed to hear. He shook his head.

"Good," Henley smiled, obviously relieved. "You had me worried there for a moment. Where was I? Oh, yes, Phase One. Okay, let me tell you about Phase Two." His eyes sparkled with delight. "Phase Two is the Game Changer. We're talking maybe eight to ten years. Two is about controlling risk. Pre-screening life's building blocks, the sperm and the eggs. Making sure they're "fit" for implantation, or if a couple so desires, "The Dish." There are a couple of monstrous benefits to mankind with this one. First, the obvious one, cost. It'll save more trillions in healthcare costs over the lifetime of the individual, and, as importantly, liberate him or her for a far more productive life. Some of our people are suggesting the increased productivity alone over a person's lifetime could dwarf the cost savings. I don't have to tell you how much excitement this has generated. The second great benefit, though, is the kicker. Scientists at Stanford University have found a way to actually coax cells from the couple's own skin into becoming sperm and eggs. This means couples can grow their own sperm and eggs, "lease a dish" in a local lab, and create the kind of new life we all want— life societies can afford— life with far more upside potential and far less downside risk."

"In a dish?" Joe asked, somewhat confused.

"Sure," Henley replied. "Over 15% of all couples of child-bearing age in the West are infertile. Do you have any idea what that portends for our survival? We're replacing at less than a rate of 1.5 children per couple; the undeveloped world is reproducing at about 3 to 4 times that. We've got to get this fixed quickly, but fixed properly so we're not simply transferring costs from the front end of life to the back end.

"Anyway, Phase Two is about commercializing new molecular discovery and changing the trajectory of the world's population growth. The goal is simple: every child a healthy child, from the moment of birth through an extended, far more productive life here on earth."

A tremor rippled through Joe's body. *If that's what "Two" is about, where in God's name are we headed with "Three?"*

"So, rough cut on Phases One and Two. Ready for Three?"

Joe nodded mutely.

If Henley noted his mental reservations, he did not give voice to it. "'Three' is really the denouement. It's about rationalizing the way man functions, conducts trade, and governs himself." Henley waited to see Joe's reaction and was not disappointed.

"Come again?" Joe requested, wide eyed.

"I thought that one might stoke your interest," Henley replied quickly. "'Three' is about "the chip" and its infinite possibilities. Think big, Joe. Then multiply by infinity." Henley paused for effect. "'The 'chip' is the mortar that will settle the concrete, the ingredient that will secure all the gains from Phases One and Two." Henley removed his wrist watch and placed it on the table between the two men. He extended his left wrist to Joe and pointed to where the face of the watch had been. "Think of a wafer thin chip implanted just under your skin, right about there," he pointed to a spot between his wrist bones. "Now, that chip carries not only all your medical records, it carries all your other personal information. It allows you to transact business, buy and sell on line, travel here and abroad without passport and visa. Think of it. No more infernal security lines at airports, Joe!" Joe couldn't help but note Henley's total conviction. *This is religion for him. Life without end in Utopia. Ten billion perfect souls ... well, maybe five.*

"Now think of this technology with an RIF capability: radio frequency. You've got a loved one and he gets lost, or a teenager with an addiction to drugs or alcohol who wanders off the reservation. The 'chip' tells you where they are, and hooks you up to law enforcement for immediate help.

"Even more importantly," he continued breathlessly, "this technology will help us to rationalize the way government and commerce work. Let's be honest, Joe. It's not working now. We both know it. Even the common man has an intuitive sense that something is very wrong. The fundamental problem is twofold; one, government is focused on the wrong question. It asks: what *should* government do? The right question is: what *can* government do? And secondly, people no longer trust private enterprise. They no longer believe it bears the promise of their dreams." He shrugged. "All this obscene profiteering, the mass transfer of jobs overseas, the unwillingness, or inability, of western corporations to accelerate the rate of innovation— no doubt as a consequence of the failure of their educational systems— this has forced their people to compete with far more advantageous cost structures in developing nations." Henley paused briefly. "The citizenry is furious." Pause. "It's just not working, Joe. Trust must be restored. It's the essential lubricant for trade."

Henley took a substantial gulp of wine and re-poured himself another half glass. Joe was tempted to grab the bottle from his hands and swill it clean. He fought the temptation off. "This technology, which by the way is already being tested, Joe— I can't tell you where— will address all of that."

"How?" Joe could not disguise his incredulity.

Henley appeared to take no offense. "It will force governments and corporations and NGO's into new alliances based on far more rationalized cost structures. For instance, governments are well positioned to provide basic services and ease regulatory barriers which will get frozen capital moving again. Corporations understand how to commercialize discovery and create new markets which in turn create jobs and stability within societies. NGO's know how to organize public and private ventures to address human need, particularly in undeveloped nations.

"There is simply too much, far too much, inefficiency today: too much duplication of effort, too much confusion of purpose, too much uncertainty of output. Our institutions need to be rationalized. We're stuck with Industrial Revolution business and operating models which barely worked for the Technological Revolution. They simply will not work for the Life Sciences Revolution." Henley shook his head vigorously. "They won't work for "4", Joe."

Joe's mind was immediately flooded with questions. He did not know how to begin to sort them out. He chose to play safe and begin at ground zero. "Chad, what's HM Inc's role in all this?"

Just then three waiters arrived, two carrying platinum covered dishes on small elegant trays. They set the trays down on the table and removed the dishes, setting them in front of the table's two patrons, under the watchful eye of the head waiter. At his command, actually the mere hint of a nod, they uncovered what they hoped would be revered as the Head Chef's masterful work. Joe immediately imagined some thought-to-be-dead-animal lunging for freedom at the moment of "presentation." No such luck. Everything on both plates appeared to be perfectly dead.

Henley immediately began carving small, thin slices of beef and re-arranging them on his plate in a way Joe thought a bit anal. He recalled that Henley began his career as an accountant and, therefore, he chose to overlook it.

"Good question," Henley grunted through a small mouthful of chateaubriand. "Didn't I tell you the food was excellent? And wait till you taste the wine: heavenly!"

The head waiter arrived with an interesting looking bottle and two exquisite glasses that appeared to be made of Waterford Crystal. He popped the cork for Henley to sniff, but he demurred and instead tapped his glass with the knife in his hand. The waiter poured. Henley imbibed. He nodded to the waiter who poured a small amount into Joe's glass. Joe sipped politely. He was impressed with the balance of full bouquet and delicate taste. He, too, nodded to the waiter, who half filled each man's glass, bowed and left.

Henley took three quick swallows of the wine and put his glass at rest. "Didn't I tell you?" he said with notable excitement. "Isn't it just superb?"

"It most certainly is, Chad. It exceeds even my own heightened expectations."

Henley smiled and nodded happily. "Well, to your question. HM Inc will play the first crucial role in all of this. As you can plainly see, this is, ah, delicate stuff. It can't be rammed down people's throats. They'd choke, and rebel. Then we will have actually greatly exacerbated the very problem we set out to solve. No, no, it's all got to be done gradually, one step at a time. It will start with fabulous new cures that will extend lives. People will relax and embrace discovery. They will see it for what it is: their last best hope on this confused and oppressed planet. Still, we must act with dispatch. It's not like we have another 20 years or so.

"Anyway, the first task is to get the right man in the right chair. I'm speaking of the '08 election here in the United States. Right now, the problem is the world lacks a world figure. There is no Ronald Reagan or Michail Gorbechev or Maggie Thatcher, or even a Helmut Kohl." Henley shook his head in disdain. "I'm not even certain our generation can produce that kind of leader, that's what really worries me. But that aside, there is great hope that America may have at least provided temporary residence for the right man at the right moment." He looked at Joe with slight amusement.

Joe bit. "Who?"

"A first term senator, a minority. Blank slate. Near-perfect Petrie dish. No paper trail to speak of. Hell, nobody really even knows where he's from."

Joe took a gulp of wine. A wave of fear washed over him. The taste was too good. He saw himself wrestling Henley for the rest of the bottle and unleashing all his old demons. "Are you talking about the guy with the Arab name?"

"Yes," Henley replied smiling.

"Never happen. Not in a million years," Joe offered, suddenly tingling.

"Why do you say that?" Henley inquired, bemused.

"It's already wired. That she-devil will win and the reptile will be back in his old haunt. Too much name recognition, too much money, too much organization."

Henley smiled knowingly. "Nevertheless, the "dark horse," as you Yanks like to say, will win."

Joe stared at Henley. He was shocked at his matter of fact certainty. He said nothing.

"It will happen, I assure you. And when it does, the world will marvel. It will be hailed as a great victory not just for the U.S., but for people everywhere."

Joe decided to tip toe in. "May I ask how?"

"Of course! We're still in the Mad Zone, right?"

Joe nodded through his apprehension.

Henley surveyed the room carefully. It was about half filled. He turned to Joe and said, "Two considerations: money and media. We've got them both. He will win. Trust me."

Joe stared blankly. His mouth formed the 'how' without a sound.

"We own a major network, remember. The playbook is all about access and coverage. The candidate grants 24/7 access, he gets 24/7 coverage: all of it quite favorable of course. But that's only half the equation. The other half is how the other candidates are covered or *not* covered. And with respect to the woman you mentioned, I remind you both she and her husband have much baggage, you would agree?"

Joe nodded numbly.

"Of course, the other consideration is money. Typically three or four hundred million is the number. Our guys have about 600 or 700 million lined up. At least half of it from off shore."

"Chad, trust me. You can't buy elections like that in America. It's still a two party system. There are too many people watching."

Henley smiled, amused, but said nothing.

"Tell me, why is it so important to get this guy in?"

"He'll loosen the foundations. He's on board with the whole package. He wants the power. He sees himself as more of a global figure than a national figure," Henley laughed. "Can you imagine?" He laughed again. "Anyway, our guys aren't concerned. He'll do what he's told. He's pretty much said as much."

"The bioengineering, the reconstitution of government and commerce, the chip, all of that?" Joe asked, unable to hide his amazement.

Henley nodded. "Once he's in place, things will begin to happen quickly. The government will look the other way on mergers and acquisitions, in the national interest, of course." Henley smiled. "We'll be able to roll up pretty much whatever we think we need to get this whole thing moving. That means the bioengineering labs on the west coast and the big pharma houses here in the east. Ultimately, we'll link the diagnostic side of the house with the therapeutic side. We're gonna do whatever it takes to get Phase One moving. We're in the catbird's seat, Joe. And that is a stroke of unusually good fortune for a couple of guys like us."

Joe smiled weakly. He looked at his plate. His appetite was gone. Worse, the night was still young. He looked at his watch. It was only 7:40. Maybe he'd spend the night in New York. Better yet, maybe he'd spend the night in the East River.

"Oh my God! This can't be happening." Suddenly, Chad Henley's feet were churning under the table and he appeared on the verge of hyperventilating. Joe turned to him and saw pure fear in his eyes. He started to get out of his seat to perform the Heimlich maneuver which he'd learned in the service, but Henley was already on his own two feet. Then he did something Joe had never seen done by a businessman in a restaurant before. He took a seat on the opposite side of the table, back to the room, and dragged his entire place setting around until it rested in front of him. Joe looked at him as though he'd taken leave of his senses.

"We must finish quickly and leave through the back door," Henley said through clenched teeth. "This could very well end up being an unmitigated disaster. I would never have thought this possible. I cannot believe it is happening."

"What?" Joe asked, looking around and seeing nothing unusual.

Henley hunched down and over his plate as if to make himself invisible. Without looking up he said, "Don't look. Please Joe, do *not* look. You're not going to believe who just walked in."

Joe looked. He didn't see anything other than a few guys settling into seats on the opposite side of the restaurant. "Who, Chad? What am I missing here?"

"Benton! He just arrived. If he sees me here, he will immediately connect the dots. The word will come down tomorrow morning for Hankinson to find out who I was having dinner with. I cannot, I just can't ... He'll know, oh Lord. They'll know, they'll all know that I've been talking out of school. You don't do that at HM Inc, you don't do it and *survive*. I thought this place was completely off the radar screen. Damn, we should have met in Jersey City. Joe, we've got to get out of here quickly and quietly. I'm going out through the back door in two minutes. Wait two more minutes, and follow me, please. We'll get a cab and finish up downtown.

Joe looked over to Benton's table. There were two gentlemen with him. One was a distinguished man in his late 50's or early 60's. He was elegant in his appearance and manner. Joe took him to be some sort of European aristocrat. The other man was older and looked familiar, but Joe couldn't place him.

"Chad, who are those guys with Benton?"

Henley looked up nervously and said, "Please don't look over, Joe. Please. You'll only draw attention to yourself, and this table, and me. These men have each taken careful note of everything that is going on in this restaurant right now. They miss nothing."

Joe looked over to the table again. The men seemed to be quite preoccupied with the task of choosing a wine. "So you're not going to tell me who they are?"

Henley looked at him and said, "The older gentleman is Stef Boros. The other man is Hanley Siliezar, Chairman of Ultra Com, the world's largest advertising syndicate."

With that he was off: bowler hat and designer suit jacket left on the chair beside him. Chad Henley's half turned body and diminutive feet were now in motion and heading toward the kitchen.

Joe looked over to the other table. No one there seemed to take notice. He stood, gathered his things, took a final gulp of very good wine, reached for his host's hat and jacket, and walked toward, and out, the front door.

# 25

John Sweeney drove his Acura through the black wrought iron gates and up the long Belgian block driveway. He half circled the courtyard with its tri-level marble fountain and came to a stop in front of the stunning three-story colonial home. Two young Jamaican men sat waiting on a small green bench next to the front door. At his arrival, both leapt to their feet and began moving toward his black sedan. John stole a quick look in the mirror and ran his fingers through his gray flecked hair; he grabbed a bottle of wine in its slender brown sleeve of a bag, and turned to open the car door, only to discover it was already open. One of the young men was standing by the door. "Good evening, sir. Welcome to the home of Michael Burns," he said in lightly-accented English. John smiled and said, "Make sure Mr. Burns pays you in bills; if he gives you coins there's bound to be more than a few St. Christopher medals in there." The young man threw back his head and laughed.

John made his way up a red brick path, through the open

wood door with its double side lights, and into a generous central hall foyer. There he was greeted by Carol Burns, whose presence in the middle of the foyer lent an elegant dimension to the gracious home. "Father, thank you so much for coming. It means so much to Michael and me."

"Wouldn't miss it, Carol. Anytime Michael Burns and liquor are in the same time zone, a Catholic priest is required to be on call."

Carol Burns' laughter was as pure as an Irish dawn, and John Sweeney marveled at the effortless beauty behind the smile. She was that rarity of rarities, he reminded himself, a woman whose physical beauty continued to peak as she aged ever so gracefully; the secret, he knew, was that her physical beauty was perpetually back-lit by a glowing interior beauty.

"So, where is that rascal?" he asked.

Carol Burns' eyes danced. "Where else but holding court in the pub?"

John handed Carol the bottle of wine and headed for the pub. He moved through about a dozen or so guests huddled around a wide assortment of hors d'oeurves displayed on a large granite breakfast bar in the kitchen. He returned greetings from the assembled and stopped for several handshakes from men and more than a few discrete hugs from women. He made a mental note to be long gone before any of those discrete hugs became borderline indiscrete later in the evening.

The entry to the pub was through a glass door in the kitchen, which opened to a covered flagstone patio. The pub's entrance featured exposed stone walls and a vaulted ceiling. John descended several steps and found himself in an authentic Chicago-style Speakeasy, which included an original reclaimed bar and oak paneling. A 60-inch high definition TV screen hung above a fireplace, which was lit despite mild weather. There was a juke box in the corner and several narrow, high tables surrounded by bar stools spread throughout the room, all of which appeared to be occupied.

Behind the bar, taking drink orders, and very much holding court was the man of the house: one Michael Burns.

At the sight of his friend and confessor, he attempted to leap over the bar for a bear hug of a greeting. His trailing foot, however, caught the inside edge of the bar, and he landed heavily on his rump on top of the bar. He grimaced and yelped, "Thank God for thick padding," to no one in particular. His guests seized the rare opportunity to skewer him. "Fire the drunken bastard," and, "Hey, Father, hope you didn't come here looking for a drink," and, "Burns landed on his brains; he's probably suffered a concussion."

Michael immediately gathered himself and began to pantomime a pole dance on the bar's surface. This further elevated the catcalls and elicited a wagging finger from his pastor. Obediently, Burns jumped down and made for the collar. He smothered John Sweeney in a bear hug and whispered in his ear "Thanks for coming, Father; now I can relax knowing these cretins will have to behave themselves."

Sweeney laughed out loud and looked into Michael Burns' earnest blue eyes and shook his head. "Aye, Michael, it's not the others I'll be a worryin' about."

Burns feigned mock indignation and said, "How about a wee bit of Jameson's, just to put you in the mood?"

"For what?" Sweeney asked. "To hear *your* confession? I'd need more than a wee bit of Jameson's, Lad."

Burns went behind the bar and poured his pastor a pint of Guinness; but John, taking note of the others, waved it off and asked instead for a Coke. Burns' eyebrows arched in response and he announced, "Men, you may want to stay clear of the 9:00 Mass tomorrow. I think our man is preparing a stem winder on the virtue of temperance."

"Father, can you at least wait till the whiskey runs dry?" yelled one man whom John recognized as an occasional attendee at Sunday Mass.

"Give it now, right here, Father. Burnsie'll show you how to get up on top of the bar," said another; this was met with raucous laughter.

John Sweeney just ducked his head and smiled good-naturedly. Waitresses carrying plates of hot hors d'oeurves circulated among the men. A college football game, Notre Dame versus Michigan, was being telecast on the big screen above the fireplace mantle. He eased his way over to Michael Burns and said, "So, how you doin' big fella, everything okay?"

Burns shot him a look of apprehension in reply. John couldn't quite read it. Burns shrugged his shoulders and said, "I'm gonna need to talk to you in a week or so."

John nodded and said nothing. He did not like what he saw in his friend's eyes.

Just then, Carol Burns appeared on the top step of the pub and announced dinner was about to be served in the dining room.

"Last call!" Michael Burns yelled to his pub crawlers, which earned him a piercing look from his wife.

John Sweeney followed the crowd toward the dining room, which, as he had noted on the way in, looked like a miniature replica of a Versailles banquet hall. Some guests entered through French doors from the large flag-stoned patio which overlooked a covered pool; others entered through the designer kitchen with its industrial-grade ovens and serving areas. John entered through the kitchen and saw Joe and Fran Delgado looking at the seating diagram. He approached them from behind and slid his arms around both sets of shoulders. Fran looked up first and smiled brightly. "Father, I was hoping you'd be here. Terry is still floating on air from her session, or whatever you call those things, a couple of weeks ago. I don't know what you said to that girl, Father, but she sure is thinking differently about everything!"

John smiled. He could not, and therefore did not, try to hide his deep gratification when he heard that his God has seen fit to use his priestly ministry to touch a heart. "Thank you, Fran. I'm delighted to hear that. She is an absolutely extraordinary young woman. I'm sure the good Lord has plans …"

"You're not going to try to make a nun out of her, are you?" Fran Delgado pounced. "Don't forget she's got two children, and I have no intention of raising them. Been there, done that!" The woman was actually glaring at him, which caught John off guard, and served to induce even more sympathy for her husband.

"Yeah, don't get any ideas," Joe added, behind eyes that twinkled with pure delight. *Just a little reminder, Padre, of what my Hell Tour's been like. Think celibacy's tough?* "Don't go pulling a Jim Jones on our kid. Hell, we'll call the bishop, won't we, Dearest?"

Fran Delgado ignored the sarcasm and made her way to her seat which she was happy to learn was a good bit away from her husband's seat.

John mouthed a silent mea culpa and squeezed Joe's shoulder. Delgado leaned in and whispered, "I need to talk to you within the next couple of weeks. Will you have time?"

John nodded. "For you, there will always be time."

John made his way into the exquisitely lit and appointed room, behind Joe. Carol Burns approached and took his arm and led him to a seat at a right angle from her husband, who sat at the head of the table. On his right was a woman from the parish whom he saw at Sunday Mass, occasionally. Across from him was the publisher of the city's only major newspaper. He was chewing on an unlit cigar and staring at him warily.

John smiled and nodded and made a mental note to avoid eye contact if at all possible. Several of his letters to the editor had been published recently; they were highly critical of the newspaper's editorial positions on what his church regarded as "life" issues. He was surprised to discover later that his letters had met with a mixed response even among his own parishioners. He'd decided some years ago, however, he'd keep his own final judgment in mind when deciding what to say, and to whom, about his church's moral teachings.

He canvassed the room. He counted 12 chairs on each side of the long, elegant table. On opposite ends sat the man and the lady of the house, barely visible to each other through the elaborate series of floral settings. He studied the couples filling the chairs. He recognized most, but not all. Many were parishioners from Narbrook's border communities, north and west of the borough. They were the professional class. The men were corporate types and white-collar entrepreneurs, with a sprinkling of physicians and lawyers. The women were mostly teachers and college professors, real estate brokers and chairs of non profits. John guesstimated that perhaps one in four of those around the table regularly attended Sunday Mass.

Suddenly, Maggie Kealey entered the room on the arm of Jim Gillespie. John literally watched heads turn, the more conspicuous among them belonging to women. She was dressed in a plum-colored satin dress with a modest neckline and accented sleeveless shoulders. She was radiant, and John felt his heart stir at the sight of her. Over the 17 years of his urban exile, she had been his most treasured confidant. Their emotional bond was forged in rejection: in her case, the rejection of a husband; in his case, the rejection of his parishioners. In time, they learned how to salve each other's wounds. In his darkest hours she taught him trust. In her darkest hours, he taught her hope.

He stood immediately and found himself moving toward her. She saw him and hesitated, then smiled warmly and reversed her steps. They met, awkwardly, in a narrow, high traffic thoroughfare at the foot of the table. They said hello and exchanged silent glances which inquired into the other's current state of heart and mind. The traffic pattern quickly forced their separation, and indeed they would not speak again that evening. John made his way back to his seat near the head of the table, and watched as Maggie and her escort took their seats near the foot of the table on the opposite side.

When all were correctly seated— a surprisingly complex ritual that offered comic overtones as one mis-seated woman rose only to fall into the lap of another, causing the second woman to spill a glass of red wine on her husband's lap— tuxedoed waiters arrived bearing trays of champagne glasses. When glasses were filled, Michael Burns rose to his feet. "My friends, we've all taken heavy body shots over the past six months," he said as he glanced at Carol at the other end of the table. "Hell, my portfolio is down 40%, and that's just from my wife's latest trip to New York." Howls of laughter accompanied a withering look from his wife. "But," he raised his glass, "America is still America, and, thanks be to God, there will always be another bright tomorrow. So, let's celebrate her on the eve of another great democratic milestone: the peaceful electoral transfer of power, from one Republican president to another." This was met by all manner of jeers and catcalls, even a few insults – all of which appeared to greatly delight Michael Burns, who sat down quite pleased with himself.

Immediately, teams of waiters appeared with the first course: a soup that was clear, perhaps a consommé.

John studied his friend as he turned to the publisher seated on his left. He was a perpetual enigma. John wondered what was behind Le Grande Soiree. With the election only ten days away, was this merely an elaborate focus group to prepare John for an important business solicitation? Was it a platform to proselytize about social or economic issues? Or did the man simply want to raise the spirits of friends whose monthly portfolio statements over the past six months had melted like spring snow?

John thought perhaps a little of each. He didn't have to wait long for confirmation. Never content to let the aimless conversation of even house guests dim the limelight, Michael was presently tapping his empty wine glass with a silver knife to quiet the table. "My friends, we have a special gift tonight for that special loser among us whose portfolio plummeted faster and steeper than all the rest. I won't tell you what it is, but let me lead the bidding. As of October 10, 2008, the Burns' are down … 38%!"

This drew gasps and, after a momentary silence, a succession of numbers from guests around the table. "… 31 … 27 … 36 … 29 … 34 … 37 …" More silence, then, "… 41 …" Heads turned to Dr. Jim Gillespie, who paused until he collected all pairs of eyes before shrugging and saying, "I bought what Maggie bought." Pause. "And somehow she's *up* 41%?" he shrugged. "I've got a call into the SEC." This elicited boisterous laughter and a light punch in the arm from his companion.

Michael Burns signaled the head waiter, who brought one red apple and a tin cup, and handed it to Jim Gillespie, who immediately seized the tin cup, stood, fixed his date with a hard stare and said with mock indignation, "You didn't say anything about random drug testing." He exited stage left amidst an explosion of laughter. He re-entered moments later, and handed the cup to Michael Burns, who immediately drained the cup of its contents— an iconic red wine from lush vineyards in the south of France— and pronounced it "vintage Gillespie." More laughter.

John Sweeney marveled at the mores of the upper middle class. *They celebrate the loss of millions with a state dinner, believing it will all return just as mysteriously as it vanished. Would that they had such trust in their Divine Lord.*

An uneasy silence descended upon the room. The only sounds were of the waiters clearing and serving, and the odd tinkle of crystal and china. John felt the awkwardness and glanced at Michael Burns to see if he would relieve it. It appeared he had no such intention. Then a voice that belonged to Philip Leighton, a center city attorney: "It *is* scary, is it not?" he said to no one in particular. More silence.

Then, Nick Becker, a center city banker: "It is our *long term prospects* that are truly frightening."

Mark Erickson, a hedge fund manager, said, "Oh nonsense. Michael is right. This is America. Yes we have problems. But great countries are filled with great people who know how to solve great problems."

Becker turned to Erickson and said, "Mark, America has entered a place of no return. Once the manufacturing and financial services sectors flip, it's over. And they've flipped."

"What does that mean, flipped?" asked Carole Hartman, a high profile realtor on the Main Line.

Nick Becker replied, "Changed places, as the lead sector in America's Gross Domestic Product: the aggregate value of all goods and services produced annually. About 50 years ago, manufacturing was 30% of our GDP, and the financial services industry accounted for about 10%. Some 20 years ago, they drew even at about 17% each. Today, manufacturing is about 10% of our GDP, and financial services are about 25%."

"And that's bad, why?" asked Deidre Flanagan, a professor of U.S. history at Rosemont College, an elite private women's college about ten minutes away.

"Because it's only happened to three other global trading empires. And in each case, it signaled irreversible decline," Becker replied.

"Which empires?" asked Carole Hartman.

"Hapsburg Spain, Dutch Netherlands, Imperial Britain," Becker ticked off. "History's pretty clear about this. Once an empire stops making and shipping things, and focuses mostly on moving money around, for all intents and purposes, it's over."

Stunned silence. John Sweeney was greatly taken aback. So many questions formed in his mind so quickly he could not sort them out. He sat mute along with the others. Then Michael Burns, perhaps in an attempt to rescue the evening, said, "Nick, now do you understand why you don't have more clients?" The laughter was spontaneous but somewhat hollowed out, John thought. It was as if a room full of anxiety found its way into throats suddenly parched. On cue, hands reached for water and wine glasses.

"Nick, what happened?" Jim Gillespie asked matter of factly. John quickly scanned his face to see if there was a joke forming in the recesses of that ever-fertile mind. He saw no such indication that Gillespie was anything less than deadly serious.

"Debt," Becker said soberly.

Jack Meyer, the newspaper publisher, nodded and added, "They say 'debt' is the 'crack cocaine' of our generation."

John watched as heads fell onto chests, up and down the long table.

Cheryl Weston, a private practice attorney on the Main Line, turned to Jack Meyer and asked, "Who is 'they'?"

Meyer nodded and replied, "The major fund managers, who of course are doing everything they can to leverage even higher multiples for ever growing mountains of our debt."

"History will record that the race to securitize our financial system was the dagger to the heart of a once great empire," said Nick Becker, spreading yet more joy among the assembled.

"Nick, can you break that down for the simple-minded among us?" It was Maggie Kealey. And from the looks of it, John thought he detected a sense of relief among most of the assembled.

Nick Becker paused and took a sip of wine. As he did so, waiters scurried about with trays of Chilean Sea Bass and six-, eight-, and ten-ounce Kansas City Steaks. "The people who run the country decided in the middle of the last decade that the 'New Frontier' for American ingenuity would be centered in the financial services industry. In other words: how we create more money from our current stocks of assets. In the world of finance they refer to it as transitioning from a 'cash flow constrained' economy to an 'asset backed' economy." Small smile. "They decided it was time to create a shadow banking system by repealing Glass-Steagall: depression-era legislation forbidding common ownership of banks, investment firms and insurance companies. The first products out of the shoot were from formerly regulated investment firms: a whole new category of stocks and bonds based on pools of loans and hard assets. Think housing. As we now know, a lot of those loans were bad, and a lot of those homes got trapped in a bubble and suffered extreme devaluation. In fact the $23 trillion housing sector alone plunged 25% in the past two years." He paused and looked around the room and shrugged. "When the bubbles began popping– first technology, then residential housing, and finally our financial markets – the whole economic order simply imploded from what you might call a cluster stress fracture."

"Nick, who are the people we're talking about here?" asked Barbara Kallelis, a private school Latin teacher.

Becker didn't flinch. "The U.S. Treasury Secretary, the

Chairman of the Federal Reserve, and the President of the United States."

"Why would they do such a thing?" Maggie Kealey asked. "It strikes me as completely irresponsible."

Becker nodded. "Obviously I have a dog in this fight, Maggie, so I am a bit biased." It was rumored Becker's bank was among the more highly leveraged, which put him high on the list for a bail out.

"Politics," Jack Meyer offered. His fiscally conservative political leanings were so well known that his comment was dismissed out of hand even by Republicans at the table. "Over 60% of all Wall Street financial contributions – personal and institutional - went to Democratic candidates in the last two elections; it'll be higher Tuesday a week."

"I think it's even more basic," said Tom Krug, a potato chip manufacturer. "It's about pure greed. When people make something, it creates all sorts of jobs. You need people to supply, manufacture, transport, distribute, market and retail the product. Everybody gets paid. And the collective nature of the work ensures that there's a basic equilibrium in the system. The people with the most capital at risk get higher proportions of the wealth that's created, as they should. But everybody gets paid and that's what allows communities to form. When you create something called a 'credit derivative' – built on incomprehensible algorithms - out of corrupt Fannie Mae loans, the only people who make money are the people who move them. And they, of course, are out of the market long before the IED detonates, leaving taxpayers holding the bag."

A sober silence fell upon the room.

"Does anybody have any idea what the current U.S. debt level is?" Nick Becker asked.

"$25 trillion?" Marge Weston, a physician, suggested.

Becker shook his head. "It's double that."

Small gasps.

"How'd you like to be a young couple starting out today, staring at a $50 trillion note, courtesy of your dad and mom?" he asked of no one in particular.

"What's the projected GDP for '08?" asked Jack Meyer.

"About 14 trillion," Becker replied.

"So, our debt is, what, almost four times our annual output?" Michael Burns asked in genuine surprise.

Becker nodded. "Debt itself can be managed, as long as cash flow is sufficient. The problem is our debt ratios are so out of whack they will cause a massive devaluation of the dollar. Add to that, diminishing pools of known oil – what they refer to as 'peak oil'— and it doesn't take a visionary to spot a 'perfect storm' beginning to form."

Suddenly Jim Gillespie sprang to his feet, and with a gusto that stunned the table, broke out in song at the top of his lungs. "For he's a jolly good fellow, for he's a jolly good fellow, for he's a jolly good felllooow, that nobody can deny." Then he led the table, who against their own instincts followed along. "That nobody can deny, that nobody can deny, for he's a jolly good felllooow, that nobody can deny." He finished by standing on his chair and leading a full throated cheer. "Give me an 'N' … give me an 'I' … give me a 'C' … give me a 'K' … give me a 'Y'. Whatta you got? NICKY! …NICKY! …NICKY!" he paused, theatrically, then bellowed, "And whatta you need? "Prozac! Prozac! Prozac!"

Gillespie sat down to a rousing ovation. Even Becker was applauding.

Gillespie took a long swig of wine, looked at Becker and said, "Holy Mother of God, Becker! Lighten up, will you! You're killing us."

Michael Burns convulsed. John thought he might actually fall out of his chair. The mood turned festive. Waiters bustled about pouring new wine into old skins. Laughter rose from private conversations. Additional trays of food appeared and made their way round and round the table. John glanced at Michael Burns. He was smiling. He looked down the table for Maggie. She was looking at him. Without taking her eyes off John, she tilted her head towards Jim Gillespie, who was holding court, and smiled and shrugged. John smiled and nodded.

From across the table, Jack Meyer began asking questions about various church positions on key electoral issues. John thought perhaps Meyer was baiting him, and worried that his answers might end up, out of context, in a social column with only a veneer of anonymity. So he set about deflecting and redirecting the questions to others at their end of the table. He was soon dismayed to learn, however, that those he had co-opted were unsure what some of those positions actually were, and appeared to care not one whit.

When waiters appeared bearing dessert trays, Michael Burns decided it was time to roil his guests some more. John just looked at him in utter amazement. "Okay, let's get down and dirty here," he said, rising to his feet. "In ten days we vote. Around the table: who's going to win this thing?"

When the count was complete, the Democratic nominee had 16 'votes' to ten for the Republican nominee. This surprised John. What happened next, however, shocked him. Michael Burns, clever as always, had a follow up question. "Who," he asked, "*should* win?" This time, the Democratic nominee actually picked up another 'vote.'

It was clear. These upper middle class Catholics had made their decision. They were going to vote Democratic, by a three to two ratio.

Burns appeared stunned. He immediately leapt in where angels feared to tread. "How?" he asked, visibly upset. "What about the babies?"

This cast an immediate pall over the table. Women shifted uneasily in their seats; men reached for wine. No one said anything for over a minute. Then Carole Hartman said, "I'm voting my pocketbook. The Republicans have had eight years to straighten this mess out, and they just made it worse."

Several heads nodded.

Jack Meyer surprised everyone. "The Democrats fielded a better candidate. They deserve to win."

Marge Weston seemed to speak for many when she said, "Look, our Church itself is split on this thing."

Maggie Kealey immediately challenged her. "How so, Marge?"

The room quieted instantly. A palpable tension seemed to materialize out of nowhere. The two most formidable women in the room were about to face off.

Marge Weston turned to Maggie and said, "Well, I thought the statement by our Bishops Conference on the election was fairly ambiguous."

Maggie appeared to gird herself. She nodded. "Yes, I suppose that's a valid interpretation. But the Church has always been clear that some issues are more consequential than others. And those issues are commonly referred to as the 'life issues.'"

"Yes, *but*," Marge challenged. "Our bishops made it clear in their statement that we could vote for a pro abortion candidate, as long as we had a 'proportionate' reason for doing so."

Jim Gillespie groaned. Heads turned. Maggie waved him off. She turned back to her debate opponent and asked, "And what might that be, Marge?"

Marge Weston didn't flinch. "War."

Maggie pursued. "War? Okay, work with me here. How many people, on all sides, have been killed by the wars in Iraq and Afghanistan?"

No one knew.

Michael Burns put the figure at 50,000. Jack Meyer said it was probably higher.

Maggie suggested, "Would everyone agree that 100,000 is probably the outer edge?"

Some heads nodded. Marge Weston's head was not among them, however. "Where you going with this, Maggie?" she asked.

"We kill over 100,000 babies every month in this country. How is the 'war consideration' 'proportionate'?"

Several people, John thought as many as four, tried to speak at once. The room was turning on his friend. He wanted in on the battle, he just didn't quite know how to enter. His opportunity came in the form of a question. "Father, is she right? It was Fran Delgado, whose eyes pleaded 'please say no.'

All heads turned to the end of the table. John felt the darting eyes and the quickened hearts. "Yes," he said simply.

A chorus of opposition stalked him from random points in the room.

"How can you take a position to the right of your own bishops?"

"What about the ethical issues surrounding illegal immigration, Father?"

"What about the Gospel's 'preferential option' for the poor?"

John held his hands up. "Please, one at a time."

"Father, are you saying that as Catholics we *have* to vote Republican next Tuesday?" Mark Erickson asked.

"No," he replied. The answer appeared to shock the table.

"Then what are you saying, Father?" Marge Weston asked.

"I'm going to tell you how one of America's finest bishop's, Denver archbishop Charles Chaput, answered that same question earlier this year. 'The proportionate reason for voting for a pro abortion candidate," he said, 'has to be a reason we could, with an honest heart, expect the unborn victims of abortion to accept when we meet them and need to explain our decision, as we someday will."

A heavy silence fell upon the table. Conversation ceased. The drinking and eating seemed suspended. Slowly the room began to empty. Within ten minutes only Michael Burns and John Sweeney were left. Carol Burns had taken it upon herself to see the others, including Jim Gillespie and Maggie Kealey, to the door.

Burns turned to John Sweeney and said, "My God, Sweeney! Remind me never, ever to invite you to another one of my dinner parties." Then he jumped up and hugged John Sweeney, and kissed him on both cheeks.

John laughed and returned the hug, before turning and leaving the room in search of the front door. He was acutely aware his words were already making the rounds in late night phone calls among his parishioners.

# 26

---

H e awoke to the sense there might be something waiting for him. He glanced at the clock on his night table. It was 6:43 a.m. He put on his robe and slippers and padded into the study. He hit the black bar on the keyboard of his laptop and waited for his mail to appear on screen. On this cold gray Sunday morning in early December, his Inbox spilled out slowly. The New York Times appeared first, then TownHall, the Philadelphia Newspapers, two posts from colleagues at the hospital, one from a friend, and then, his heart leapt. There it was. Her name on the screen. He just stared at it for several moments trying to imagine what the next click would reveal. Would it be purely professional? Might it contain an invitation of some sort? *Any chance of a marriage proposal?* Heart racing, he shut his eyes and clicked.

"Jim, any chance we could get together sometime today to talk about the onsite NFP clinic?"

He read it five times. Try as he might, he couldn't find even a hint of a marriage proposal.

He typed in a response. "Sure, your place or mine?"

He looked at it on the screen in front of him for several moments and fought off the temptation to say something more. He clicked the send button. Immediately he was flooded with a tsunami of guilt. He feared she would regard his reply as too personal. It was, after all, Sunday. Worse, he reminded himself, it was Sunday morning. She was probably dressing for church, or maybe undressing to shower for church. *Stop it! Stop it! Get hold of yourself, now. Next thing you know, desires will become thoughts, thoughts will become fantasies, fantasies will become soul-deadening sin. No Holy Communion. No sanctifying grace. No mystical fortification for re-immersion in the rancid culture. Helluva way to start the week, idiot!*

Amidst his self flagellation, a reply came in. Its suddenness stunned him. He was afraid to open it. He stood and started out of the room, only to come back and click open her reply.

"How about a walk in Valley Forge Park instead? It's supposed to clear up some. Can you pick me up at noon?" It was 'signed' simply: J

His heart was thumping so hard he thought he'd have an aneurysm. He stared at the symbol and tried to read everything into it imaginable. She was happy they were going to be together. She was anticipating a chance to talk about 'the future.' She simply couldn't bear to be away from him for a whole weekend.

*Who are you kidding? She wants you to advise her, not court her. She'll probably reimburse you for the gas.*

How to reply?

"Any chance I could take you to the Inn for brunch before we head out?" He fretted over every word. Would she think him too aggressive? Perhaps a cast of mind too 'social' for a business discussion? Maybe a bit too ... cloying? He clicked 'send' and waited for a reply.

In an instant, it appeared.

"Love to, but Grace and Scott are here with the little ones. They spent the night. I'm on kitchen duty again! I hope to God I haven't forgotten how to make pancakes; it's flour, milk and eggs, in that order, right?

Jim Gillespie groaned in the peculiar way of the love sick. He quickly searched for the 'print' icon and clicked. Her reply was in his hands in moments. He opened his top desk drawer and withdrew a manila folder with the word Maggie written in large letters on the outside. He held the string of correspondence and read it through top to bottom several more times before closing the file and placing it back in the drawer. He walked slowly back to his bedroom and fell across the bed horizontally. He stared at the ceiling. He put his right hand over his heart in a vain attempt to still and soothe it. *Lord, will you please remove this thorn from my heart? I don't think I can continue this way much longer. I love this woman. I crave her company. I want to be with her, Lord, morning, noon, and night. Yet I can't have her. She is the forbidden fruit in the garden. I get it, Lord. I do. But please, what am I supposed to do with this fire in my heart, this ... dare I say ... love? Where did it come from, if not from you? For whom do you intend it, if not for her? What would you have me do with it? I didn't ask for this, Lord. I didn't see it coming. I do not want to offend you in any way. But, how many cold showers can a man take? My skin is turning pink. I'm starting to look like an albino, Lord! Please rescue me before I do something that shocks my mother. On the other hand ...*

He closed his eyes and in a moment entered another realm. He saw her coming down a magnificent center aisle in an exquisite white dress with an impossibly long train. Her dark hair swirled high like a soft, lush honeycomb under her lace veil. Her sapphire eyes pierced the veil and revealed an unspeakable beauty. Her skin was redolent even from a distance. He felt his palms moisten and his heart leap into his throat as she drew closer. Suddenly her arm was linked in his, and she briefly laid her lovely head on his shoulder. A surge of purifying energy coursed through his body and he thought he might simply explode in pure joy. Together they made their way up to a white marble altar enshrouded in mist. On the top step waiting for them was Father John Sweeney. He appeared to be laughing more than smiling, and beckoning them with open arms. As they approached, he rushed down to embrace them and his tears fell upon their cheeks and necks. Maggie started to cry and buried her head into his left shoulder, squeezing his arm tightly for support. He could feel her body as it nestled against his and he could smell her warm, sweet breath on his cheek. So boundless was his joy that his first thought was that he was in heaven.

He awoke with a jolt when the phone in his bedroom pierced the silence. It was her. "Thank you, Jim." Brief pause. "We're good for noon today, right? If the weather doesn't break, we'll find a little diner and have some hot chocolate and talk this through, okay?" Another pause. Jim Gillespie, for the first time in his life, was speechless. His mind was churning in a futile effort to separate fantasy and reality. Suddenly she was speaking again. "Jim, Jim, are you alright?"

"Yes," he mumbled into the receiver. He struggled to clear the fog that had settled into the frontal lobe of his brain, and sat up in an effort to keep the room from spinning. "I'm fine. Noon it is, Maggie."

"Oh, thanks Jim. This is such a momentous decision, we just have to get this right."

*Which one? The decision to marry? It's really not all that difficult, love.* "Yes, yes. I agree. We'll wrestle it down together, figuratively speaking, of course."

The sound of her laughter washed over his heart like a soft ocean breeze. "Okay, Dr. Gillespie. Assuming we do end up outside, feel free to bring one of those smelly cigars if you want."

Jim heard himself laugh. "Okay, I get the hint. I'll bring two."

He cradled the phone as he listened to the surprise in her laughter. Gently, he set it down in the receiver.

He sprang from the bed to prepare for Mass. He glanced again at the clock. It was 7:22, too late to make the 7:30. He'd go to the 9:00, the family Mass. He immediately went in search of cotton balls.

• • •

By the time Jim Gillespie wheeled his navy blue Porsche through the main entrance of Valley Forge Park, the sun had managed to fight its way through the clouds. The air temperature had climbed a good five to seven degrees. The lot was only half filled, and he found a spot near the Welcome Center. He jumped out and, after suggesting Maggie remain in the car, walked briskly to the Center for a map of the trails. He was in jeans, a windbreaker and an old blue Brooklyn Dodgers baseball cap. He exited the shop waving the map in his left hand and wearing a bemused smile. She got out of the car dressed in maroon corduroy slacks with a crimson pullover and a dark blue scarf. As he approached he reported, "That cute young lady on duty asked if I wanted a private tour." Pause. "I think she was hitting on me."

Maggie Kealey laughed, "It's the Porsche, Jim. It's the only reason I asked you instead of Ciancini."

Jim was stunned that even artful repartee could pierce his heart, *if* it came from her and hinted rejection. As he fought to banish the sound from his ears, he knew, much later in the evening, he'd be fighting to banish the pain from his heart. "Yeah, I know. Even Mother won't be seen with me, unless she's behind the wheel," he added good naturedly.

She studied him as he studied the map. She both liked and greatly admired Jim Gillespie, she conceded. But even if she was free to marry, and she certainly was not, she would not choose to marry this man. She needed someone more physically vital, more circumspect, more … like Bill. She immediately chastised herself for thinking about her former husband. She reminded herself how ruinous those first seven years had been after he left: all but completely destroying her self esteem, not to mention her mental, emotional and physical health. She remembered crying herself to sleep far too many nights, praying he would return. Some nights she begged God to take her before morning. Every time she looked into the face of one of their five children, she felt a fresh wave of guilt and shame. They were now, officially, children from a broken family, she told herself. Each of them was now statistically far more likely to suffer through a divorce of his own. *Why, Lord? Where did I fail? To this day, I can't accept it. Can't you put us back together? I'll take him back, I swear. He can't be happy with that woman, can he, Lord? How can he be?*

She studied Jim Gillespie's receding hairline, plain oval face and frumpy body. *This is a good man, Lord. And I thank you that he is in my life. But Lord, please that it remain only and always professional. Please God, that I never in any way lead him on. You know my heart, Lord. I gave it away 35 years ago in a sacred covenant. I seek nothing now but a clean heart which finds its rest in yours.*

They decided on a trail that passed the famous Potts House, which General Washington used for his headquarters during the severe winter encampment of 1777-1778. The trail itself was of lesser consequence than the need to stretch their legs and talk about some serious business. They walked perhaps 100 yards or so in silence. With the Potts House in view, Maggie suddenly said, "Isn't it just remarkable what these men risked for an ideal, Jim?"

"Their honor, their fortunes, their very lives, as they themselves formally recorded it," he replied.

"Jim, how is it men were willing to do the heroic then, from these tents, exposed to all manner of disease and danger and discomfort; but today we can't get our men to sacrifice even momentary pleasure to safeguard their wives and families and communities?"

"Ah, far too many Viagra commercials?" he guessed, impertinently.

If she heard him she gave no indication. "And at what cost! The entirety of our spiritual patrimony, all but exhausted in a single generation. We've wiped out 12 generations of labor and sacrifice in one." She turned to him with eyes he simply found irresistible. "Oh Jim, what's going to happen to our children?"

"Yes, the children. Precisely why I didn't have any. By the way, I also had the foresight to buy Microsoft at 12 dollars."

"What are we leaving them?"

"Well, they seem happy with the iPods."

"Jim, if our men aren't going to stand up and do the right thing, *we've* got to stand up and do it."

"Yes, yes. It's up to us women!" he declared triumphally.

She stopped and tugged on his arm. "Jim, we've got to throw them all out, the whole Ob/Gyn department, from Ciancini on down, and just start over. They're all 'at will' employees. Legally, there's no reason we can't do it, right? So, how *do* we do it?"

He stopped and looked at her. Her boldness aroused his protective instinct. He knew she was prepared to lay everything on the line for what she believed. He also knew she would be chewed to pieces. He saw her suddenly as an old woman in a nursing home, telling a disinterested young woman visitor, perhaps a niece, what she once tried to do, and why it failed. *Please God, don't let her do this. Please guide her to the true and the good in some other, less ruinous, way.*

"Ah, maybe if you gave them an ultimatum first?"

She blinked. "Why? They're Catholic physicians and they've been killing Catholic babies, in a Catholic hospital. They ought to be excommunicated."

"You want to just terminate them, all of them?"

"Yes."

"Is a firing squad in the courtyard out of the question?"

She fixed him with a withering stare.

"Ah, perhaps one or more of them would be willing to change?"

"Too late. They've made a mockery of their oath to abide by the Church's Ethical and Religious Directives. And even if our broken church doesn't take those directives seriously, I do! Besides, Ciancini has known my position on the matter. I presume he shared it with the others. Far as I can tell, it's been business as usual over the past six months." She paused, then shook her head. "No, Jim. Time's up."

"Maggie, they'd walk out with nearly all our Ob/Gyn

business. Our own two private practices in the Women's Clinic combine for less than 20% of the business those fellows bring in."

She looked at him with fire in her eyes. "I don't care," each word coming forth slowly and with emphasis.

He decided to try another tack. "What about the impact on hospital morale? You're building something very special, Maggie. I'd hate to see you disrupt it."

"Disrupt it!" The fire returned. "What I intend to disrupt is the killing!"

"But we doctors are odd ducks. We tend to band together. And if pushed into a corner ..."

"What are you suggesting, that I'll have a full scale revolt on my hands?"

"Well, maybe not 'full scale,' but you may lose a good number of the others doctors, and never really know it until it's too late."

"The hell with them."

He turned to her as they walked and drew closer. He spoke softly. "Maggie, you can't run a hospital without doctors."

"Then the good sisters will have to close it."

He searched for a delicate way to broach the highly probable. "Maggie, suppose the good sisters don't want to close it?"

She grew silent.

He could feel acute pain in her silence. He anguished that his simple question had summoned it.

"Then I will have been obedient," she said softly. "A 'useless servant,' nothing more. And it will be time for me to move on."

Now *he* felt deep pain. He reversed field. "Maggie, what if we *were* to replace those four? Who would we replace them with?"

"Hank Seelaus."

"Maggie, Hank Seelaus is only one man. He couldn't possibly handle that volume, on top of his own patient load."

"Well, we'll just have to recruit NFP doctors to work under him."

"And where would we find these doctors?"

"Hank will find them."

"And if he doesn't?"

She stopped abruptly. She looked deeply into his eyes. He felt his heart stir. "Jim, we have to trust. We can't go into this doubting whether God will help us."

*Lord, what do I do with that?* "Maggie," he said, choosing his words carefully, "what if God is busy working on that situation in the West Bank, or what really happened that night in Michael Jackson's bedroom?"

She laughed. "Oh Jim, honestly! Do you think God cares about some rock star's autopsy?"

"If you're referring to mine, I hope to God he does."

She was reduced to giggling like a school girl. Her laughter had a lovely lyrical quality to it that he found irresistible. In these moments it took every ounce of self mastery to restrain himself from throwing his arms around her and hugging her so tightly he could feel her heart beat. "Maggie, we need to think this through."

"Jim, I've been thinking of little else since the night of the Gala. That was the night Stan Koblinski told me what was going on in that department." She paused and continued walking. With no other options, he followed. "It's happening on *my* watch now. I can't *not* act. This killing of human embryos *will* stop. At least in *my* hospital."

He decided to try yet another tack. "How about if we could get the Cardinal Archbishop to *order* you to do it?"

She crinkled her nose. "O'Hallaran?"

"Sure, why not?"

"Michael Burns says he's, ah, less interested in pastoral matters than he is in raising money."

Jim nodded. "That's true. He does tend to see his legacy in fiscal terms. But, if you were to drop this mess in his lap and ask him if he thought its becoming public would help or hinder his money raising efforts, who knows?" Small smile. "He may just *order* you to go back and clean it up."

"Really," she seemed intrigued.

"Sure. Then, you're just doing what the good bishop asked

you to do. I mean, after all, a Catholic hospital should be in conformance with its Church's teachings, right? Hell, even the nuns might understand that." Slight pause. "Well, some of them."

She seemed buoyed by the possibility. "Jim, do you really think the cardinal would do that?"

*Hell no. You'd have a better chance of getting a loan at prime plus two from that one.* "Well, we won't know until we try."

They walked on in silence. The sun had slipped back into the clouds and a chill swept off the hills from the west. He saw her shiver and bundle up. He was about to suggest they turn back when she said, "Jim, how do I get in front of him?"

He paused before replying. "I roomed in college with his right hand guy, Bishop Bancone. We still get together from time to time. I could ask him to arrange a one-on-one with the cardinal for sometime before Christmas. I think he'd do that for me. Of course, I'd have to promise you'd bring a satchel full of unmarked c-notes."

To his great surprise, she did not laugh. "Really? Do you think he'd want money, Jim?"

"Maggie, every once in awhile ... I say something, I don't know, something not actually meant to be taken literally. You might think of it as a ... joke ... but perhaps that would be a bit presumptuous on my part."

"Will you call the bishop?" she asked with a sense of hope that both surprised and calmed him. He consoled himself that at least she was no longer thinking mass executions.

She shivered again and looked at him with evident concern. "Maybe we should head back?"

He nodded and said, "Can't wait to get me alone in the Porsche, right?"

She threw back her head and laughed.

He gently put his hand on her shoulder and turned her around. Together they walked into a stiff wind toward the car and home.

# 27

---

" ... And this is the famous Aaron McKenna, entrepreneur, raconteur, athlete, confidant to the rich and famous, including our governor and mayor, and world class marketing talent. *This* is the man who will lead Women's Right into the promised land."

Aaron McKenna stood up as Michael Burns sat down. The Women's Right conference room was somewhat smaller than Burns had expected, given the scope of the organization's ambitions. It was painted in soft pastels, set off by garish post-modern art work hung at what appeared to be random intervals. The neo-modern conference table swallowed most of the room. There were five women seated around the upper end of the table, all in sneakers. They did not look happy. As Michael Burns was extolling the creative virtues of Ed Mobley, each of them was busy twittering on their Blackberrys. There hadn't been a single question for Mobley, an ad industry Hall of Fame creative talent, which left Michael Burns smoldering.

"So, how come you sold out?" The first question was directed to McKenna by the Executive Director, Rachel Hobson, a slight, short-haired woman who appeared to be in her mid-to-late 30's.

Burns sat bolt upright. He looked up at McKenna, who smiled magnanimously and deflected the question easily. "Got an offer I couldn't refuse."

"Aren't you going to miss being your own boss?" This was a follow up from Hobson, who clearly did not like being dismissed so summarily.

"Oh, but I will be," McKenna replied through an engaging smile, eyes darting to the others in hopes of eliciting a less hostile line of questioning.

"Yeah, how's that?" Hobson bore in.

"Michael and I have an understanding," McKenna replied evenly, refusing to be goaded.

"Yeah, what is it?"

"That's none of your business," Burns snapped. This had gone far enough. Immediately after the Ultra Com transaction closed, he'd transferred over $8 million into his portfolio after buying out McKenna on his own, paying capital gains, and cleaning up the rest of his children's private debt. As far as he was concerned, he didn't even need the balance from the "earn out." Though he wanted more, he had enough. And that meant he could afford to have had enough of Ms. Hobson.

"Now, now, Michael," McKenna soothed. He turned his attention to the Executive Director. "Our understanding is: Michael doesn't bother me, and I don't bother him."

"Aaron is going to manage all our government business," Michael Burns interrupted, in an attempt to recover." He paused for effect. "The benefit to Women's Right will be twofold: one, this young man knows his way around City Hall and Harrisburg, which will be of enormous help in securing additional grants; and two, he understands how to very creatively lobby the large minority community, which will help you build your customer base, which in turn will strengthen your case for additional grant monies."

"We know how to reach minority women. We don't need

Burns Advertising, or Aaron McKenna, to do that," Ms. Hobson suggested airily.

Suddenly Michael was aware of Ed Mobley stirring on his right. Mobley owned a well deserved reputation as an anarchist. His dossier included peeing on a client's office plant after the client criticized one of his TV boards, throwing a cell phone at a female client who meddled during a commercial shoot, and flipping off just about every CEO who had the misfortune of managing him. The very last thing Michael wanted to do as one of Hanley Siliezar's new employees was to explain how he managed to blow up the Women's Right account on the first day.

Ed Mobley stood up, knocking his chair backwards in the process. He did not bother to pick it up. Turning to Michael, he said, "Well, I've heard enough from ol' Butchie here. I'd quit the business before I'd write an ad for these dykies in Nikes ..." And with that, he was gone.

Michael looked at McKenna who merely shrugged.

Rachel Hobson smiled and said to Michael, "Well, we outted that bigot rather easily. Now, how about you two?"

"You just chased the best creative director in America out your door," Michael said, careful to make eye contact with the other women. "Not very smart."

As Hobson was about to reply, Aaron McKenna headed both her and a Michael Burns meltdown off by interrupting, "Ed will get over it, ladies. Trust me. Then he paused and did something that Michael Burns did not think he had in him. "Rachel, ladies, it's clear Burns Advertising wasn't your first choice. We understand that. But give us a chance. We believe in the work you are doing; and no one will work harder to help you succeed."

At this Rachel Hobson fell momentarily silent. Then she pointed to Michael and said to McKenna, "What about that one? He's a pillar of his church. We hate that church and all it stands for. Why should we want him in here, on the inside?"

Burns shuddered. *So that's it! Why didn't you just tell Proper Parenthood to get lost when they suggested you hire us? Gutless?"*

McKenna nodded. "Rachel, you're right," he replied, patiently. "I don't blame you. I wouldn't want him around either. In fact," he added with a magnetic smile, "I don't even like him hanging around Burns Advertising."

The ladies in sneakers laughed. Even Rachel Hobson smiled. Michael did not know what to do, except keep quiet. It was now and forever the Aaron McKenna show at Women's Right, and that suited him just fine.

McKenna made a point of engaging the other women. To no one in particular, he said, "Could someone tell me what this important organization wants to accomplish in the next several years?"

A bulky woman in a crew cut and a dark blue University of Pennsylvania sweat suit, answered, "We want to do more *with more.*"

Aaron McKenna laughed and looked at Michael Burns. "Finally! I found a client after my own heart!" Then he turned to the woman and said in a tone pure urban chic, "What's your name, sister?"

Michael felt a current of energy sweep the room. His thoroughbred was breaking from the pack. The young lady appeared to relax her game face. "Melissa," she answered with a trace of a smile.

McKenna elevated the charm offensive. "Melissa, as in Etheridge, my favorite female country singer?"

The young woman laughed self consciously at the gratuitous reference to the iconic lesbian.

McKenna turned to the others. "So, which one of you accomplished women is going to answer my question? Just what is it you sisters want to get done over the next few years?"

A tiny little lady on the far right of Rachel Hobson said, "How about you first tell us what you know about Women's Right?"

Michael Burns flinched. He did not think his horse would navigate this hurdle so easily. Research was not something that arrested the attention of Aaron McKenna. He was wrong, again.

"Well, my little one, I can tell you that you were founded as a coalition of existing women's groups in the mid-70's. Your mission at the time was to defend the dignity of all women, which was something that was not very popular back then. You set out to end wage discrimination, to help abused women, to protect women from rape and its after effects, and to end the days of men telling women what they had to do with their bodies. In all of this you were heroes, true pioneers."

Michael watched a bond forming between the man sitting to his right and the women at the far end of the table. Their eyes seemed to lighten. Their faces lost their hardness. And their body language was saying something different, though Michael was hesitant to presume precisely what it was suggesting.

Rachel Hobson actually smiled and said, "Do you happen to know where we got our first grant?"

"I do," McKenna replied matter-of-factly. "It was $50,000 from the William Penn Foundation. And I'm well aware that you've managed to put $20 million on the street in service to women in need over the past 30 years."

Michael thought he heard one women actually giggle. Rachel Hobson looked at Burns with a blank expression, and turned to McKenna and said, "I'm impressed, Mr. McKenna."

"How about we drop the Mister, Sister?" McKenna replied with an engaging smile. Two of the other women laughed, which forced a smile from the Executive Director.

"Fair enough," she said. "Let me tell you what we're going to do over the next couple of years, and what we're going to expect from Aaron McKenna." She stared at Burns to make sure the insult found its target. It had.

"First," she said, still staring at Michael Burns, "we're going to lobby Harrisburg to overturn the 24 Hour Waiting Period for teenage moms. Then, we're going to take dead aim at the president's health care legislation, and make damn sure there are no restrictions in it when it goes to Congress, and when it comes out of Congress."

"Restrictions?" McKenna interrupted.

"To women's God-given reproductive freedom," she replied icily. "And finally," with a brief pause for dramatic effect, "Women's

Right will organize the Gay/Lesbian community to lobby for a Marriage Act within two years here in Pennsylvania."

Michael Burns saw his whole life pass before him. It concluded with him being strapped down to a cold table in a small windowless chamber. His children were making sure the leather straps were properly fastened, his wife was approaching with a syringe filled with a lethal injection, and behind the glass the cardinal and archdiocesan hierarchy were nodding approval.

"My, my, Ladies," Aaron McKenna said after a lyrical whistle. "That is one damn fine, and damn formidable, agenda!" He paused and smiled. "And I am absolutely certain Burns Advertising will be able to help you get all three of those things done."

"How?" Rachel Hobson inquired, still testing.

Aaron McKenna didn't miss a beat. "Ladies, your time has arrived," he announced a bit too triumphally, Michael feared. "You've been laboring in the vineyard for a long time, under a hot noonday sun, but now your ship has come in!" Michael blanched at the mixed metaphor, but it wasn't at all clear the ladies took note of it. They were fairly swooning under McKenna's Baptist preacher cant. "It so happens," he said after a dangerously extended pause, "I'm playing pick-up basketball with the President of the United States in two weeks. I will ask him to have his point person for the health care legislation contact Rachel for Women's Right input."

Rachel Hobson's eyes widened to the approximate size of half dollars. The other ladies in sneakers turned to each other with mouths agape. Not a word was said. They were simply speechless.

McKenna continued. "Now, as far as repealing the 24-hour Waiting Period, I'll tell Ned, uh, the governor, to start gearing up. We've got a window with a D in the chair in Washington. Now is the time to get *all* of our agenda passed." He paused and stared down Rachel Hobson. "And I do mean *all of it.* And that goes for the Marriage Act too. You good people have been discriminated against for far too long. We're gonna change that within the next two years."

Michael didn't know whether it was McKenna's deployment

of the word "our" with respect to the Women's Right mission—which signaled the politically potent fusion of minority agendas—or whether it was his utter and unabashed conviction, but whatever it was, the squeals of delight which greeted his proclamation of victory sent chills running up and down his spine. The ladies were actually hugging each other. Michael was suddenly fearful that clothing might come flying off. *I'd be the only safe one in the room.*

Rachel Hobson stood and walked toward the other end of the table. She brushed past Michael without so much as looking at him. She thrust her right hand toward Aaron McKenna. Michael glanced quickly to see if there was hair on the knuckles. McKenna took the proffered hand in both of his and stood. "Come here, ladies," he beckoned with his shoulders. The others immediately stood and walked quickly to their Executive Director and their new Leading Man.

Michael was suddenly in the awkward position of having a revival going on around him, without an invitation to participate. He stood to make room for the small, intimate assembly. He walked toward the far end of the table, stopping at the mid-way point.

McKenna was oblivious to all of it. His eyes directed the women to form a small circle around him. Then he asked "for hands."

Michael was flabbergasted. *This son of a bitch is going to lead cheers! Tell me this isn't happening!*

All five of the women now had their hands on McKenna's smooth ebony fingers. Their heads were leaning into the small huddle. "Ladies," he soberly intoned, "This is our time. Let us pledge to each other, right here, right now, that ... *we ... will ... not ... stop...* until we get ... *all* ... the rights we deserve as Americans."

One of the women started crying. This induced tears from two others. Hobson and Melissa Etheridge were hanging tough.

"Ladies," McKenna began, with eyes that were now watery. He even dared to slip, seamlessly Michael thought, into a badlands street vernacular. "Nomo bigotry ... Nomo prejudice ... Nomo second class citizenship." Pause. "We all God's chillum! We all got God-given rights."

He paused again, looking down upon them with apparent affection. He was at least a foot taller than the tallest of them. "Lord God, help us go forward to do your work. Guide us, Lord, to help our women get their just due." His voice ascended majestically. "Empower us, Lord, to right these wrongs and bring the American promise to all of your children ... *now Lord* ... in the fullness of your time."

And with that, Aaron McKenna lifted their hands and threw them high in the air and began hugging them one by one. The ladies returned the affection with tight, prolonged hugs of their own. Even Rachel Hobson hugged him tightly and mouthed a quiet 'thank you.'

Michael Burns took the scene in and realized he was now, officially, a dead man walking. But at least he knew a glowing report of Burns Advertising's first meeting with the leadership team of Women's Right would reach the desk of Hanley Siliezar.

And Mr. Siliezar's happiness was now very important to Michael Burns.

# 28

It was half past seven when Joe Delgado arrived home from work. A light snow was falling as he parked his new Lexus 460 in his garage. He entered the kitchen from the garage and immediately dodged a flying truck thrown by one of two resident al Qaeda mini-terrorists. He smiled painfully at his daughter, who was commencing a counter attack, weapon of some sort in hand. He shuddered at the prospect of hand to hand combat in his own kitchen, and walked into the den where he picked up a phone and dialed an old friend.

"That you, Joe?" the voice on the other end inquired.

"Yes, Father. How's 8:00?"

"Works for me. Want me to have Carmella set out a hot plate?"

"No thanks, Father. I can't have you spoiling me at this point in my life." He heard a soft chuckle on the other end, followed by a click. He set the phone down and headed back into the kitchen where he was greeted by his victorious daughter, who appeared to have banished the enemy. "Hi, Kitten. How was your day?" he asked, opening the refrigerator and removing a bottle of cold water.

Terry Delgado approached him in a full-length apron with a spatula in hand and gave him a one-arm hug. "Hi, Daddy. Same old, same old. How 'bout you?"

"Well, there's something to be said for 'same old, same old,'" he said, inspecting the penne pasta simmering in a large copper pot on the stove. "Hey, is this for me?" he asked startled.

"Sure is," she answered cheerfully, while tossing a green garden salad in a bright red ceramic bowl.

"Why?" His defenses kicked in reflexively. *She found a job and wants me to hire a nanny. She found a home and wants me to buy it. She's on a mission from her mother to get my approval for a major capital expenditure, probably a face lift.*

His daughter turned around to face him; there were tears in her eyes. "Because today is your birthday, Daddy."

Something caught in his throat. He couldn't speak. It was true, of course. He had taken congratulatory calls from two of his three brothers and all four of his sisters. Each told him this 60th year of his would be "momentous," or words to that effect. Paula Gomez came to work with a small, beautifully wrapped gift: a copy of St. Francis DeSales' classic *Introduction to the Devout Life*. He immediately assumed she was sending him some sort of message about what it was like to work for him. Other than that, certainly nothing "momentous" had happened, at least not as yet. He assumed he would go home to a cold, empty home and a cold, empty plate. *This* he was not prepared for. He didn't know which was the greater surprise: a daughter in tears at a milestone otherwise unacknowledged in his own home, or a pot full of irresistible hot pasta in blessed marinara sauce. Perhaps he would just tell his daughter to set the pot down in front of his place at the table and forget the plate.

"Thank you, Sweetheart. This means a great deal to me," he said as he advanced and enveloped her. He heard her soft groan under the pressure. He pulled back and looked at her watery eyes. "*You* mean a great deal to me, Terry," he added. He stopped and looked down. He felt a thickness again in his throat and did not trust himself to say more.

"Oh, Daddy! I so wish it was different," she said, her voice breaking. "We should all be here celebrating your life. You've given so much to all of us. This is wrong. Just wrong ..." She began to cry and hugged him again. The wave of gratitude coursing through his being so surprised him that he decided not to attend the tear stains on his favorite silk tie.

"Well," he said softly, in a voice not quite resolute, "*we're* here: you and I. And I am very, very grateful for that, Kitten."

She picked up the end of her apron and dried her eyes to no avail; the tears continued. She thought of the sacrifice he'd made for her many years ago, and how it seemed to have flattened his career trajectory at Pittman Labs, effectively trapping him in a world alien to his very nature and purpose. She thought of the unbearably cold silence that now permeated the home of her childhood and left an entire family divided. She thought of this new development in his career and whether it brought new opportunity or merely new anxiety. "Daddy," she said, searching for her voice, "I just want you to know how grateful I am for everything you've done for me, and for our family. You have been a rock."

He nodded, head down, then looked up and brightened. "Kitten, I think *boulder*: big, round, falling *boulder* might be the more accurate term."

She laughed and a small tear-spawned air bubble formed under her left nostril; rather than be repulsed by it, he found it endearingly reminiscent of the child he used to love to tease about growing up far too quickly. She lifted her apron again and dabbed at both her eyes and her nose, and looked up at him and said, "So, Pop Pop, what kind of dressing do you want on your birthday salad?"

He looked at the assortment on the counter and said, "How about French? I'm getting sick of the English."

She eyed him coolly and said, "What's that supposed to mean?"

He shook his head unconvincingly. "Absolutely nothing, Kitten. Just Pop Pop talking nonsense."

He went over to the small table in a nook on the far side of the island counter and sat down heavily. His neck and shoulders ached from a mounting tension he was hoping would be relieved, at least partially, later tonight. A new president of the United States had been elected under an unprecedented avalanche of cash, much of it rumored to have originated off shore; the candidate, of which very little was known, appeared to catch his competition flat-footed. His opponents, on both sides, claimed he had benefited, quite unfairly, from an unapologetically sympathetic major broadcast network which appeared to set the tone for the coverage of the candidate by competing networks. The HM Inc rollup of Pittman and Rossiter had proceeded without government interference, as had the rollup of the three leading Silicon Valley biotechnology firms focused on embryonic stem cell research. Virtually overnight, HM Inc had become the world's leading force in a rapidly nationalizing health-care industry, despite an outcry from its competitors in both the diagnostic and therapeutic sectors.

Joe Delgado had benefitted quite handsomely from all this. He was promoted to Executive Vice President and Chief Financial Officer for HM Inc's new Therapeutics Division, which included HM's now consolidated acquisitions of Rossiter and Pittman. He now reported to Chad Henley, who had been named the new division's Chief Operating Officer. Henley reported into the division's newly appointed Chief Executive Officer, Phil Hankinson.

They made it easy for him to stay on. He was allowed to convert his Pittman shares into HM Inc stock, which immediately jumped in value over 35%, and left him with a pre-capital gains position worth a little over $6 million: not enough on which to retire at age 59, he decided. So he accepted the job and its terms: an $800,000 annual salary, a bonus in the projected range of $200,000 to $400,000, and an initial package of options worth half his existing HM position when fully vested. More importantly, they acceded to his wish that he spend only three days a week in Manhattan; the other two days he was permitted to work out of his old office at Pittman Labs, a mere ten minutes from home. This made it possible for him to retain Paula Gomez, who turned out to be the only executive secretary to keep her position in the bloodbath which immediately followed the HM acquisition. In all, 106 jobs were lost, including one belonging to Pittman's CEO, Hal Fairfax, or, roughly 12% of the Pittman headquarters workforce.

This left Joe feeling conflicted. He knew some portion of those lost salaries helped fund his new position. At the same time, however, he needed his new job for several reasons, not the least of which was his sanity. He didn't think it was fair that he was paid so much, at the expense of those who had lost the little they had. But, unfortunately, that was the capitalist business model in the Knowledge Economy. He had no hobbies and few outside interests. For better or worse, he often reminded himself, his work was now his life. It was a refuge from a failed marriage and a fixed coordinate in a world he believed was spinning perilously out of control. He found his only consolation in his ability to perform at a high level professionally, and in being the "go to guy" for senior line officers in the corporation. No one knew the therapeutic business better than he did, certainly not the HM Inc Diagnostic team of Hankinson and Henley. He took great comfort in the fact that these men were now playing in *his* arena and were largely dependent on *his* industry knowledge and experience.

Terry put a plate of steaming joy in front of him and popped a cork on a bottle of red wine. She poured it slowly and sung happy birthday. When she had half-filled her own glass, she raised it, smiled and said, "Happy Birthday, Daddy."

"Thank you, Kitten," he said with a pained smile. The circumstances of their far too private celebration weighed heavily on his heart. His little one, too, was a victim of a failed marriage. He didn't have to project to feel her pain; all he had to do was to look into her eyes. She was very much his daughter and she wore emotional pain as he did: a 24/7 hair shirt. They understood there was nothing either one could say to the other to diminish pain, and therefore wasted no energy trying. In the banal idiom of the day: it was what it was.

She sat down across from him. He looked at her plate. There was a small portion of pasta and a slightly larger portion of green salad. This worried him. She'd begun taking on that preternaturally thin look he thought too many divorced women felt obliged to fashion. He understood, of course, but he did not like it one bit. The thought of his first born "back in play" in a fetid jungle full of older carnivores pained him greatly.

"How you doin', Kitten?" he asked with a gravitas intended to brook no evasion.

She looked down at her plate. "I'm struggling a bit, Daddy," she answered,then added, brightening "like you."

He smiled. "Well, as your grandmother used to say, this is, after all, nothing more than a 'vale of tears'."

She laughed. "When I was little I could never understand what she meant; but *now* I sure do."

"Father John says suffering is a great mercy."

"I know, Daddy; he told me that too."

"Do you understand it?"

"Not fully, no …"

He laughed and said, "Probably just as well …"

She brightened again. "So, how do you like your birthday dinner?"

He straightened. "Great food, even better companionship: what's not to like?"

She looked at his plate which was nearly empty. "Let me get you some more, Daddy."

His eyes danced as she reached for his plate. "Go ahead, spoil me. Of course, if I fall dead asleep on Father Sweeney, I'm blaming you."

She re-filled his plate and set it in front of him; she re-filled his wine glass and set it next to his plate. He studied the steam as it arose from his plate and evaporated somewhere above him. "So, any plans, Kitten?"

She looked up in surprise. The question appeared to catch her off guard. "I'm thinking about doing some volunteer work in the spring."

"Really? Any particular organization?" he inquired, discretely.

"Yes, Grace Peters' NFP clinic up in Bucks County."

"Isn't that Maggie Kealey's daughter?"

"Yes, I talked to her on the phone last week. Father John suggested it," she said, her eyes searching his for support.

He chose not to raise the issue of the al Qaeda cell upstairs; he presumed they'd be shipped off to Gitmo in chains. "She's not a physician, right?"

"No, she's not a doctor, Daddy. But she has an affiliation with a wonderful NFP physician up there who has a private practice in his own home. His name is Dr. Hank Seelaus."

He nodded as he ate. This one cooked not like *her* mother, but like *his* mother, he decided. Somewhere out there, he knew, there was a 200-pound man who would someday be a 300-pound man. "Well, that all sounds very promising, Kitten." Slight pause. "Any idea what you'll be doing?"

"No, not yet. But I think eventually I'd like to be trained to work directly with young married women."

He smiled wryly. "Good, Kitten, as long as you don't forget *you're* still very much a young woman."

"Oh, Daddy, I'm over the hill."

"No, you are *not!*" he snapped. The mini-explosion shocked her and embarrassed him. He paused to recover. "Sorry, Kitten. I just don't want to see you thinking that way. Don't let anybody tell you who you are but you." It was clear he was referring to her ex-husband "And me," he added with a smile that disarmed her.

She got up and came around to his chair and hugged him. "Oh Daddy, I don't know what I would do without you." She started to cry again. He reached up and guided her thin frame onto his lap. He hugged her and misted up. "And I don't know what I'd do without you, Kitten," he replied through a voice he found impossible to lighten.

She squeezed extra hard and got up. "Daddy, I think someone is waiting for you."

His head swiveled around expecting to see the enemy in its camouflage fatigues. "No," she laughed, "I didn't mean the kids. I meant Father Sweeney."

He laughed and rose and pecked her on the cheek. "Thank you, sweetheart. I really appreciate what you did for me tonight." He looked down and mumbled into his chest. "You're too good to your old man." Then he grabbed his suit jacket off the back of his chair and started for the door which led to the garage. He turned and said, "Don't wait up, Kitten. I may be awhile."

She nodded, her face frozen in concern.

• • •

The light snow had not yet accumulated and it took him a little over six minutes to drive the two and a half miles to the rectory. He pulled into the driveway and parked his car in the back by the garage. He did not want to raise suspicions, lest he be observed. He walked across the grass and up the front steps and knocked on the front door. There was no sound inside and he immediately suspected a miscommunication of some sort. He glanced at his watch. It was 8:03. He heard the sound of a door opening and closing to his right. Coming out of the upper church was John Sweeney. "Hey, Joe," he called.

Joe heard the voice before he saw the face. Sweeney momentarily appeared bathed in light from a pair of flood lights on the roof of the church. With small flakes of snow gently swirling silently about the priest's head, the scene struck Joe as ethereal. "Hey, Father," he replied, extending his hand. "Thanks for making time for me on such short notice."

"You never need notice, Joe. How many times do I have to tell you that?" John smiled as he hugged his visitor. "My door is always open to you," Sweeney added, suddenly struggling to open his own front door. "It's just not always open *to me*," he said, laughing. He turned to Joe and said, "Maybe Carmella flipped the dead latch. I suppose I really should stop complaining about the food."

Without warning, he bounded down the rectory steps and headed toward the back of the house. "Wait here, Joe," he called out. "I'll either get it open or we're both spending the night at your house."

Joe immediately had visions of his wife, bearing an uncanny resemblance to Kathy Bates, standing at the kitchen door of their home barring entry with the aid of a pick axe. Within moments, the front door opened and John Sweeney, smiling sheepishly, welcomed him inside. He entered and basked in the warmth coming from the old radiator in the narrow center hall. He blew on his hands and held them a few inches above the radiator. Sweeney took note of his discomfort and beckoned him into the parlor. "C'mon, it's nice and warm in here." Then, he said as an aside, "This is where Carmella reads her romance novels."

Joe took a seat in a wing chair next to a radiator. John pulled a matching chair from its setting and positioned it opposite Joe's. The room was lit by two end table lamps on either side of a large couch in front of the room's only window. Joe found the warm, informal lighting to his liking. For reasons he never fully understood, he had always recoiled from the sharp glare of overhead lighting. Even in what were now his two work offices, he insisted on lamps as the sole source of interior light in winter months.

"What can I get you, my friend?" John Sweeney asked before settling himself.

"A pint of Jameson's," he replied to instant laughter.

"Now wouldn't that be a sight for poor Carmella in the morning? The likes of the two of us passed out on the parlor floor."

"Who do you think she'd call first, the bishop or your mother?"

John winced and said softly, "I would hope my mother; the bishop has the long memory."

"Ah, Father, forgive me. I know not what I do."

John waved his hand dismissively. "No offense taken, Joe. I'm afraid Mother is not long for this world, and that's the good news."

"What are the doctors telling you, Father?"

John shook his head slowly before letting it fall to his chest. "Not long, not long," he mumbled.

The thought of a mother of a priest slipping the veil under the anointed hands of her son struck Joe as a richly textured act of mercy for both. The faith of the one giving life to the ministry of the other, who prepares her to be re-born, in death, to eternal life. *Exquisite. It is the stark beauty of death that dresses life in its most poignant cloak.*

"I'll pray for her, Father, and for you and the family," he said softly. "What a blessing for a mother to be attended to by a good priest, a priest she herself conceived."

John fell silent for a moment. "Joe, she has no idea who I am," he said with manifest pain.

"Hey Father," Joe engaged him directly, "now *that's* the good news."

John Sweeney threw his head back and laughed. Joe watched layers of concern all but vanish around the folds of his friend's eyes. *How true it is that laughter cures more ills than medicine.* That association triggered another. Was this, perhaps, the explanation for Maggie Kealey's friendship with Dr. Jim Gillespie? Gillespie was one of the funniest men he knew; Maggie Kealey's life had been otherwise bereft of humor for as long as he'd known her: going on 30 years now.

"Hey, Father, how is Maggie doing?"

"Keep her in your prayers, Joe," John answered quickly. "She's got quite a lot on her plate at the hospital." He paused. "I'll tell her you were asking after her; I know she'll appreciate that."

"Father, tell her if she needs any help, business or whatever, I'm available."

John nodded. "I will indeed, Joe. That's very kind of you." He paused again and said, "Now tell me about the world of Joe Delgado."

Joe flinched nervously. "Father, I need a little guidance."

John thought back to the first time he heard Joe Delgado's confession. It was now almost 20 years ago. He'd started the same way. Did John dare? He did. "Joe, if it's only a *little* guidance you're looking for, once again, you've come to the right place."

Joe laughed reflexively and John thought he saw a flicker of recognition of that moment, of a time when each was a different man. Neither had quite gotten things right back then, but this was a new day, John reminded himself. And the God they both served had proven Himself to be a God of second chances.

"Father, I almost don't know where to begin."

"Start at the end," John suggested with a shrug.

Joe looked down at the floor to collect his thoughts. "Father, there is some very bad stuff going down. And once again I've found myself, if not in the middle of it, at least close enough to be able to smell the sulfur. It's now come to a head, and I don't know how to proceed, or even *if* I can proceed."

John sat back in the wing chair and exhaled. "Oh my ..." He sat there in silence for several moments then leaned forward and said, "Okay, lay it out for me, Joe."

Approximately 40 minutes later Joe Delgado finished. John Sweeney had not said a word. He was quite simply awestruck at the scope of what he heard. He sat speechless as his friend shared the HM Inc business mission and how it fit into the larger framework of a global revolution in Life Sciences. The plan's pure audacity numbed him. A number of times during the account, he thought of the scriptural passage where Christ tells his disciples it was not what entered a man from outside that was impure but what originated in the interior of his being. The "designs of men" were an endless source of mystery to John Sweeney. He recalled that Pope John Paul II liked to quote the church fathers when he referred to these designs as the "mystery of iniquity," which were, he reminded the people of God, nothing more than the "absence of good."

John thought what he just heard was something more than simply the absence of good. He had questions and he needed time to formulate them. But he also needed more information. "Joe, do you think there is a "mission control" for this global black market in human embryos?"

"Father, I don't," he replied quickly. "At least, not yet."

John Sweeney stared at him expressionless. "Who are the major players, at this point?"

"The U.S., the Brits, the Israelis, and the Chinese."

"What's the going rate for a single embryo?"

"Father, it ranges from $2000 all the way up to $50,000, depending."

"Depending on what?"

"On origin. If the sperm and eggs came from what they call "productive lines," *countries* will pay a premium; if they come from high achievement lineage, *couples* will pay an exorbitant premium.

"So the governments of these countries are actively involved in acquiring these embryos?"

"Yes, Father." He paused. "But they are careful to make sure they have plausible deniability, lest their citizenry question why they are diverting tax dollars for something so, ah, speculative. The morality of it in Europe and Asia is not an issue. This of course gives them an unfair advantage, or so our scientists claim."

"But our new president is going to change that?"

"Yes, Father."

"Which is precisely why he named an evangelical Christian as his point man at the National Institute of Health."

"Yes, Father."

"So, it's a foot race: a global foot race. With all the developed nations throwing money at this thing, assuming it will pay out in, what, patents for new discoveries?"

"Yes, Father."

"And these new discoveries will be used to enrich a few fortunate countries?"

"Yes, Father, and bend the cost curve for healthcare delivery, which is now the aging developed world's most intractable problem."

John Sweeney gazed out the window. He saw the snow falling more heavily now under a street lamp and beginning to drift on a neighbor's driveway across the street. "But the beneficiaries will not be the aged or infirmed?"

"No, Father."

"And who is going to tell these people they don't, what, qualify?"

"The government."

John Sweeney thought of his mother, dying slowly, seven blocks away. *Hurry mom. Please hurry.* He fell silent. Neither man spoke for several minutes.

"I don't see it, Joe," John Sweeney said, breaking the silence. "Man's been here before. It didn't work. What *is* all of this but a new Tower of Babel? Do these people think the Creator of the universe is going to stand by and allow His creation to create new life on their own, in *their* own image, in a *laboratory*?" He paused in deep reflection. "I just don't see it."

Joe smiled. "Well, Father, you may be right. But I can assure you the nations of the earth are quite busy constructing that tower, and regard it as having life or death importance to their economic survival. They see this fourth great revolution as the new line of demarcation between haves and have nots."

John Sweeney nodded soberly. "Which brings us back to you, Joe. Is HM asking you to get involved in any of this?"

"No. At least, not yet, Father. I don't have, nor do I expect to have, any oversight role in Bio Freedom, the company HM formed from the rollup of the three largest U.S. biotech firms focused on embryonic stem cell research."

"So, what's the problem?"

"Well, if Bio Freedom is successful, HM's Therapeutic Division will be commercializing those discoveries."

"Which means you'll be directly involved in the marketing of these, what, "miracle cures?"

"Well, not directly involved in the marketing, but I *will be* directly responsible for the division's profitability, and this is expected to be an important part of that."

John Sweeney's eyes clouded. "Joe, tell me how this thing would work."

Joe shifted uneasily. "Father, what Bio Freedom will no doubt do is to use the financial world's model for buying "futures.""

John nodded. "Okay, how does *that* work?"

Joe paused before replying. He was now acutely embarrassed and about to become more so. "Basically, Father, you find the biggest, most reliable 'source pools' in the world for these embryos, and you just throw money at the scarcity, and the people who control it. The countries, or private firms, with the biggest bags of money command the supply. When the embryos come onto the market, they're already under contract, so to speak. They're directed to *your* supply chain and into your laboratories."

"Where they are chopped into pieces and used for therapeutic discovery?"

"Yes Father," Joe replied softly.

"And HM Inc has the biggest bag of money?"

"Well, yes and no," Joe answered, surprised by the question. "They have, uh, assets they can sell to raise enough cash to outbid whole nations."

John's interest was piqued. "Joe, can you give me an example of one of these assets?"

Joe hesitated before replying. "Father, this is totally confidential, right?"

Sweeney smiled. "If you're asking am I going to go out and buy HM stock on a hot tip, the answer is no. I'm still trying to pay off Visa from my last vacation."

The thought of a priest with a Visa credit card balance was too rich for the accountant in Joe Delgado at this late hour of the evening. He waved his arms in front of him signaling he did not want to hear any more. Then he collected himself for highly sensitive disclosure. "Father, HM owns one of the three major broadcast networks. The network, uh, fulfilled its mission. It helped elect the man they wanted to the highest office in the land. He has repaid them in kind. He has liberated U.S. scientists, and their commercial patrons in return. They are now free to conduct any research they want on human embryos, and the actual research itself will be funded by American taxpayers. The network is now in the process of being sold, and some portion of the net proceeds will be earmarked for 'human embryonic futures.'"

John Sweeney shuddered. The barbarism simply left him numb. "And this division of HM, this Bio Freedom, will be given some portion of that money to buy 'futures contracts' for large supplies of these tiny little people for HM's research labs?"

"Yes, Father," Joe replied.

"But you won't be involved in any of that."

"No, Father. I will have no involvement in any of that."

"Bio Freedom has its own chief financial officer who does what you do for this new pharmaceutical division?"

"Yes, Father."

John Sweeney looked away. "Suppose it doesn't work?"

Joe Delgado's eyes glazed over. "Father?"

"Suppose these Bio Freedom scientists fail? Suppose they can't get these mysterious little embryonic stem cells to work for their intended purposes? From what I understand, nobody's had any success with them. It's only the adult stem cells which have shown any promise."

Joe eased back in his chair in momentary silence. "Well, I suppose HM would be forced to acknowledge the failure, and, I suppose, sell the unit."

"The unit?"

"The business unit, Father. Meaning the company: Bio Freedom."

"Then what? What would that mean for you?"

Again, silence. "I really don't know, Father." He shook his head. "I really don't know."

John Sweeney sat back in his wing chair. His head was pounding. Tonight would be a difficult night. He knew it would end, not in a bed, but in a pew in a darkened church.

# 29

---

The doors swung open, the music began, the procession started. Maggie Kealey counted 62 priests in two columns inching forward from the back of the church. They were followed by six bishops who were followed by one cardinal who was, in turn, followed by one very sad priest.

The funeral rite for Mary Kate Sweeney had commenced.

Only 12 of the bishops and priests could fit on the small St. Martha's altar at one time; the others occupied the first three pews on either side of the main aisle.

The crowd that came to honor the mother of a priest spilled onto the church steps and beyond. Narbrook police hastened to cordon off Narbrook Avenue and re-route traffic. The little church's pews held 320 souls. Police estimated there was double that number outside.

The family sat in three pews behind the priests on the right hand side of the aisle facing the altar. Barry, Kevin and Brendan flew in with their families: 12 children among them. Eileen sat between Brendan's twin boys in the second pew. John sat as though transfixed on the top step of the altar. The cardinal sat on the right side of the altar in a scarlet cassock with white surplice. Next to him sat the Archbishop of Cincinnati, Joseph J. McManus, in a magenta cassock with a white surplice.

When the church was fully settled, John stood, his back to the tabernacle. He looked at the casket at the foot of the altar for a long moment. The church fell silent. Slowly, deliberately, he made the sign of the cross, and in a voice husky with emotion he began the introductory rite. "Let us begin, together, this celebration of the life, death and resurrection of our faithful sister in the Lord, Mary Kate Sweeney, in the name of the Father, and of the Son, and of the Holy Spirit …"

He finished the Opening Prayer and sat down to await the readings. Cardinal O'Hallaran nodded to him consolingly. The readings, and the music, were selected by Eileen. No one in the family contested her choices.

The first reading was from Wisdom, chapter 3, on the souls of the just. The responsorial psalm was taken from Psalm 40 on prayer and gratitude. The second reading was from Peter's first letter on Christian suffering. They were read in succession by brothers Barry, Kevin and Brendan.

Even before Brendan had returned to his pew, John was on his feet and moving to the pulpit. He was wearing his game face. He gazed out at the congregation, held up the large red lectionary with both hands and intoned, "May the Gospel of our Lord Jesus Christ be in my mind, on my lips and in my heart."

He then set the lectionary back on its stand, stole a glance at the casket, and began to read from the Gospel of The Beatitudes from Matthew 5. When he had finished, he waited for the sound of over 1000 souls to settle inside and outside the church; he looked yet again at the casket of the one among them who was now and forever sitting, settled, in paradise.

He looked through the doors at the rear of the church and saw a portion of the throng assembled out on the steps and down into the street. It was an unseasonably mild early spring day, with a surprisingly high sun melting the vestiges of a recent snow storm. His eyes canvassed the familiar and unfamiliar people sitting below his feet. He saw relatives from Ireland. This astonished him. What was it about being Irish, he wondered, that permitted such a pre-ternaturally intuitive understanding of death?

He saw family and friends and former coaches and teammates. He saw those he at one time knew but whose names he could no longer remember. He was certain some of them were friends of his brothers and sisters. In the day, as houseguests, they were fel-low anarchists scheming ways to roil the fragile order in Mary Kate Sweeney's home. Many were parishioners. His eyes sought Maggie Kealey. He saw her sitting between two large men, neither of whom was Jim Gillespie. He recalled advising her to be careful to avoid Gillespie's companionship in anything other than business or business social settings, lest she give scandal as a woman whose marriage to William Kealey, not having been declared null, was still valid in the eyes of her church. He saw Michael and Carol Burns. Carol's smile was pitch perfect for the occasion. He also saw Joe and Fran Delgado. Their body language said, 'Only for you, Sweeney.'

His eyes rested on his brother priests. *Immaculate Mother, how is it I see my pain in their eyes? What men! Thank you, thank you, thank you, Mother, for the great privilege of being counted among their number.* His heart was so stirred at the sight of so many of them drawn to *his* pain, he had to fight off the urge to blurt out his love and gratitude. He briefly reflected on their struggle to live holy, chaste lives in imitation of their Master. Indeed, it was *his* struggle, and the pas-sage of time had not made it any easier. These men, he reminded himself, were imperfect in the way of all men. But they were good men, whose pursuit of holiness was the single animating force in their lives.

He looked down at the Lectionary, briefly. He looked up and glanced at the choir in the loft. He fixed his gaze on his mother's casket one last time, cleared his throat and began what his parishio-ner's would later refer to as "The Funeral Sermon on the Mount."

"To live the Beatitudes is to live the life of Christ.

"Mary Kate Sweeney lived the Beatitudes.

"She was a woman poor in spirit. She had an Old Testament filial fear of the Lord, anchored in a bedrock hope for his mercy. She never knew, or permitted herself to know, indulgence. Nor would she permit her children's direct exposure to it in any form. She well understood its corrupting nature, its power to make the trivial appear priceless and the priceless appear trivial. I remember showing her my first paycheck as a priest and asking her what she thought dad would have thought of it. She said, 'Your father would have told you to go back and demand a raise.'" Laughter reverberated throughout the church. "Mom, I said, 'what do *you* think? She looked at me as only a true believer could look at another and said, 'I think you should return it.'" There was a sound of rippling 'ahs'. "She lived a life of authentic interior poverty. When I told her that in her later years, she said, 'Well, I suppose you have to credit your father's cheapness for part of that.'" More laughter. "The truth, however, was that she never lost a sense of what was important, what was *most* important, in this temporal life. Her love and devotion to our blessed Lord in the Eucharist, in the Tabernacle, and in the Monstrance, was the ordering principle in her life. And because it was the ordering principle in her life, it became the ordering principle in the lives of her children.

"Because Mary Kate Sweeney was poor in spirit, she was able to mourn with true piety. She mourned the premature death of a husband she loved dearly. She mourned the shocking and terrifying death of her second son, buried alive in an avalanche of steel on 9/11. She mourned a daughter who gave up a personal life to care for her in her decline. She mourned with and for friends and family during their dark nights of purgation. Time and again I've been told by relatives, even as recently as this weekend, that it was my mother, taking on their yoke of suffering, who helped them through the most difficult moments of their lives. She mourned our hopelessly fractured church that she loved with a mother's heart. She mourned the decline of a once great country that would no longer offer her grandchildren the hope it offered her grandparents. At the end of her life she mourned, along with the rest of us, the loss of a mind as keen and penetrating as a cosmic laser."

He paused. "Mary Kate Sweeney mourned with the heart of Christ because she understood what the French poet Paul Claudel said to be a fundamental truth of human existence: 'Jesus did *not* come to explain away suffering or to remove it,' Claudel wrote. 'He came to fill it with his presence.'

"And because she mourned, she was meek. I can remember when we were growing up, friends would visit and they would tell mother what they thought was wrong with Holy Mother Church. 'She doesn't respect women.' 'She got the birth control question wrong.' 'Priests should be permitted to marry.' 'She should dial down the moral truth message— no one wants to hear it— and concentrate on social justice, which is what Christ really came to teach us.' Mother would always listen politely. Invariably, when the friend would finish she would just look at them and simply say, 'Oh.' This would often confound them; they would repeat their critique. She'd nod again and say, 'Oh.' It was her way of letting them know, in perfect meekness, she had indeed understood and she was not prepared to argue the faith, even with friends. She believed the faith was to be *lived*. And she lived it with a meekness that belied her exquisite mind and passionate Irish heart. She understood it to be the 'pearl of great price' that none of us deserve, but all of us who receive it must give an accounting for. And this allowed her to live a life of gratitude which, itself, bears the unique imprint of meekness.

"And because my mother was meek, she was able to hunger and thirst for righteousness. How passionate she was, how faithful, to the plight of the unborn! She'd pack us all up on Saturday mornings to carry placards outside the very hospital that employed her. Doctors and nurses and administrators would wave to her on their way in. Some even saluted her; although it wasn't until I got older that I learned that particular signal wasn't actually a salute!" Loud roar. "She taught us through her example that what Pope Paul VI said was true: 'There can be no peace without justice.' She saw this great issue of our day as a matter of simple justice. Children who were conceived were already alive and deserved the same constitutional rights and protections as the rest of us. A number of times I heard her beg women, particularly minority women, who were going in for abortions to please deliver their children and let her adopt them. We'd be standing beside her when she was talking to these women. The women would just look at her, and all of us, and laugh." Pause, small smile. "I used to tell our younger brothers and sisters we were going to put all those little babies in their beds, and it would be their jobs to feed and change them." Raucous laughter again.

"And because mother hungered and thirsted for righteousness, she was able to show mercy. First and foremost, she was merciful to her sons." Laughter. "After squinting into the red glare of one of Barry's report cards, she asked for a pair of sunglasses." More laughter. "Yet his only 'punishment' was mandatory tutoring from his oldest brother. The next quarter we both flunked math." Explosion of laughter. "Over the years, I saw mother show mercy routinely to those in her own family who let her down, and in some cases, even betrayed her. But mother's greatest manifestations of mercy were extended to those who deliberately hurt her. I watched her interact with people in the parish who had criticized her severely for the way she was raising her family. These were women who had husbands and half as many children, mind you." Mild laughter. "Yet I never saw her sense of mercy strained beyond endurance. She would greet these ladies time and again as though they were ardent admirers. I don't have to tell you what an indispensible lesson that was for a future pastor." Prolonged laughter.

"And because Mother was merciful, she was favored with a pure heart, which is itself a great gift from almighty God. St. Augustine said the Beatitudes were a ladder we ascended only one rung at a time. But John Paul II said the Beatitudes were like a fountain perpetually sustained by an underground spring. He said the great upsurge in souls was a work of the Holy Spirit working through his seven gifts, lifting us from one gift, one virtue, one Beatitude, to the next. He said true purity of heart was the penultimate Beatitude because it alone permitted the soul to be a peacemaker.

"And Mother was a peacemaker. She understood the need for, and value of, reparative suffering. She didn't court suffering, ever; nor did she make it feel unwelcome when it arrived. I saw this first hand in our own family, in our extended family, at the hospital where she worked as a nurse for 32 years, and here in the parish. She always sought the high ground in any dispute, and had the wisdom to 'work back from love,' as she called it. I once asked her what that meant, and she explained that in virtually any situation in life there is a solution anchored in selfless love, and the Christian's task is to find it. She always reminded us we had to look no further than the Cross to understand what true, unconditional, selfless love looked like.

"The reason only the pure of heart can be peacemakers is because it is only the authentic peacemaker who can be persecuted. The true peacemaker understands the work of true and lasting peace is the work of repairing the disunity brought about by sin. The true peacemaker understands that this work necessarily requires that they must be persecuted by a world that rejects the very notion of sin, and, by extension, the need for a Redeemer. At its core, this persecution is merely yet another face of the demonic. GK Chesterton saw this clearly. Toward the end of his life he wrote that in the final analysis the great ideological battles in the modern and post modern ages are not between the progressive and the traditionalist, the statist and the republican, the collectivist and the capitalist, but between the Catholic Church and her enemies. He said if the Catholic Church is *for* something, her enemies are against it; if she is *against* it, they are for it. In our time, the persecution has begun anew. Mother saw this coming and prepared us for it. She told us the church in our children's generation would be "smaller and holier" because the persecution would grow in intensity. We are already seeing this, are we not?

"We know Mary Kate Sweeney lived the Beatitudes because she died in that glorious mystical wellspring that is the indelible mark of the Beatitudes.

"One month ago today, Barry initiated a family teleconference with Dr. Burke. He told us mother would not live to see Spring." Long painful pause. "She would die, literally, in the winter of her years." Longer pause. "Dr. Koblinski, from the U.S. Catholic Bioethics Center, was also on the call, for which the family is forever grateful.

"The question became: what do we do when mother's system begins to shuts down? Specifically, what do we do when she can no longer swallow, which is the signature calling card of death in an Alzheimer patient? Do we insert tubes to provide an unspecified number of hours of nutrition, or at the very least hours of hydration? Or do we accept this sign as the finger of God at work in a good and faithful servant?

"Dr. Koblinski re-iterated church teaching on end of life. Ordinary measures, he advised, can be viewed by loved ones as extraordinary measures when the body itself is shutting down and the soul is preparing for departure.

"We understood. We did. Yet we could not reach a consensus on what to do. None of us was able to advise the rest of us. So torturous was the dilemma, we could not even discuss it among ourselves. Who among us would have denied the mother who suckled us water? Who among us could have stood by to see her, in pain, uncomprehending, her body being invaded by tubes at the very moment it had begun to collapse under the weight of a lifetime of suffering?

"By the infinite mercy of God, we were spared. Three days ago, Eileen called to tell me she could no longer get mother to take food or water. She was not able to swallow. I hung up and went to the church to pray. I didn't know what else to do. I came out with the intention of calling Barry to hastily arrange another teleconference. When I re-entered the rectory, Carmella told me Eileen had called again. I immediately returned the call. She answered sobbing. I instantly knew."

The church was completely still. The only sound was of women crying.

He paused to compose himself. "Clearly, God didn't have a high level of confidence that the Sweeneys would get this thing right." Pent up explosion of laughter.

John waited for it to settle. "He determined, alone, that a woman whose life had made visible the Beatitudes in our time and place, whose human failings had been purified by a lifetime of suffering, whose reparative suffering for her family, her church, and her country had been, at long last, exhausted, was finally, sufficiently prepared for the glorious gift of gifts, the crown of all crowns: a face to face encounter with her Creator."

He paused for effect. "We accept His decision."

He paused one last time. "Mother, pray for us."

He turned and walked back to his chair behind the altar. As he did so he began chastising himself. *Why? How dare you turn your own mother's elegy into a tutorial? Why the social and political commentary? Why the family secrets? What is the matter with you! You are an absolute disgrace!*

As he approached his chair, he observed both the cardinal and the archbishop of Cincinnati. He was startled to see tears streaming down their faces. He was even more surprised to observe that neither man was making any attempt to either mask or dry his tears. He turned and sat down and was shocked to see a sea of white handkerchiefs in the pews. For a nanosecond, he thought he had happened upon a late inning Phillies rally. Then he saw men and women dabbing eyes, drying cheeks, blowing noses. He looked quickly for his own family. He almost burst out laughing. It appeared they were all sharing a single hanky. He caught his brother, Barry's eyes. The look said everything. He immediately felt peace in his heart. *Thank you, Immaculate Mother. Thank you for not allowing me to blow my own mom's eulogy. God, how I love you and need you. Would you please tell my mom how much I miss her? Please ask her to pray for me, for all of us, every day: that we all make it home safely.*

He felt a tap on his knee. It was his best friend, the archbishop of Cincinnati. He was signaling John to stand and begin the Prayer of the Faithful in preparation for the Offertory. He stood and recited the prayer. As he did so he was aware of a warm, ethereal current of energy coursing through and around the sanctuary. He thought he smelled lilacs, or perhaps it was roses. He wasn't sure. But all of a sudden the altar felt, and smelled, like a great garden in the midst of some celestial greenhouse. He quickly looked at the other bishops and priests on the altar to see if any were experiencing what he was. It appeared they were. They had strange smiles on their faces and were opening and closing their eyes in a state of what looked to be mild euphoria.

The organist struck the opening notes of the Offertory Hymn, *Be Not Afraid*. From the choir loft came the sounds of Cherubim and Seraphim. John glanced up quickly, checking for wings. Soon the entire church seemed bathed in a light, mystical mist. Problems and anxieties, urges and impulses, grievances and resentments, all seemed to loose their temporal moorings and drift toward some unseen distant horizon. John, now beginning the Offertory, and feeling all of this most acutely, immediately wondered if his mother's holy life had drawn the favor of a brief foretaste for those assembled in her honor.

After the Communion, four different Sweeneys marched to the pulpit to eulogize their mother. Church protocol called for one, one limited to four minutes. But John made no attempt to mediate that firestorm. To be Irish was to crave only one thing: a captive audience. Each of his brothers, even his sister, insisted on having their own four minutes in front of a captive audience.

They each spoke for roughly 10 minutes. *Four, forty, hey, what's the difference?*

To John's everlasting shock, the congregation appeared to actually enjoy the odd alchemy of reverent reminiscence and irreverent irrelevancy. Only brother Brendan appeared to stumble when he spoke of summer 'day trips' to the sea shore. He noted that the family packed a cooler of sandwiches and Kool Aid to avoid having to pay boardwalk food prices that his father characterized as "highway robbery." And rather than pay $2 for a single changing locker—*for all of them*— they changed in the car: *all of them.*

That would have been fine, reasonably harmless, John thought. It was not, however, reasonably harmless enough for Brendan. He insisted on sharing the dialogue of the epic battle between his mother, who adamantly refused to change in the car, and his father, who was equally adamant he was not going to shell out $2 when all of them would promise "to look the other way."

"Poor Mom," he related. "She ended up having to sit on the hot beach in a house dress."

John immediately looked at his other brothers and sisters. They're heads were bowed, and in their hands. *So much for that mystical mist.*

At the end of Mass he came down from the altar to read the funeral rite and sprinkle holy water on the casket. He couldn't put a finger on what exactly he was feeling as he did so.

And too quickly, it was over. John stood frozen for several moments as the pall bearers began slowly moving the casket to the back of the church and down the steps, and into the hearse for what would be his mother's final ride. Behind him, the cardinal nudged him gently and he began moving. In the loft, the choir began the final hymn his mother would never hear: *He Will Raise You Up.*

John followed the casket out of the church and down the steps. He was squinting into the strong sunlight.

# 30

The mansion was set back about 100 yards from the street, accessed by a long crescent driveway that began under a stone portico with a small guardhouse attached. It was built in 1920 on a bluff overlooking center city Philadelphia about ten miles away. The men who built it were, by and large, artisans and stone masons from the Italian and Irish communities south and west of City Hall. That it was ever completed was believed to have required a miraculous intercession on the part of the archdiocese's patron saint, St. John Neumann ... a German. The money to build it came from a generation of European immigrants who saw it as a statement that *they* had arrived in the New World; *their* bishop would now take his rightful place among the city fathers.

In recent years, however, the mansion had become a subject of controversy. When the scandal broke, it became a target, along with other archdiocesan "hard assets," for trial attorneys and their client victims. O'Hallaran fought like a lion to keep the state legislature from opening up a "look back" period to allow victims to sue beyond the statue of limitations. And although his legal team succeeded, the net effect of the controversy was a loss of good will among a suddenly restless flock. Conventional wisdom argued for a sale of the property, with proceeds going to the victims, and the mansion's only resident, the cardinal, taking a modest suite of rooms at the nearby archdiocesan seminary. From all reports, the cardinal himself did not think much of the idea.

On a wet, positively dismal spring morning, Maggie Kealey drove through the black wrought iron gates and proceeded up the driveway, through the portico, in search of a place to park. She saw three unmarked spots, two of which were empty, about 40 yards from the mansion, and pulled into the first one. She turned the ignition off and paused to gather herself. She was nervous and the chemical disturbance triggered recollections of what she used to feel before concerts, when she held first chair in the oboe section of the Philadelphia Orchestra. She closed her eyes and prayed. *Blessed Virgin, please accompany me. I am so anxious right now. Calm me. Guide me, that I may make our case in a humble, convincing manner. Let the cardinal see that I only want to do what is right for our young Catholic families. Stir his spirit through your spouse, Mother, that we will live what your son's church teaches.* She paused and remembered Father Sweeney's counsel in prayer. *But it is not success I seek this day, heavenly Mother, but rather faithfulness to the work I have been given to do.*

She pulled an umbrella from the back seat, gathered her dark leather attaché and got out of the car. She opened the umbrella, 'bleeped' the car door lock with the remote, and briefly reflected on the propriety of locking a car on a cardinal archbishop's gated, and guarded, grounds. She slung the shoulder strap over her right shoulder and made her way to the front door.

She rang the bell and the door opened. She was taken aback at the sight of Kathleen Hamilton standing behind it, smiling. Kathleen was a former classmate of Maggie's in high school and college, and had married Jim Hamilton immediately after graduation. Hamilton was one the city's most successful developers and one of the church's finest sons. "Maggie, his eminence told me you were coming; I stayed just long enough to say hello, and goodbye."

Maggie entered the foyer, momentarily flustered. She did a quick sort to account for the co-incidence and came up empty. "Kate, what a surprise! How is Jim?" On a beautiful moonlit night during the summer of her junior year in college, while Bill Kealey was away at Harvard's summer football camp, Jim Hamilton had proposed to Maggie on a sand dune in Avalon. Shocked into speechlessness, Maggie never responded. She couldn't remember a time after that when she didn't feel tension in his presence. It was acerbated when the two couples would double date, prior to, and after, their weddings, which were intentionally scheduled only two weeks apart. When Bill left, they had drifted apart. Maggie couldn't remember the last time she had seen Jim or Kate Hamilton, other than in the society pages.

"Jim is great, Maggie. But how are *you?*" Kate's eyes revealed genuine concern, which greatly irritated Maggie.

"Oh, holding up best I can, for a grandmother," she replied, ever mindful that the Hamiltons were childless. "What brings you here? I hope I'm not interrupting?"

Kate Hamilton went into overdrive to assure Maggie Kealey she was not interrupting anything. "No, no, I was just leaving! Honestly. His eminence is a dear friend of ours and Jim asked me to do some interior design work on the first floor. Pro bono, of course." She handed Maggie a business card. "Jim has me doing more and more of this kind of work for his clients. I actually like it, and it gets me off the golf course." Small smile. "I mean there are only so many days a week you can play golf."

*My, my, Kate. I'd almost forgotten how tedious you really are. But thanks for reminding me. Now I remember why I haven't called you in, what has it been, 30 years? And as for the business card, I'll be sure to give you a call when we re-model our emergency room.* "Well, this has certainly been a treat," Maggie said, smiling diplomatically. "Ah, do you suppose his eminence is in?"

Kate laughed awkwardly. "Of course he is! Here I am,

monopolizing your time. Shame on me. But it's just so good to see you, Maggie, after all these years." Her eyes narrowed slightly. "Now, let me tell his eminence you're here." She turned and departed with an abruptness that surprised Maggie. *Well, I certainly hope I didn't offend.*

Presently, his eminence appeared. He was alone. Maggie imagined Kate Hamilton sitting at the prelate's desk writing a personal note in elegant long hand, advising 'his eminence' of Maggie Kealey's disastrous marriage to Bill Kealey and how she had yet to file for annulment, and then leaving her business card next to her signature.

"Well, well, if it isn't Philadelphia's most celebrated woman executive," O' Hallaran said as he approached, hand extended, behind a wary smile. Maggie immediately sensed his discomfort.

"Thank you, your eminence, for making time to see me. I can only imagine how many demands there are on your schedule," she replied with a trace of nervousness.

He made a modest attempt to put her at ease. "Come, let's go into the parlor. We'll be more comfortable there."

She followed him, staring at his scarlet skull cap and crimson sash. She noticed he waddled a bit and wondered if there was a treadmill in one of the mansion's reported 16 rooms. They passed through at least two smaller rooms she thought would have been ideal for their discussion, before coming to a large formal sitting room with elegant furnishings. She followed the aging prelate to two facing couches, separated by a large glass coffee table, in the center of the room. Without waiting for Maggie, O'Hallaran walked to the farther of the two, turned and sat down, unceremoniously. Once settled, he gestured for her to sit opposite him. She removed a coat which no one had offered to take, and carefully set it, along with her umbrella and a slightly moist attaché, on the thickly carpeted floor beside her feet.

She sat and immediately reached down to open the attaché and remove a thick folder marked Regina Hospital: NFP Clinic. She placed the folder on her lap and folded her hands, resting them lightly on the folder. She inched forward on the sofa until she was sitting on its edge. She leaned forward slightly in the position of a supplicant, the very position she had intended to avoid. The prelate made no such attempt to engage. He sat deep in his thick sofa, knees slightly more elevated than his robed bottom, eyeing her carefully.

*He's inscrutable. What was he told? Will he listen with an open heart?* She waited for him to speak. When he was certain she was ever so slightly unnerved, he did. "Well, Mrs. Kealey, your friend, Bishop Bancone, who speaks highly of you, incidentally, tells me you have a problem."

*WE have a problem, your eminence.* "Actually your eminence, Bishop Bancone is a former college roommate of our chief of oncology, and the new head of our Women's Clinic, Dr. James Gillespie. I've never had the privilege of meeting his Excellency." *There, off to a good start, are we?*

His eminence was not accustomed to being corrected, certainly not by supplicants. "Well, it seems I was misinformed," he replied, blanching slightly. "So, what is it you wanted to talk about Mrs. Kealey?

*Ok … should I begin, or wait for the interpreters?* "I've come to request an archdiocesan audit of Regina Hospital, your eminence."

O'Hallaran shifted uneasily. "A what?"

"An audit, your eminence," she replied evenly. "A complete review of our OB/GYN practices in light of the USCCB's ERD's."

He nodded slowly. "You mean the Ethical and Religious Directives for Catholic Health Care?"

"Yes, your eminence."

"Why an audit?"

She paused and replied, "I don't believe our hospital is in compliance."

"Don't you have a Director of Mission, someone from the Order?"

She nodded. "Yes. Sister Kathleen Sullivan, she's our DOM; but we need someone more familiar with the Directives."

O'Hallaran stared at her. She had no idea what he was thinking and it temporarily distracted her. "Mrs. Kealey, perhaps you could give me some specific indication of what your concerns are?

She had prepared for the meeting by working back from this single question. "I can, your eminence," she said quickly. She opened her folder and removed a two page memo she'd prepared in anticipation. Although she had taken great pains to memorize its contents, she chose to reference her talking points to heighten the gravitas.

"We have four Ob/Gyn physicians on staff. They are all dispensing oral contraceptives to our Catholic patients. They are also referring infertile Catholic patients to the Mid-Atlantic Fertility Clinic, in an adjoining suite, for In Vitro Fertilization procedures. We have reason to believe they are also referring young Catholic women in their 20's to this clinic, which is paying them up to $5000 for their eggs, which they then freeze and sell at a premium to women in their 40's ... whose own eggs have a much lower success rate. They are believed to be doing the same thing with our young Catholic men, building a sperm bank for future desperate couples who will be willing to pay anything to have children."

She paused briefly and added, "We have reason to believe our doctors may be profiting from these, ah, transactions."

She sat back in the sofa to assess his reaction. There was nothing to assess. *What sort of man rises through the ranks to accept the Crosier and Miter in today's American Church? Holy Mother of God, where do they find men like this?* "These men, and they are all men, are also dispensing the Morning After Pill." *That's not good, can we agree?*

Nothing.

She soldiered on. "There is also the serious matter of a paper trail, for business transactions. We advertise the services of this fertility clinic in our on-line directory. In exchange, we exact annual "directory dues" of $500. This is in addition to the monthly rental income we receive for the Fertility Clinic's suite, and the ancillary revenue we receive for blood work and MRI's, and other such procedures."

Still nothing. *Am I speaking into a dead phone?*

"There is, of course, a serious, if unintended, consequence of all this, your eminence," she said, her patience nearly exhausted.

His left eyebrow lifted ever so slightly.

"The new president is said to favor legislation that mandates all hospitals provide access to 'reproductive services'. Catholic attorneys are telling us our hospitals stand a much better chance of resisting this mandate if we can prove we're not already providing similar services."

"Similar? Aren't you referring to abortion legislation, Mrs. Kealey?"

*He speaks!* She bit her tongue and prayed silently. "Your eminence, hormonal contraceptives are abortifacients."

This drew blood. His face turned a shade of crimson that, she thought, nicely matched his sash. "I am, of course, aware of that, Mrs. Kealey."

*Ah, sweet unfettered clarity.* "And, of course, the destruction of human embryos, either before or after they are cryogenically preserved, is also a form of abortion, or perhaps infanticide," she replied evenly.

"What is your intention, Mrs. Kealey, in bringing this internal matter of yours to *my* attention?"

Maggie smiled despite herself. Her patience was all but depleted. "Your eminence, if these ERD's are ignored in one hospital, what's to prevent them from being ignored in other Catholic hospitals? In fact, from what I understand, it is well known that they are being ignored!"

She paused as he squirmed. "And if these so-called 'Directives' are ignored in our Catholic hospitals, what are the faithful to conclude, except that their Church does *not* take these 'life issues,' as she refers to them, as seriously as she claims to?"

"Then put a stop to it!" The vehemence with which the cardinal spoke seemed to surprise them both.

Maggie reclined, slightly, as if from the force of the words. "I intend to," she said flatly. "I was hoping you'd see this as an opportunity to collaborate, and in the process send a signal to the other 12 Catholic hospitals in the region."

"I am not in the business of sending signals, Mrs. Kealey." Slight pause. "That is not what we bishops do."

She felt a blast furnace open somewhere in the pit of her stomach. "Then, what exactly is it, your eminence, that you bishops *do* in circumstances like this?"

He eyed her carefully to see if the insult was gratuitous. He hoped, more than thought, not. "*We teach*, Mrs. Kealey. That's what we bishops do. We teach. And the very ethical directives you cite are a direct outcome of the teaching authority of the U.S. Bishops. We have issued these directives, through the proper channels, that is to say our Conference, precisely to guide Catholic administrators like you. So that you, *you the laity*, can leaven the public square, as indeed it is your duty to do."

*In for a penny, in for a pound. She always found that a rather strange aphorism. Not today.* "And, your eminence, what if the directives are ignored? Whose responsibility is it to *enforce* them?"

"It falls to the people whose competence has placed them in a position of authority. People like you, Mrs. Kealey. You are the health care professional, not me. You have the moral responsibility to form a right conscience and act on it in the public square. Clearly, all of these things you have brought to my attention are serious violations of the moral order. They are grievously sinful acts. They must be opposed!"

*Now we're getting somewhere.* "Your eminence," she said softly, attempting to change speeds like a baseball pitcher. "I intend to close our Ob/Gyn department and open a Natural Family Planning Clinic. I'm going to bring in a NaPro technology team, with high level expertise in the Creighton Method, developed by Doctor Thomas Hilgers at the Pope Paul VI Institute. I want to set up an adoption agency on site for couples who are simply not able to have children. I want to offer NFP courses to Catholics and non-Catholic couples, every night of the week. I want to set up a teaching center for other Catholic hospitals, for our priests and seminarians, for our Catholic physicians."

She halted. He was staring vacantly. *Is he listening? Where is he? Has he left for his next appointment?* "Your eminence, please work with me on this. Let's create demand, a real market, for the sacred transmission of human life. Let's build a prototype for the whole archdiocese. Who knows? Maybe it'll end up being a prototype for the whole nation, just like our Catholic school system once was." She paused. "Our people are hungering for this, your eminence. I have met them and talked to them, and grieved with them. And they *are* grieving: grieving from wounds that are still a mystery to them. And why wouldn't they be? Those wounds were self-inflicted with the most unlikely of accomplices: Catholic doctors in Catholic hospitals."

She paused. "Let's fix it, your eminence. You and me. Send an archdiocesan team out to Regina Hospital to conduct an audit. Have them report their findings, privately, to you and to me. Then draft a personal letter to me requesting I address the issues raised in the report, and prepare for a follow up audit in one year. And—"

"Why? Why, Mrs. Kealey?" he interrupted. "Why do we need to go through all that? You know that what is going on in your hospital is in serious and direct violation of Church teaching. You have the competence and the authority, not to mention responsibility, to address these issues, privately, as you say. Why do you insist on bringing me into what is clearly an internal matter between you and the Order? You well know I have no jurisdiction in these areas. Regina Hospital is owned and operated by the Regina Order. Take the matter up with them."

She recoiled as though doused by cold water. *Holy Mother of God! Mother, what would you have me do with that? Is this simply Episcopal indifference or cowardice?*

"Your eminence, less than one percent of our fertile, Catholic child-bearing couples are using Natural Family Planning! The rest are either using abortifacient contraceptives, or are infertile from sexually transmitted diseases. We are now told septic abortions are responsible for a minimum of *five times* as many abortions as surgical procedures." She summoned the energy for a final salvo. "Is it any wonder we're closing schools and parishes?"

She missed. His body language told her none of this was of particular concern. She seethed at her futility. She had only one arrow left in the quiver. She removed it slowly, deliberately, took dead aim, and released. "Your eminence, perhaps I misunderstood. I understood Directive 71 of the *Bishop's* ERD's was to be taken, well, literally."

She did not see so much as a flicker of recognition in his eyes.

She looked down at her notes briefly to ensure she would not fumble the wording. "Anyway, this is what Directive 71 says, your eminence: 'The diocesan bishop has the *final responsibility* for assessing and addressing the issue of scandal ... considering not only the circumstances of his diocese ... but the regional and national implications of his decision ...'"

She paused and sat erect. "Now, your eminence, what am I missing?"

The cardinal engaged in a fierce struggle to get to his feet. He won, but not without a somewhat protracted battle. She immediately stood. They were separated only by a coffee table. She noted she was slightly taller than he was. He straightened his bearing, looked at his watch and said, "Nothing, Mrs. Kealey. You're not missing anything. But I will be if I don't get moving. Thank you for coming in, and please give my warmest regards to Sister Kathleen."

And with that, he was off, leaving Maggie to find her own way out.

Suddenly alone, she gathered her things and left.

# 31

Peter Feeney approached Maria Esposito's desk warily and asked, "Who's in there with him?"

She looked up from her coffee and danish, smiled, and said, "Good morning, Peter. Didn't smell you coming." She nodded toward the large aromatic cup of Starbucks on her desk.

He forced a laugh. She studied him closely. "Hey, why the long face? Mary Ellen okay?"

"Yep, fine."

"Peter! What's going on? You look terrible. Have you been sleeping?"

He was surprised by her prescience. "No."

"Why?"

"Oh, stuff ..."

She rolled her eyes. "Oh, that's real helpful."

He stood there shifting his weight from one foot to the other. "Who did you say was in there?"

"I didn't," she smiled.

"Well, who is it?"

"Oh, just stuff …"

He laughed. "It's Mobley, isn't it?"

It was her turn to laugh. "Always a safe bet on a Monday morning."

"What'd he do now?"

"Oh, I'm sure it has to do with what he *didn't* do."

"Understand he caused a bit of a ruckus with, uh, the ladies."

Her face crinkled in momentary puzzlement.

"Uh, the Women's Right ladies?"

"Oh. Well, that's the least of Mr. Mobley's difficulties."

Just then the Monday morning voice of Michael Burns rose above the clacking of nearby personal computer keyboards, above the laughter drifting up the corridor from the Account Management department, above even the din of street traffic ten stories below. It was a voice absent any lyrical quality.

Presently, a door opened, and Ed Mobley exited, shoulders hunched, eyes down. He walked quickly between Maria Esposito and Peter Feeney without acknowledging either. He did not look pleased.

Suddenly, Michael Burns appeared at the door. "Mornin' Feeney." He paused ever so briefly and said, "What the hell are you doing here?"

"Got a minute, Michael?"

Michael Burns was nothing if not a deeply intuitive man. His CFO's simple question triggered an early warning system in the pit of his stomach. He did not like the sounds of either the question or its tone. This was something serious: perhaps very bad news. He immediately suspected Feeney had received a call from Glenn Ackerman, Ultra Com's Chief Operating Officer. Maybe Henley Siliezar had received a bad report from one of Burns Advertising's clients, probably Women's Right. *I knew I couldn't trust those radicals.*

"Sure, c'mon in," he replied, trying to appear unconcerned. Peter Feeney crossed the threshold of his hopelessness and entered his CEO's suite. Before Michael closed the door after him, he glanced at Maria Esposito. Their eyes met. She shrugged her shoulders. Michael grimaced and returned his attention to his CFO, who was now standing in front of Michael's desk.

"Sit down, Peter," Michael said quietly but firmly. He noted Feeney chose to sit on the opposite side of his desk rather than in the more comfortable sitting area beyond. He studied Feeney's eyes for a hint of an agenda. *Irony*, he thought. *I taught this man how to play poker.* Once Feeney was settled and looking at him, he said, "Now, tell me. To what do I owe this unexpected pleasure?"

"I'm resigning, Michael," he said evenly.

*Holy Mother of God! What? This can't be happening. How will I explain this to New York?*

He gathered himself and replied. "May I ask why, Peter?"

"Conscience ..."

Michael knew instantly. On the train back from their trip to Ultra Com headquarters in Manhattan, Peter had bared his soul. To him, Hanley Siliezar was the anti-Christ. Entering into a business deal with him was nothing less than a Faustian bargain. He wanted no part of it. Michael had tried his best to accentuate the positives: the national profile, access to new resources, better new business prospects, more money, more money ...

Feeney had fallen silent. At the time, Michael did not think this a good sign.

"Would you like to tell me about it?"

Peter Feeney leaned forward in his chair. "I can't live with myself. It's really that simple."

Michael felt a lance thrust through the middle of his heart. He winced visibly. "I assume you're speaking of the Ultra Com deal?"

Peter shook his head. "No, Michael. That's only part of it, actually. I don't like the Women's Right deal. I don't like McKenna 'Bogartin' his way around the firm as our new Messiah. I don't like the financial reporting straight jacket Ultra Com has put us in. I don't like the attitude I smell in the halls. We've lost that sense of unity of purpose, that cohesion that made us the one firm in town everyone wanted to work for."

Michael stared out the window. From his office terrace he

could see the city's skyline, the river, and the major league sports complex. There were times he pinched himself. This was not one of them. He understood Feeney's broadside to be directly aimed at his leadership. He resented it. He struggled to control himself. "Peter, we had to expect some dislocation, did we not?"

"It's not the dislocation that's bothering me, Michael," he said softly. "We've sold out. I can feel it. And I think the others can too."

Michael flinched. "Well, yes. We certainly did sell out. And it personally enriched each of us."

*Ah yes, money. The ultimate elixir.* "Michael, I can't do this anymore. I'm sorry ..."

"You're leaving at least $1.35 million on the table if you leave now. That's not insignificant for a father of three school-age children."

Peter nodded. "It is quite significant, Michael. And I thank you for the opportunity you've given me here. It wouldn't have happened anywhere else. And I'll always be very grateful for that." His eyes fell as his voice fell.

Michael Burns studied his young protégé. He had long expected that Peter Feeney would replace him as CEO; the Ultra Com deal took that hammer out of his hands. They both understood that. He thought perhaps this was the real reason he was fielding a resignation in his office at 9:22 on a Monday morning. "Is it a matter of succession, Peter?" he gently probed.

Feeney shook his head. "No, Michael." He paused to find the right words. "No disrespect, but I wouldn't want to run the firm I see Burns Advertising becoming."

Something all too familiar detonated in Michael Burns' stomach. "That's a cheap shot!" he exploded. "Where do you get off coming in here and, and, and disrespecting me? You ingrate! I grabbed your scrawny butt out of accounting when you were just a pup and put you on a fast track to financial independence. And this is the way you repay me!?" He fought off the temptation to throw his ex-chief financial officer out of his office. He didn't want 14 years to end this way.

Sensing the inevitable, Feeney stood. The sight of him on his feet drew deep and instant remorse from Michael Burns. He was a Godfather to Feeney's first-born; they frequently talked about their faith journey on business trips, their wives collaborated in several non profits. "Peter," he said with quiet desperation, "what is this really about?"

Feeney looked down at his friend and mentor and was shocked at how small he suddenly appeared. "Michael, I just don't want any part of destroying human embryos, whether it's in the womb or in the laboratory. I think what these people are about is, is pure evil. And I can't tell you how disappointed I am in you. I never, ever, figured you would buy into anything like this! And for what, a few extra million! Michael!"

Michael Burns' head fell on his chest. He immediately understood the wound to their relationship was mortal.

Peter Feeney fought off the temptation to add something conciliatory. He opened a folder and removed a neatly typed three paragraph letter. He dropped it on Michael Burns' desk and said, "Michael, I'm prepared to work the two weeks' notice if you want me to." He paused ever so briefly. "If you don't want me to, I can be out of here today."

The figure in the chair did not look up.

Peter Feeney quietly took his leave.

* * *

They walked hand in hand down the Ocean City boardwalk. The weather and the crowd walking, jogging and biking suggested late June. It was, however, a glorious Saturday morning in early May. Michael and Carol Burns were re-tracing 40 year old steps from the spring of their youth. Heads turned as they passed. Carol Burns was 58 going on 38, a stunning beauty still capable of drawing the attention of men 15 years younger. Michael Burns, though rugged and formidable, had not aged as gracefully. Long hours, late dinners, and too little exercise had speckled his hair, shifted his weight, and slowed his step. Still, he told himself, it was *his* hand that held the hand of the most beautiful woman of her generation.

"Why so quiet?" she asked, as they passed the 9th Street Pavilion. As kids they used to "make out"— in the innocent, if non-descriptive expression of the day – underneath this very pavilion on star-lit summer nights.

"I didn't realize I was being quiet," he replied a tad more defensively than he intended. "I was just enjoying this magnificent salt air."

She knew enough not to probe. Some lessons learned over 35 years of marriage became deeply ingrained. They fought loudly and repeatedly early in their marriage. Her problems with chronic depression and his career difficulties drew them closer over time. From the bottom of her own black abyss, she had become addicted to pain medication; he had once been fired, out of work for 100 excruciating days, with a wife and five children to support. They survived by learning to lean on one another; over time they found themselves graced with a bond that was unique among their married friends.

A little over 12 years ago, they'd bought a second home on an elite private lagoon on the northern tip of the island. It quickly became the family's summer headquarters. Initially, they took great pleasure in weekend getaways in autumn, even winter. Then cometh *the* phone call from Lower Merwood Police Chief McCray. It was a few minutes past 2:00 a.m. on a Saturday morning in late October.

"Michael, ah, it's Jim. Are you aware now you're hostin' a party for over 100 high school kids at your home in Penn Valley?"

Michael remembered sitting bolt upright. He thought he was dreaming. He looked at Carol sleeping soundly beside him. "Jim? Jim, is that you?"

"Aye, t'is, Michael," Police Chief McCray replied soberly. "The neighbors are complainin' something fierce, Michael. I think it's the band that's the biggest problem. It's outside and it's quite loud. Can you hear it now, Michael?"

Michael's head shot back from the phone receiver as though it was struck. "Jim, put my sons on, either one! Those little …." Muffled sounds.

"Michael, your sons aren't here. Apparently they put to flight."

"Put to flight? You mean they took off? How the hell do you flee *your own* home?"

"Ah, Michael. Now me and the good Sergeant Harkens here, we were wondrin' the same thing."

That closed the summer home in winter, and every other season, until the little rascals had graduated college, which took only six years apiece.

Newly liberated from the perils of midnight phone calls from police chiefs, Michael and Carol Burns had taken to escaping Friday evenings on random autumn and winter weekends. Their routine seldom varied. It began with a late dinner in one of their favorite restaurants in Margate, one Barrier Island north. This was followed by snuggling on an area rug in front of a burning fireplace, where they could also watch a heavy snow falling softly into a gentle rising tide.

On Saturday mornings they would have breakfast at a small shop in the center of the island, then walk the boards. They would putter around the house until mid-afternoon and then drive to Cape May for a candlelight dinner at a favorite seaside Victorian Inn. When they returned home, Michael would put a movie in the DVD player and they'd sit on a couch, under blankets, in front of the fireplace and share popcorn. Sometimes the movies were not movies he wanted his wife to see. On those occasions, he'd end up ripping them out of the DVD player and throwing them into the fireplace. They seemed to trip wires from a past life. Generally, in those moments he'd reach into their home library of classics. If it had been a particularly grueling week, often as not, he'd pull *What about Bob*, the Bill Murray comic epic from the '90's. It had become something of a Burns family album. At least once a year, the entire clan would gather, somewhere, to see it. The family sport was shouting out upcoming lines at just the right moment.

Sundays began with Mass on the island and brunch at a hotel on the boardwalk. Then, depending on weather, they would either hang around the house and read or head back to their home in Penn Valley, where Michael would begin preparing for the week ahead. The residual hangover from his having to wrestle with work problems on a Sunday afternoon or evening was usually cited as the triggering factor for his legendary Black Mondays.

"Peter Feeney resigned," he said suddenly, as they passed the children's pavilion at 6th Street.

She wasn't sure she heard him correctly. "I'm sorry, honey. What did you say?"

He paused and said, "Should we turn around now?"

"Oh, yes, if you want." She fell silent for a moment, then asked, "Is everything okay at work, honey?"

He stifled a groan he nonetheless heard rising within his heart. "Well, I've taken a bit of a body blow," he offered softly.

The breeze picked up from the ocean and muffled his words. For over a year, Carol had tried to hide her deteriorating hearing from him. She panicked. "Honey, are you okay? Did you say the car was in the body shop?"

Michael smiled. He loved his wife. No one made him laugh, cry, and plant his feet in adversity the way she did. Some nights all it took was a look. They had been chaste in their marriage and in the period leading up to it, their teenage kissing under the board-walk notwithstanding. The fruit of that virtue, as Father Sweeney was fond of reminding them, was the depth and purity of the love they now shared.

"No, no. The car is fine, honey," he replied, taking great pains not to mention they had driven down to their shore home in it. He turned to her and said a bit deliberately, "I was saying Peter Feeney resigned Friday."

"Oh my, Michael!" she said, her eyes wide with alarm. "Why would Peter do such a thing?"

"I'm not sure you ever get the real reason," he replied, now wanting to dismiss the issue and arrest her alarm.

"Well, what did he tell you? What's he going to do?"

*Good question. Forgot to ask. Damn.* "You know, I don't really know what he's intending."

He had not succeeded in allaying her concern. "Honey, that is so strange. Maybe I should call Mary Ellen and probe her a bit. I'll bet we can fix this. Maybe it's a mid-life crisis of some kind."

"No!" he thundered, causing heads to turn in what were now unwelcome stares. "Ah, let me handle it sweetheart, "he backtracked. "Sometimes you just have to let a little time go by."

"Okay," she said before falling into an uneasy silence. He knew what was coming. She was now homing in, a one woman, heat seeking, truth commission. "Honey, what reason did he give you? I mean, after, what's it been, 14 years? He must have had a reason."

"He's no longer happy at Burns Advertising," he replied warily. "He says he doesn't like the way Ultra Com is managing us, or some of the changes he's noticing in our people's attitudes."

"Such as?" she wanted to know, suddenly alert to trouble.

Michael hedged. "Oh, you know how it is. Now that I've sold the hammer, I don't have the clout I used to have. I can't spot reward and punish performance in quite the same way. That tends to change things, Honey. It's human nature, I suppose."

Carol Burns was nothing if not intuitive. What she was hearing did not in her judgment pass the smell test. She decided to try one more plunge. "What, specifically, doesn't Peter like about Ultra Com, Michael?"

Cornered, he retreated, tactically. "He doesn't like Hanley Siliezar. Doesn't trust him. Doesn't like his plans for Ultra Com, and he doesn't like the role Burns Advertising will be asked to play in those plans."

She stopped suddenly. She released his hand. Her eyes narrowed. "Michael, what haven't you been telling me?"

Michael fidgeted. He knew his wife. She would not stop until she found the source of Peter Feeney's anxiety; and, heaven forbid, it was an anxiety she shared but he didn't. "It's actually very complicated, Sweetheart."

"No it isn't, Michael," she replied icily. "Obviously, it's about right and wrong. And that just ain't all that complicated, Honey."

He felt trapped. *Pandora's Box. So this is what it feels like opened. What to tell her? That her husband is part of a demonic plot to create a New World Order ushered in behind a Trojan horse called the Life Sciences Revolution. 'You know Honey, the one that kills off all the old people, and as many of the defective new little ones as they can ... so they can keep all the ones in between producing more and costing less.'* "The Life Sciences Revolution offers a lot of promise, Sweetheart. But its actual delivery might cause some initial pain."

"To whom?" she asked pointedly.

"To the elderly, who will have their healthcare rationed, for one."

"Who else?"

He did not want to go there. He resisted with all his powers of evasion. "Little people."

She gasped. "Who?"

"Human embryos, they will become the new lab rats."

"You're not involved in any of that?"

"No, of course not!" he said defensively.

"Then what is it exactly they want from *you*, Michael?"

She struck a nerve. He immediately sought escape routes. "I'm really not totally sure. They're talking vaguely about me helping scope out potential new markets for, I don't know, new drug treatments, I suppose."

"What kind of new treatments?"

They were now at the car. He was not one for locking doors. They climbed in and she quickly fastened her seat belt. He was not one for fastening seat belts. He started the car and did a U-turn in the middle of the street to head home. He was also not one for traffic regulations. After her groan, she resumed the interrogation. "What kind of new treatments, Michael?"

"Well, I know they're going to home in on the most expensive diseases: Alzheimer's, diabetes, breast and cervical cancer, that kind of stuff."

"Well, that all sounds good." She paused to reflect. "As long as they're not going to chop up little human embryos to do it."

"I really don't know how it's all going to work, Sweetheart. I'm supposed to get more information the end of this month."

"Really!? What's going on?"

"I've got a meeting with Siliezar and some of his people in New York."

An uneasy silence invaded the car. He was keenly aware his wife was now deep in thought. He could almost read the brain waves. *She'll send me to Father Sweeney.* "Honey, I think you should talk to Fr. Sweeney before you get in too deep. I don't like this thing. I smell sulfur."

"That's a good idea, Sweetheart."

Another heavy silence. "Maybe I should go with you."

He felt the onset of a sudden panic attack. "No, Sweetheart. I can handle it. I really can. I'll take care of it."

She turned to him. He could feel her penetrating gaze. For once, he was in no hurry to take his eyes off the road. "I know you can, Honey," she said firmly. "It's just, well, you know how trusting you are. People know they can take advantage of you. You're not always so discerning." Small smile. "I think that's why God made wives."

*Ah, finally. The answer to one of life's true mysteries.* "Well, let me get a better idea of where this is headed, then I'll check in with Fr. John."

She nodded reluctantly.

He pulled into the driveway, got out of the car, and immediately walked around to the dock behind the house. He picked up a small beach chair sitting by the garage and walked it out to the end of a floating dock. He opened the chair and set it on the edge and sat down. The tide was up and he was tempted to remove his Docksiders and let his toes dangle in the water. But he decided the water might be too cold. He just couldn't afford to put his health in jeopardy.

# 32

Rami Schatz headed for the podium clutching several sheaves of papers. His light red hair gave every indication of having been dried in a wind storm. He dropped the papers unceremoniously on the podium and nervously tugged on the lavaliere mic attached to the front pocket of his checked sports shirt. He surveyed the small group of HM Inc executives gathered in the Fountainhead conference room of the Ritz Carlton Hotel in Stanford, Connecticut. It was a seasonably warm, cloudless Saturday morning in late May, and ten of the other 11 executives were already glancing at their watches and thinking about tee times. Seated around the elliptical conference table were HM Healthcare's senior business unit managers and their corporate bosses: HM Inc's CEO Geoffrey Benton, CFO Thomas Shillingford and COO Ralph Bryant. At the moment only Benton appeared interested in what Schatz had to say.

Schatz was Bio Freedom's mercurial CEO. He had flown in the day before from his Silicon Valley headquarters on the HM Inc Gulfstream. He brought with him David Bedein, his chief molecular scientist, and Ira Berkowitz, his chief financial officer. Phil Hankinson, HM Therapeutics Division's CEO, was in the room with his two lieutenants, COO Chad Henley and CFO Joe Delgado. HM Diagnostic's new CEO, Connie Neumann, and his COO Gary Hess and CFO Don Thurlow had flown in from London on HM Inc's Challenger.

The "On the Cusp" agenda included a late dinner in a private room at the hotel on Friday evening. Saturday's sessions were scheduled to run from 8:00 a.m. through 2:00 p.m., followed by golf or tennis, and another long business dinner. Sunday morning's agenda was scheduled to begin at 9:00 a.m. in deference to those who might want to attend a morning service. A "wheels up" departure for those flying east and west was scheduled for 2:00 p.m. following a final luncheon.

Benton himself had fashioned the agenda. He wanted "the 12"— as he referred to his senior team— all on the same page. As he had explained during last evening's dinner, "The heavy brush is being cleared away." The message: the time has come for each of us to step up and deliver.

On this morning, following a light breakfast, each of the three teams would "report out" against forecast. The focus: are we "on plan?"

Bio Freedom was first up. In the back of the room, Joe Delgado studied Rami Schatz. He was said to be a brilliant engineer and businessman, a unique combination in a country known for developing technologies but not for managing companies or marketing products. Schatz had initially made his reputation as the man who had led the Israeli team that created Intel's fastest chip, and, later, developed software for local area networks that doubled the speed of data transmission. When one million Jewish immigrants fled the Soviet Union after its collapse, it was Schatz who convinced the Israeli government and American expats to set up technology incubators to put them to work. He was an iconic figure to the young Israelis who worked with him, and a bad rash for those who had to manage him. Geoffrey Benton, like all Fortune 100 CEO's, believed he could manage not so much anyone as everyone. Joe Delgado noted Benton had not taken his eyes off Schatz since the moment he arrived at the podium.

"Good Morning, America!" he said in thick dialect behind a disarming smile. "My English ... not so good." He shrugged his shoulders. "But," he tapped the side of his head with a forefinger. "This veddy, veddy good." The room exhaled into easy laughter. Joe glanced at Benton, who was nodding and smiling.

"First, let me say, we are happy with U.S. President. He's doing all good things. He appoint Dr. Collins at NIH. Dr. Collins wave some restrictions on embryonic stem cells. More to come, yes?" Big smile. "Then your president, I should say: 'my president,' gives us Biotechs one billion U.S." He paused. "Not bad for start ..." More laughter. "Now I understand what Geoffrey mean last night when he say 'the brush is finally being cleared away.' I will not worry about what else this President do for HM, but his thank you is veddy, veddy good. 'It's all good,' as America likes to say."

The room tensed immediately at the reference to the U.S. president and his most significant corporate patron. Joe, realizing Schatz had yet to be acculturated to American boardroom etiquette, thought he might be witness to a train wreck. "We are all happy no one remember HM promise that it would not harvest human embryo cells." The laughter was now all his. Joe could not believe what he was hearing. *This man is tone deaf!* "I'm happy HM has amnesia," he said while holding his forefinger to his lips and making a shushing sound. "Because not only are we going to *harvest*, we are going to *plant* too! And we are going to *water!* And we are going to *cultivate!*" He paused, wide-eyed. "We will do more with these little human embryo cells than anyone else. And we will change the way research is done, and people live, and countries enter the new world that is to come."

The silence was unnerving to all but Schatz. He plowed ahead unmindful of the land mines he was gaily tripping along the way. "So the question is: is Bio Freedom on plan?" He paused ever so briefly and looked at Benson. "The answer is: Bio Freedom is *ahead of plan*."

Joe thought about clapping to add to the comic surrealism, but thought Hankinson, in particular, wouldn't appreciate being embarrassed.

"First, the team is built." He pointed to Bedein and Berkowitz. "These men I bring from the Kibbutz." Big smile. "I leave back home all our wonderful scientists and technicians. Second, we are organized around tissue discovery. Our priority targets are Alzheimer's, Diabetes, and Parkinson's, all things happening to Boomer Babies." He stopped and pointed to Delgado. "Like him!" The laughter returned. Delgado shrugged it off. *It's a long season.* "Third, everyone working veddy, veddy hard. Into the night, every night. But happy. We will make history. Everybody sings all the time. We love our work."

He stepped away from the podium and lifted a small laptop from an adjoining table onto the flat surface below the light and the mic. He clicked on his power point presentation. Immediately an intricately shaded map of the world materialized on a large screen behind and to the left of the podium. Joe squinted to read the legend. He thought his eyes were playing tricks on him because what he was reading made no sense.

"Welcome to the Great Easter Egg Hunt!" Shatz proclaimed with all the grace of an East European politician. He removed a compressed silver laser pointer from his shirt pocket and extended it to its full length. He pointed to a chart that explained the world-wide ratio of bunny rabbits to human eggs. Then he pointed to the difference between Bio Freedom bunny rabbits, which were colored red, white and blue, and all the other bunny rabbits which were colored egg white.

"We talk now about supply chain. What we see is: Bio Freedom is winning the Easter Egg Hunt! Look ..." He pointed to China. "The bunnies represent fertility clinics. We have signed contracts with more than half the clinics in the country. Our next closest competitor is a country!" He paused to let that settle before pointing to Russia. "This is all government oil money, corrupt oligarchy, and they are unnecessarily bidding up what should be commodity prices," he said with evident contempt. "But as you can see, we are buying more eggs and sperm from them than they are able to buy from themselves!"

His glee was off-putting. "This is what I say to the Russians: 'to compete with us, you too must sell off a big American network!" Then Rami Schatz did something Joe Delgado had never seen done in a corporate boardroom before. He grabbed the underside of his right forearm with his left hand and thrust it vigorously in the air toward the country on the map called Russia.

Big smile.

Big silence.

"Excuse me," Joe said a bit too sharply.

Heads turned. Joe immediately had second thoughts about the wisdom of an interruption. "Yes, Mr. Boomer," Schatz immediately replied. "Am I going too fast?"

Joe felt a familiar warmth in the pit of his stomach. It rose quickly despite his efforts to stifle it. He felt hot coals lodge in his throat. *What does he resent? That I'm staff and not line?* "Do I understand you to be saying we are in the business of buying more eggs than we could possibly use?"

Heads turned back to the podium. "Of course," Schatz exclaimed in the manner of a man who had discovered it is always better to beg forgiveness than ask permission.

"Why would we be doing that?"

"Because the people with the most eggs at the end of the game … win."

Joe's mind was racing to seal off borders. "Why?"

"Because we are in a footrace with the whole world. Everyone needs the eggs: universities, private companies, whole countries. Sperm is easy. Men are always prepared to pleasure themselves. It's a waste to pay them!" Big smile. "But, no eggs, no embryos. No embryos, no tissues. No tissues, no discovery. No discovery, no products. No products, no company. No company, no jobs." Brief pause, small smile. "I don't know about *you,* Boomer, but I like to work."

Joe was dogged by nature. He understood Rami Schatz was an intellectual gymnast. Schatz was the hare in this race. *Still ...* "But, and please correct me if I'm wrong, *and understand you do so at your peril,* Bio Freedom's mandate is tissue discovery for HM Healthcare's commercialization. What does operating a black market for women's eggs, and men's sperm, have to do with that?"

Henley said later he could hear "swords being unsheathed." Schatz looked at Benton. Benton looked at Schatz.

"We are in the business of making money, yes, Boomer?" Schatz fired back. "So, would HM shareholders object if we create ancillary revenue streams?"

Joe's eyes never left the other man's pupils.

Schatz read this, mistakenly, as acquiescence. "Americans do not want their government to create and destroy embryos for research purposes, but that doesn't mean *we* can't!" Smile. "There are too many research labs here and around the world that will come to depend on us for their supply. Many of these labs are on university campuses. Big, green, wealthy American campuses. This will become big business for us."

"We are in the business of healing suffering and extending life," Joe replied with an edge. "Check the mission statement."

"That's the difference between us line guys and you staff guys," Schatz said, upping the ante as he looked at Benton. "We create markets; you create documents."

Benton stood. He was a large man with a large head and even larger shoulders. Joe estimated maybe 6'4" and possibly 275 pounds. He had been a football player, an offensive tackle, at Michigan, and won All Big 10 honors in both his junior and senior seasons. The mere sight of him standing, hands on hips, saying nothing, induced stillness in the room.

Benton sat down. Joe was impressed. Not a word had been said. Yet the whole room changed temperature. Benton waved at Schatz to continue.

Schatz clicked on his next slide. "Well, as I was saying, there are whole countries competing for egg futures. Look at England: their government has committed $8 billion over the next ten years; Russia, $12 billion; China, $6 billion; even Canada, $4 billion." He glanced at Joe. "And here in the U.S. we have states competing with each other. The California state legislature has committed almost $1 billion; Connecticut, $350 million; Florida, $600 million; Illinois, $400 million; Maryland, $700 million; Massachusetts, $800 million; Ohio, $300 million; Virginia, $400 million." He paused and scanned the room and settled on Joe. "Do I need to go on?"

No takers.

Save Joe Delgado. "So, what are we paying for these eggs?"

"Going rate is about $5000 for one retrieval cycle," Schatz replied. "Of course, when you buy wholesale..." Toothy grin. "In global markets we buy for less," he said as he shrugged his shoulders. He was not in the habit of divulging trade secrets, even among corporate partners.

"How about the high end stuff? Chad Henley asked.

Schatz smiled. "Up to $50,000 for the 'good' DNA."

"What's the definition of 'good'? Thomas Shillingford demanded.

"Ah, well, there the beauty is in the idea of the beholder."

"Speak plainly," Shillingford snapped impatiently. Joe sat up in his seat. This was getting interesting.

If Rami Schatz felt defensive, he gave no indication. Joe had read with great interest stories about the Israeli culture. Every man, woman and child believed themselves to be a sovereign. Soldiers could remove a company commander if they did not believe he was up to the job. It was a nation of *bitzu'ists*, a Hebrew word meaning people who get things done. Golda Meier was once asked how she liked being the state of Israel's first woman Prime Minister. She replied, "We have three million prime ministers."

"Ah, yes. 'Good' means university professors to some, Olympic athletes to others, and," small leer, "swim suit models for still others."

"Schatzy," Joe said to instant laughter around the table, "this egg thing, this is, what, step one?"

Rami Schatz nodded warily. He didn't know where this was going.

"Then what?"

"Supply chain," he said tersely. "We must establish continuous supply so our lab can stay ahead of the discovery curve."

"Yes, yes, I get that. Then what?"

"First, we *discover*, then, we *scale* ..." he said enigmatically. He was trying to get back to his power point, without success.

"What the hell does that mean?" Shillingford pounced.

Again, no visible reaction from Schatz. Joe was impressed.

"'Discovery' means taking eggs from our supply chain, injecting sperm from our contracted sperm banks, and making embryos. Then we remove tissues from the embryos and test for targeted cures."

"'*Scale*' means step two," he said, nodding in Joe's direction. "We target cures to populations as directly as possible to minimize rejection. So ..." Slight pause, small smile. "We want eggs and sperm from Jews to develop cures for Tay Sachs. This minimizes the need for immune suppressant drugs, which are cancerous and infectious. We want eggs and sperm from northern Europeans to make cure for multiple sclerosis, and ..." Big smile. "American embryos for Alzheimer's." He laughed so hard he sputtered into a violent coughing spasm.

The room was otherwise quiet.

He paused and glanced at Benton. "We set up supply chain to wholesale these human embryos for ancillary markets, where people try to do the same things, but *not* in therapeutic classes where *we* are making cures." His face suddenly contorted and turned red. "Like mental illness in Russia!" Again, the little Israeli turned to the map on the screen behind him and gave his old landlords the clenched and raised forearm. This time the room erupted. He shrugged his shoulders.

"Schatzy," Delgado pierced the humor. "So we're focused only on the Big 3: Alzheimer's, Diabetes, Parkinson's?"

Schatz looked at Benton, which escaped no one's attention. Benton didn't so much as blink. Schatz interpreted the non signal as a signal to answer the question. It was only later he learned, in America, non signals are not signals.

"Well, mostly," he shrugged.

"What's that mean?" Shillingford asked, impatiently.

Another glance at Benton. Again, nothing. "We keep this secret, right?" He didn't bother waiting for an answer. "We are all in the hunt for the jackpot." Small smile. "I speak of the Fountain of Youth."

"The what!?" Shillingford cupped his ear theatrically.

Schatz walked to the side of the podium. He unclipped his lavaliere mic. It was clear to all he did not want what he was about to say amplified. Indeed, what he was about to say did neither need nor want amplification. "Let me say it to you this way." Pause. "How does man reverse the aging process?"

Rami Schatz did not wait for an answer. "He changes his heart. He replaces old parts with new parts. The new parts are young parts. The young parts will come from human embryos. The adult stem cells have failed. That game is over. The race to the pot at the end of the rainbow will be found in the lab that creates the breakthrough: old hearts become young hearts. Young hearts that will live forever!" He laughed at the pure audacity of it. "Brought to you by Bio Freedom, a wholly owned subsidiary of HM Inc!" He bowed toward Benton who shifted uneasily in his seat.

The room fell quiet. It was several long moments before anyone spoke. The next voice heard belonged to Joe Delgado. "Let me see if I have this right, Mr. Schatz," he began. It was vintage Lieutenant Columbo. "The rich buy eggs from the poor, and sperm from the demented, so they can make lab babies, which they then kill so the rich can live longer?" He paused to allow a stillness to settle in the room. "Do I have that right, Mr. Schatz?"

Benton stood up abruptly. "Men, time for a brief coffee break."

The men around the table got up and moved slowly to a large table set up outside the room. The table had several urns of blended coffee and a number of plates of breads and cakes and pastries. As Joe passed Benton, he put his arm on Joe's forearm and said, "Can I talk to you a minute, Joe?"

Joe didn't like the hand on his arm. His training made a reflexive counter more likely than he cared to admit to himself. He looked at the hand, then at Benton, and slowed his step. "Okay."

Benton relaxed his hand and made himself smaller. It signaled conciliation. "Joe, I know this initial supply chain work comes across as borderline unethical. But, believe me, nothing could be further from the truth. We are at work at the corporate level to bring this, these transactions, above ground. One of my interests is to create a global supply chain that feeds the university labs and private bio labs in every country with safe and transparently documented sourcing." He leaned in and said softly, "I've worked my whole life at HM, and I've never known the company to cut corners. You will find we strive to embrace integrity with the same passion we strive to embrace innovation."

Joe nodded. He'd heard what he expected to hear. The game was on.

# 33

---

J ohn Sweeney picked himself up off a thick Persian rug in front of a darkened altar and blessed himself. He departed the sanctuary and walked quickly to the vestibule, where he glanced at the clock and involuntarily yielded back a sliver of the peace he had just been granted. It was 8:08 and he was, as customary, running late.

He left the church through the back door and entered a sublimely weatherless evening in early June. He crossed the street and made his way up the hill to the Parish Hall where at least a couple dozen young 20-something's, holdovers from his popular Theology on Tap program, were waiting to hear him speak about the "source and summit" of the Catholic faith.

The Parish Hall served as a school cafeteria for 286 children during the day. It was built, literally, into the side of a hill, the highest point in Narbrook. Above it sat the school gymnasium where the legends of Brigadoon were born. The little school had almost had its doors closed several times in recent years. Only the successive demise of surrounding parish schools had saved it.

John thought his favorite living Catholic philosopher, Peter Kreeft, put his finger on the problem, when he declared, "the Pill has proven more destructive than a nuclear bomb." Ultimately, without a robust and immediate "New Evangelization," he knew his school, the school of his youth, would simply run out of new souls, its oxygen supply, and it, too, would be forced to close its doors.

This sobering reality helped him focus attention on the evening's talk. Nothing so enlivened his priestly fervor as the opportunity to speak to generation next. He loved them with an all consuming passion and it was in the moments he spent among them that he'd come to understand the source of John Paul II's mythical wellspring of energy.

Tonight, he would open his heart and speak of the greatest love of his life: his love for the body and blood, soul and divinity of his incarnated Lord present in the Holy Eucharist. Nothing else. He entered the Hall and was immediately struck dumb. His eyes filled with tears, which began a quiet, gentle descent onto his cheeks and down the front of his priestly collar. There, sitting with their backs to him, were somewhere between 80 to 90 souls. They were praying the rosary. Terry Delgado was leading them.

He stepped back outside and wept. He cried from the depths of his being. *Lord God, Lamb of God, have mercy on me a sinner. Depart from me, O Lord, for I am accursed. I have no right to be entrusted with the gift of these precious souls who hunger and thirst only for you. Please Lord, I beg you! Send them a better shepherd. Is your heart not moved with pity for them, Lord? Why me, Lord? They deserve better, Lord. Please, please, Lord. I am not worthy to speak in your name.*

He walked around to the concrete steps leading up to the gymnasium and sat on the third step. He wept openly and unashamedly. His whole body convulsed in a relentless spasm of joy and pain. In moments, the waves of the emotional tsunami began to slowly recede. Reflexively, he reached into his back pocket for a handkerchief. Nothing. He began pawing at his eyes and tears with his hands.

He stood and sucked air in quick bursts to still his heart. He felt cleansed, at peace. In an instant, he understood. He had received the gift of tears. *Now* he was ready to share the deepest yearnings of his heart. He immediately felt self conscious about eyes he knew were now quite red. This would be noticed by the young people. He didn't want them distracted. *Should I put sun glasses on? Should I put reading glasses on?* He decided to trust. *Those tears were your gift to me, O Lord, at precisely the right moment. Why should I be ashamed of them?* He started walking slowly to the back door of the Parish Hall. *How true it is that He seldom arrives early, but He is never late.*

Reaching the door, he opened it and re-entered. From across the large room, Terry Delgado spotted him and nodded, smiling warmly. He stood in the back and pulled out his beads. The children— *what else to call them*— were on the fourth sorrowful mystery, the carrying of the cross. He joined in the responses. The sense of peace in his heart seemed somehow to seep into the entirety of his being. He began to mist up. *Get hold of yourself! Think of the mystery. The Lord fell enough. He doesn't need you tripping over him.*

As he prayed he slowly paced the back of the Hall, beads in hand. He meditated on the Passion. *What made him keep getting up? What did he think when he looked out into history and saw the present age? Did he find his hope in the age to follow?* He glanced at the young men and women sitting on folding chairs. Again, he gave interior voice to the gratitude in his heart for the gift of priestly ministry. *Of all the men available to you, Lord, why me?* His heart began to stir. He recognized a familiar warmth in the pit of his stomach, equal parts excitement and anxiety. It reminded him of game days in high school and college. It was precisely the same feeling. The ball— a football in the fall, a baseball in the spring— would be given to him as quarterback or pitcher and he would be expected to do something productive with it. Tonight it would be a small microphone sitting atop a makeshift podium. He looked at it from a distance. He blocked everything else from his vision. He imaged himself behind that microphone opening his heart, emptying it, transferring its animating force to those seated before him. Tonight these souls would be fed. The Lord himself would see to it. And not merely fed, but *filled*. He bounced lightly on the balls of his feet. He was ready. The fire within was crackling. He pined for human contact.

The rosary was brought to conclusion. Terry Delgado stepped to the podium and introduced him simply as, "Father John, the priest who says 'yes' to God." Immediately, his feet started moving toward the front of the hall. As he passed row upon row of young adults, they turned in their seats to get a glimpse of him and, as they did, they began to stand and cheer wildly. He felt something loosed deep within him. He fought it. Reflexively, he clenched and unclenched his jaw and thought of his sins. Sins of pride and sloth and anger. *Show them those, Lord! Let them see me for who I am.* He arrived at the podium, tapped gently on the mic, smiled and motioned for the audience to both quiet down and sit down. At his gentle summons they sat en masse with an alacrity that startled him. He leaned into the mic and said, "I'm not at all persuaded. I know you just wanted to stretch after that long rosary."

Bedlam.

*Whoa, what's going on? The Spirit is fully alive in this building tonight. Stay focused, and feed his sheep. Love them, and feed his sheep. Trust them, and feed his sheep.*

He began tenderly. "My friends, may I talk with you tonight about the animating force of my very existence?" He waited for heads to nod. What he saw instead very nearly derailed him. Their eyes were luminous and moist. They were listening to every word with an active, palpable hunger. He felt a unity in the room, a communion of spirits, a holy communion of souls. "I speak, of course, of what the Church Fathers called the 'source and summit' of our Catholic faith: the Holy Eucharist, the Body and Blood, Soul and Divinity of our Lord Jesus Christ, the incarnate and eternal word of God."

He paused and looked out at the freshly scrubbed faces of the new Church Militant. He saw many familiar faces, including two of Maggie Kealey's daughters, Kathleen and Colleen, and Michael and Carol Burns' twin sons, Patrick and Michael, or Paddy and

Mike, as they were known. He loved those boys. He'd tried to seed thoughts of religious vocations, with Carol's support, as early as high school, but found it impossible to compete with the reigning prep school trifecta of sports, alcohol and girls. Paddy was now a partner in a downtown building construction firm; Mike was a policeman in a nearby suburban township. Turns out the lad, an amateur boxer, had a few scrapes in his youth, at least two of which were filed under the heading 'aggravated assault.' Legend had it that one of his father's friends asked his son, a township policeman, to call the Burns home to invite young Mike to "make the rounds" with him one Friday evening. The idea was to see if maybe Michael Jr. might like police work. Michael Sr. answered the phone. He listened patiently as the young policeman explained the reason for the call. Then, reportedly, asked if his son "could ride in cuffs in the back seat, so he'd be more comfortable."

John swept the crowd and marveled at the sheer number of unfamiliar souls. *Where did all these young people come from, Lord? Why don't I know them? Please God, I will do them no harm.* He continued softly. "In John 6, Jesus referred to himself as the Bread of Life, and said that whoever comes to him will never hunger, and whoever believes in him will never thirst." He paused. "Then he went even further and said, 'Amen, Amen I say to you, unless you eat of my flesh and drink my blood, you do not have life within you."

He paused and inquired, "What is Jesus saying to you and to me as we gather tonight in his name?" He paused again. "Is he saying, *He* is the 'stuff' of life, its very essence? That man is more than simply molecules, and must be fed another kind of bread?" His sparkling eyes swept the room. "He answers these questions for all time in the very next sentence. 'Whoever eats my flesh and drinks my blood has eternal life and I will raise him up on the last day."

He paused again. "But, He goes even further. Listen to what He says. 'My flesh is *true* food and my blood is *true* drink. Whoever eats my flesh and drinks my blood remains in me and I in him.'"

He swept the room again searching for a wounded heart. He found a slight young woman dressed in black. She appeared to be alone. He saw anxiety and discontent in her eyes. To her he said, "What is the Redeemer of all mankind saying in this passage?" Pause. " Clearly, he's saying *three things*: one, there is a *life* within us that transcends the physical dimensions of our existence; two, it is *this life* that determines our eternal destiny; and three, that there is such a thing as objective moral truth, and it originates in the flesh and blood of the Word Incarnate!"

In that instant, he saw a cloud lift from the young woman's eyes.

"Let's break this down," he continued. "First, our age has told us God doesn't exist. That nothing unseen, unproven, unverifiable, can be *proven* to exist, and, therefore, should be regarded as though it does *not* exist. Our Lord is contesting this, 2000 years in advance. He's saying, 'Oh, the unseen exists, alright. In fact, the natural order, creation itself, is built on it.'" Pause. "He's saying the natural order 'overlays' the mystical order, which is its foundation. Indeed it was the Word of God as we read in Genesis that established the natural order, proclaimed its purpose and defined its limits.

"As John says in his prologue: '*In the beginning was the word*, and the word was *with* God, and the word *was* God." Pause. "Then, in the very next sentence, he identifies this person, who was *with* God, and who himself *was also* God. He calls him a '*He*." He writes of this '*He*.' '*He* was in the beginning with God. All things came to be through *him* ... and without *him* nothing came to be."

Pause. "Then John descends deeper into mystical truth. He writes: 'what came to be through him,' *this he*, 'was *life*, and this *life* is the *light* of the human race.'

He smiled. "Now my dear friends, if what John is saying here is true, what is the inescapable conclusion?" No takers. "The conclusion is this: God himself is a unity of 'persons.' He ordained that creation would mirror the unity of its creator. And it is *this* unity, the unity of life-giving love, which is man's true source of light."

Pause. "So what happens?" He swept the room. "Man, the pinnacle of God's creation, created in His own image and likeness, falls. He sins. The sin begets a disruption, a disunity, in the natural

order. And that disunity begets a darkness within man himself."
Pause. "My young friends, this is profound! The full meaning,
the inescapable conclusion, of this is too wondrous to even contemplate: it is therefore only and always in the Eucharist, the true
flesh and true blood of the incarnate word, made present *only* in
the sacrament of love, that God restores man, who is then able to
restore light, and through that light restore a measure of unity
within creation."

In that moment, he could feel a roomful of young hearts, and
the heart of a middle-aged priest, beat as one. *How true it is, that
Truth is a symphony.*

"The second truth concerns man's eternal destiny. We were
created, as John Paul II often said, in love ... by love ... for love.
Our destiny is not of this world, anymore than Christ's kingdom
was of this world. We have a rendezvous with death, each of us.
And after death, a judgment. And after our judgment, a destination. And we are told, and we believe, there are only two possible
destinations for each of us.

"In our age, man has convinced himself there is only one destination. And that destination is attained simply by being tolerant.
If we accept fallen man as he is, and do not judge him, accepting
his personal, subjective truth as equal to our own, we will have led
a good life and have earned our heavenly reward."

Pause. "But that's *not* what our Lord is saying to us in John 6,
is it? He's saying something quite different." Another pause while
his eyes found the eyes of the young woman again. "He's saying the
door to heaven is marked with the blood of the lamb. He's saying
we must eat his flesh and drink his blood to have this eternal life
we seek. And it is only this life within us, and no other, that insures
Christ will raise us up on the last day.

He paused and lifted his voice. "It is *not* about tolerance. It is
*not* about the acceptance of every blasphemy and immorality con-
ceivable in ourselves, and in our fellow man, that merits eternal
reward." As an aside, behind a smile he added, "Let me correct
myself: actually that behavior *does* merit an eternal reward, just not

the one we wish." Waves of laughter immediately built and receded quietly. He paused and thundered, "It is the life of Christ, and only the life of Christ in us, that prepares us for eternal joy beyond all telling."

He paused and tears filled his eyes. He proclaimed, "It is only and always the Holy Eucharist! It is now and forever the Holy Eucharist! It is for one and for all the Holy Eucharist! *This* is what assures us of life eternal. And we know this to be true, because Christ himself told us it is true."

He paused and unselfconsciously thumbed several tears out of his eyes. "There is a third truth inherent in these scriptural references on the mystery of the Holy Eucharist." He paused. "And that is the nature of *Truth* itself. Our dear Lord knew these 'hard sayings' would not go down easily. He knew he was talking to hard-hearted skeptics. He understood that many would leave him because they simply could not accept these flesh and blood truths, if you will. *That's why* he emphasized their intrinsic truth. Listen again to what he says. 'My flesh is *true* food; my blood is *true* drink.' Then lest there be any confusion about this he adds, 'Whoever eats *my* flesh and drinks *my* blood remains in me, and I in him.'" Slight pause. "And, again we ask, who is it who is saying this to us?" Another slight pause. "It is the one who referred to himself as The Way, *the Truth*, and The Life."

His eyes swept the hall in search of another lonely soul. They rested on a young man who appeared to be in his early 30's. He was overweight and wore a baseball cap, backwards. His body language said he had tuned out, but his eyes were engaged. To him, John said, "So what is Christ saying to us?" He paused. The body did not move. *Perhaps the mind?* He thundered on. "He is saying *truth* is not made objective by subjective opinion. Its power does not rest upon its affirmation." Brief pause. "Truth simply *is* and it is immutable, regardless of how it is perceived or received in one age or the next."

The wide body in the chair stirred. "Christ is telling us that the essential *truth* of his real flesh and real blood is found in its being the point of entry for a true living oneness, a Holy Communion, with God himself. This is a great mystery. It cannot be proven to a skeptical age that demands empirical proof. Yet saints have lived on the Eucharist alone and died of natural causes. They discovered Christ's words to be true, *literally true, life giving true.* They fed on the Eucharist, and in so doing fed on the life of Christ within them. His body and blood, soul and divinity nourished their body and blood, soul and humanity. And because he remained in them, he permitted them to remain in him. Not merely in time, or for a time, but for all time. For eternity."

The young man was now leaning forward in his chair, elbows on knees, listening intently.

John looked down for a moment to collect his thoughts. He felt himself being tugged in a direction he had not intended to go, indeed did not want to go. He submitted. "About 70 years ago, Pope Pius XI wrote in a papal encyclical, Mystici Corporis, 'It is a great mystery that the salvation of the *many* depends on the holiness of the *few* …'"

He paused to get a sense of where the Spirit was going with this. He felt a thread. "The holy in every age are *made* holy. Holiness is a 'you can't get there from here' destination. It is an action of God. But our merciful God has chosen to *facilitate this journey* through the sacramental encounter with his incarnate word." He paused. "It is in the eating and drinking of his *true* flesh and *true* blood that the '*remaining*' in him, and him in you, begins. And it is in this 'remaining,' where holiness is conceived, nurtured, and ultimately born in our works of mercy."

He paused and swept the hall. They sat in rapt attention. *All good. Thank you Lord. Now where?* "Now, what are we to make of what we are hearing tonight?" All eyes transfixed. "Just what is the Spirit saying to us?" Pause. "Clearly, he's saying that our Holy Communions can and do benefit others, if they are holy." He saw heads beginning to nod slowly. "But there is a corollary, is there not? If *worthy* Holy Communions benefit ourselves and others, what is the effect of *un*worthy, or even sacrilegious, Communions?" He paused and thundered, "Let me tell you what the effect is: when

Holy Communion is received unworthily, or in a manner which is sacrilegious, its reception does real damage! It damages the proclamation of the Gospel of Life and Love! It damages sacramental grace and unity! It damages *bodies and souls!*"

The nodding stopped. No movement. All eyes staring intently. *There … Lord? You want me to go there, here, now?* Suddenly he felt a small quiet gust of love fill his lungs. He searched for its voice. "Let me be clear," his voice trailed off. He really didn't want to go where he was being led. "The taproot of *all* the problems in the Catholic Church today is unworthy and sacrilegious Communions."

He was surprised to see heads beginning to nod again. He felt a voice rushing into his heart. "The problem we now have, and it is pandemic, is too many believe proper reception of Holy Eucharist is simply a matter of individual conscience. There is no such thing as mortal sin, short of murder. You can receive Holy Eucharist whenever you want, even if you're living in sin. There is no need for confession and absolution. No need for penance and repentance. After all, who's to judge? If there is no objective moral evil, who cares about the subjective opinion of another, even the 'opinion' of an institution like the Church?" He stopped and shrugged his shoulders. "In the idiom of the day, 'no harm, no foul.'"

His heavy heart lifted his strong voice to a different level: "But, there *is* harm, harm to the individuals *and* harm to the Church. St Paul makes this clear when he says in Corinthians, 'Whoever eats the bread or drinks the cup of the Lord *unworthily* sins against the body and blood of our Lord, and eats and drinks a judgment on himself.'"

He paused. "The problem today, and it is unique in the history of the church, is that no one is calling *any* fouls. We Catholics operate on an honor system. You know the rules; you call your own fouls. But because we no longer accept, or even understand, the mystical reality, we no longer accept, or even understand, the harm to the mystical body of Christ. And because we do not understand the harm, we do not call the fouls. We approach the sacred altar unworthily. We invite our lacerated redeemer into hearts darkened by grave sin. We disrupt and further destroy the unity of love between God and man."

Pause, then in quiet rage he enunciated, "The result: massive and unprecedented damage to the source and summit of our faith, a church divided and tragically impoverished."

To his utter astonishment, he heard applause. A mere trickle at first, then a cascading wave, and finally a thunderous roar. Even the wide body in back was pounding his hands together and putting his hat on front to back. The applause continued to lap the podium and surround the stage. John was careful not to wear it. He was ever attentive to the possibility the Spirit might have more to say.

He did.

"My precious young friends, The Bread of Life and Love is inseparable from the Gospel of Life and Love. The more there is devotion *to* the *one*, the more there is devotion *to* the *other*. The more damage to the one, the more damage *to* the other." He paused and thundered, "We cannot have a holy church with unworthy and sacrilegious communions! We cannot have holy families with unworthy and sacrilegious communions! We cannot have a holy people with unworthy and sacrilegious communions! And make no mistake, America will not preserve its cherished freedoms unless we Catholics cherish and preserve the Eucharist."

Standing ovation.

John filled up. He smiled through tears and nodded toward all corners of the hall. He saw Terry Delgado approach the podium. She was carrying a liter of bottled water. She handed him the bottle and leaned in to the mic and said, "Such is the power of a simple 'yes' to God." The roar swelled and gradually ebbed. Terry turned to John and smiled. "We promised you'd take questions." John nodded. More applause. Immediately a hand went up in the back. It was a man who looked to be about 35. He was holding hands with his wife seated beside him. "Father John, what's the most common source of these unworthy and sacrilegious Communions?"

He didn't blink. "Artificial contraception."

"Contraception?" the young man repeated, confusion clouding his features.

John looked at the young man with great love and nodded slowly, deliberately. "Hormonal contraceptives are abortifacients and are responsible for roughly five times as many abortions, called septic abortions, in America as surgical procedures. Yet few of our people have been told this. So, we now have what one of our bishops said was a condition in the Church where 'contraception has become a spiritual cancer eating away at the mystical body of Christ.'"

He was surprised at the number of heads nodding swiftly in unison. The man wanted a follow up. "Why don't our priests do something about it?"

"I believe they are waiting on the bishops," John replied quietly.

A voice from the other end of the hall sounded. A woman's voice. "Then why don't our bishops do something about it?"

"They're waiting on the pope," shouted a young man in the middle of the audience, eliciting loud spontaneous laughter.

John hastened to set the record straight. "No, no, no," he said, shaking his head. "Our popes have been clear on this. About 20 years ago, during one of his papal visits, a U.S. bishop asked John Paul II publicly about this "hard saying," if you will. He basically said, 'our people don't want to hear us talk about why contraception is wrong. So what are we supposed to do, chase them out of the church?'"

A chorus of low groans.

"John Paul II's response was quite enlightening. He said, in essence, 'many Catholics think they can ignore this teaching and still receive Holy Communion. This is a grave error. And it is a direct challenge to the teaching office of the bishop.'"

Silence.

Then, a voice asked, "So what happened?" it belonged to young Michael Burns. John was delighted to take his question.

"Nothing happened, Mike. The Catholic media never reported the exchange. So Catholics never heard about it."

"But Father, then why didn't the bishops teach it in their dioceses, and ask their priests to teach it too?" asked Colleen Kealey. John was stunned at how much the daughter looked like her father.

"Good question," John replied with a tight smile. "For reasons I perhaps don't fully understand, they seem to have made a decision to handle contraception as a pastoral matter, not a doctrinal matter *and* a pastoral matter."

"What's that mean, Father?" inquired the young woman in black.

John made it a practice not to duck tough questions, particularly from the young. He had learned some years ago that bad answers have bad consequences in the lives of real people. "It means, in an attempt to keep as many people as possible coming to church, they've basically decided to let Catholics make up their own minds, with or without the aid of objective moral truth."

"Wait, what? That can't be right," Patrick Burns said.

"No, Patrick. It is not right." He replied directly. "We Catholics are called to form what are called 'right consciences.' And those 'right consciences' are supposed to inform and guide the decisions we make. Clearly that becomes very difficult to do without a straightforward presentation of the Church's teachings on the great moral issues of the day."

Terry Delgado stood to ask her question. John wished he could have sat to answer it. "Father, if young people aren't being taught that use of contraceptives is against church teaching, are they really culpable in the eyes of God?"

John marveled at her prescience. He leaned into the mic and said tenderly, "In my opinion, and in a very general sense, no, Terry. But the people who were responsible for teaching our young people these truths: *they* are culpable."

A rush of hands shot up in the air. John pointed to one young lady in the first row. "Father, are you saying a couple can cohabitate and contracept and still receive Holy Communion?"

"No," he replied evenly. "Cohabitation which includes sexual intimacy is fornication. It is a serious sin. Contraception which separates the divinely ordered purpose of the love- and life-giving act is an intrinsic evil. Reception of Holy Eucharist under these conditions is inherently unworthy."

The young lady's face had a cloud cover that his answer had not lifted. "Father, I'm confused. So are contracepting married couples living in mortal sin?"

"They are living in *grave* sin. Objectively, what they are doing is intrinsically evil. Whether it is *also* mortal sin is a matter for the couple and their confessor. There is no question the first condition for mortal sin is met. The matter *is* grave. The question is whether the couple *understands* it is grave, and is able to "sufficiently reflect" on its gravity, and, finally, whether they *fully assent* to what is gravely evil, now that they correctly understand it to be so."

He paused. "What we can never lose sight of is that the Church alone was given the power, from Christ himself, to "bind or loose" sin, and the 'binding or loosing' is best done in the sacrament of Reconciliation, where Christ is present in the alter Christus."

He paused and added, "Let me point out, however, that the Church also holds, as John Paul II made clear, that these couples must be told very clearly that what they are doing is seriously sinful, and asked *not* to present themselves for Holy Communion."

He lifted his chin and voice and said, "We have entered a new period in Church history. For the first time we have a whole generation that is uncatechized. In fact, many have been taught by Catholic high school religion teachers and Catholic university theology teachers that they have not only a "*right*" to dissent from this teaching, but a "*duty*" to do so because it has not been "infallibly proclaimed." He smiled and added, "Of course, neither has murder." Pause. "As John Paul II once said, 'This Church doctrine on the sacred transmission of human life has been 'definitively proclaimed,' and that is more than sufficient."

He raised his voice. "This is why Paul VI and John Paul II repeatedly called for a New Evangelization. The young, like all of us, have a responsibility to seek truth. They also are entitled to find truth when they seek it. Today, too many young people are *not* seeking truth; and too many of those who are seeking are *not* finding truth.

"This is causing irreparable harm to the mystical body of Christ. It is causing irreparable harm to the mortal bodies and immortal souls of young couples. It is causing irreparable harm to families and parishes and whole dioceses."

Terry Delgado shot up out of her seat again. "But Father, in some cases we have confessors telling us that contraception is the lesser of two evils, that it's better than divorce. What are we supposed to do with that?"

John paused before answering. He scanned the room. He took a long slug on the water bottle. He adjusted the mic. He clenched his jaw and tried to unclench it … and failed. He looked directly at Terry Delgado and said, "First, Terry, I'd say that is a matter between that confessor and God himself; second, as an intrinsic evil contraception is never, ever permitted under any circumstances; and finally …" He raised his voice again and thundered, "Married couples using Natural Family Planning divorce at a rate of 1 in 100." Pause. "I believe that speaks to the issue of 'lesser evil.'"

A heavy silence fell upon the room, subduing hearts and voices.

Then a young man in the back yelled, "Our age needs another Jonah."

Spontaneous eruption. Into the middle of it, Terry Delgado shouted, "We have one. His name is Father John Sweeney."

A smattering of uneven applause greeted this remark. John immediately shook his head vigorously. "No, no! We had a modern day Jonah. His name was John Paul II.

His eyes misted up, his throat burned, and his voice broke. "We just didn't listen to him."

# 34

Lori Needham burst into Maggie Kealey's office breathless with excitement. Maggie's first thought was: *she must be pregnant.* Her second thought was: *please, God, an extended maternity leave.*

Maggie had never been altogether blind to the Miss Wiggins quality in her secretary. She chewed gum, teased her hair, and processed information very slowly, if at all, in a spot-on imitation of Tim Conway's young secretary on the old Carol Burnett Show. Several times Maggie had to abort attempts to give her dictation, such was her involuntary reaction to the young woman's facial expressions as she assiduously took her shorthand, only to read back pure gibberish. Maggie would send her for coffee instead and ask her to close the door behind her, whereupon Maggie would simply giggle like a schoolgirl.

"Yes, Lori?" Maggie asked, pleasantly.

"Mrs. K, Fran Delgado's on the phone and she sounds very happy."

*And this is what sent you bouncing in here at 9:10 a.m.? If one of my children was injured, God forbid, in a traffic accident, I would have found out about it, when? On my way out to lunch?* "Why thank you, Lori. Do you think we could take her number and tell her I'll call her back?"

"Well, I don't think that one's gonna work this time, Mrs. K."

Maggie stared frozen featured over her bifocals and asked, "And why would 'that one' not work this time, Lori?"

"Well, she asked me if you were busy, and I was like, 'no, not really.'"

"Lori, do you remember our last conversation about these personal calls from friends? *It was only last week, for crying out loud!* And how we agreed we would always explain that I was busy, uh, busy working, Lori … and then take their name and number, and promise I would get back to them as soon as possible?"

Blank stare. Then, a vain attempt to blow a bubble … with chewing gum. "Uh, not really."

"Okay," Maggie all but chirped. "Then by all means, let's *do* put Mrs. Delgado through."

She smiled the smile of the vindicated. "Okay."

In the briefest of moments, Maggie was neck-deep in quicksand with a decidedly inebriated Fran Delgado. She had never mastered the art of escape. She thought perhaps it was its seeming incompatibility with Catholic social teaching, or perhaps just the habits she had developed as an attentive nurse who also happened to be a single mother.

She put Fran Delgado on the speaker phone and searched her desk for a mindless administrative task. She saw a stack of correspondence awaiting only her signature. She reached for a pen and began. Every now and again she'd murmur an "unh hunh," to affirm she was hanging on every slurred word. She found it interesting that people like Fran Delgado did not so much want a mind or heart on the other end of the phone; they simply wanted a pair of ears. Maggie wondered if the Life Sciences Revolution would produce just such an artifact for moments like these. *Here, Fran. I'll be out of pocket for the next week, just talk into these until I get back.*

The rant was always the same. Joe didn't love her. Joe never talked to her. Joe only took the job in New York to be away from her. Joe never fully appreciated what he had in her. Joe would never have made even Vice President at Pittman Labs without her, much less Executive Vice President at HM Inc. Joe would never have been admitted to Philadelphia Country Club if it wasn't for her family name. Joe really came from a lower middle class family. Joe would never survive if anything happened to her. Joe wasn't loved by his own children, like she was. Joe didn't really have any friends, like she did. Joe had no life outside work like she did.

This last always intrigued Maggie. Did Fran Delgado believe she was still working? And if she did, what kind of work did she see herself doing?

The conversation always proceeded around an ellipse. On any given day there could be anywhere from three to six laps. Never less, seldom more. The details rarely varied. The raw pain on the other end never ebbed.

These calls often triggered Maggie's own painful memories, memories of a husband who walked out on her after their daughter's suicide and moved in with his secretary. Memories of being a single mother with five children and no visible means of support other than half her husband's pay check. Memories of physical and emotional and spiritual pain without end.

The first Christmas brought the worst of the pain. She and Grace went to buy a tree. They lugged it home and hauled it into the house to decorate with the other children. On Christmas Eve, she filled the house with her own family, so her children's Christmas would be filled with a sense of complete joy, rather than a sense of partial abandonment. In the middle of the night, a paralyzing migraine attacked her in her sleep. As she hurried into the bathroom to clutch some pills and dampen a cloth, she heard a terrible crash. She quickly descended the steps only to find the tree, improperly secured, had fallen to the floor, damaging half its contents. Earlier in the evening when the home was filled, the tree had been a magnificent centerpiece of radiant joy. Now that the room was empty and she was once again alone, the tree had coming crashing down and lay at her feet broken and helpless. The pain and futility of it sent her crashing to the floor next to the fallen tree. She too was broken and helpless. There was no husband, no man upstairs to help her right the tree for the children. She was alone. It was Christmas and she was alone.

It was after Moia's suicide she learned it was physically impossible to swallow water and cry at the same time. She began carrying plastic liters of water everywhere, even in public. She also learned very quickly that public tears were a luxury she could ill afford. Every time a random memory of Moia or Bill burst a dam in front of the children, their eyes revealed the depth of the fear in their hearts. After some of those moments, she would steal away to the shower. The hot water soothed, and its sound muffled her lamentations.

Many a night she waited for the children to fall asleep, and left home to pay a visit to a dear friend in the tabernacle. Alone, she would cry out in her anger and shame and demand answers of a silent God that were never forthcoming. Nonetheless she began to realize this friend of hers never let her leave empty handed. Pain itself never lessened. But virtue, particularly fortitude, was strengthened. And in time, she developed capacities she did not know she possessed, that enabled her to carry a cross of biblical proportion.

All families, she believed, begin with a measure of unity, some more, some less. The death of a child severs unity, if the grief is not shared; divorce severs unity, precisely because it *is* shared. The fragments of unity become like heat-seeking shards of shrapnel piercing flesh and tissue until they find the pulsing heart. There they impale themselves, living an indulgent half life in the incompleteness that is the broken family.

In the years that followed, loneliness ate away at bone and sinew. With Bill beside her in bed, she never knew fear. When he left, she began sleeping with most of the lights on in the house. On her first New Years Eve alone, she watched the ball drop in Times

Square, on television. At midnight, the host cast about the crowd for his wife, pulled her on stage and kissed her passionately. Alone, Maggie cried herself into the New Year.

Perhaps the biggest shock was the reaction of friends to Bill's departure. Married women friends began to slowly distance themselves. They grew to resent the attention she was getting as a single woman from their husbands. And the married men advanced like a swarm of locusts. They would arrive at the house to cut her lawn or fix her sink or teach her little ones to play ball.

She knew, of course, what was being said of her. That she was a religious zealot and Bill Kealey had simply had enough; that her unstable reaction to Moia's suicide had chased Bill away; that she was a remote, impersonal figure incapable of intimacy. It was these rawest of wounds that ultimately drove her back into church. She discovered statues didn't recoil when she cried out in the darkness and begged her God for answers. There were no answers, of course. She came to understand answers only come much later in the journey, when the soul is prepared to accept.

In time she was able to reflect on her life with Bill. Carol Burns once told her she was a trophy wife. Every young man "in the day" had designs on her affections; this triggered an alpha male response in Bill Kealey. She remembered his violent outbursts if she even talked, much less danced, with another young man. She could recall him often telling her how beautiful she was; she couldn't ever recall him telling her how much he admired her love of truth and beauty.

In the final years of their marriage, the bone crushing, spirit sapping burden of Moia's bi-polar illness and demonic oppression chased Bill into the seclusion of his work and his mistress. She blamed herself for the failure of the marriage. She understood it to be irrational, yet she found a strange peace in accepting it as punishment for her placing her husband's *need* for 'on demand' physical intimacy above God's *want* for their purity and oneness of hearts. She recalled the traumatic night of her stroke and her physician's interrogation about her use of the Pill. And every time she looked in a mirror, she was reminded of the stroke's calling card. She came to believe the partial paralysis around the corner of her mouth was a perfect metaphor for the imperfection of her soul.

She knew she would never get over the loss of her daughter. The years dulled the pain without in any way ever diminishing it. She saw Moia's face in every counter clerk, every young nurse, every driver idling in the next lane. Yet in recent years, she had been granted a gift of surpassing peace. She had come to realize Moia's death had liberated Grace's life. A haunted, tormented Moia would have drawn down Grace's reserves and deprived her of the single-mindedness necessary to pursue life and love on her own terms. There would have been no Scott in her life. And without a Scott, there would have been no Paul, no Mary, no James, and no little Martha. Too, there well might not be scores of other children whose mothers never would have been able to conceive and bring children to term were it not for Grace's Natural Family Planning clinic.

It was Grace who persuaded her mother to return to school to become a Registered Nurse. She pointed out the work would be intrinsically healing. It also, of course, offered the opportunity of shift work, which was quite attractive to a single mother of five children.

Ultimately that is where Maggie Kealey found her peace. In the heart of a God who knew how, and when, to bring joy from sorrow, hope from despair, and new life from death.

Suddenly the door to her office opened and Jim Gillespie entered. Maggie was surprised to see an edge in his eyes. She quickly wrapped up the call from Fran Delgado. "Gotta go, Fran. Bye." Click.

"Jim, what's up?"

He walked quietly to the formal sitting area on the other side of her office. He sat down on one of the two sofas and waited for her to join him.

She got up immediately and walked over and sat on the facing sofa. She was inclined to offer him coffee, but her instincts told her this was neither a business nor a social visit.

His reserve triggered anxiety in the pit of her stomach. He made no move to relieve it. She felt like a school girl called into the principal's office for something she didn't do. At least she hoped she didn't do whatever it was that brought Jim Gillespie to her office on a day which had already started poorly.

She was just about ready to say, 'out with it,' when his mouth opened. It closed almost instantly. It was now clear to her that whatever he was about to say was going to be difficult.

"Maggie, I just got off the phone with Bishop Bancone." She immediately felt a sharp pain in her stomach, which quickly morphed into a dull pain in her heart. Instantly, she knew what was coming. She was about to be dressed down by a man who worked for her. Dressed down by a man who held her in great esteem. Dressed down by a man who had gone out on a limb for her in arranging the meeting with the Cardinal Archbishop of Philadelphia.

"Maggie, you insulted the cardinal," he began, softly. He was not looking at her. It was clear he was disappointed *in* her, and had been embarrassed *by* her. "He was deeply offended by some of the things you said to him."

She struggled to hold her tongue. *Let him finish. Let's get it all out on the table. Then we'll see where we go from there.*

"He is said to be furious at how you corrected him, then lectured him, and finally challenged him. He said you all but called him a fraud! Made him feel like he was a useless idiot. He told Bancone no one has ever spoken to him that way, not even his parents."

*Perhaps if they had?*

"Bancone says the cardinal felt ambushed. He's blaming Bancone for not vetting the meeting in advance. Bancone is livid. He all but said it will cost him his own diocese. He stopped just short of blaming me, though not short enough." He paused briefly.

"Maggie, you just lost an ally you needed; and I just lost a friend I didn't need to lose."

He was looking at her now. His face was a mask of agitation. His words were tumbling out faster than he could edit them. "What in hell were you thinking?" He was standing now, pacing the room, waving his arms. She had never seen this side of Dr. James Gillespie. He was a force, a powerful storm just now hitting land. "Are you going to go through the rest of your life, Maggie, unloading old wounds on unsuspecting victims?" He stopped, and for a split second she thought he was about to physically accost her. "Get yourself some help, will you!" He was loud and getting louder. "What you did in that mansion will spread quickly throughout the archdiocese. It'll find its way back to this hospital. Your enemies will laugh and nod and file it away for the day you step forward to do them harm."

He resumed pacing. "You just blew up your own agenda! You just tipped off the other side you're coming after them, with nothing!" he half shouted.

Her mind was in retreat and looking for a safe house from which to re- group and mount a defense. Her heart, however, had cast a dense fog over her ruminations. There was something in what she was hearing that was drawing a strong emotional response, and she didn't understand it.

He stopped behind the sofa facing hers and leaned his forearms on its high back. He struggled to control himself. "How could you be so reckless with our agenda? Why must important work, work God himself may have called us to do, be held hostage to your need to fight every enemy, real or perceived? I'm telling you," he began pacing again furiously, "you may have just set us back two years!" Then he turned and exploded. "How many little lives will that end up costing?"

Jim Gillespie didn't wait for an answer to any of his questions. He whirled around and left, slamming the door after him.

Maggie sat frozen. She didn't move for at least ten minutes. She had never seen Jim Gillespie angry. It stirred something deep within her she didn't understand. She kept repeating slowly in her mind key phrases that had impaled themselves in her heart: "… important work … God may have been calling *us* to do … how could you be so reckless with *our* agenda? You may have set *us* back two years …" Gradually it dawned on her that she had a partner: a man who would stand with her and protect her and fight for her. For the first time in her life she had a man in her life, a real man who would not abandon her when the going got rough.

Ever so slowly, and ever so quietly, Maggie Kealey began to cry. Within moments she was awash in tears. They cascaded down her cheeks and onto her neck and chest. She tried to stop them and failed. She tried to wipe them away and failed. She gave up and submitted to the sweetest pain she had ever experienced.

It was at that moment that the door opened and Miss Wiggins entered and said, "Uh, Mrs. K, I forgot to tell you. Dr. Gillespie wanted to see you."

Maggie, back to her secretary, did not turn. She regained her composure and said, "Thank you, Lori. We just had a wonderful little chat."

When she heard the door close behind her she got up and went back to work.

# 35

After 35 years of toiling in the vineyard, Michael Burns felt he had finally arrived. He entered Ultra Com's large, elegant boardroom, professionally appointed in Brazilian marble and African tusk and leather. He glanced quickly around the room and marveled at what he saw. *It's a mini United Nations!* There were perhaps 20 men in dark leather captain's chairs, seated around what was reputed to be the largest conference room table in New York. They were clustered in micro delegations representing Russia, China, India, South America, Europe, the Islamic world, Japan and America. Another 20 men, apparently their lieutenants, sat behind them in matching but smaller leather chairs, ringing the oversized elliptical table on three sides.

Michael saw two vacant chairs in the back of the room and immediately set out to commandeer one. He dropped his leather carry bag next to the chair and removed his sport coat and draped it over the back. He spotted a coffee bar at the back of the room. It was positioned next to floor-to-ceiling windows overlooking Central Park, some 42 stories below.

It was early summer, and despite the exhilaration of the moment, he resented being called away from his beloved 38-foot Riviera Sport Fisherman for an all-day Saturday business meeting. He glanced at his watch. It was 7:53 a.m. *By this time the boys and I'd be hauling butt back from the Canyon with about a thousand pounds of Marlin.* He didn't buy the confidentiality argument for an "off hours" weekend meeting. *Who takes notice of anybody else in New York? Everybody thinks they're somebody important up here. Why not a Thursday night meeting, or even a Friday morning meeting?*

As he sugared his coffee or, as his friends liked to needle him, coffeed his sugar, he looked at the early morning joggers some 400 feet below. He watched as they made their way briskly, like so many ants, through leafy trails around small ponds and ball fields. *They just don't know what to do with all that energy. That's why they left Peoria. They'll run till they drop in this city. And when they drop, the next wave in will simply run right up and over their backs. Ah, the raw beauty and animal magnetism of capitalism.*

Michael turned to sit down and almost had a coronary. There, standing next to the empty chair beside his, now dropping his bag and removing his sports coat, was Joe Delgado. Once settled, Delgado looked up, searching for the coffee bar, and saw Michael. His eyes widened, but the rest of his face froze. Instinctively each man sensed it would be better if the other went unacknowledged. Michael nodded imperceptibly and Delgado half winked as they wordlessly passed each other.

There was a buzz of excitement in the room. Each man was there by special invitation. They were about to be initiated into the most selective of fraternities, deputized as co-architects of the world's fourth great revolution, or as Geoffrey Benton of HM Inc liked to say, simply: "4."

They were men of science and technology, government and commerce, blue chip think tanks and senior Non Governmental Organizations, what were referred to as NGO's. They represented the power interests of countries and corporations, intra govern-mental agencies and interlocking global alliances. At the head of the seemingly endless table sat Hanley Siliezar. On his left sat Stefan Boros. On his right, Geoffrey Benton. It struck Michael immediately that he was looking at an unholy trinity. He found himself staring at Boros. He was stunned by how much older the man appeared in person. Whatever spark may have once illumined his dark eyes was now gone. His head hung at an angle Michael found odd. It was though the thought of centering it required more energy than he cared to expend. Michael glanced at Benton. He found the corporate legend off-puttingly cool and imperious, and large, very large. He looked at his boss, Hanley Siliezar, and was alternately proud and puzzled by his supreme confidence. *He's convinced he was born for this moment.*

Suddenly, Siliezar was leaping from his seat in a burst of raw energy. He arrived at the podium in three quick purposeful steps. He wore a lavaliere mic and his turbo charged pace signaled he would not long be bound by a podium. In very short order Michael knew Siliezar would tap into a great field of energy, sending it coursing through the room and drawing each man into his orbit.

"Good morning," he intoned with both hands on the sides of the podium. "Thank you for coming." Big smile. "I am sure we are all excited to be here, especially on a beautiful summer day, yes?" Some groans, polite laughter. "We will only meet once. In the future, we communicate by internet, and when required, by satellite. All our communications will bear the highest level of security.

"Why are we here?" Slight pause, small smile, big boom. "To save our troubled world!" Michael was immediately surprised and a bit disturbed that no one, other than him, had laughed. "There must be an intervention, yes?" Heads nodded. "Things are out of control." More heads nodded, more quickly. He looked at the Islamic delegation. "The clash of civilizations proceeds under a nuclear Sword of Damocles." He glanced at the African delegation. "The Third World is now hopelessly roiled, mere pawns in this clash." He looked at the European and American delegations. "Debt is raging out of control in the First World. Governments are imperiled. Anarchy threatens. Wealth, great wealth, our wealth, is on the verge of being destroyed forever." An eerie chill filled the room. "This must be prevented!" Barely perceptible pause. "At all costs!"

The volume and intensity of the applause caught Michael by surprise. He had been invited to attend by Hanley Siliezar and he didn't think declining the invitation was an option. Siliezar had said simply, "Maahkill, this is an important meeting. Many, many important people. I think you should come." Now as he looked around at his new colleagues, he asked himself, *Who are these people? What are they doing here? WHAT AM I DOING HERE?*

"This morning we share the plan to close the door to the Open Society here in the west. Make no mistake. This is step one. Then we show you how we attack the biggest impediment to our success, Gulliver himself, and how we tame him. And finally, we share how we succeed through the creation of a new Trojan horse, the introduction of man's fourth and final great revolution: the Life Sciences Revolution."

Hanley Siliezar stepped back from the podium and glanced at the other two men before stepping forward and introducing Stef Boros. "Please welcome the true visionary of our time. A man we all admire for his courage and fortitude. The one man in the world today whose very name divides continents, countries, even households. Stef Boros!" The applause was generous and sustained. Michael found himself clapping politely and was surprised to observe his friend Delgado was not applauding.

Boros, stooped and frail, walked with a slight limp to the podium. Michael prepared himself for an underpowered voice and message. What he heard was anything but underpowered.

"Good morning," Boros said, in a loud clear voice. Michael couldn't place the dialect. It sounded part German Austrian, part east European. "I have long been an advocate for the Open Society." He paused dramatically. "Now, I am questioning myself."

Boros looked around the table at each man. It appeared to Michael that he knew each of these men personally. He did not bother to look at the men in the chairs behind the table. They were not important to him. They were not the men who made decisions. They were men who carried out the decisions.

"As a young boy I saw firsthand the errors, and the ruthlessness, of Nazi persecution and Communist oppression. I became a big believer in personal freedom – freedom of speech, property rights, free elections. But, the re-election of George W. Bush in 2004 forced me to reconsider the concept of Open Society. Here was the oldest and most successful democracy in the world violating its own principles. Here was America violating basic human rights in the name of fighting a war on terror, and invading Iraq on false premises."

The spontaneity of the applause was exceeded only by its intensity. Michael felt Joe Delgado's elbow gently nudge his right arm. Neither man said a word. The sound ebbed.

"I blame Bush, yes; but I also blame the American people. The purpose of thinking is to acquire a better understanding of reality. Clearly this did not happen in the 2004 election. The manipulative function took precedence over the cognitive function. This is the great undiagnosed weakness of an Open Society. Truth can be separated from public discourse by ruthless men who gain control over the means of social communications. I speak of course of unprincipled advertising men." From his seat behind the podium Hanley Siliezar offered a stage wink that drew laughter, which appeared to surprise Boros.

"Enlightenment philosophers put their faith in *Reason*. Reason was supposed to work like a searchlight illuminating reality. This singular idea gave rise to the Renaissance, to the first revolution: the industrial revolution, and to societal revolutions which freed man from the chains of religious oppression. But the Enlightenment thinkers did not grasp that man was incapable of differentiating the laws of the natural sciences from those of social sciences. They did not grasp that there would come a time when the Open Society produced men who would subvert the primacy of the cognitive function with the age old alchemy of the manipulative function."

Michael felt the "second team" seated around him begin to stir.

Boros did not.

"I haven't altogether abandoned my support for the Open Society. But I have come to the conclusion that it needs help. We can no longer afford to let those who would manipulate political discourse, robbing it of the power of reality, override the cognitive function. This must be addressed, and addressed systematically!"

If Boros was expecting applause he had to be sorely disappointed. The men around the table were fidgeting. They had not come to hear useless platitudes, the ruminations of an aging pseudo-intellectual.

"We cannot accept that we live in an age that is not concerned with truth. Two generations of deceptive advertising and legions of manipulative opinion makers have put the democratic project itself at risk. We must rescue political discourse from its own demise. And we must begin here in America!"

Suddenly, there was applause so raucous and sustained Michael thought for a moment he had wandered into a college football locker room, the locker room of an opponent.

"So, how are we to begin?" Michael was suddenly aware that there was a striking absence of sound in the large room. All eyes were now riveted on the man behind the podium. "Change must be systemic if it is to last." He looked at the third man seated on the right side of the table and bowed slightly. "Graham could decree a Fairness Doctrine in the broadcast industry tomorrow, but it wouldn't last." Michael recognized the gentleman Boros had addressed as FCC Chairman, Graham Forrester. "The media, even the mainstream media, would circle the wagons and denounce it, and demand it be rescinded." Pause. "I have no doubt we could push energy and health care legislation through this c Congress, but if it is done too soon, and done in too coercive a manner, the manipulators will lead the people to push back and our work will be set back years."

He eyed the room coolly. "No. This is not the way to do

change. Change must be organic. It must be seminal." He paused for effect. "It must be *constitutional*." He pulled his arms off the sides of the podium and let them hang by his sides. "In the fall of 2012, one of my organizations will introduce a revised U.S. Constitution for public review and debate. I will share it with each of you in the coming months. We will posit that this document is *necessary*, that it is *inevitable*, that it is *urgent* that it become *the* constitution for America's next 200 years. The document is currently in draft form and is being vetted by key members of the academy, the media, and the three branches of federal government."

He straightened and gazed royally around the room, nodding slightly at several notables. "How is this document different, you ask?" He smiled. "Well, for one thing, instead of limited rights based on maximum freedom, it will promote maximum rights based on limited freedom." Another smile. "The structural deficiencies of the first U.S. Constitution will be addressed head on. What *should not* be done by government in the name of individual rights will be replaced by what *should* be done by government in the name of civil society." Slight pause. "This will of course include equal access to universal entitlements for education and health care.

"The reactionary manipulators will of course attack this truth. They will *not* accept that the ratification of this document will be America's only opportunity to survive the 21st Century intact. They will raise the level of hysteria to undreamt-of heights. But the priceless treasure that is immutable reality will set in. The marketplace will fail them. Debt will impoverish them. Representative government will abandon them. Slowly it will begin to dawn on the brighter among them that the America that *was* … no longer *is*. The America of the future will be a more sober, more responsible, more cooperative citizen of the world."

Great spontaneous applause.

"Ultimately, the mass of people will turn to power to protect them from one another. That power will reside in the hands of people we hand pick. People who think as we think." Pause.

"People who will work with us to secure a future worthy of man in the age to come.

"We will not succeed in year one. Nor in year two. But all these legislative efforts we have championed will have their effect. They will batter the fortress that is American public opinion as molded by the manipulators. The timeline is of lesser consequence to us. We are prepared for a generational war. The current generation of Americans has now been weaned of its umbilical recourse to righteous indignation. There is little if any moral outrage left in them. This is our moment to strike. We will go underground with a shadow Constitutional Convention in 2014, and if all goes well, bring the discussions into the public square by 2016. In time, we believe by 2020, the soil will be fertile for the passage of a new U.S. Constitution." He lowered his voice and leaned into the mic. "America will once again by guided by law. Law based on truth. Truth which reflects reality. Reality that reflects the lived experience of *all* Americans, not merely *some* Americans, and is accessible to a restored cognitive function that is beyond the manipulation of reactionaries."

Another burst of spontaneous applause.

He stood erect and waited for the room to settle. "Then, and only then, will America have the enduring, systemic change it needs. It will no longer be a land of haves and have nots. It will be a fairer, stronger, more virtuous country. It will finally become the country its Founders envisioned. And most importantly, it will take its rightful place, no more and no less, in a far better organized family of nations."

He paused. "So I would ask each of you, please embrace this work that I am doing on behalf of our children. Speak well of it. Defend it from unjust attack. Regard it as a strategic umbrella for your own work, for the work we are all doing, to protect and preserve our world from those who would destroy it in the name of a self-centered pursuit of profit and power."

He bowed slightly from the waist and returned to his seat. Some 45 men rose as one and applauded as though the speaker had just announced a stock split. As he stood applauding politely, Michael glanced at Joe Delgado next to him. He was also standing but he was not applauding. Delgado leaned in and whispered, "This sedition must be exposed."

Michael Burns shrugged his shoulders equivocally and sat down.

Hanley Siliezar again approached the podium. He stood quietly waiting for the room to settle. When it did, he leaned into the mic and said, "Thank you, Stef. You are a man of vision. A man who is willing to risk his good name, his fortune, and his very life for all that is true, good and beautiful. You are a man after the Founders' own hearts." He paused, a small smile playing at the corners of his mouth. "I don't suppose I could sell you any advertising for your new constitutional campaign?"

The room erupted in laughter. Boros grimaced reflexively before permitting himself a small smile.

Siliezar gripped the podium with both hands. Michael thought he detected a trace of tension around the corners of his eyes. The elegantly attired Brazilian looked around the room and thrust his shoulders back involuntarily. He leaned into the mic slightly and began, "My dear friend, Stef Boros, and I agree on many things. This morning you have learned two things on which we do *not* agree." Small smile. "We disagree on the social merits of advertising …" Spontaneous laughter. "… And we disagree on the strategic role of a new U.S. Constitution." The room fell silent.

"I believe the work of serious, radical change is best done at the grass roots level; and I believe, therefore, the role of Stef's new U.S. Constitution will be to *ratify* that change, not to inform and guide it." He paused and swept the room. "Now you say to yourself, why does Hanley draw this distinction without a difference?"

Theatrical pause. "I say this because there are times when power must be seized. We are living in one of those times. The nicety of constitutional conventions, shadow or otherwise, is an artifact of another age. The U.S. Constitution provided a measure of continuity for the first two revolutions, the Industrial and Cultural, but we all see how it broke down in the third, the Technological Revolution of the late 20th Century. Once information itself, the currency for all progress in the post modern age, is universalized, the time and energy required to move large ships of state into a fundamental harmony with one another is prohibitively excessive."

He paused for the ritual nodding of heads before continuing. "The United States of America is Gulliver on the world stage today. But like Gulliver, her lethargy borne of indulgence will permit her to be bound by the wishes of others. These will take two forms: those which will be initiated from within, and those which will be initiated from abroad. The internal will be lodged in the private sector which still controls the wealth of nations. Regulatory reform will be the chief mechanism of the transfer of this wealth." He paused and smiled. "Some of you are directly, dare I say intimately, involved in this work already. The Secretary of the Treasury will soon own the nation's banks and be given power to seize any company's assets, in any sector which he believes is in danger of insolvency, and whose failure would cause systemic damage to the U.S. economy."

He smiled. "That is the first step. The second step will be to nationalize healthcare to force rationing, which in turn will force mass dependency. It is precisely this dependency which will mobilize support for an even accelerated rate of wealth transfer."

Another smile. "And finally, we will nationalize U.S. energy policy in accordance with a new UN created NGO responsible for taxation, enforcement and redistribution. Emission reduction targets will be assigned for each First World country." Small smile. "The targets for America, I'm told, will be quite rigid." Michael was startled by the suddenness and the volume of the laughter which accompanied this aside. "And the penalties more so!" More laughter. "This will occasion a great transfer of wealth from the First World to the Third." He nodded gratuitously in the direction of the Islamic and African delegations. "This is essential if we seek an enduring peace based on an enduring social justice"

He paused and reached under the podium for a cup of

something. Michael knew far better than the others that what Hanley Siliezar was now sipping was not coffee. "Those are the grass root changes we pursue from within. Let me tell you about those we pursue from abroad.

"First, let me tell you a story. And let me start by acknowledging the truth in one of Stefan's main arguments this morning. The greatest challenge facing mankind today is the challenge of distinguishing reality from fantasy. Some like to call this the Information Age. I call it the Disinformation Age. Try as he might, man is never quite able to entirely rid himself of the nefarious influence of religion. If you suppress it in one form, it merely re-emerges in another. We must acknowledge this reality and bend it to our own purposes."

He paused for another sip. Michael guessed it was a varietal from a vineyard Siliezar owned in Southern France. *Probably to relax him.* "So, what have we done?" Small smile. "We have mapped the traditional Judeo-Christian belief system and adapted it for the *only* 21st century religion that will have a sustainable global flock. I speak of course of the religion we call 'Environmentalism.'" He shrugged his shoulders. "This is nothing more than a reincarnation of socialism. 'Red' morphing into 'green.' But, as we are plainly seeing, 'green' is far more adaptive to the power of myth."

Michael saw heads nodding in unison throughout the room. *True believers, all.*

"So, what do we have?" Pause, smile. "We have our own Eden. We have a state of grace and unity with nature. We have a fall from grace into the state of pollution as a consequence of eating from the tree of knowledge. And, therefore, we have a judgment day fast approaching. We have energy sinners who are doomed to die. We offer salvation for those 'with eyes to see and ears to hear' in the form of 'sustainability'. A sustainability that relies on global and national emission targets, regulated and governed by a world body."

He stopped and glared imperiously over the heads of those assembled. Michael was embarrassed for the first time. The man behind the podium was bathed in pure arrogance.

"The national sinners will be sent to the docket in the World Court. There they will be tried and convicted. And when convicted they will be separated from their national wealth as bishops were once separated from their heads in revolutionary France."

Pause. "So what will happen to individual citizens in America for excessive and unauthorized consumption of carbons will happen simultaneously to America as a nation, a nation whose economy is currently 85% carbon based. As wealth is being transferred from individuals to nation, so too will that same wealth be transferred from nation to a world governing body, in this case the World Bank, under the auspices of the International Monetary Fund."

Michael sensed some confusion in the room. He wondered if Siliezar's renowned instincts would serve him well.

They did.

"Let me stop here and perhaps clear a few things up." He stepped away from the podium momentarily and reached for his cup. He drank from it without any apparent self consciousness. He pushed a button on the podium and a large screen descended behind him. He grabbed a remote and walked over to the screen. He clicked once. A diagram filled the screen. The diagram had three interlocking circles and a thin line protruding from its core out toward the margin. Siliezar studied the visual for a moment then whirled and faced the room. "Our three loosely aligned governing bodies: The United Nations, The International Monetary Fund, The World Court." He stepped back and paused to assess the comprehension level in the room.

He pointed to the core of the diagram and said, simply, "The Executive Council." He clicked again and a slide appeared with 12 photos and brief bios in three symmetrical rows. Michael immediately understood that all 12 men were in the room. Siliezar nodded and smiled.

He clicked again. The new agenda for the United Nations appeared in the form of five bullet points. Siliezar commented on each item briefly. Michael sensed the room was in full accord.

He clicked again. The agenda for the International Monetary

Fund appeared in six bullet points. Siliezar went through these points with greater care and precision. Aspects of how the IMF would mechanize the transfer of wealth among nations seemed complex, and Michael sensed there were others in the room who, like him, did not fully comprehend what they were hearing.

He clicked again. The agenda for The World Court appeared in five bullet points. Michael found this the most fascinating of the slides. He had a hard time imagining the America in which he was raised permitting its military and government officials, its entrepreneurs and its financiers to be accountable to anonymous foreign entities whose agenda was shadowy and suspect.

Now finished, Siliezar paused and leaned an arm on the edge of the podium. He set the remote down on the top of the podium. His eyes swept the room. "Okay, I will entertain questions."

Michael thought the 70 to 80 seconds which followed to be among the most awkward of his professional experience. He noted Siliezar appeared completely relaxed.

A dark hand went up. It belonged to a very large person dressed in some sort of silk robe which was green and black. Siliezar nodded in the direction of the man and called him by name. "Maboir."

The man did not stand. He lifted his voice which was lyrical to its core and said, "Tell us about the money." This elicited a few laughs. Siliezar himself smiled. "Ah yes, the money." He looked around the room, a twinkle in his eyes. "Always a good place to start, yes?" Another smile. "Let's begin here in America." Pause. "The natives have grown restless. As some of you know, there is a movement afoot to reign in the Federal Reserve." He shook his head. "Not to worry. Americans, lazy as they clearly are, will *never* trust their elected representatives with the money supply. So the Fed will continue to expand it to levels even beyond what they did during the serial bubble years. This will ultimately cause hyper inflation here, which will spread quickly throughout the developed world. This hyperinflation will cause the currency, the U.S. dollar, to crash and burn. The dollar will ultimately lose its peg in world financial markets. This, in turn, will force sovereign nations to depend even more on the IMF for loans to keep their governments afloat." He paused and smiled in a way that sent a chill running up Michael's back. "And the *terms and collateral* for those loans will of course involve more than restrictive repayment schedules and national assets. They will involve *policy*! What policy, you ask?" Another, darker smile. "*Economic policy, energy policy*, and of course, *universal health care policy*." Pause. "The very policies which have sprung from the fertile minds of the men in this room."

A smattering of applause built slowly and escalated into the thunderous affirmation peculiar to true believers in collective wisdom. Michael glanced over at Delgado. He appeared to be napping behind dark glasses.

Siliezar asked if there were any other questions. No one in the room stirred. He concluded by thanking the men for their attention and proceeded to introduce Geoffrey Benton. "I promised you a Trojan Horse, yes?" This drew the expected laughter. "Well, a Trojan Horse must have a Trojan Warrior to direct it, yes?" Several heads around the table nodded. He paused and smiled indulgently. It was clear to Michael that Hanley Siliezar held Geoffrey Benton in very high regard. "I am proud to introduce to you the most brilliant man in America. The Chairman and CEO of the world's greatest conglomerate, and its most important health care companies, HM Inc." Pause. "I give you the ultimate Trojan Warrior of our time, Mr. Geoffrey Benton."

Michael couldn't read it. He'd never seen Siliezar defer to another man. Clearly there had to be a unique financial interest in play somewhere. He resolved to uncover it. There had to be room in there for him.

Geoffrey Benton approached the podium in the manner of a rock star. He walked slowly with a feigned lack of self consciousness. A cynical smile, what else to call it, played at the corners of his mouth. The applause was warm and generous and sustained. He made no attempt to hide his intention to revel in it. Michael instantly felt an intense dislike for the man. He wondered if Benton had negotiated the right to be the final speaker of the morning session. He again wondered what kind of deal he had cut with Siliezar in all of this, and wondered if Boros knew or even cared.

He wore a lavaliere mic and brushed past the podium without even looking at it. He began to pace the room, circling the table, prolonging the applause. Michael read the signal. He was younger and more vital than the others. Smarter too. He was the man of the hour, the man with the secret, the man who was about to reveal where all this was all going.

He stopped in the front of the room several yards from the podium. He turned to Boros and Siliezar and bowed in feigned deference. Then he turned to the room and began. "The problem with myth, is myth." He smiled enigmatically. "Yes, it has power over the imagination, but it lacks enduring power over the *heart*." He resumed pacing. "It is the heart which holds the whip hand in man's decisions and actions, precisely because it is the heart which holds man's deepest secrets and yearnings."

He arrived at the back of the room. He smiled and nodded respectfully to Joe Delgado who, Michael observed, returned the nod ... without the smile.

"Every man, in his heart, feels he has been cheated by life. Myth offers *an* explanation, but it does not offer *the* explanation."

He resumed pacing slowly toward the front of the room. Were it not for the tone and cast in his voice, he was simply a man talking aloud to himself.

"Every man who ever lived has wanted to live forever. The Patriarchs, we are told, lived 1000 years. Yet Modern Man, the restless pilgrim who is in the process of discovering the very secrets of creation, lives well less than 10% of that.

"Why?" He stopped and opened his hands and turned them back to front, shrugging his shoulders slightly as he did so.

"Let me posit an answer." Pause. "Man dies so relatively soon after his birth because he has transferred the whip from his heart to his head." Pause, voice rising. "He has accepted the myth! He has accepted limits he believes have been established by his creator! And so he lives a short, brutish life in a dark and dangerous world."

He was once again in the front of the room. Michael noted Benton was picking up the pace. *He's good. I must give the man his due. He's insufferable, but he's good, very good.*

"This is tragic!" Dramatic pause, booming peroration. "Why? Because man has confused secrets with limits. He has confused myth with reality. He has denied the deepest longings in his heart and yielded to the simplest of rationalizations in his head.

"For the first time in 300 generations this myth will be challenged!" he thundered. "We in our generation will speak to generations past and those to come. We will instruct them. We will demonstrate that the very secrets of life eternal are embedded in the existence of matter itself. We will reveal that these secrets are as so many imbedded micro chips in the big black box computer that is the physical universe."

He paused and swept the room. "Then we will lead man by the hand to the fountain of eternal youth. We will show him all that is now possible." Large smile. "And we will show him how all that is now possible can be his *in this lifetime.*"

Benton closed his eyes momentarily. Michael had never seen this done. He knew the man wasn't praying. *My God, I hope he knows where he's going with this.*

Benton opened his eyes and smiled. "As many of you know, HM recently rolled up the three most promising Silicon Valley biotech start ups. We brought them all under one roof about a year ago, branded it Biotech Freedom, and hired a top Israeli engineer and entrepreneur to run it. We have an aggressive agenda. Within ten years we expect to discover and patent the use of embryonic stem cell tissues to replace clogged and worn out arteries and ventricles in aging hearts, making them young again. We expect to add up to 20% more lifespan to the average *productive* life in the west, and reduce by 30% the cost of its maintenance by 2025." Michael felt Joe Delgado stir beside him.

"But this is only the beginning. It is simply the Trojan Horse, as Hanley referred to it. This development will have mass appeal and create great expectations. It will generate what Hanley and his

Madison Avenue buddies like to call 'permission to believe.' It will move men to act, to accept, even to embrace what we call 'The Golden Lock'." He removed from his pocket a wafer thin computer chip roughly the size of a postage stamp. He held it high between his thumb and forefinger for all to see. Then he removed a second chip from his pocket and started each of the two chips circulating down and around opposite sides of the table. As they moved from one pair of hands to the next, Geoffrey Benton continued.

"This puts us in the game," he said, pointing to one of the chips which was being inspected by the leader of the Islamic delegation, dressed in a western business suit. "Men the world over will line up to have HM licensed subcontractors insert these chips beneath the skin just above the wrist. Once *they* are in, *we* are in. For *man* it is access to healthcare, with additional benefits for trade and travel. For *us* it is access to all manner of living atomic and molecular material from which the New Man will be created."

Benton paused to let that sink in. Michael was not at all certain he had heard what he heard. *What New Man? What the hell is he talking about?* He glanced over at Delgado and was surprised to see him sitting on the edge of his seat, chin in hands, elbows stuck in his thighs.

"We have a laboratory in Tel Aviv, under the direction of David Moskowitz." He stopped and acknowledged Israel's iconic nanotechnologist who was sitting in the back on Michael's left. "And in that laboratory, under Dr. Moskowitz's direction, we have pierced the veil." He paused before lifting the shroud. "We have penetrated the foundation of human physical reality. We are now able to turn sub atomic particles and elements into something entirely different. By changing a material's atomic structure at the sub atomic level, which only nanotechnology makes possible, we can transform that material into something else, with entirely new properties, which have never before been seen in nature."

Michael sensed something profound at work in the minds of the men around him. They were being ushered into the sanctuary of 'the new promise." The excitement in the room was palpable.

"Dr. Moskowitz does not believe the human species in its current form represents the *end* of development; he believes instead we are in an *early* stage of development. Am I correct, doctor?"

The small, gaunt figure to Michael's left stirred. He turned and saw the man's head moving in the manner of a bobble head doll. This brought an indulgent smile from Benton.

"David and his men believe there will be an early form of "post human" man by the middle of this century. This New Man will be an amalgamation of nanotechnology and nanopharmaceuticals, interfaced with microchips and nanorobots. He will boast cloned human parts, altered superior genes, alpha animal tissue, mechanized bones and muscles and, of course, one very smart microchip. He will be smarter, healthier and happier. His own lifetime will span several lifetimes, as will his productivity, and cost his government but a fraction of the cost we are currently paying to extend the unproductive lives of our seniors."

Michael felt the air in the room suddenly disappear. He sat up and tried to breathe. He felt the onset of a panic attack. He glanced again at Delgado. His mouth was open and his lips were moving.

"Our men are even talking about removing stem cells from human embryos and bathing them in neural brain cells to grow connections to high tech sources of artificial intelligence." He paused. "Literally computer brains." He smiled. "Programmable computer brains."

He strode purposefully to the podium and settled in behind it. "Genesis 1: God creates man in His image and likeness." He paused dramatically and swept the room with an undisguised air of triumph. "Genesis 2 Man creates man in *his* own image and likeness."

With that Geoffrey Benton turned in the direction of Stef Boros and Hanley Siliezar and bowed slightly. Then he took his seat.

Unlike the aftermath of Siliezar's presentation, the room now grew very still. Michael couldn't detect its pulse. For a long while no one said anything, yet there appeared to be no visible sign of discomfort anywhere in the room. *Maybe they're imagining their grandchildren in that world, trying to hang on to their inheritance.*

Suddenly, Hanley Siliezar leapt to his feet and bounded to the podium. He smiled and leaned into the mic. "Well, I promised you not only a Trojan Horse, but a Trojan Warrior to direct this Trojan Horse. So tell me, did I deliver on my promises?"

The room stirred fitfully. It was clear many, if not most, were now somewhat uncomfortable with the ramifications of what they had just heard. Siliezar read it flawlessly. "I know you have many questions." Small pause, large smile. "I do too." He let his body go somewhat limp to ease tension in the room. Michael was astonished. He felt his own tension begin to ebb. "Questions ... questions ... questions ... that is what our afternoon session is about." Another pause. "That, and, of course, another round of presentations from some of the senior government and finance officials among us. These men will give us an overview of how our agenda will be sequenced over the next one, three, five and ten years. When we leave tonight, I assure you, all your questions will have been answered."

He stepped back from the podium and said, "Lunch is served next door. Please follow Michael Burns. He is the man in the back in the light blue sport jacket. He must always be first to the food and the beer."

Michael felt the room turn to him. He shrugged and headed out. He suddenly needed a cold beer, maybe two.

# 36

---

In retrospect, Joe Delgado realized it was an omen.

At Michael Burns' insistence he'd left New York immediately after the final "Revolution 4" session, and driven to the Burns' summer home on a quiet lagoon in the northern end of Ocean City, New Jersey. The drive on a Saturday evening in June took a little over two and a half hours. The large home sat at the mouth of the lagoon and had an iconic widow's walk standing guard above its third floor roof that was part of the island's lore.

The home itself faced northeast on a double lot, and offered breathtaking views of the ocean, bay and lagoon from its 100-foot pier and its upper floors. A heated pool sat just off a large first floor back porch which ran the entire width of the home. Sunrises were magnificent; sunsets more so. Delgado had been to the home on two other occasions. Each time he'd left thinking Michael Burns lived the most charmed life of any one he had ever known. He was married to the most beautiful woman he knew. He had five accomplished children all making their way in the world with a little help from their influential father. He had a remarkably successful business that employed hundreds and offered him entree into the power corridors of both city and state. He had a wide assortment of friends and admirers, including several princes of the Catholic Church who routinely petitioned him for counsel and financial support. He lived in two designer homes, one hour apart, which allowed him to entertain on a lavish scale. In his garage, he had an elegant, black Mercedes 550 and an egg-white Range Rover for his wife. At the end of his 100-foot pier, which jutted out into the Ocean City bay, he parked his 38-foot Cabo Sport Fisherman and a 24-foot Chris Craft that was said to reach speeds of 72 miles per hour.

Joe begrudged his friend none of his earthly treasures. He knew Michael had earned every one of them. Not merely because he had taken risks and worked hard like countless entrepreneurs before and after him. Michael Burns, Joe believed, had been blessed abundantly for another reason. At a critical moment in his earthly journey, Michael had chosen faith over career. And his God had simply rewarded him in kind.

Joe, too, once had such an opportunity. He'd let it pass. It had all but cost him his marriage and his relationship with at least two of his three daughters. That was the least of it. His health had suffered. His career had stalled. His faith was, if not lost, largely missing in action. What pained him most, however, was knowing he had become a shell of the man he'd once been. And now, far too late in life, he'd entered into a Faustian bargain with a corporation run by a man he believed was evil. He was confident that his friend saw what he saw in New York today. This was the decisive factor in his agreeing to spend the night in Michael Burns' vacation home and join him on a sea cruise the following morning. Joe Delgado wanted to talk to Michael Burns about what they had witnessed, and more importantly, what they should do about it.

Joe parked his silver 750 BMW in an open spot just off the driveway, which sat at the end of a small cul de sac. There were four cars in the driveway, none of which Joe recognized. In the reflected light of a street lamp, he was able to make out two Acuras and one Honda SUV; he assumed they belonged to the children.

It was an exquisitely beautiful evening and the stars seemed to beckon from half the distance, far from the lights and emissions of a large city. As Joe approached the home he heard music and laughter coming from inside the home. He knocked on the screen door. Carol Burns, dressed in a peach tank top and shorts, appeared. When she saw him, she smiled and opened the door and held out her arms for a hug. Joe immediately understood. He had become a sympathetic figure in his old circles. "How are you, Joe?" she said as she hugged him. Joe let his arms hang by his side rather than return the hug. It had been a long time, and he simply did not trust himself. "I'm fine, Carol. How are you?"

She pulled back and he saw genuine concern in her eyes. He shrugged in response, not wanting to say more. "Michael arrive?"

She shook her head and retreated. "C'mon in, Joe."

He walked through a short center hall and into a bright, airy family room with a large bay window and several smaller ones. The soft twinkling lights coming from the lagoon's other houses and boats produced a stunning effect from inside the home. Joe saw that Michael Burns' sons were entertaining several friends. At the sight of him, both young men leapt to their feet and approached, hands extended. Joe, like nearly everyone else, liked Michael Burns' boys, mostly because they favored their mother's humility and kindness.

"Hey, Mr. Delgado," in stereo, "it's good to see you."

"How 'bout a beer?" asked Patrick.

Carol intercepted, discretely. "No, Mr. Delgado is going to have an iced tea with me on the back porch."

Joe felt a yearning ripple through his heart causing slight pain; in that instant he yielded involuntarily to a flash of deep envy. He had never known the kind of consideration Carol Burns had just extended him. Not from his mother who was tough and taught her children to be tough. Not from his wife who saw him as an extension of her enabling and improvident father. He let her put her arm around his and escort him to the back porch. She directed him to a row of large white rockers with fluffy nautical blue cushions. He sat in the first one and expected her to sit next to him, but she remained standing and said, "Joe, have you had any dinner?"

He had not. "Yes, thank you, Carol."

"Can I bring you a light snack with the iced tea?"

"No, just the iced tea, thanks."

She departed and he sat in the silence of a light breeze coming off the water. The expansive beauty of the setting was breathtaking. *So this is what God will do for a man who puts Him first.* He felt privileged to know such a man, and to be able to call him friend. *Maybe … if I hang around this guy more … some of that gold dust will fall on me.*

Carol returned with two glasses of iced tea and a plate of cold cuts which she put on a small table next to his chair. He looked at the plate and smiled. "Not very convincing, am I?"

She laughed and shook her head, and in that instant he thought she might just be the loveliest woman he'd ever seen. "Once a mother, always a mother."

He reached for the plate and made no attempt to disguise his hunger. There were small dinner rolls which had been sliced open to ease entry for the roast beef, ham, turkey, cheese, tomatoes and lettuce. There was a small cup of mayonnaise on the edge of the plate. Carol handed him silverware wrapped in a matching blue linen cloth. "Okay, you make crumbs, I give you a broom," she said with a smile.

He made quick work of the plate, then downed the glass of iced tea in one long, uninterrupted chug.

"So glad you weren't hungry."

He smiled and set the plate and glass and dinner knife on the small table. "You know me too well."

She turned away in slight embarrassment. When she returned her gaze she said, "Joe, I'm sorry Michael is not here. He does this sometimes."

His felt his stomach stir. "Does what?"

Her eyes gave evidence of a measure of pain and embarrassment. "He stops in Atlantic City on the way down."

"What on earth for?" he was incredulous.

"He stops at the casinos."

"The casinos?"

She nodded and fell silent.

The thought of Michael Burns with a closet gambling jones just didn't compute. Everyone knew he had a volcanic temper, but he was believed to be a man of few, if any, other vices. "How long's this been going on, Carol?"

"Too long, Joe." Then, in an ever so slight breach of discretion: "Ever since he sold Burns Advertising."

Joe was familiar with the disease. Once successful men entered the High Net Worth fraternity many had a tendency to think the rules no longer applied. They also came to understand they were perpetually measured by the others. They navigated their way through the power salons with numbers on their forehead. A 12, as in million, did not get the same respect as a 25. A 25 was not given the same respect as a 50. A 50 was not accorded the same level of respect as a "telephone number." In the beginning, Joe was astonished that successful men knew the total net worth of other successful men. Then, as he occasionally found himself among them, he understood. The men themselves told the others.

There were elephants on this porch, Joe realized. His wife's drinking, Michael Burns' gambling, Joe's own bout with alcoholism, the state of his marriage, the appearance of a slight tremor in his host's marriage. It was, he understood far too well, merely the inevitable cracks and crevices of aging concupiscence.

They sat and talked about anything and everything else. He delighted in her intelligence and sense of humor. Tired as he was from the long session of the preceding evening, and the stunning agenda and disclosures of the day, he was prepared to stay up with her until her husband returned. He noted out of the corner of his eye, however, that she was stifling a yawn as she was retelling a story about her son the policeman. Seems he stopped a speeding motorist a week ago on a back county road and told him if he wanted to speed he ought to do it on the interstate highway, 'cause that's what I do.'

"Carol, you've been ever so gracious, as always, but I'm a bit tired. I hope you won't mind if I turn in?"

She smiled. "I'm sorry, Joe. I should have spiked those iced teas, or at least mine."

He laughed and shook his head. "Carol," he paused awkwardly; he did not trust himself to finish his thought.

She waited a moment to see if he had anything further to say; when his silence convinced her he didn't, she arose and said, "Okay, follow me. I'll show you where you're bunking for the night. I think you'll like it."

She led him to a back staircase that reminded him of his childhood home. The memories of he and his seven brothers running up and down those steps in reckless pursuit of each other flashed through his mind like an extended video montage. *How could that have been 50 years ago? Is it possible those years are gone, forever?* He followed her up to the second floor, crossed a long corridor to another doorway to the third floor, and, finally, entered a small passageway which led to the widow's walk. It took three final steps to scale the heights, and when they arrived Joe was rendered speechless at the incomparable vista from the island's highest peak. Carol pointed to a small-pull out bed that had been made up for him. From it, a guest could lie on his back and look up at the stars through a small retractable dome. He marveled at the 360-degree vista of land and sea. Carol pointed to a small pull-out head and a mini bar stocked with all manner of snacks, bottled water and soft drinks. There were two small built-ins which held a number of leather bound classics. "If we don't see you tomorrow morning, we'll understand," she said laughing. He noted someone had neglected to remove the last bottle of beer.

"Mass at 7:00. You know Michael. He likes to be on the water early."

"Okay," he smiled gamely.

She put her hand on his forearm. It was light to the touch. "Joe, thank you for being such a good friend to Michael."

He looked at the floor self consciously. She lingered a moment, then left.

He immediately removed his clothes and dropped into bed exhausted.

*   *   *

Sunday morning broke clear and cool. From the flying bridge of the Cabo Sport Fisherman, the two men lowered visors and used hands to shield their eyes from the glare of the sun as they headed due east through a small inlet less than a quarter mile from the Burns' dock. The tide was out and the shoals that marked the inlet were tricky for boats that drew five feet of water.

Michael Burns carefully monitored his Garmin GPSMAP for depth, which Joe noted seemed to change abruptly and force constant course correction. It took nearly ten minutes to clear the shallow inlet and when they finally did, Michael opened the engines and headed toward the horizon.

Fighting the stiff breeze, Joe glanced over and studied the profile of his friend. He saw a look of pure contentment. He was a man in full, a man in command of his own destiny, a man who was heading into open seas in the prime of his life.

About 15 miles off shore, with no land in sight, Michael Burns cut the Caterpillar 715-HPm diesel engines. The boat slowed, stopped, then started to drift. The Garmin marked the ocean depth at 68 feet. The screen was full of fish swimming beneath and around the hull of the boat. Michael jumped from his captain's chair and waved Joe to follow him down into the cabin. The living and dining areas and the small galley were attractively but not elaborately appointed, and offered a glimpse of a somewhat Spartan sleeping area that could accommodate up to five guests. Michael opened the refrigerator and pulled out a Heineken and a pitcher of orange juice. He handed the pitcher to Joe and smiled. "We're out in the middle of nowhere. I could be persuaded to look the other way."

Joe shook his head and said, "No thanks. The only person I'd be cheating is myself."

Michael led him to the stern and a small sun deck. He pulled two forest green, high backed, director's chairs out of storage. He opened them and set them next to each other on the deck. He hopped into one and draped his legs over the stern. Joe followed, nearly spilling his orange juice. They sat in silence for several moments. The wind, coming from the north, kicked the swells up to two to four feet, which caused the Cabo's 12-foot beam to rock as though automated. Both men zipped their golf jackets to their chins. The salt air invigorated and the rolling sea soothed.

"You are one blessed man, Michael."

Michael Burns turned in surprise. "We're *both* blessed men, Joe."

Joe choked back a response and drifted again into a momentary silence.

After a few perfunctory questions about his health and family, his host turned the subject to Joe's career decision. "How's that HM thing working out? You happy up there?"

Joe took a moment to reflect. He did not want to leap into a major conversation with an unknown outcome. "It's okay," he answered.

Michael Burns laughed. "That good, huh?"

"How 'bout you?"

"Can't beat the money," Burns retorted with a laugh.

Joe smiled. "That good, huh?" His friend's comment didn't settle well. He decided to wade into the deep water. "Sometimes I ask myself what in hell I'm doing."

Burns glanced over and nodded but did not comment, which surprised Joe. "I'm making more money than I ever thought possible, Burnsie, but I'm beginning to question what I'm doing for it."

"How's that?"

Joe hesitated momentarily. "Well, I really didn't sign up for Armageddon."

Burns half turned in his chair. "You don't take those guys seriously?"

"Oh, I think they are quite serious."

"Well, sure, they're serious. But no way they're gonna pull off any of that crap. Just can't happen." He shook his head emphatically. "Won't happen!"

"How can you be so certain?"

"Look at the room. Bunch of think tank egg heads, NGO clerks, government flunkies. They're a joke!"

Joe was stunned. "Michael," he said patiently. "I can't speak for your guy, Siliezar, but I can tell you Geoffrey Benton is no joke. Stef Boros is no joke. Their Trojan Horse is no joke. I've seen the plans, the sources of funding, the state of the science. These people are quite serious."

Michael Burns was not accustomed to people contradicting him. It tended to produce a sputtering, vituperative anger. Joe understood it to be a disease peculiar to CEO's. "You're dreaming, Joe. Nobody's going to force a new U.S. Constitution down the throats of American citizens. No one. And there is absolutely no way Americans are going to let a bunch of Euro wimps indict and convict American citizens and soldiers in a World Court. No way. And the whole idea of, what, Post Humans?" He shook his head in disdain. "What a load of crap that was. I can't ever remember hearing anything so ridiculous."

Joe thought he might be observing the interplay between denial and rationalization. He decided to tack to starboard. "What if I was to share with you some highly confidential information, extremely sensitive HM Inc corporate files, that document in great detail everything we heard in New York yesterday?"

Michael Burns shook his head again, reflexively. "Plans do not a global revolution make, Joe." He looked out to sea and dropped an expletive. "As kids we were taught that if we wanted to hear God laugh we should tell him our plans." He turned and looked at Joe. "I don't know if God's laughing about now, but I sure as hell am."

Joe noted Michael Burns was sure as hell *not* laughing. "Burnsie, I don't know God as well as you do, but I have a strong feeling He's not laughing at Man's plans to do a makeover of his creative masterpiece."

Michael Burns fell momentarily silent. "What are *we* supposed to do about it anyway? Stand in front of the tank like that little guy in Tiananmen Square?"

Joe recognized the sound of tactical retreat. "We're supposed to do what you did in New York, and I didn't do in Philadelphia 20 years ago. Stand on principle, defend truth, even to the shedding of blood. Wasn't that what you said to Father Sweeney the night of the parish sesquicentennial?"

Michael Burns leapt out of his seat and flung his bottle into the sea. He turned on Joe and let loose a full measure of the purple rage for which he was famous. It was only with great difficulty that Joe remained in his seat. "I don't need to be lectured on standing up for the faith!" he bellowed at the top of his lungs. "I've paid my dues! People know what I'm about! I don't cut and run, never have, never will!"

He turned and paced the sun deck. A four-foot swell almost caused him to lose his balance. He looked up to the heavens and let out a primal scream. The sound was part man, part animal, accompanied by a violent shaking of the upper torso. Joe believed his friend was in the midst of a meltdown. But just as suddenly as the storm arrived, it appeared to depart with equal suddenness. Burns turned to his guest and said in a voice now decidedly raspy, "I need two more years, two and a half at most. That's all. Then I'm done. I walk away forever. At that point, if this thing has reached a point where I think it's real, a serious threat to our children, I'll stand with you."

Joe was stunned. A tremor of extreme sadness penetrated his heart. He couldn't bear to see a man he'd looked up to for so long be reduced so irretrievably by his own words. "We're talking about your earn-out, I presume?"

Burns turned away.

"How much are we talking about, Michael?"

For a long while, Michael Burns stared at the gently rolling sea. Joe thought he may have heard his final word on the subject. But Burns abruptly turned and said quietly, "$12 to $15 million …"

Joe stared at him unblinking. He shrugged his shoulders and said, "Well, I suppose that is a helluva lot more than 30 pieces of silver."

Burns, snorting fire, was all but on him in three long strides. Joe jumped out of his chair primed for battle. Burns stopped three feet away. Joe took one step forward. They were all but chest to chest. Joe knew well Michael Burns was a seminal force of nature. His strength and toughness were urban legends. On his 60th birthday, he was said to have chest pressed 300 pounds. He had a 48"chest and a waist only slightly thickened at 36"; his neck was 18" and his body fat was said to be 12%. He had been an elite athlete in his prime and was known to be absolutely fearless.

Joe believed he could handle his friend without too much trouble. At 6'1" and 220 pounds he was slightly larger, and he knew his three round sessions with CC three times a week would give him an edge in pure endurance. He stood confident and relaxed, bent his knees slightly and adjusted his gaze to Burns' sternum so he could instantly detect motion. He expected one or both of the arms he was tracking out of the corner of his eyes to be set in motion at any second. He was trained to respond, reflexively, with equal or greater force. He tingled with excitement knowing his victim would not know what combination of punches, carefully sequenced, had separated him from his senses until much later, if ever.

There was a great stillness in the boat. It was as if the elements themselves had taken note of the imminent mayhem and waited in hushed anticipation.

Then, in a flash: movement. A five-foot swell struck the

drifting vessel flush on its port side. Both men were sent sprawling to the deck. Burns landed on his right knee and rolled over twice. Joe was sent crashing against the fiberglass tackle box, injuring his right shoulder. For several minutes neither man spoke as the boat rocked through the aftershock. Burns was the first to stand. He flexed his knee in pain. Both his knees had been scoped twice. He knew instantly he was in trouble. He limped over to where Delgado was laying and stooped over his friend. Neither man would give the other the satisfaction of acknowledging pain.

Michael slowly and with great difficulty climbed the ladder to the flying bridge. It was 13 rungs to the top. He sat down gingerly and let his right leg dangle over the side of the platform. He fired up the diesel engines and turned the boat toward shore. Within minutes he was cruising at 22 knots.

The tide was in by the time they reached the inlet, and he headed over the shoals at 15 knots. He was tracking his pier and saw his sons readying the Chris Craft for an afternoon of waterskiing on the bay with friends. They were gone by the time Michael reached the large slip. He eased the Cabo into the slip stern first with minimal difficulty. He cut the engines and reached for a 10-foot stainless steel pole to lift the lines from two pilings. As he did so he was surprised by the familiar syncopated sound of a passenger's two feet landing heavily on a wood dock. He turned to see Joe Delgado moving briskly down the pier. He did not turn around.

Michael eased himself down to the dock and secured the vessel himself, irritated at his guest's breach of nautical etiquette. He reached for the long green dock hose and opened the faucet. The spray flew upward toward the flying bridge. He adjusted the nozzle to the rinse position. Methodically he worked his way down to the roof of the cabin, the long bow with its stainless steel guard rail, the cabin's large windows, the vessel's spotless hull and, finally, the small sun deck which had almost hosted Ali-Frazier 4.

As he worked, he bridled at his guest's accusation of betrayal. The indignity burned a laser-like hole in his heart and left him simmering in quiet rage. For several moments he even entertained the idea of following Joe Delgado home and challenging him to settle what they had only started.

Blinded by his fury he did not at first notice a large vessel entering the lagoon. It was a 67-foot Viking Motor Yacht and it was headed to a dock on the opposite side of the mouth of the lagoon. Michael's heart began to race. He knew from the quiet purring of the engines, they were twin 1100 horsepower Common Rail Man's. He guessed there were four staterooms with probably three bathrooms. The flying bridge was open and as large as a living room, and looked every bit as comfortable with its white plush captain chairs and sofas, and its smooth, burnished teak flooring. He estimated the technology alone built into the radar bar was worth over $500,000. The lower aft deck held a silver 12-foot automated launch. Michael had never seen a sleeker, more elegant yacht in all his life. And, in that moment, he vowed that he, too, would one day own such a yacht.

As he watched its smiling owner joke with guests while easing the stunning white ship of state into an oversized slip, Michael Burns made a private vow on the spot where he stood. That yacht, or one very much like it, would be the very first thing he would buy with his Ultra Com earn out.

He replaced the hose and closed the faucet. He turned and headed down the long dock leading to the island's most storied home.

He was suddenly feeling much better.

# 37

John Sweeney pulled off the road and angled his black Acura into the first open parking space outside the Sunset Village assisted living facility.

He turned the motor off and shut his eyes and prayed. *Lord, my presence here is but a pale reflection of the love you have for this man. May he feel the true depth of that love in the time we spend together, and the true depth of the gratitude in my heart for the gift he has been in my life.*

He opened his eyes and looked at the exterior of the building. Its design was neo-Victorian. The color scheme was neo Montessori – blended shades of mauves and pastels. He was not a fan of nursing homes. In his mind, they were places where hearts forever young went to die. His sister had given up a meaningful portion of her life to keep their mother out of one. He never left one feeling anything but sadness for the poor souls waiting patiently in death's vestibule. He thought, in general, the elderly should live with their children, and that the rapid expansion of America's nursing home industry deprived each generation of something indispensible.

He got out of the car without locking it. He immediately

thought of his father. One summer evening many years ago, a wealthy physician in the parish invited the large and barely civilized Sweeney family to Philadelphia's most prestigious country club for dinner. As they followed their host to the terrace, John beheld the most spectacular setting he had ever seen. Lush, rolling, exquisitely manicured countryside as far as the eye could see. A stunning array of elite golf holes cast in three shades of green dotted the landscape. There were rushing streams which fed into large ponds, with bright red Koi and back lit fountains accentuated by a magenta sky at dusk. He was 14 at the time, and he remembered thinking he had just stolen his first glimpse of paradise.

After dinner, the Sweeney family parted company with their host and walked through the parking lot to their car — a seven-year-old Ford station wagon. They passed Mercedes Benzes, BMW's, Lexuses, and at least one Bentley. When they arrived at the family car, John noted it was the only car with its windows and doors locked. That was his first real recognition that perhaps his father was indeed a bit different.

He entered the nursing home and immediately saw an elderly woman with a raised cane struggling to attack an older man who was sitting in a chair staring vacantly. Whatever the man had said or done, it was clear he had not the slightest recollection of it.

John looked around hoping to see an employee rushing to intercept the woman. None appeared. He gently removed the cane from the woman's frail hand and guided her to a nearby sitting area where several other women seemed to welcome her return. He sat her down on a couch, a puzzled expression creasing her otherwise unremarkable face.

He walked to the front desk and asked for Hal Schwartz. A young woman, John guessed in her early 20's, immediately picked up the phone to ring the room. As she did so she smiled and asked him to sign the guest register. He did. Under "Resident" he wrote, The Coach.

The young lady returned the phone to its cradle and said, "He's not in his room, Father; he must be in the dining room."

John nodded, turned and headed into the small dining hall just off the main entrance. There were about a dozen tables, each with four chairs. He checked his watch. It was 1:10. He made a mental note to leave by 3:00 in order to pray and prepare himself to hear Saturday afternoon confessions.

He was surprised to see that all the tables were filled. He'd assumed on a beautiful summer day friends and relatives would arrive early to take residents out for some fresh air. He spotted his friend at a table in the back of the room near a bay window overlooking the street and its traffic. The old man was holding court with three elderly ladies in waiting. It appeared the women were either keenly interested in what he had to say or, more likely, feigning interest as the requisite price of companionship. John did not think his former coach and mentor either noted or valued the distinction.

One of the ladies recognized him. "Oh, it's Father Sweeney. He must be here to see you, Hal."

The other women immediately turned in his direction. John saw indifference in the eyes of one, thinly veiled hostility in the other. He reflexively thought of his childhood when the mere presence of a priest sent men, women and children scrambling to their feet. *Mea Maxima Culpa, Lord.*

Hal Schwartz started to stand but John gently pressed down on his right shoulder to hold him in place. Undeterred, the older man struggled to his feet to hug his visitor. He laid his head on John's neck and kissed it. He smelled of lentil soup. John clasped him on the back and held him tight.

The woman who appeared to resent John's intrusion said, "He's here to hear your confession, Schwartz."

Hal Schwartz tugged himself apart, looked him up and down, and shook his head. "Nah. If he was, he'd have brought an overnight bag."

John laughed. "Hey, Coach, if I'd known I was going to be cutting into your social life—"

Schwartz smiled at the ladies. "You blew it. I almost had him convinced I was still celibate."

John winced as the women giggled on cue. He had been reliably informed even nursing homes, veritable vestibules for Judgment Day, had not been spared the long reach of the sexual revolution.

Schwartz turned and grabbed John by the arm. "Let's go to my room."

John started to protest but the older man, even in his weakened condition, retained a vise-like grip. Hal Schwartz reached for his walker and steered it toward the entrance of the dining room. He beckoned John to follow.

As he watched the stooped figure in front of him slowly make his way out of the dining room, he thought of the man he first met as a 12-year-old boy at the Narbrook playground. In those days of innocence, Hal Schwartz was an urban legend. He was the most successful coach in Lower Merwood High School's long and storied history. He'd won seven state championships, sent dozens of former players to the Major Leagues, and routinely rejected offers from Division One universities to come fix their broken programs.

He was even more beloved as a U.S. history teacher. He was a bona fide hero, a man who fought and nearly died on a beach at Normandy. He was an unabashed patriot and a believer in American exceptionalism, with its robust domestic and overseas accountabilities. His retirement, 17 years earlier, was the event of the year on Philadelphia's historic Main Line.

The school gymnasium was filled with the rich and famous and the not so rich and famous. Four open mics had been set up and the tributes flowed for over four hours. Although he had not been a student of Hal Schwartz, simply one of his summer league baseball players, John had stood on line not so patiently waiting his turn to talk about the man who had changed the whole trajectory of his life, twice. And when that moment arrived, he was forced to leave the tribute unfinished and turn away from the mic with tears streaming down his cheeks.

The loss of his wife of 47 years, chemotherapy treatments for prostate cancer, and a recent triple bypass had taken their toll. Hal Schwartz now moved like a man who anticipated, even welcomed, death. His eyes were sunken and hollow and his chest heaved from the effort simply to fill his lungs with air.

They arrived at his first floor room and entered, John shuffling his feet awkwardly to keep from overtaking his host. The room was small and unkempt, a lifetime of possessions reduced to unseemly clutter. The older man made his way over to an overstuffed chair with clothes draped over its back and several books resting awkwardly on its arms. He sat down with a dull thud, sending the books plunging to the floor. He waved John into a straight backed desk chair adjacent to his. John approached the chair and removed several cartons of partially-eaten Chinese food. He looked for a place to put the cartons and, not seeing one, set them down by his feet.

He was aware his host was watching him carefully. He sat and settled himself and looked the older man in the eye and held his gaze. "Coach, how are you doing?"

Hal Schwartz allowed his eyes to fall to the floor. For a long moment nothing was said. John was crushed. He felt tears welling up inside him and he feared they would make an unwelcome appearance at the very moment the other man raised his own eyes and unburdened his heart.

"I envy you your belief, John."

A lance split John's heart. Tears formed quickly forcing his head to drop to his chest. Within moments the tears found their way to the front of his black short sleeve shirt, staining it. He couldn't speak. The pain in his heart, instead of ebbing, intensified.

"I know you will say I am carrying my cross, but I know no such theology."

John struggled to clear his throat and still the tremor in his voice. It took several moments. In the distance he could hear an argument escalating down the hall. "One of our elder sisters in the faith, a Jewish woman by the name of Edith Stein, once referred to it as 'the science of the Cross.'"

Schwartz stared unblinking.

John regarded this, incorrectly, as an invitation. "She believed the Cross was uniquely the destiny of God's Chosen People."

Nothing.

"She was gassed at Auschwitz." He paused awkwardly. "John Paul II canonized her."

"I remember. It caused a bit of a ruckus, didn't it?"

John nodded.

"Our peoples have such a long history."

"It's quickly coming to a glorious close," John replied. The thought, now given expression, seemed to surprise them both.

Schwartz' eyebrows arched. "A Kumbaya moment?" Small smile. "Before or after Armageddon?"

John grimaced. "God chose well, Hal. Your people did the job He gave them to do."

"Then why have you Christians persecuted us for 2000 years?"

It was a stunning 'first taste' of an unknown recrimination. For 45 years, they had carefully avoided the forbidden zone. "Not all of us, Hal. And those who did were wrong. That's why our Pope went to the Wailing Wall and apologized on behalf of all of us."

The old man stared hard. "One apology? 2000 years?"

John nodded, pained. He did not know this man. "Inadequate, yes. But it is a start, no?"

The old man nodded. "That pope, he knew how to pope."

*Where to go with this?* "He loved your people, and he taught us to love your people."

"Oh, I grant you we are not always that lovable."

"I always thought you were."

The old man smiled. "Well, I hope I don't say anything today to change that opinion."

"Impossible!" John replied with vehemence.

"Well, we Jews may seem at times a bit difficult to understand."

"By God's own design. From the beginning you were a people

set apart. It's in your DNA." John smiled and added, "He didn't want you contaminated by us Gentiles because it was from the Jews that salvation would come to all men."

The old man looked startled. "Then why have we always been accused of being Christ killers?"

John blinked. His friend, in the manner of those nearing death, had thrown discretion overboard. "You didn't kill Christ, Hal. I did." He paused and added, "Anyway, the Old Testament reveals nothing about God, if not that he is a God of the remnant. The Messiah was to come as a gift for the faithfulness of the people of the covenant."

Hal Schwartz nodded glumly.

John sought to stir his friend's spirit. "The New Testament confirms this and proclaims that the Redeemer gave up his life willingly for the sins of *all* men. Even in our day, we continue to see this same God acting through a faithful remnant. This is how He has always dealt with humankind. One of our popes wrote in the '40's: 'It is a great mystery that the salvation of the many depends on the holiness of the few.'"

Schwartz frowned. "So, am I now to believe we Jews are not a plague on all of humanity?"

John winced. "Because of a faithful remnant in every age, yours is the election *and* the incarnation. Not bad for a small, 4000-year-old tribe, huh?"

The old man smiled.

John seized upon the smile. "And, thanks to *that* remnant there are almost a billion and a half Christians in the world today." He paused. "Yes, I think any fair minded person would have to conclude God chose his people well."

A long silence ensued. Each man was lost in his own thoughts about the other and a relationship spanning nearly half a century.

The silence was broken by a classic Jewish lamentation. "Our God died in the Shoah."

"Or so it *might* appear," John replied, too quickly.

The old man let the remark pass. "As Eli Wiesel once said, 'the meaning of the Holocaust is that it implicates not only Abraham but his God. It was there that the covenant was broken.'"

*Lord, how to explain that the stumbling block to this man's faith is the cornerstone of mine?* "Hal," he began gently, "Evil is evil precisely because it always attacks what God has chosen. And how else to look at the Holocaust except as evil's desperate action against those who were waiting in patient expectation?

The old man waved his hand wearily to dismiss the notion.

John advanced. "In what we call 'the economy of salvation' grace is always purchased by suffering. Clearly the Incarnation was preceded by near constant Jewish suffering which culminated in the 'slaughter of the innocents' under Herod. There are those among us who believe his Second Coming has also now been preceded by the unprecedented suffering of Jews, principally the slaughter of the innocents in the Holocaust."

Schwartz stared numbly. "Are you here to convert me, John?"

The question stung. John recoiled as though tasered. "How can I be what you helped me to be, and not share with you what I've become?"

"As Wiesel also once famously said, ' if you Gentiles would stop thinking about our salvation, perhaps our cemeteries wouldn't be so full.'"

John leapt to his feet and made a move to go but the old man implored him to stay. "John, if we can't be honest with each other at this point in our lives, then when?"

John didn't want the friendship to end in contention. He struggled to find a bridge to another subject but the old man was having none of it. He lifted a single finger in John's direction and said, "Our faith was built on three axioms: God is all loving; the Jews are his chosen people; and good will be rewarded in this life." He paused. "The holocaust presents a problem. Clearly one of the three axioms is not true. Many Jews in my generation concluded it is the first."

John had never heard this explanation. He immediately thought of the turbo charged secularization of western culture, primarily through the elite universities after the war, and wondered if this was its animating force. "What a tragic irony, Hal, if the chosen people at the end of time embrace a notion their forefathers resisted at the beginning of time."

The old man merely shrugged.

Once engaged, John always found it difficult to back off. "I mean, why give evil the posthumous victory your generation denied it?"

"Hitler was a baptized Catholic. You know that, John."

"He was indeed. But he turned his back on his faith. He was a practicing occultist. Just as there is an economy of salvation, there is an economy of perdition. Each has a central figure. Hitler was baptized in Christ; but he worshipped Satan."

"That is Christian revisionism," the old man snapped.

"It is *not*," John fired back with a vehemence that surprised them both. "It is a matter of their own historical records that the Third Reich was intended to be the Messianic Era on earth: a 1000 year reign with Hitler taking the place of Christ, the Aryan race taking the place of the Jews as the Chosen People, and blood purity taking the place of holiness as the essence of salvation."

This appeared to surprise Schwartz which greatly surprised John. *How is it we have passed the better part of 50 years together and never, ever, discussed what is core to our being?* "That reptile was indeed the devil incarnate," the old man said after a long pause.

John nodded quickly. "From the moment in the Garden, Satan's mission has been about nullification. What God creates in love, Satan seeks to destroy in hate. The Incarnation opened salvation to all, in effect nullifying the nullification."

The old man blinked.

"The Jews have been in his sights since Abraham foreshadowed the Cross with Isaac. The First Coming signaled the end of Satan's reign on earth. The Second Coming marks its end. He is obsessed with its imminence. The Holocaust was his attempt to delay it."

Hal Schwartz slowly shook his head and a smile formed around the corners of his mouth. "Well, at least one good thing came out of that hell on earth." He paused. "We Jews don't have to worry about you Christians trying to convert us anymore."

John leveled his gaze. "That is our guilt over-riding the Gospel imperative to evangelize the world."

The old man laughed. "Ah, the Irish! We Jews give thanks for the Irish, the only people on earth whose guilt rivals our own."

John smiled. "The primordial influence of mothers."

Hal Schwartz's head bobbed and his eyes danced with delight.

John took the measure of the moment. "The devil has sown his confusion well. Jews believe the Nazis were practicing Christianity, which the Nazi's own documents make clear they were not, and many Christians believe *we* were responsible for these horrific crimes against humanity, which we clearly were not."

Each man fell into a tranquil silence, content nothing said, or unsaid, had gone unheard.

Finally, the old man shook his head as if to clear it. "Well, anyway, the Nazis are gone but the persecution continues."

In that moment, John glimpsed for the first time something of what it meant to be a Jew.

John nodded. "As a history teacher, you well know how the Arab world rallied around Hitler in the '30's."

Schwartz didn't respond.

John pressed the issue. "The historical record is clear, Hal. There were direct Arab links to the Nazis at the highest levels of government in half a dozen mid-east countries."

Nothing.

John shifted his approach. "Hal, we Christians believe our enemy is not flesh and blood but principalities and powers."

Silence.

"Hal, think about nullification, just for a moment." Pause. "What better way than through a false religion?"

The old man's eyes narrowed.

"I mean there are many, many good Muslim men and women, but what else to call its core doctrine of eternal reward in the

Hadith? It's not about the pure joy of being in God's presence; it's about the basest of sensual pleasures: food and drink and sex. What are we to make of that?"

The old man smiled. "That sounds pretty good about now, John."

John allowed himself a small smile. "Hal, if you and I were Satan, why wouldn't we want to prevent the Second Coming? And if we couldn't prevent it, at least delay it. And what better way to delay it than by focusing on the Jews as a race and Christianity as a faith?"

He smiled. "Yeah, well, the Muslim world does seem to hate America as much as they hate Israel."

John leapt. "Let me tell you what I think. This is not the Church speaking. It's John Sweeney ..."

"When John Sweeney speaks, I always hear the Catholic Church speaking."

Tears immediately formed in John's eyes. "Nothing you could say, whether you meant it as a compliment or an insult, could ever mean as much to me—"

The old man started to protest but John waved him off. "Not important, Hal." Slight pause. "Not important. I think we may be seeing a glimpse of the Divine Plan in all of this. Abraham, at first, isn't quite sure about what God told him. He sires Ishmael after God promised him a child by Sarah. When he sees God is worthy of his trust, he is even willing to sacrifice the child of the promise, Isaac. God intervenes. Ishmael becomes father to the Muslims; Isaac to Jews." He paused, eyes twinkling. The old man was listening intently. "Now imagine Ishmael's offspring being the force that produces Armageddon, the conflict that culminates in the coming of Isaac's offspring, the Messiah." Dramatic pause. "How about the biblical narrative ending like that some 4000 years later?"

The old man was captivated.

"Hal, in the grand scheme of things, what was the 20th century about if not the systematic Nazi attempt to wipe out Europe's Jews, and when that failed because one third survived, the no less systematic Islamic attempt to wipe the new state of that surviving third off the map?" He paused briefly. "And if indeed the Jews are God's Chosen People, once and forever, what is that if not diabolical to the core?"

Hal Schwartz began slowly nodding. "It does feel like some sort of culmination is at hand."

"In your own circles, do your people ever discuss any of this?"

"No."

"Why?"

"I think I made that clear, John. Were you listening?"

John felt the sting of reprimand.

The old man had arrived at a point of departure in his life when all the ballast had been hurled overboard. There was never a reason not to say what you thought; and never, ever, a reason to apologize if it gave offense.

John changed his tone. "You know, Hal," he began gently. "As a Jew who became a cardinal once put it, 'The great grace given to Israel is, in the Messiah, given to the pagan. The Church is Catholic, or universal, precisely because she alone reunites the two categories which divided history: those who participate in the Election, and those who do not.'"

"Why do you speak only of Jews who became Christians?"

"Because they speak of something profoundly important in our time. They remind us it was only through, at St. Paul says, a temporary veiling of the Jews' eyes that salvation came to all the rest of us." He paused and continued softly. "And every Jew I know who has converted refers to it as a 'return.' They all say the same thing: becoming Catholic turned out to be the most Jewish thing they have ever done."

The old man's eyes began to moisten.

"These men and women say Christianity is the continuation of Judaism: its fruit, its very hope." John was surprised to discover his heart was pounding. He had come to Sunset Village on this day intending only to provide a small measure of comfort to a man who had become a surrogate father to him when he lost his own father as a college student. But something in the man's eyes and voice on this day engendered something in him he did not know existed: a desire to unite two peoples divided by the events of a weekend 2000 years ago. "What I have heard them say, Hal, is that in becoming Catholic they did not change their religion, they fulfilled it."

The tears were now running down the old man's face. His hands began to shake. He looked at John and shook slightly. "John, what am I to do? I don't have this, this faith, that you have."

He was sobbing now. John rushed to his side and knelt next to the chair. He wrapped the man's head and shoulders in his large arms and pulled them gently to his head and kissed the man again and again on the top of his bald and badly sutured head.

"We will pray, the two of us, to know God's will in this matter, Coach. If grace arrives, you will know it. It will flood your heart and make all things new. Then you will call me and I will come to you." His voice started to break and he stopped abruptly.

He knelt until he felt strong enough to depart. He grabbed the old man's chair and lifted himself with some difficulty. Four surgeries had left his knees in painful disrepair. He reached down and clasped the old man's hands in his and looked into his eyes with a great and tender love. He pulled him to his breast, his tears rinsing the old man's head and shoulders. "I love you, Hal. I love you for everything you have been in my life, throughout virtually the whole of my life. Please know that I pray for you every morning when I raise the sacred host." His voice caught. "Know, too, you have been father to my vocation."

He moved quickly, head down, tears streaming, through the door and into the corridor. Within moments he was outside squinting into a bright summer sun and wiping tears from his eyes with his bare forearms.

With a heart made heavy by the weight of pure love he moved slowly to his car.

Hal Schwartz died in his sleep that night.

# 38

Maggie Kealey arrived a bit flushed and well after the others.

It was Father Sweeney's practice to invite parishioners attending the 9:00 and 10:30 Sunday Masses to join him once a month for a continental breakfast in the parish hall.

On this shimmering bluebird day in early autumn she was stopped coming out of church after the 10:30 by a nurse from the hospital who claimed to be experiencing marital difficulties. She divulged her husband was an alcoholic. The woman seemed intent on drawing Maggie into the middle of the struggle in a desperate attempt to confront her husband and persuade him to seek help. Maggie wanted no part of it, but the nurse refused to accept her CEO's protestations of limited influence. It was a good 15 minutes later before she finally wrested herself free of the woman and made her way down the steps to the church basement that was the site for the Sunday morning socials.

Upon entering the hall she immediately searched for Jim Gillespie and saw that he was entertaining a small circle of women on the far side of the room. One of the women, an attractive widow named Colleen O'Boyle, appeared to be taking an unusual interest in her Chief of Oncology and Director of the Women's Clinic. All Maggie knew of the woman was that her husband had been a successful commercial realtor who died of colon cancer over two years ago. Maggie thought the woman to be in her mid-to-late 40's, though she looked a good deal younger. She was short and blonde and cute and quite personable; she also possessed, Maggie was disappointed to observe, a stunning figure. Maggie did not know if she had children, she thought perhaps she did, but her body language suggested she was certainly open to having one or two in marriage with Dr. James Gillespie.

Maggie approached the small group warily. She was looking for some time alone with the good doctor and clearly this was neither the time nor the place. Her arrival was noted first by the widow. "Oh, Maggie, please join us. Jim is telling us some of his hospital stories."

Maggie winced and shot an accusatory glance at her Department Head, who merely shrugged his shoulders and continued. Gillespie was in rare form and she marveled that this enigmatic man could summon his trademark humor on demand, even at a small parish social on a Sunday morning. Maggie left the group momentarily and returned with a cup of hot coffee and a small cheese Danish. She felt a bit tired and was looking for a place nearby to sit, when she heard Gillespie punctuate another story with her name. The women were laughing uproariously and looking at her for corroboration. Her eyes made their way to Gillespie and she noted his arm was now encircled within the arm of the widow.

It had been 40 years since Maggie felt the flashing pain of jealousy. She remembered watching Bill dance with a sorority sister, each with both arms draped around the other, at a campus mixer one night, and being shocked at the depth of the resentment she suddenly felt toward each of them. She felt humiliated, and resolved to confront him, yet was unable to summon the courage. Something in his manner always intimidated her. He was an alpha male, and she watched a number of young women in those years respond biologically to his sheer physical presence. So she seethed in private and looked for opportunities to spark a retaliatory measure of jealousy in him. It never quite worked out. Bill would immediately size up his competition and decide he was in no danger of losing his footing, and would just move on to whatever, or whoever, attracted his attention in that moment.

Maggie was so unsettled at the sight of her colleague suddenly "in play," the object of an attractive younger woman's heightened attention, that she was unable to speak. The others seemed to enjoy her discomfort, though she couldn't be sure of that. It was Gillespie who rescued her. He came over and stood beside her and began talking about the remarkable work she was doing at Philadelphia's largest Catholic hospital. Within several minutes the others withdrew one by one, the widow last among them. Now alone, Jim turned to Maggie and said, "Woman, is there no one left to accuse you? Then I do not accuse you. Go and sin no more."

Maggie turned to face Gillespie, leveled a steady gaze and said, "Jim, would you take me home?"

Gillespie mimed wiping his face with a handkerchief as if struck by a glass of water. "How did you get to Mass?"

"I drove."

He immediately parsed two possibilities. One, she was jealous of Colleen O' Boyle's sudden interest in him; two, she was still seething over the dressing down he had administered in her office after her meeting with Cardinal O'Hallaran.

He tended to think it was the latter.

"Okay. I brought the pickup. You want to ride in the front with me, or alone in the back, which is open, by the way?"

She ignored him and turned to leave. As she did so, she encountered her pastor. "Maggie, are you leaving? You just got here."

"Oh, Father, I'm so sorry. Jim and I have a very important meeting tomorrow. In fact, may we ask for your prayer support? This one is critical."

Sweeney's smile froze. "Is this the meeting with Sister Kathleen?"

Maggie nodded.

"We're going to demand she fire all non Catholics," Gillespie intoned.

John and Maggie glanced at him as though he was an impudent child. "Maggie, you have my prayers." He turned to Gillespie and, tongue firmly planted in cheek, said, "And Jim, you have my absolution."

Maggie did not wait for Jim Gillespie. She turned to leave, and in moments was outside walking slowly to his Porsche Carrera. He caught up in several purposeful strides. They walked together in silence and reached the car just as a small cloud momentarily shadowed the sun.

It was a six block drive to Maggie's home. The journey was briefly interrupted by the town's only traffic light. Maggie Kealey chose this moment to respond to Gillespie's broadside earlier in the week. "You know, Jim, you were really out of line coming into my office and raising your voice about my meeting with O'Hallaran. That was demeaning, doing that within earshot of others. It was also entirely too personal. You made references to my emotional scars from Bill and Moia. Where do you get off doing that? What have I ever done to you to deserve such treatment?" She quickly stole a glance to gauge his reaction. He was staring straight ahead as the purring car scaled the town's only bridge. She raised her voice in protest. "Why humiliate me? Why, Jim? Who does such a thing to a person they claim to respect?"

No response.

"Are you going to just sit there and ignore me?"

He sat and ignored her.

Her voice began to crack. "I don't know what I'm supposed to do. That man, the cardinal, he's not interested in the church's mission. He cares only about his capital campaign. I challenged him. I challenged him to do the right thing for the right reason. Why don't I have that right? And why must I be humiliated in public for having done so by someone who acts like he's my friend?"

Nothing.

Quietly, she began to cry.

Gillespie turned right onto Winchester Lane and moments later pulled into the fourth driveway on the left. He inched up to the home's front entrance which was on its port side. It was not lost on him, as he stared straight ahead at the one-car detached garage at the end of the driveway, that he was looking at the designated site of Moia Kealey's final solution. He left the car idling, suspecting he may not get an invitation to follow his hitch hiker inside.

Maggie Kealey sat in silence, tears streaming down her cheeks. She appeared to be waiting for a response, any response, before she would open the door of the car and take her leave. Sensing none was forthcoming, she suddenly turned in her seat and faced Gillespie. "Do you despise me, Jim? Is that what this is about? Tell me if it is! I don't need anyone standing with me who is *not* with me. If we're not together on this, I will go into that meeting alone. And I will come out of that meeting, alone; and I will do what I have to do, alone!" She lifted her voice several decibels. "Are you listening to me, Jim? Are you with me or not? I need to know, now!"

Jim Gillespie sat with his hands in his lap. He was looking at them. It was not at all clear he was prepared to say anything. Indeed he was not.

After several awkward moments, Maggie Kealey burst into tears and turned to leave. Blinded by her tears she couldn't find the door handle. Suddenly, she felt a strong hand on her left shoulder. It was turning her against her will back toward the car's driver. In one motion the hand was replaced by another and the original was now behind her neck and gently pulling her toward the driver. Maggie Kealey was so stunned she simply submitted. Jim Gillespie, eyes filled with a faraway look she did not recognize, inched closer. He paused for a nanosecond to permit a protest. In its absence he enveloped his passenger in his arms and kissed her passionately on the lips. The embrace was so strong and the emotion in the kiss so filled with repressed longing that she found her body relaxing involuntarily.

Gillespie blew through any stop signs that may have existed. He kissed her again and again, on her lips, her cheeks, her neck, each time with greater passion. With each kiss, years of all but uncontrollable desire seemed to be released.

Maggie, now engaged, raised her arms and cupped his face with her hands; she returned each kiss with a tender passionate kiss of her own on his lips and cheeks and hands.

In the passion of the moment, it did not seem to occur to either of them that they were now necking in broad daylight, in a car, in front of her home, on a Sunday morning ... after Mass.

Once he pulled back momentarily only to lurch forward with even more intensity. Soon she was simply overwhelmed and lay back in her seat with her hands gripping his to ensure they did not roam unsupervised.

In minutes, Jim Gillespie, passion finally spent, sat back in his seat and said soberly, "Now, if there is anything in my response that you find unclear, I suggest you communicate it through the proper inter office channels."

Maggie, hair and dress slightly askew, laughed. She found the doorknob which had eluded her earlier and opened the small door to disembark. Remarkably, she found herself turned again for a final kiss of transcendent emphasis. "What's a letter between friends without a little post script?" Jim Gillespie inquired politely.

She looked at him dreamily. "8:00 a.m. tomorrow in Sister Kathleen's office, Gillespie. And don't make me come looking for you."

"Now there's a world class disincentive if I ever heard one."

The car door shut and Maggie Kealey quickly scaled the two steps to her front door. She was humming. Jim Gillespie watched her with the eyes of a basset hound. He waited until she was inside and turned to smile at him and blow a kiss.

Only then did he slowly ease the car back out of the driveway.

Sister Kathleen was late for her own meeting. Maggie Kealey and Jim Gillespie, each with a requisite Starbucks in hand, stood in the formal sitting area of the office chatting about secrets. Presently, the good Sister arrived. It was 8:23 a.m. There would be no explanation.

Instead, her eyes widened at the sight of Jim Gillespie. "Hello, Jim. What a surprise." Then turning to Maggie she said, "I didn't know Dr. Gillespie would be sitting in our meeting this morning."

Maggie refused to allow the Order's point person for the Hospital's mission put her on the defensive, a favorite tactic. "Good morning, Kathleen. How are you today?"

The nun nodded imperceptibly, a small smile frozen on her pale face.

"Dr. Gillespie has a firsthand account of a meeting with a potential strategic partner that I believe will prove useful."

Kathleen Sullivan glanced at Jim Gillespie, who smiled, she thought, a bit too brightly.

"May we sit, Sister?" Maggie inquired politely.

"Yes, of course," she replied perfunctorily. She waited until Jim and Maggie were seated, then sat down in a slightly larger wing chair near the room's only window. Once seated, she began methodically brushing invisible crumbs from the lap of her skirt. Maggie stared hard at Jim, imploring him with her eyes not to comment.

"Care to borrow my whisk broom, Sister?"

Maggie moaned softly. The nun stared absentmindedly at Gillespie, then turned to Maggie and said, "So, tell me about this new strategic initiative of yours."

"I bring you a problem and its solution," Maggie began directly. "I've learned Regina Hospital is not in compliance with the U.S. Bishops' ERD's." Jim had asked her not to start with that simple statement of fact. She immediately saw that he had been right.

"Specifics, please," the nun replied tersely.

Maggie pounced, precisely as Jim has importuned her not to.

"Number *one*, our entire Ob/Gyn staff is dispensing oral contraceptives; *two*, they are referring infertile couples to Mid Atlantic for IVF procedures; *three*, Mid Atlantic is actually doing the procedures in our building; *four*, our docs have set up a egg bank for younger women and a sperm bank for younger men; *five*, they are selling these eggs and sperm to older infertile couples; *six*, our docs are profiting from the sale; *seven*, we are advertising Mid Atlantic's services in our on-line directory; *eight*, we profit from our transactions with Mid Atlantic in three ways: a) they pay us for the advertising, b) they pay us rent for their suite, and c) they send our own patients back for blood work, ultra sounds and MRI's, which we bill *them* for; *nine*, we believe, but cannot yet prove, there is a black market for our patients' eggs which are cryogenically preserved and sold to major pharmaceutical houses, state universities and biotech firms for embryonic stem cell research purposes. We suspect our doctors are profiting from this trade as well; and *ten*, although not all of this is known within the hospital and community, some of it is widely suspected. The consequence is a growing skepticism about the hospital's stated mission of 'providing Christ's compassionate care for the poor.'"

*Strike three*, Jim Gillespie muttered under his breath. He didn't understand why otherwise successful women couldn't, or wouldn't, apply the brakes when a precipice loomed. He sat as if in a towing truck awaiting a 911 call from his local dispatcher.

The nun turned to him and said, "Do you concur, Dr. Gillespie?"

It was the one question he feared. Certainly, his CEO had the facts correct. It was the opinion encasing the facts that troubled him. "I do."

Kathleen Sullivan sat looking at her lap for several awkward moments. Jim was certain she was yearning for a few crumbs. She looked up in weary resignation. Clearly, the content of this meeting now explained her tardiness. She had one reason to get up in the morning – to ensure Regina Hospital was living its mission. She had just been told the devil himself had stolen the mission and replaced it with his own while she slept. She did not appear over-joyed to learn this.

"And the solution?"

Maggie Kealey, game face unchanged, leapt. "I'm going to close our OB/Gyn Department and open a Natural Family Planning Clinic."

"What?"

"I'm going to bring in a NaPro technology physician named Hank Seelaus to staff it and run it. He'll also oversee our on-site Adoption Agency and our NFP Education Program for couples, physicians and priests."

"You'll do no such thing."

Abrupt silence.

Jim Gillespie, sitting in his ringside seat, thought a knockout blow had just been delivered. Then again, he reminded himself, this was Maggie Kealey, and she had demonstrated nothing in her life if not an extraordinary capacity to rise from the canvas.

"Oh, I *will* do it, Sister. I am not here to ask your permission. I am the Chief Executive Officer of this hospital. I am responsible for all of its operating decisions. This is an operating decision. I have made it. This is what's known as a 'heads up.'"

Silence. Gillespie thought he saw icicles forming on the edge of his coffee cup.

Kathleen Sullivan surprised them both by switching gears. "I dare say you'll start a stampede for the door. Physicians tend to circle the wagons, do they not, Doctor Gillespie?"

"It's a distinct possibility, Sister," he responded evenly.

"And the patients would of course follow?"

"Perhaps," he replied.

Brief, awkward silence. Then the good nun resumed her patient cross examination in an attempt to divide and conquer. "I suppose we would then be forced to shut our doors?"

He just shrugged.

The nun now turned her attention to Maggie. "And this

would *advance* our mission to provide compassionate care to the poor in the name of Christ?"

Maggie was prepared. "Oh, as you might imagine, I see a quite different scenario." She paused briefly for control. "I see us creating America's first commercial market for the sacred transmission of human life. Something truly counter cultural. A prototype for all Catholic hospitals in the country. I see good NFP doctors coming from all over America and drawing patients from all over America. I see us building residence halls with child care centers for couples from out of town. I see us building residence centers for priests and seminarians coming from all over the world to learn NFP and going back home and beginning a counter revolution in their own countries."

The good Sister appeared unmoved.

This did not deter the impassioned advocacy of her CEO. "This will do the one thing I have been charged by the Board with doing: change our payer mix. This is the only way it can be done. We are kidding ourselves if we believe we can attract better cardiologists, oncologists, gastroenterologists than Jeff or Penn. We cannot; we will not. The women with full health care coverage will continue to come into the city to see those physicians for their serious illnesses and procedures. And we will continue to provide the best care we can manage to the uncovered masses, requiring millions in annual subsidies from the Order. One day, the Order will simply run out of money. On *that* day, the doors will close." Maggie paused to assess the damage and concluded it was negligible. "On *that* day Kathleen, one might ask, how did the Order's decision to cling to the status quo serve the long term mission of providing compassionate care to the poor in Christ's name?"

As pure theatre, Gillespie thought it pretty good. As intramural polemics, he was less certain.

"I suppose one would have to say on that day that Divine Providence had spoken, Mrs. Kealey," the nun replied flatly.

"Spoken?" Maggie appeared on the verge of an outburst. Gillespie sat up on the edge of his chair. "Divine Providence is speaking now, to all of us. He is saying, 'do the right thing.' Do the *mission* thing. He's saying, 'Create a Culture of Life oasis amidst a Culture of Death. I will bless that. Trust! Trust above all else. For all things are possible for one who trusts.'" She shifted gears and spoke in softer, gentler terms. "This is the moment of our visitation, Kathleen. The Spirit is speaking clearly to us. We are either going to act in conformance with the Church's magisterial truth and bear fruit that will last, or we are going to turn away and wither on the vine."

Maggie stood abruptly. This drew surprised reactions from each of the others. "On my watch, we will choose life." She looked at Jim who rose and stood beside her. "I'm moving forward, Sister. If the Board disapproves, it can fire me."

The nun's face registered shock.

"I stand with Maggie, Kathleen," Jim said quietly but firmly.

Kathleen Sullivan's countenance was now decidedly ashen. There was a discernable remoteness at the edge of her eyes as though she were imagining a conversation with her superiors. She said nothing.

Jim looked at Maggie and signaled a departure. They turned together and left Kathleen Sullivan in silence.

Jim suddenly reappeared at the door. He stared at the hospital's sitting Director of Mission and said, "Forgive me, sister. I forgot to mention. You'll also be looking for a new Head of Oncology." He paused and added, "human cancer, I'm trained to deal with; institutional cancer, I'm not."

He turned without waiting for a reply and left the conference room for a second and final time.

Jim Gillespie and Maggie Kealey went in search of Hank Seelaus. They had an idea they wanted to discuss with him.

# 39

Michael Burns did not like being summoned to New York. It was one thing to schedule a meeting himself for specific business purposes; it was another to have one scheduled for him without being told why.

Cliff Ackerman had been characteristically tight-lipped on the phone. All he would say is, "It's important you be here Monday morning."

Michael couldn't fathom what might possibly constitute an agenda for a one-on-one meeting with Ackerman. Siliezar's absence was troubling. He was said to be "traveling." Michael couldn't read that. In the year since the acquisition, he had never been asked to meet with Ackerman alone. He wondered if Siliezar knew of the meeting, and concluded he most certainly did. Cliff Ackerman did not make decisions; he implemented them.

Michael sat erect in his Metro Club Car seat. He held coffee in one hand, a folded Wall Street Journal in the other. His stomach was churning. He read and re-read the same Page One story on HM Inc plans to be a significant player in multiple areas of the coming Life Sciences Revolution. The story, of course, contained no new revelations. He found it mildly amusing just how far the general press lagged current business stories. He knew large corporations were a big part of the reason, measuring every disclosure for its likely impact on share price; but he believed, at root, it was a consequence of the world of higher education being captured by committed leftists. In their view, he believed, commercial trade was a necessary evil. It was permitted to exist, more or less, only to create wealth that was to be redistributed in accordance with their grand designs.

His stomach refused to allow him to compartmentalize his pending meeting. He kept reviewing several likely scenarios. Siliezar had a specific mission for him on the Life Science Revolution front. Siliezar had concerns about Burns Advertising's first and second quarter Income Statement. Revenues were off 12% due to some softness in the general market, and costs were up 17% due to several new account ramp ups, Women's Right being the chief offender. And speaking of Women's Right, there was always the possibility of a formal complaint that had made its way, first, to Proper Parenthood, then on to Siliezar directly. Michael did not trust women who weren't women. He was only too happy to have off-loaded that problem to Aaron McKenna, who seemed delighted to be developing the business without interference from him.

A burly conductor punched his ticket and asked him what he thought about the Philadelphia Eagles' fortunes this season. It was early October and the town's beloved Birds had won three of their first four games. "They'll win ten games, as they always do, and get bounced in the first playoff game, as they always do," he replied with certainty. The conductor laughed and said, "Man, you got that right."

Michael laid the newspaper on his lap and opened the tray table in his seat. He set the coffee on the small table and the newspaper next to it. He pushed the button releasing the seat and reclined, head resting a bit uneasily against a small blue pillow. These were the moments when he liked to do a "current state assessment" of his life. He always began with family. The three girls had married, two well. One was going through a difficult divorce. A child was involved. He greatly liked his son-in-law; the problem was his daughter was not as fond of him. There were six additional grandchildren between the other two daughters. Carol told him repeatedly he was not allowed to have favorites. He never made any attempt to hide the fact that a three-year-old he called Boom Boom was his favorite. The child was built like a beer keg, and had discovered early in his young life that he could pretty much head butt his way into, or out of, anything. He was, Michael liked to tell perfect strangers, a seminal force of nature.

His sons were each doing well. He was proud of both. Paddy was a builder, a natural leader of men, quiet and intelligent and other-directed. Mike was a rough and ready Irish cop with a heart big as all outdoors. He didn't let too many people get close, but those who did were especially fond of him. Neither man was married, though each was dating. Carol took a much more active interest in her sons' social calendars than he did. He only cared that the young ladies were practicing Catholics from good homes.

His thoughts drifted to Joe Delgado. He did not like how their boating excursion had ended. In fact, it troubled him greatly. Their friendship spanned three decades. They met as young parishioners of St. Martha's parish in Narbrook in their early 20's. It was a source of surprise and amusement to each to discover they had played baseball and football against each other in high school. Joe was a catcher and a center; Michael was a pitcher and a quarterback. Joe loved teasing him that their schoolboy positions reflected the differences in their personalities and need for recognition. Privately, Michael concurred. He esteemed his friend's low-profile, "blue collar" ethic, and wished he possessed a portion of it.

In the weeks after the incident, he had checked his e-mail regularly to see if perhaps there was, not an apology necessarily, but a signal of some sort that the matter was now behind them. In its absence, he tried to formulate just such a correspondence, but was unable. What does one say when one's character has been assailed by a dear friend and the action, or inaction, which set the issue in play is as yet unresolved?

Michael found it interesting that friendships built on principle were more easily sundered than those built on mutual interest. To be bonded in the Holy Eucharist, he believed, was to be connected at the deepest level of man. All ruptures had to be offenses against the sanctity at the core of the bond, something of which concupiscent man was all too capable. Missing a four-foot putt in a Member-Guest somehow didn't have the same disruptive force.

He conceded his friend had a right to feel what he felt, even to think what he thought, about Michael's unwillingness to co-pilot a kamikaze mission into the Life Sciences edifice. His problem was with how that disappointment was expressed. There had been the unmistakable ring of utter disdain. After all, he reasoned, it wasn't as if he hadn't laid himself out in New York years ago, while Delgado remained frozen in time.

He had a penchant for brooding. Mentally, he began taking his friend to task. *Now you want to move, and move at your pace, and I'm supposed to move in lock step with you? And if I don't, I'm a disgrace? So I'm headed, where? Hell?* Michael felt his blood begin to run hot. He suddenly saw himself face to face with Delgado again. This time his veins were bulging and he was suggesting, not so politely, that he give careful consideration to a certain biological impossibility.

It took several moments for his heart rate to return to normal. He sipped his coffee. It was no longer warm. He picked up the newspaper. It no longer held his interest. He decided this was not a particularly good day to complete his current state assessment. He pushed the button inside his seat and reclined all the way back. He felt tired and he shut his eyes, hoping to catch a catnap before the train arrived in Manhattan.

. . .

Michael arrived at the 48th floor reception desk for Ultra Com Inc about four minutes early for his 9:15 meeting. He was announced and asked to wait. Not a good sign, he concluded. There had always been someone to greet him upon arrival. Now he sat as though a vendor. *Sit tight. We'll get to you.* He was surprisingly sensitive to slights, and a master at sending and decoding their signals. He felt an edge building somewhere deep within him. He hoped, for Cliff Ackerman's sake, he had good news.

He picked up a magazine to read. He read a lengthy piece about the United States' economic woes and the likelihood, which was thought to be high, that the U. S. dollar would soon lose its peg in global currency. When he finished he looked at his watch. He was now 11 minutes into his wait. Another bad sign, he brooded.

Presently, Cliff Ackerman appeared in the reception area and walked toward Michael with a large forced grin and an outstretched hand. He was in his shirtsleeves, tie neatly in place. "Michael, so good of you to come up. Thank you."

Michael took his hand and felt its indecision. "Not like I had a choice, Cliff," he replied with a tight smile.

Ackerman winced. "Michael, how was your weekend? Were you out on the boat?"

Michael was now trying to silence a Geiger counter in his stomach which always portended the imminence of trouble. "No. Carol and I attended a christening for one of our grandchildren. Never made it down the shore. Next weekend, hopefully."

They passed Ackerman's office. Michael was surprised they weren't meeting there. Instead, Ackerman led him to a small conference room down the hall from the Executive Suite. There were no windows, and, Michael quickly noted, no coffee cart. This would not be a social visit.

When they were seated, Ackerman came quickly to the point. "Michael, we have a small problem."

Michael felt a right hand land solidly in his solar plexus. "Just how small is small, Cliff?"

Ackerman flinched. Michael felt a left dig into his ribs. "Well, it's a problem."

"Cliff, that part I'm getting."

"Michael, the problem is in our Philadelphia office."

"Uh, that would be Burns Advertising?"

"Yes."

"Care to let me in on it, Cliff?"

"Aaron McKenna and Ed Mobley have threatened to resign and take several of the agency's largest clients, and a significant portion of the agency's revenue, if you're not replaced as CEO in 40 days."

Michael never saw the crossing right hand that landed flush on his jaw and sent him spiraling to the floor in search of equilibrium. He was in a free fall. He tried to get his mind around what he was hearing, but failed. Every time he thought he had a grip, he lost it. He found himself realizing nothing in his life had prepared him for such treachery. It was a way of thinking, a course of action, that was simply outside his code of behavior.

He immediately thought of McKenna, whom he had mentored over the past 12 years. He'd been father to the young man's hopes and dreams, his very career. He'd made him wealthy in his early 30's by buying his agency, and had promised him, at the time, succession within four years. It was unfathomable, simply unconscionable, that a protégé would reward kindness in such a lethal manner.

He thought of Mobley, whom he saw as a despicable human being who despised everyone and everything, even the very business that had afforded him a measure of wealth and fame. Certainly, Mobley was the initiator. Michael quickly convinced himself that Mobley had carefully cultivated McKenna, plying him with influence and affirmation, and had secured his compliance in the palace coup by promising him far greater riches and fame in their new collaboration.

He looked at Ackerman who was staring blankly at him. He suspected his cold war enemy was taking great satisfaction in this assignment. Michael immediately thought of Siliezar. Why hadn't he been the one to break the news of the coup? In fact, why hadn't he simply fired the two traitors on the spot? What changed? Why was Siliezar suddenly willing to go along with this, this absurd plot? When, how had he fallen out of favor?

He felt like getting up and leaving without saying another word. He had one slight problem; he didn't trust his legs. The room was still spinning.

What did this mean? How would he explain it to Carol, to the children, to his friends? How would it be announced in the agency itself, to the public? Would there be a public execution? Would he have to stand on a stage while the new coronation takes place? Would he be given an office? Would he ... what about his deal? What about his contract? He must call his lawyer immediately. There must be a clause in there, somewhere, to protect him from such treachery. The public humiliation alone demanded it.

"Did they define 'several' and 'significant portion' for you, Cliff?"

Ackerman's head dropped. He stared at the table. It was empty save for his sweating palms. "Yes, they did, Michael." It was clear he was not enjoying the rear naked choke by which he now controlled his adversary's movement. He identified two large accounts and several mid-sized accounts, one of which was Women's Right. Michael immediately calculated the losses. It represented over 30% of his firm's annual revenues. Recovery was possible, but unlikely: particularly if his best marketing and creative talent walked out with the felons.

"Give me 48 hours, Cliff. That's all I ask." There was an air of desperation in the plea which further heightened Ackerman's anxiety.

"Can't, Michael."

Michael didn't hear 'no.' It was a capacity he developed over time and, some believed, it lay at the root of his success. There was no mind that couldn't be changed once he turned the after-burners on. "I guarantee you, Cliff, I'll get half of that business back in 48 hours, and the other half in less than a week."

Ackerman stared past Michael. If anyone had told him a year ago he would flinch when it came time to pull *this* trigger, he would have laughed at them. But here he was, flinching. "Michael, Hanley approved it. It's done. There's no court of appeals with any jurisdiction."

Michael blinked.

An awkward silence fell upon the two men.

Michael was the first to speak. "Cliff, what happened?"

"They got to him, Michael. That's really the heart of it."

"How?" This was asked in a hushed tone of disbelief.

"He likes McKenna," Ackerman replied with a shrug. "You trained him too well. In fact, Hanley said as much. 'Thees one, he remind me of Maahkill. But, he is 20 years younger and much less expensive.'"

Michael was flabbergasted. "What about my contract?"

"One of our attorneys will be dispatched to work out a cash settlement with your attorney." Ackerman paused and added, "You will find Hanley very generous in these matters, Michael."

"Generous! Generous? I don't want generosity. What I want is justice!" Michael's voice had risen several decibels. "This is a travesty. No firm of any stature conducts itself in this manner. You should be ashamed." He paused to launch a blow dart. "Aren't you ashamed, Cliff?"

Ackerman surprised him. "I don't like it, Michael. If that's what you're asking, no, I don't like it."

"How could Hanley bless such treason?"

"To him, it's simply business. He made a few phone calls to the clients and concluded McKenna and Mobley had not exaggerated their strength. He viewed their strength as your weakness. Hanley despises weakness. He sees it as an opportunity to get younger and tougher, and shed a very large, unproductive expense." Ackerman paused and added, "Those are his words, Michael, not mine."

"What about all the talk about me working with him on the project, on the Life Science Revolution?"

Ackerman appeared to bite his lower lip. "Michael, he said you didn't show him enough initiative soon enough."

The room began swimming again. Slowly, the oxygen was being suctioned out. All the exits were sealed. Michael felt a stabbing pain in his chest. "Enough initiative?" his voice trailed off. "What was he expecting? We hadn't even scoped out what he wanted me to do."

"Michael," Ackerman said with some hesitation. "He thinks you retired after you cashed the first check. He says everyone has their number. He thought yours was higher. McKenna and Mobley convinced him otherwise. He's a guy who cuts his losses and moves on."

Michael's heart began to race. He saw his whole life crumbling around him. He'd have to sell at least one of his homes. There'd be no Viking Motor Yacht. He'd have to find something else to do, but what? At 60, he was too young to retire and too old to start over in the advertising business. The private and public humiliation would be extreme. His wife would be greatly saddened at the way his career had ended. His children would feel pity for him. His friends would offer consolation and encouragement, to be sure. What they really thought, he would never know. Maybe he did know.

"What's next, Cliff?"

"It'll be done with dignity, Michael. There will be a press release saying you are being promoted, effective December 1st, to Executive Vice President of Ultra Com Inc in New York. One week later, a follow up release will go out announcing McKenna and Mobley's promotions as CEO and COO, respectively. The subtext will be clear: it required thought and two men, to replace you, one of whom is your hand-picked protégé. You'll be quoted liberally, saying all the right things. On Friday, November 30 there will be a public reception to honor your legendary contributions to the Philadelphia Advertising community. Your family and friends will be invited. The governor and mayor will be there, along with assorted other Philadelphia dignitaries." He paused and shrugged. "All grace and style, Michael. Hanley is superb at public funerals."

Michael's heart sank to uncharted depths. He felt like he had just been mugged, then bound and gagged and left in a gutter. The attack, he now realized, was directed at the very core of his being, his identity. To the *who* he thought he had become. There would be no recovery from this wound. It was mortal.

"So, all that left is the lawyering up?"

Ackerman nodded grimly. "Pretty much."

Michael stood on uncertain legs. He looked down at Ackerman who continued to sit, avoiding his gaze. Then he turned and left.

For a second time in his career, he was leaving New York without a job.

This time, he left without hope.

# 40

---

US Airways flight 2012 to Ben Gurion airport in Tel Aviv departed from Philadelphia International airport over an hour and 45 minutes late. Wheels went up at 10: 47 p.m. eastern standard time and set down at 3:43 a.m. Israeli time. Other than the delay, the transatlantic flight was entirely uneventful for HM Healthcare's CFO Joe Delgado, flying in Business Class.

He did not sleep one minute of the 11 hours. It had been 14 years since he had been diagnosed with Sleep Apnea— a condition which had gone undiagnosed for eight years— and overseas flights with their late evening departures were nothing short of hell tours. He slept only with the aid of a CPAP machine, which could not be used on airplanes. The machine featured a Hannibal Lecter mask that he liked to don to frighten the junior al Qaeda cell that had invaded his home. It never failed to draw a sharp rebuke from his daughter, which was an added bonus. There was something ferociously appealing about being lectured by your children for misbehaving with their children.

He arrived exhausted and irritable. The warm October air and the hyper intensity of the terminal's lighting heightened his sense of teetering on the outer edge of civility. He searched in vain for a burly man holding a sign bearing his name. So much for their Israeli operation's attention to detail. He checked his watch. It was 4:01. He looked for a place to sit down. He didn't see one. He immediately understood why. No one was sitting down. No one was motionless. The entire terminal resembled a high school assembly at closing bell.

Joe stuffed his hands in his pants pockets and just watched. He watched people walk from one end of the terminal to another, from one group of passengers to another, from one shopping area to another. Motion itself seemed to define purpose: movement for movement's sake. Movement because *not* to move was to invite, what exactly? Enemy attack? Time frozen? Personal obsolescence?

Out of the corner of his eye, Joe saw a darkly complexioned man of considerable density approaching him. He appeared to be in his early 30's. His head and body were those of a man who had found them useful in making his way in the world. Joe turned in his direction. The man was now no more than 40 feet away. He still had not signaled whether he was friend or foe. Joe subtly shifted his weight. Front foot at 1:00, back foot at 2:00. He drew a bead on the man's circuitry just above what he guessed was a 20-inch neck. He lifted off his back foot slightly so he was up on his toes, ready to spring. They were now maybe 20 feet apart. The man's face was effortlessly menacing. Joe suddenly saw himself on an operating table with an Israeli surgeon inserting a pin in his right hand. At ten feet, the man's pace slowed. At five feet he pulled up, expression unchanged, and said, "Josef Dugooda?"

Joe stood down. "Close enough."

The man extended a massive hand which completely enveloped his. "Where's loogage?"

Joe pointed to the baggage tray with his flight number posted above it. Just then a loud buzzer went off, and the conveyer lurched forward noisily. The bagman's eyes were trained on the eclectically tagged bags spitting out the mouth of the cargo hold. Suddenly, he turned to Joe and said, "Point!" Joe noted that the man's index finger, which was pointing instructively in the direction of the tray, was easily the width of any two of his fingers. He thought the man's height to be about 5'10" and his weight about 275 pounds. He guessed his body fat to be in the 12% to 14% range. Joe thought it unlikely he would hear another word from the stranger until he dropped him off at the King David Hotel in Jerusalem.

He was right. The drive took the better part of 90 minutes. The driver spent an inordinate amount of time on his Blackberry. Joe marveled that the man was able to get fingers that looked more like toes to dance on its micro keyboard. He was also astonished at the number of cars on the road before dawn on a Saturday morning.

The country had grown tremendously in population and, Joe thought not so coincidentally, economic achievement since his last visit nearly 20 years ago. He believed the Israeli miracle was the most underappreciated, and therefore the most undertold, story in the world. A Jewish friend recently told him there were only about 800,000 Jews in the country at its founding in 1948; today, he claimed there were over seven million. Over those 60 years, the Israeli economy was reported to have increased 50 fold. There was no dearth of explanations. His friend said it was the Israeli himself. In all the world, he was unique. He was independent, tough, smart, curious, entrepreneurial, perpetually dissatisfied, relentlessly adaptable, and stunningly resourceful. He was all these things and more, and had been so for over 4000 years, regardless of where he laid his head.

Joe thought the neighborhood demanded nothing less.

He also believed enlightened self government hadn't hurt. The Law of Return had famously guaranteed every Jew a right to make Israel home. This brought the return, most notably, of the inestimable Russian Jews. Almost one million strong. They represented 30% of Russia's doctors, 20% of its engineers and scientists. What impressed Joe was the Israeli government's decision to create a Ministry of Immigrant Absorption, with living stipends and free language immersion classes for entire families. Jews, he concluded, understood survival. Americans, he wasn't so sure.

The lobby of the King David was all imported and buffed mahogany and marble. Like all great destination hotels it whispered of mythic moments past and the grand adventure of promised moments present. The driver lifted his stuffed black suitcase with two fingers and a thumb and hoisted it onto the bell captain's luggage rack; he stuffed several indecipherable currency notes in the man's hand and turned and left. Joe half expected to hear him introduced at the scheduled 2:00 meeting as HM Israel's Head of Human Resources.

His room was borderline four stars and overlooked a large outdoor pool, which was ringed with gaily colored canopies. He unpacked and hung the only business suit he had brought. He carefully removed a diary with periodic entries chronicling progress of The Project and hid it under his pillow. Then he pulled his workout clothes from the suitcase and changed. He knew from experience the best catnaps after overseas flights were earned.

He threw a long towel over his shoulder and left the room, key card in hand. He descended to street level and followed signs to the health club. It was 6:21. The room was full. He found a treadmill and programmed a 30-minute workout. When he finished, he lifted for 15 minutes. Then he hit the sauna for ten minutes. Sweating profusely, he left. He stepped into the elevator with three other guests. The other three passengers exited, a bit hastily he thought, on the second floor. He rode alone to the fourth.

Back in his room he showered and shaved and brushed his teeth. He pulled on a pair of white boxers and studied himself in the mirror. At 6'1", 218 pounds, 12.8% body fat, he was in the best shape of his life. He did not know what the future held, for himself, his family, his country. But, he consoled himself, at least he'd be fit.

He unpacked his CPAP and overseas adapter and plugged it into the socket underneath the night table. He called the front desk and left a 1:00 p.m. wake up call. Then he climbed into bed, adjusted the mask, turned on the machine and, finally, slept the sleep of the righteous.

He dreamt he was being followed in the Old City. He ducked in and out of small shops and back alleys in the Muslim Quarter before finally being cornered by UN police. He was arrested as a spy and sentenced to hard labor. Geoffrey Benton showed up at the arraignment and promised him he'd never serve a day. It was the last time he saw him. The first night in jail he was tortured. The second day, a letter arrived. It was from his wife. It said she loved him and missed him and urged him to come home. He saw himself, furious, throwing the letter on the dirt floor of his cell. He lay down and begged God for death. He couldn't feel his tongue. It was swollen and distended. Slowly, his ability to breathe was compromised. He began sucking air in a panic. He awoke dripping wet. He was on his back. The CPAP mask had slid off.

The wake-up call sounded like a jackhammer. He grabbed the phone and threw it against the wall behind the bed. He looked for the clock. It was on the floor next to the bed and it was not working. He had unplugged it to install the machine. He got up and went to the desk and picked up his watch. It was 12:57. Maybe his watch was slow. He dressed quickly: light sport jacket, open collar dress shirt and tan slacks. He headed down to the small dining room overlooking the pool. He ordered a seafood salad of some unknown formulation, and an iced tea. As the food arrived, he saw Rami Schatz enter the room. Their eyes met. Schatz responded as though Joe was a wealthy uncle. He threaded his way through the room's tables at a half gallop and arrived with a huge grin on his sunburnt face. "Boomer boy, how's by you?" he said, without hint of an edge.

Surprised, Joe stuck out his hand and said, "Sit down, Schatzy, and tell me what I've just ordered."

Bio Freedom's CEO sat and a waiter arrived immediately. He looked at Joe's plate and said, "Bring me the catch of the day, broiled in a light curry sauce."

The waiter nodded. "What are you drinking, sir?"

"I'm *not* drinking. It's far too early," he laughed at his own witticism. The waiter winced and left. Schatz called after him. "Iced tea."

He turned to look at Joe, smile undiminished. "I think you shook the boys up in Connecticut."

Joe felt a pin prick somewhere near an artery or ventricle. "I was just asking questions all of us should be asking," he replied defensively. "I guarantee you, others will ask those questions, including stockholders, and HM Inc better have answers."

Schatz laughed dismissively. "Believe me, Boomer, nobody cares as long as we make money. And if we don't, we're not here anyway," he laughed again, and it reminded Joe of why he did not like this man.

"So what to make of the big 'hush hush'?" Joe asked tentatively.

Schatz shrugged his shoulders. "They will show us the future. Then tell us to go make it happen."

"Where is this lab?"

"Somewhere outside Tel Aviv."

"Then why lodge us here in Jerusalem?" Joe asked, now perturbed.

Schatz smiled. "Get with the program, Boomer. In less than one hour, we will leave in twos and take different routes. No notes, no recorders, no cell phones. We will get a taste, that's all. Just a taste. The idea is to whet our appetites so we will go back to Europe and the States and run in place harder, longer."

The cynicism surprised Joe. He knew Schatz to be fully invested, and vested, in Project 4, as it was called in the senior executive suite at HM Inc headquarters in Connecticut. Maybe the irascible Schatz hadn't entirely bought in. Joe was intrigued by the possibility.

Schatz's food arrived. He ate the way he worked and lived. Within several minutes he was finished and waved the waiter over. "Check, please. I'll sign for both." That business dispatched, he turned to Joe and tapped his watch. "Let's head over to the Golda Meier room and check in on the others."

Joe looked at his watch. It was 1:46. He nodded and followed Schatz out of the room. Together, in silence, they walked the steps to the mezzanine level. The Golda Meier room was the smallest of the meeting rooms. It was cozy, minimally furnished and handsomely appointed in dark teak and leather. As they entered, Joe immediately saw Chad Henley and Geoff Benton, their backs to him, chatting up David Moskowitz, HM Israel's top scientist and the man responsible for today's tour. In the corner, he saw Phil Hankinson standing alone. He immediately walked over to say hello. Hankinson was cordial but guarded. Presently, HM Inc's CFO Thomas Shillingford arrived with HM Diagnostics CEO Connie Neumann.

There were eight men now in the small room. Chad Henley nodded to Geoff Benton, who slowly made his way to the front of the room. He placed his drink, it appeared to be a varietal from the continent, on a coaster at the edge of the table, and motioned the others to sit.

"Welcome to the Big Hard." Large, gracious smile. Joe noted Benton was completely relaxed. *Maybe it wasn't a varietal.* "Welcome to HM Israel." Smile fading. "Welcome to the future." Smile gone.

"Good. Then you are prepared to cash us out?" joked Rami Schatz, and Benton reacted as though he was ready to return to the bar.

"Not quite yet, Rami," he finessed. "But as you, indeed all of us, will see today, we are much closer than anyone could have imagined to realizing man's greatest dream and his crowning achievement." He paused and went back to the small bar and grabbed a bottle of Evian. He removed the cap and consumed half the bottle without a hint of self consciousness. "And what we will see," his voice was suddenly sharper, more vibrant, "could only happen here, in Israel." Pause. "Israel, the most remarkable country in the world." Joe interpreted this as Benton's way of ratcheting up the pressure on David Moskowitz. *We're betting the ranch, son. Got me covered, right?* He glanced over to Moskowitz. He was smiling, head bobbing like an adolescent's Adam's apple.

"Simon Peres once said, 'the greatest contribution of the Jewish people is dissatisfaction.' He noted 'this is bad for politics, but good for science.'" Benton smiled at Moskowitz. He then proceeded to talk about the unique contributions of the Israeli economy to the rest of the world. He spoke of boundary-morphing new technologies called "mashups," and neighborhood-centric private/public ventures called "clusters," and ideas that generated other ideas— which he called "meta ideas"— and said that although the Israelis hadn't invented them, they certainly had perfected them. And that, he said, was why HM Inc had bet the farm in Israel, even as the Iranians were enriching uranium and the Chinese and Russians were blocking UN resolutions to sanction them. *Armageddon, maybe. Profit, absolutely.*

Joe struggled to follow. He had come to believe Benton's core competency was obfuscation. He glanced and saw he was not alone. Eventually, Benton began winding down. To his everlasting relief, Joe heard him say, "So let me bring David up to tell you a little bit about what we're going to see this afternoon."

David Moskowitz, reed thin and preternaturally anxious, stood and walked to the front of the room. He swiftly launched into a brief history of the laboratory as an early settlers kibbutzim, a military barracks and currently, a state-of-the-art science lab, employing over 100 of the top nanotechnologists in the world, which was to say, Israeli scientists.

He spoke in hushed, precise terms about the way the laboratory was organized to create nanotechnology "mashups" and "meta ideas" that would lead to the development of whole new industries. He talked about its investors, which included the U.S. government and Stef Boros and Warren Buffet. He talked about "outcomes," and how they were being developed with the help of the HM Inc senior management team.

When he finished, Benton popped back up to explain the travel protocol to and from the laboratory. Schatz had been right.

They left in twos, each with a driver and a different route. They would reconnoiter at an abandoned school a mile away from the laboratory at 5:00 p.m. Once they were assured no one had followed any of the four nondescript cars, they would proceed together in a van to the laboratory.

Joe made a mental note to include the itinerary in his diary entry.

The HM management team entered the laboratory at 5:21. The interior reminded Joe of an old airplane hangar. It was large and open and chaotic in the manner of a Middle Eastern bazaar. It had the feel of retail science; it was so loud and disputatious that Joe found it difficult to believe any serious work was getting done.

They were met in the makeshift lobby by two balding, middle-aged men in dark business suits. Moskowitz introduced them as if they were fraternity buddies. One was the Israeli Minister of Finance; the other was said to be the Executive Director of something called "Yozma." Moskowitz explained Yozma, Hebrew for "initiative," was a government program created in the early '90's to develop ten new venture capital funds. Each fund had three co-partners: an Israeli venture capitalist in training, a foreign venture capital firm, and an Israeli investment bank. According to Moskowitz, the $100 million initiative had grown to over three billion dollars under management in less than 15 years. It had become the rocket fuel for the world's "Start Up Nation."

Moskowitz moved the group through the laboratories within the laboratories. They toured the nanotechnology lab, the nano-pharmaceuticals lab, and the nanochip and nanobot lab. They were also led through conventional labs where work was being done in optics, electronics, and wireless data transmission. At each stop, Moskowitz paused to ask surprisingly young men to describe the work they were doing and how it fit into the overall framework of The Project. Though clearly pre-rehearsed, undoubtedly for countless prospective investors, Joe found it stunningly coherent and persuasive. There was no doubt the serious men in white coats believed they were on a mission of profound importance.

The tour ended at 6:54. Joe noted no one in the laboratory had left, no one had stopped for dinner, and no one was working at any less frenetic a pace than when the HM management team showed up over an hour and a half ago.

Plans called for a rendezvous at the King David for 9:00 p.m. cocktails and dinner, in the Menachim Begin room. Joe left the lab with Tom Shillingford and a driver who was probably in her mid 20's but looked 16. On the way down, she mentioned casually she had been a tank commander in the war with Hamas in Lebanon.

They arrived at the hotel at 8:41 and Joe immediately went to his room for a quick shower and a change of clothes. When he entered the room he immediately sensed something amiss. His suitcase, which he had left open on the floor, was now sitting diagonal not flush against the wall. His CPAP mask was draped over the machine not the bedpost. His electric razor, which he had left charging, was unplugged.

He immediately went to his bed and pulled back the covers. He removed all three of the pillows, tossing them gently onto the floor. It was gone. The diary was missing. His heart began racing. He sat down to slow the world down. He picked up the phone and asked for the hotel manager. The front desk said the manager was gone for the evening, but the assistant manager on duty would be happy to come up to the room.

Within several minutes there was a sharp rap on the door. Joe, in boxers and shirtsleeves, opened the door. The assistant manager was an attractive woman in her early-mid 30's. She strode in like a drug enforcement agent. "What is the problem, Mr. Dugadoo?"

"Somebody's been in my things and removed valuables. I want an immediate investigation."

The woman walked to the small table at the far end of the room and picked up a notepad and a ball point pen. She walked back and stood facing him. "Okay, what is missing?"

"Before we get into that, could you explain how such a thing could happen at a four star hotel?"

The woman let the notepad fall to her side, leveled her gaze and said, "Mr. Dugadoo, we have 126 rooms at King David Hotel. We do not have 126 security guards. A professional saboteur can enter any hotel room in the world and take whatever he wants. This is precisely why we provide secure vaults for our guests where they can put their valuables."

Joe nodded. He decided against throwing a punch in frustration. He had a pretty good idea he'd only end up on his back with Israel's reigning Judo Champion standing over him, not a hair out of place. "Okay," he said soberly. "I'm missing a personal diary. It was a six inch by nine inch black leather-bound book. It is of extreme importance to me."

"I'm sure it is, Mr. Dugadoo." She stood and said, "I will have a police detective come to your room within 30 minutes."

Joe shook his head. "No, I'll be in the Begin room with a private party. It'll have to wait until I get back to the room, sometime around midnight. Will that be too late?"

The woman arched an eyebrow. "Can it wait until tomorrow morning?"

Joe nodded petulantly. He was not happy. Depending on who had possession of his diary, and what their intentions were, this had all the potential of a career-ending disaster.

He led the night manager to the door and headed into the bathroom for a shower. It was 9:03. His late arrival, he knew, would be noted, perhaps even anticipated.

It was 9:17 when he entered the Menachim Begin room, where the HM management team was assembled. They stood, drinks in hand, in the far corner of the room where a bar had been set up. Joe was surprised to see the two Israeli officials standing among them. One of them, the Yozma executive director, introduced as Benjamin Rosenbaum, was holding court. Chad Henley was the first to notice Joe. The look in his eye, and the manner in which he turned away, sent a chill down his spine.

Joe walked over to the bar and asked for a Diet Coke. He saw Benton notice him and start to turn away, before turning back and smiling grimly. Rami Schatz also took notice of his arrival and came over to agitate him about something or other, knocking into him and causing his Diet Coke to splash onto the cuff of his navy blazer.

Presently, Benton motioned for the group to take their seats. Joe immediately went to the end of the majestically appointed table and sat down. Connie Neumann, HM Diagnostic's CEO, sat down beside him. He immediately began waxing euphoric about their afternoon tour, and how extraordinary it was to be alive at this very moment in man's journey into a brave new tomorrow. Joe probed his eyes to see if he really believed what he was saying. He decided he couldn't tell.

Benton labored through another interminable pre-mumble about man's new launching pad. Joe thought precipice would have been a better metaphor. Finally he wound up, or down, and sat down. There was a momentary silence, then Rami Schatz started the bidding. "Moskowitz, when will you have this creature for us to see?" He laughed and looked around to see if everyone else found this as funny as he did. It was clear the others did not; it was equally clear this was entirely lost on Schatzy.

"2020 is our target," David Moskowitz replied tersely, stealing a glance at Benton.

A thick, uneasy silence settled around the table. Each man appeared to be alone with his thoughts. Then, Connie Neumann gave voice to the question in the minds of most. "Will he look different?"

"What makes you think it will be a 'he'?" Benton interrupted, sending the room into a forced paroxysm of laughter.

"Will he have a soul?" Joe's simple question forced another protracted silence. This one was different in kind. There was a palpable anxiety lying beneath its surface.

David Moskowitz glanced at Benton, who turned to Joe and glared. "Those are metaphysical matters. And those we leave to the philosophers," he said evenly.

Joe wasn't finished. If his diary had fallen into enemy hands, then it was now a footrace to a loose whistle. "Suppose the philosophers decide, well after the fact, that this 'post human' human was not such a good idea after all?"

"On what basis might they come to such a conclusion, Joe?" Benton asked, clearly baiting him.

Joe didn't flinch. "I wouldn't know, Geoff. I'm not a philosopher."

"But clearly you have problems with this initiative. Why don't you share them with us?"

Joe felt every head in the room turn. "Who said I had problems?"

Benton upped the ante. "Joe, it was clear in Connecticut. It is clear now in Jerusalem. You are struggling with certain aspects of this work. Why not share those doubts with us. After all, you're among friends." Large, benign smile.

Joe pulled his cards closer to his vest. "I'm troubled we haven't thought this through. There has been no constructive devil's advocacy. Our history shows we have problems when we rush hell-bent into what proves to be an expensive black hole. Remember Fire-Freeze and Sani-Save. They cost us about a quarter of a billion dollars all in. What was the HM Blue Ribbon panel's bottom line?" He paused to assess the depth of the wound he was inflicting. Both industrial new product debacles had happened on Benton's watch. "They suggested there was, and I quote, 'insufficient constructive devil's advocacy.'"

He saw Benton's jaw clench and unclench. He awaited a response that did not come, at least from Benton. The next voice to enter the fray belonged to his boss, Chad Henley. "Joe, that's patently unfair. We're talking about 31 consecutive quarters of double digit growth. Geoff's performance is historic by HM standards."

"This isn't about Geoff, Chad."

"I agree with Joe," Benton interjected. "It's about the future. It's apparent Joe and I have very different perspectives on what businesses HM ought to be in."

Joe took the measure of the comment before responding. "I

would disagree, Geoff. We agree on the businesses; we disagree on the products." He said this with an equal measure of acerbity.

"You are speaking of David's work, am I correct?" Benton replied, in an effort to further draw him out and isolate him.

"I am speaking of man as a product," he replied with pronounced emphasis.

"It is *you* who are calling it a product."

"'It'... Geoff...?"

Benton grew flustered. None of those in the room had ever seen Geoffrey Benton sputtering. "You're playing word games, Delgado," he said, voice rising.

Joe felt a preternatural peace in his heart. He lowered his voice and modulated it for heightened effect. "What precisely would you call what David is trying to create, Geoffrey?"

Benton's head dropped momentarily onto his chest. Suddenly, it bobbed up and he spat, "The future!"

The room froze. A hush fell upon the table. Joe thought he observed even the waiters moving more quickly in an effort to get out of the icy blast.

Nothing more of consequence was said. The dinner became an exercise in forced diversionary conversation. One of the men said later, it reminded him of his childhood when his parents fought. He used to eat, he said, with his head down and his fork in constant motion.

Joe was the first to finish and the first to leave. When he returned to his room there was a handwritten note from the assistant manager. It read: *Mr. Delgado, Detective Bilsky will call your room from the lobby at 8:00 a.m. You will find him relentless and efficient. Please advise if there is anything else the hotel's management can do to assist you in retrieving your missing document.* It was signed, *Sara Weinstein.*

*Stolen diary, Sara. Not missing document.*

Joe crumpled the note and threw it in the small wastebasket next to the table in the corner of the room. Then he knelt by the bed and prayed.

# 41

John Sweeney was nervous. It was well past 5:00. Carmella Francone had not yet returned from the grocery store, and company was coming. Important company. Dr. Koblinski, head of the Catholic Bioethics Network, was scheduled to arrive in less than an hour. He had agreed to update Dr. Jim Gillespie and Maggie Kealey on the Church's current concerns in genetic science. John had also invited Joe and Fran Delgado and Mike and Carol Burns. The Delgados accepted; the Burns declined. He didn't know which surprised him more.

At 5:23, John heard Carmella walk through the back door. He rose from the chair in his office to greet her. "Carmella, do you need help with the bags?"

"Of course I need help, Father. Do you think I'm a pack mule?"

He smiled sheepishly and banged through the screen door and down the steps to the car with its doors and trunk open. There were eight bags full of groceries. *Holy Mother of God! We're talking dinner for four, okay five. What are we going to do with all this food?*

He grabbed four bags in his strong hands and arms and hoisted them out of the car and inside to the small kitchen table, where he set them down, almost covering its surface. "Carmella, are you sure you bought enough food? What happens if Maggie Kealey wants seconds?"

The housekeeper was emptying and storing the first bag and didn't bother to look up. "You'll call Bonzo's pizza."

He went out and brought the rest of the bags in and set them on the table's chairs. "I'd love to help you, Carmella, but somehow I doubt you'd think of it as help."

"Drinks and hors d'oeurves at 7:00 and dinner at 8:00, yes Father?"

*In other words, get lost.* "Yes, Carmella."

Jim headed back to his office, grabbed his book of prayers and made a beeline for the church. He wanted to get his prayer time in before his guests arrived. This tended to eliminate anxiety if an evening ran long, which he thought was quite likely tonight. It was a bit of an eclectic group, he conceded. The wild card was always Fran Delgado. He never knew how a few glasses of wine would affect her. Sometimes they would trigger a withering assault on her long-suffering husband; other times, she'd just fall into a blessedly silent stupor. He would pray for a stupor tonight.

It was 6:35 when he left the sanctuary and emerged in the cool, late October night air. He glanced at his watch and decided he had time for a shower and shave. He welcomed the warm water with its power to soothe and cleanse. He wanted to be a good host and that meant, first, being awake and, second, being relaxed. A hot shower promised both.

The door bell rang for the first time at 6:58. It was Stanley Koblinski. John heard Carmella let him in. She would not be happy he was not downstairs to spare her the interruption. He could feel the cold dead-eyed stare already on the nape of his neck. "I'll be right down, Stan," he hollered.

He put on a fresh shirt and pressed bib and collar, and grabbed a drycleaned black suit jacket from his closet, knocking the wooden hanger with a pair of black slacks still in it to the floor. He stooped to pick it up and felt a sharp pain in his lower back. He rose stiff and unsteady. He slipped the jacket on and buttoned the middle button. He embraced the pain, which mitigated it slightly. It was now the price of whatever God willed for the evening.

He descended the steps gingerly and saw two figures through the curtain and opaque glass in the front door. He opened the door and saw Joe and Fran Delgado, just as Joe was reaching for the buzzer. He was stunned to see Fran's arm wrapped in Joe's.

He opened the door and exclaimed, "Joe, Fran, so good of you to come."

"So good of you to include us, Father," Fran replied. John couldn't help but note she was smiling. "Yes, thank you, Father," Joe added. "We've been told this place serves the best pasta on the Main Line."

The ice breaker. John admired that seemingly effortless facility in men of the world. He led the Delgados into the front parlor, where Stan Koblinski rose to meet them. Carmella appeared with four glasses of chilled white wine and a tray of warm stuffed mushrooms. She also took the opportunity to flash John her dead-eyed stare. He smiled sweetly in return.

The buzzer rang, and John put down his glass of wine and slowly extricated himself from the chair. He looked to see if the others noticed his discomfort; they hadn't. He exited the parlor, entered the hallway and opened the front door to greet Maggie and Jim. "I hope we're not interrupting your bed time, Father," Jim said, flashing a big grin. "We won't be long, promise. As Maggie said, 'let's just eat and run.'" John quickly glanced at Maggie who was suddenly ashen. *Please, Lord, let this woman know love again. This time, authentic love … selfless and pure.* "Maggie, why do you insist on wearing this hair shirt? Last time I checked, Lent was still four months off."

Her face eased into a large smile. "Jim is good for my humility, Father. He sucks the air out of every room I enter."

John led them into the parlor where they exchanged hugs

with the Delgados and handshakes with Dr. Koblinski. "Doctor, I'm assuming tonight is some form of penance," Jim Gillespie said in greeting. "So I'm not going to ask you how you're doing."

Koblinski laughed easily and moved to hug his tormentor. Gillespie mimed pulling back and said, "Hey, that sin, whatever it is, and I don't want to know what it is, although I'll listen if you want to share it with the rest of us tonight, it isn't contagious is it?"

"We're all just hoping against hope *you're* not contagious, Gillespie," John quickly interjected. "Which is why you'll be eating alone in the kitchen."

Gillespie bowed graciously and lifted two glasses of Chablis from Carmella's tray, handing one to Maggie. As they sat, John noticed Maggie looking at Jim Gillespie in a way he had never seen her look at another man. He filed it away for the ruminations of another day.

The conversation was light and discursive. They covered the obligatory grounds of parish activities and children and weather and summer holidays abroad. The heavy issues would remain until Carmella rang the bell for supper and graced the table with her one of her unique pasta creations.

At what John thought the opportune moment, he nodded to Carmella outside in the hallway. The bell rang and all eyes turned to John. "Class begins," he beamed, leading them out of the parlor and into the dining room. The room was warmly and simply appointed. There were seasonal flowers at each end and attractive place settings in matching hues. There were also two extra chairs at the table which drew Maggie Kealey's attentive eye. "Father, have the Burnses had a change of heart?"

"No, Maggie," he replied matter of factly. Carol had called and said she simply couldn't get Michael to come. No other explanation. She was clearly embarrassed, and John had made a mental note to double back and check in on his friend. "I've asked two wonderful young men to join us for coffee and dessert. Bill Fregosi and John Wallingford. They're single, in their mid-20's, and they're discerning religious vocations. I thought it would be good for them to get an in-the-trenches view of the Church's struggle in the brave new world of Catholic Health Care. I will vouch for their circumspection. They are men of honor."

"More than I can say for me," Gillespie responded. "Of course, when I was single— oh wait, I am single— is a religious vocation out of the question, Father?"

"Remember, Jim. The Good Lord never asks more of us than we can handle," John replied, smiling.

Gillespie laughed good-naturedly and glanced at Maggie Kealey sitting next to him. John was startled to see her unobtrusively clasp the doctor's right hand which hung by his side below the table.

Carmella appeared with a large tray of Penne alla Puttanesca. She set it in the middle of the table and winked at John. This signaled she was pleased with her work, and that his guests soon would be too.

John responded with the affirmation he knew she treasured. "Carmella, you are a wonder. If I didn't know better, I'd have thought you spent the entire day in the kitchen."

She looked at him with a small smile playing at the corners of her wide mouth. "And who's to say I didn't?"

Jim Gillespie laughed and said, "Carmella Francone in the kitchen, John Sweeney in the pulpit: that's why this parish works. In that order."

John filled the wine glasses with a light red Merlot. He stood and toasted his guests. "You are the salt of the earth; you are doing the Lord's work to leaven our society. God loves you in a singular way. And I love you in a special way. To your health … your families … and your blessed work and collaborations."

"Here, here," intoned Jim Gillespie, first to imbibe.

They sat and John got the conversation started, as the platter made its way ever so slowly around the table. "Maggie, maybe you and Jim could catch us up on what's happening at Regina Hospital."

Maggie smiled and looked at Jim, who said to no one in particular, "Ah, yes. The SS Titanic."

"Oh, it can't be that bad, if Maggie's in charge," Fran Delgado fairly chirped.

There was a brief silence while Maggie regrouped. "No, it's *not* that bad. But we do have our, our challenges," she said quietly. "We've got to shut down our entire Ob/Gyn department." She waited for a response that was not forthcoming. This seemed to surprise her. "Our doctors are dispensing contraceptives to Catholic couples, and referring our patients to an IVF clinic, which unfortunately is on site."

"I'd like to think they're dispensing to and referring the same couples," Jim deadpanned, causing Joe Delgado to guffaw.

"Where's the problem in any of that?" Fran Delgado simply inquired, threatening to derail the evening at its outset. John was alarmed. He'd prayed for stupor. Slowly, he slid the wine bottle closer to Joe who was sitting next to him. Joe smiled in recognition, took it and refilled his wife's glass. "Oh, nothing much, Dear, unless it's being done in a Catholic hospital," he said softly.

"When will you do that, Maggie?" Dr. Koblinski asked.

Maggie, again, looked at Jim and said, "This week, Doctor. I'm meeting with the Physician's Board to notify them of my plans on Friday morning."

Koblinski appeared taken aback. "What will you do with the department?"

"We're going to overhaul it. Bring in an NFP physician, open an NFP clinic and teach the world, or at least those with eyes to see and ears to hear, about the sacred transmission of human life."

Silence.

"Yes, we're going to reclaim fertility as the unique province of Irish Catholics," Gillespie proclaimed, deepening the silence.

"That's quite a bold action, Maggie," Koblinski said.

"The time for bold action has arrived, wouldn't you agree, Doctor?" she replied, testing him.

"I would indeed," he answered quickly. "Would that we had more Maggie Kealey's running our Catholic hospitals."

As he helped himself to a portion of the pasta, John turned to the doctor and said, "Stan, tell us where the science is going, and what that's going to require of the Church."

Koblinski took a moderate swallow from his wine glass and lifted his linen napkin to his lips. He had not planned on giving his tutorial so early in the dinner. "IVF is raging out of control in the U.S. We're now sitting on upwards of three million children conceived: only about 20%, or 600,000, have lived. Over 500,000 of the 600,000 are now living in about 300 storage freezers around the country. The remaining 100,000 are alive, and, please God, well, somewhere in our midst. I say that because the Center for Disease Control in Atlanta reports IVF children have lower birth weights, which are associated with heart disease and diabetes."

Fran Delgado gasped. Joe bit his tongue.

"Not to get too heavy, Stan, but can you break down the bio ethical principles in play here?" John asked.

Koblinski glanced quickly around the table. He understood he was the "featured guest" of the evening, but he did not want to monopolize the conversation, which he knew he was all too capable of doing. "Yes, of course, Father. There are two quite distinctive views of the power of modern biotechnology: the Catholic view, which sees healing in terms of its Founder's mission and gives primacy to the soul's destiny; and the secular view, which seeks only relief from suffering and measures progress by the quality of man's material life."

"Is the dichotomy reconcilable?" John asked.

"Unlikely," Koblinski answered abruptly. "It has given way to two different systems of health ministry. The secular system now views medicine in salvation terms. Man can be reengineered to eradicate his genetic defects. It sees the Church, particularly its moral teachings, as anachronistic and obstructionist. This has the practical effect of eliminating the question of what *ought* to be done and replacing it with a much simpler question: what *can* be done? This puts the issues of right and wrong in the public square without benefit of adequate moral reflection. They become subject to the political process, which is to say public manipulation, both nationally, and in the years to come, internationally."

Joe Delgado felt his heart begin to race.

"At the cost of Man's inherent dignity," John added.

"Precisely," Koblinski replied. "God chose man, the species, for the Incarnation of his only Son. This and this alone is the source of his inherent dignity. This dignity begins at conception and ends with natural death. Man's task is simply to preserve the dignity. He confers nothing."

"Doctor, where is the science going?" Maggie asked with a sense of alarm.

"Where it dare not go," Koblinski answered quickly.

"All I ask is that I live to 1000, like Abraham," Jim Gillespie deadpanned.

John turned to Maggie and said, "Think God will hear that plea?"

"Oh, He'll hear it. That much is certain. Whether He grants it or not will depend on whether he really is a God of Mercy … to those left on earth," she replied with a smile. This made Gillespie laugh, and once again John caught a quick hand squeeze below the table. He was finding this whole sideshow fascinating.

"The Human Genome Project is the ultimate game changer," Koblinski said. "It opened up virtually everything – mental disorder, physical defect, sexual orientation, intelligence, personality, beauty – to genetic reengineering. There are 40,000 human genes. These genes code for protein. Protein is the major structural and functional component in the human body." He paused for dramatic effect. "There will be 10,000 protein targets for pharmacological intervention by 2015. Half a trillion dollars in biotech venture capital is now chasing what they refer to as biologically active agents. It is these active agents that hold the presumed promise of healing as liberation from human misery: all that is unwanted, unattractive, imperfect."

Silence.

Into the silence stepped Carmella Francone. "There is still food on that platter. I am not happy."

Joe Delgado reflexively reached for the platter and helped himself to another portion. The other men extended their palms as if their mothers had given an order. One by one, the men took second helpings. When the last, John Sweeney, had taken the final portion, he handed the platter back to his cook and housekeeper and said, "Carmella, you have outdone yourself. This is superb by any standard."

The others quickly concurred, and Fran Delgado inquired as to the provenance of Penne alla Puttanesca.

"Oh, you don't want to know," she demurred coyly.

"Oh, but we do," Jim Gillespie demanded.

"Well if you insist," she smiled, eyeing John Sweeney whose stomach suddenly set off an alarm. "The legend back home in Calabria is that the recipe was one of necessity. It was said, once a year, the women in the village would take off with their lovers. When they returned home they scoured their cupboards and threw everything they could find into a giant pot and created a special sauce from the remnant ingredients. They served it to their husbands, who ate themselves into a stupor and, therefore, asked no questions of them."

John Sweeny appeared to gag. Stan Koblinski set his wine glass down and stared at the floor. Joe Delgado's eyes widened as he reached for his glass. Maggie Kealey and Fran Delgado giggled like school girls. Jim Gillespie eyed the cook levelly and said, "Carmella, how many husbands have you killed with this recipe?"

The woman laughed and launched into another anecdote. She was cut off by her pastor. "That'll be quite enough, Carmella. I'm sure our guests will be interested to hear more at another time ..."

She took her leave, dignity gracefully recovered.

"Where were we?" John asked no one in particular.

"I don't know about the rest of you, but I was being scandalized by your cook," Jim replied in mock dudgeon.

The rectory buzzer rang. It was a harsh, unpleasant sound

from another era. John did not wait for Carmella to answer the door. He leapt to his feet and said with palpable excitement, "That must be Bill and John. Wait till you meet these young men!"

Momentarily, he returned with two wide-eyed young men in tow and made the introductions. Each shed a light jacket and wrapped it around the back of his chair and sat down. Carmella appeared with a fresh bottle of wine and poured. She asked if the men had dinner. They replied they had.

"Yes, but did you have a School for Scandal fable recited at yours?" Gillespie inquired.

The men just looked at John who waved dismissively. "Men, we were just talking about the future of medicine in the shadow of the Human Genome Project," he said, bridging the discussion back to biotechnology. "Fascinating ... and terrifying. Dr. Koblinski was just telling us where all this is headed. Doctor?"

Koblinski nodded toward the men and resumed. "Yes, well, researchers are now talking, not so circumspectly I might add, about Cyborgs, Hybrids, even something called Posthumans. The problem they will run into, I believe, is genes are not Legos. Most genes affect many traits and many traits affect most genes. We will find there simply are tradeoffs that cannot be managed away. There is an irreducible complexity, in Michael Behe's immortal phrase, to the mystery of man. Man will try, is indeed now trying, to create a new Tower of Babel. But I do not believe he will be any more successful than his ancient ancestors were."

Joe could no longer hold his silence. "I've seen that future, doctor."

All heads swiveled. The young men sat up on the edge of their chairs. "In California, Joe?" John asked, connecting dots from a previous conversation.

"No, Father," he replied. "In Israel."

The room seemed to lose oxygen, as if the mere mention of that fully loaded biblical name and place held an immutable power.

There was a pregnant pause. Joe understood no one was prepared to ask him to elaborate, for fear of violating some corporate confidence. So he took it upon himself to elaborate. He told them of his recent trip, and the tour of the HM laboratory outside Tel Aviv which was home to mankind's grand new project. He talked about the plans and the depth of HM's corporate resources and the duplicate teams it had gathered and were now subsidizing. He spoke of Dr. Moskowitz and the bold project milestones he now wore as performance mandates and metrics.

Then, with the table's attention rapt, he circled back to the Grand Design. He spoke of Siliezar and Boros and Benton. He shared the outline for Revolution 4 and its promise as man's final revolution: the one which would finally decode the secrets imbedded in matter itself, and reengineer, indeed even reshape, its very particles and sub particles to eliminate disease and extend life to its point of origin. He talked of alliances— private and public, national and international – which were being knitted together behind the scenes to ensure this Final Revolution would arrive on time, accompanied by a new U.S. Constitution, which would deed over national sovereignty and serve as a boilerplate for other nations. He talked about the strategic significance of government policy, developed by deep monied interests off shore, in healthcare, energy and mass education, and how it would be shaped to gain full control over the human project before the end of the current era. He finished by talking about the clear absence of any moral voice in these deliberations. It is, he concluded with a nod to Stan Koblinski, only about "whether it *can* be done; not whether it *should* be done."

The silence which ensued was as deep as it was protracted. Nothing was said for several minutes. At one point, Carmella Francone arrived to assess the silence, and having taken its measure, left without comment.

Finally Maggie Kealey said, "Father, where is our Church in all of this?

John Sweeney smiled and pointed to Stan Koblinski. "Right there," he said with quiet emphasis.

Koblinski's head fell to his chest.

"I guess what Maggie is asking is what is she, the Church,

actually doing?" Joe Delgado asked, discretely, lest he set his wife off on a minor rant.

Koblinski sipped his wine and let the question settle. "Well, I spend a lot of time with our bishops. We talk about the things I've been discussing here tonight, although I'm certainly not privy to what's going on in Joe's circles," he said as he looked at Joe with undisguised awe. "We publish the best of our Catholic ethicists' reflections on all this in our quarterly journal. We develop and distribute white papers for our influencers – our university and hospital presidents, the bishops' conference in Washington, our Catholic publishers and media leaders. We put ourselves in the service of any bishop or priest or lay leader with a question or a problem in this area." He paused in some discomfort. "I don't know what else to tell you."

Maggie felt a pang of guilt. "Doctor, I'm sorry. I didn't mean to suggest in any way that you are not doing all those things, or that they are not helpful." She struggled to find the right words. "I guess what I'm asking is, are our bishops taking any of it seriously?"

Koblinski glanced at John before answering. He shrugged. "I don't know what to tell you, Maggie. Maybe it's just too early to tell."

Another uneasy silence descended upon the table.

"Won't they, our bishops that is, won't they have to speak out on all these genetic screening programs? I mean their intent is clearly just to prevent the birth of children with defects?" The question came from one of the young men at the end of the table, Bill Fregosi, and John welcomed it.

"Yes, I would certainly think so, Bill," he replied.

"I'm not as optimistic as Father," Koblinski interjected. "I think our Catholic medical community is unprepared to meet what will be a ferocious demand to abort fetuses with genetic abnormalities. And when the federal government effectively nationalizes health care, and mark my words it will not be long before it does, its minions will begin to threaten closure. I tell you," he added, voice rising, "neither the Church's sacred healing mission, nor the private consciences of its doctors and nurses will be a consideration." He paused for emphasis. "Then we will see how many Catholic doctors we have in our Catholic hospitals."

"And how many Catholic bishops we have in our chanceries," Joe Delgado interjected quickly.

Maggie Kealey cleared her throat. "Doctor, if the bishops do not take a stand, soon, it will be too late."

Joe Delgado nodded. "Maggie, I'm afraid it's already too late. Those guys have lost their moral influence, if not authority. Who listens to them anymore?"

"We can't have it both ways, Joe," John challenged. "Either they have moral influence or they don't. Weren't you and your friends claiming not long ago that their 2007 pastoral, Faithful Citizenship, helped decide the election for the pro abortion candidate?"

Joe fell silent.

From the end of the table, John Wallingford sought to ease the tension. "Doctor Koblinski, what about this new trend in the Pro Life movement, the adoption of frozen embryos?"

Koblinski nodded, welcoming the change of focus, if not subject. "It's an unsettled issue at the moment," he said equivocally. "The argument for its permissibility claims it is morally warranted because it is the only possible means of saving the life of the human embryo. Its proponents suggest it is not materially different from wet nursing."

"And the argument against?" Bill Fregosi asked.

"It's essentially the unity argument. What the Council in Gaudium et Spes argued is the 'unity of total meaning.' Motherhood has three intrinsic dimensions: it is genetic, gestational, and social. It is a purely holistic, indivisible reality arising intact from the marital act itself."

"But, if the 'end' is the saving of a human life? "John Wallingford all but implored.

Stan Koblinski was nothing if not a patient man. He nodded sympathetically. "John, I hear you. But we have to consider the

Church's received wisdom on the nature and purpose of the conjugal act. She believes it is inherently unitive and procreative. She sees the whole process of fertilization, implantation, pregnancy, birth, and the rearing of a child as seamless. Embryonic rescue causes a rupture in this process, and therefore a rupture in the unitive dimension of motherhood."

"But what will happen to all those children? That's what they are: mere children. Must they remain motherless?" Wallingford pleaded.

Silence.

"Father, why can't the Church get out in front of all this and head it off?" Maggie asked.

John Sweeney arched his eyebrows. "How? The science is beyond our competence. And, as you can see, at least some of the moral issues divided us."

"The shadow of Galileo," Joe Delgado suggested.

John nodded. "Yes, that trial did indeed cast a long shadow. Holy Mother Church doesn't want to revisit that sad institutional memory." Then he felt a surge of energy that triggered a sparkle in his eyes. "But, ultimately, she always gets these great *moral* issues right. She bats 1000 on those. Just as her Founder promised."

"Then what will happen to the half million frozen embryos, Father?" Bill Fregosi asked.

"I don't know, Bill. I simply do not know," he replied, shaking his head. "But, as I listen to Doctor Koblinski I'd have to say the 'unity of meaning' principle has a certain ... philosophical gravitas. God Himself is a unity. His creation was a unity, before the Fall. He seems to favor the unity of created things and to oppose their disunity. I don't know."

An air of disquiet filled the room. Man in his hubris had taken a step across a metaphysical line from which there appeared no retreat. The men and women around the table seemed lost in contemplation of the incomprehensible.

John Wallingford spoke for all when he sliced through the

introspection with one final searing question. "Father, what do you think God will do about all this?"

John Sweeney shook his head slowly. "John, I can only imagine. And, frankly, I don't like to think about it."

The evening ended with a prayer.

# 42

———

Maggie Kealey was cautious by nature but life had taught her there were times one had to be prepared to take a prudent gamble.

The evening before the meeting with the Regina Hospital Physician Board, she decided to bring her Ob/Gyn Department Head, Dr. Frank Ciancini, in for a chat. She thought it best to do it alone. She feared Jim's presence would perceptually lessen her authority and, perhaps, incite a confrontation.

She told Ciancini he would not be coming to the meeting on the following morning. Then she explained why. She advised she knew he was accepting kickbacks from the Mid Atlantic Fertility Clinic for IVF referrals, and that he was also profiting from the Clinic's egg and sperm banks, which his referrals were helping to populate. She offered him a chance to resign or face criminal indictment.

He laughed in her face. In the hideous animus of his response, she caught sight of a demon loosed in her hospital. It chilled her to the bone. He called her unstable and told her her action would spark a full scale revolt among her physicians. At one point he said, "You'll end up without a hospital, or a job. That will be your legacy, Nurse Kealey. You will do what war and depression and societal convulsion could not do in the 20th century. You, singlehandedly, will end 90 unbroken years of the Church's healing ministry to the poor of South Philadelphia." He threatened a defamation law suit and left in a rage, slamming the door behind him.

She sat shaking, chastising herself for the clumsy attempt. When she told Jim later that evening, he had merely grimaced and said nothing. She explained she wanted to clear away the brush for the meeting, and thought getting Ciancini out of the way would open the door for, perhaps, a unanimous vote of support. Jim had hugged her, but its force, she thought, carried the unmistakable signal of resignation.

She sat quietly, head bowed, in the back pew of St. Martha's church. She had just received the Body and Blood of mankind's Savior, and she implored Him to empower her in confronting evil. She tried to focus on prayer, but the image of Ciancini's face continued to torment her. She made a stupid mistake, she told herself. She had deeded over the element of surprise. Ciancini probably tipped off the other physicians. He now controlled the narrative, if not the agenda. All was lost. She started to feel overwhelmed.

She heard Jim stirring next to her in the pew. The sound of his presence returned her attention to the mystical reality now within her breast. She thanked God for the gift of this faithful man's support in this critical hour. She wondered half aloud whether she could continue absent it. Her muffled sounds drew a strong arm around her slender shoulders. He pulled her closer. She heard him pray, sotto voce, for God's blessing on their work, and petition his holy will for Catholic medical professionals.

Then, abruptly, he was helping her to her feet. He held her wrists loosely, looked deeply into her eyes and kissed her gently on the forehead. They genuflected together before the tabernacle and departed the empty church for Jim's car and the 35-minute drive into South Philadelphia. It was 7:05. The meeting was scheduled for 8:00 a.m.

They rode in silence, each deep in dilemma. For Maggie Kealey, this was a 'bet the career' proposition. She was proceeding without management's approval. She expected the Order would back her, if she won support from the Physician's Board. If not, she would be cast adrift. The mere thought of that possibility filled her with dread. She didn't know what she would do or how she would support herself. She worried about her reputation. She thought of the children and how they would receive the news she had been fired. She thought of her husband, Bill, and wondered what his reaction would be when he heard. Not that she cared, she told herself.

For Jim Gillespie, the terrain was no less treacherous. He'd built a reputation as a highly skilled oncologist over the past 30 years. He had risen to Department Head early in his career, at 43. His reputation as a caring teacher and administrator spread beyond the borders of the city. He had offers to move laterally several times to the prestigious center city hospitals, Penn and Jeff, but each time he declined. He felt serving in the minority community, helping the good sisters maintain a Catholic healing presence there, was a vocation. Unmarried, it had become his only vocation. Now he was risking it all. He knew the three other doctors on the Board would reject the plan out of hand. And he knew Maggie Kealey well enough to know she would not back down. In this matter, he would not have the luxury of choice. He would stand with his woman. They would go down together.

They arrived at the hospital at 7:42 and parked in the underground garage. They entered the building through one of its three rear doors and took the elevator to the fourth floor executive suite. It was dark when they stepped out into the wide hallway, and Maggie muttered disappointment that Lori Needham had not yet arrived to greet the caterer with the coffee and pastry trays.

She began moving in haste to turn lights on in several of the offices and in the executive conference room at the end of the suite.

She did not want physicians arriving in the only part of the building not yet operational. She caught Jim staring at her and he gestured to her to slow down, pushing his hands palms down in the direction of the floor. She stopped to settle herself before entering her own office. She dropped her coat on the back of the closest wing chair and set her briefcase on her desk. Without bothering to sit, she opened it and removed the file marked: *NFP Clinic*. She flipped to her talking points and reviewed them.

She heard a knock on the door and turned to see a sheepish Lori Needham standing in the doorway. "Sorry, Mrs. K. I missed my trolley."

Maggie's heart softened when she saw the fear in the young woman's eyes. She saw only a daughter in moments like these. "It's okay, Lori. But do make sure we're all set up with the coffee and pastries."

"Do you need your laptop set up for a power point?"

Maggie turned and smiled. "No. No power point today. Just me."

"Okay," she replied, reprieve now in hand.

Maggie heard voices in the common area. She immediately recognized the voice of Dr. Woo, Regina's Head of Cardiology; the other she assumed belonged to Dr. Novoa, Head of Internal Medicine. Her stomach tightened. She looked at her watch. It was 7:55.

Jim ducked his head in the door and said, "Lee and Novoa are here. You can join us at any time."

Maggie nodded and flashed a worried look. Jim started toward her but pulled up short. He smiled reassuringly and turned to join the others in the executive conference room. She shut her door and went to her couch and sat down. Then she slid to her knees and prayed. *Lord, I am weak flesh. This is all too much. I come to do your will. Will you accompany me into that room? Will you send the Holy Spirit to guide me in what I say, and should not say? Will you change the hearts of men? Is this dream possible, Lord? Can we retrieve the sacred in the sacred transmission of human life in our time? Can it be done, here, Lord, in this hospital?*

She heard a knock on the door. "Maggie, we're ready for you." It was Jim. She bowed her head and concluded. *Your will be done, Lord.*

She stood, resolute, and said, "Coming." She smoothed out her dress, pulled her long black hair back and clasped it into a bun, grabbed her file and headed for the conference room.

The first face she saw as she entered the room was Hank Woo's. He had come to America as a young boy from Hong Kong, where he had been educated at a Jesuit boarding school. He graduated Harvard, entered Penn medical school, and started his career at John Hopkins in Baltimore. He fell in love with a South Philadelphia girl and moved to the city while in his mid-30's. He was hired by the nuns to help start a Cardiology Department and, at age 41, became its director. He was a kindly and cautious man. He had mastered the art of avoiding confrontation and controversy through silence and redirection. Jim had told her she would have to press him hard for a commitment.

Hank Woo stood as she entered the room and bowed graciously. He walked around the end of the eight-foot rectangular conference room table to greet her. "Good morning, Maggie. How are you doing?"

"Good, Hank," she replied, reaching for a cup and saucer. She poured herself a cup of black coffee from a small decorous urn, hoping it would take the chill out of the late autumn air still clinging to her bones.

"Mornin', Maggie." It was Al Novoa, Head of Internal Medicine. Novoa was a Cuban who had fled the Communist regime on a makeshift raft in his early 20's. Against long odds, he and two friends landed on a dune just off the Florida Keys. They were helped ashore by a local fisherman who set them up with a Cuban family in South Beach. He went to work immediately as a short order cook, and enrolled at the University of Miami evening school, where he earned an undergraduate degree in biology in six years. His prodigious work ethic attracted the attention of a Cuban professor who sponsored him for medical school. He graduated at the top of his class at the University of North Carolina medical college and came to Philadelphia as an intern at Jeff. Six years later, the nuns hired him to replace a retiring internist. He was appointed the Head of Internal Medicine at age 48. Maggie knew him to be a tough political infighter. Jim told her not to expect his support, regardless of what she may hear in the meeting. This, she reminded herself, was why getting Ciancini out of the way the night before was critical.

"Good morning, Al," she replied perfunctorily.

She took her seat at the head of the table. She looked at her watch. It was 8:05. She looked at each of the three men and nodded slightly. "Thank you for being on time. I've got something important I want to talk to you about this morning. We're going to talk about the future of Regina Hospital, and what I need from each of you to ensure her survival."

She opened her file, careful not to look at her notes. "We are a Catholic hospital in violation of the U.S. Bishops' ethical religious directives, referred to as ERD's." She paused for a reaction; the physicians sat stoned faced.

"Our Ob/Gyn physicians are dispensing oral contraceptives. They are referring infertile Catholic couples to the Mid-Atlantic Fertility Clinic for In Vitro Fertilization procedures. They are directing our younger patients to donate to the Clinic's egg and sperm banks, and arranging for older, infertile patients to purchase eggs and sperm from the Clinic."

She paused again. Still no reaction. She thought perhaps Ciancini had indeed tipped Woo and Novoa off. "In all this, we believe our Ob/Gyns are profiting. We will take that matter up separately.

"There is also the matter of the Clinic's advertising in our on-line Directory Services, and of course the monthly rentals we collect for their suite here at the hospital. We also collect ancillary revenues from the blood work, ultrasounds and other procedures they order here at the hospital." She paused. "This I regard as blood money."

Silence.

She looked at Jim. He, too, sat frozen and mute. "This is unacceptable," she said matter of factly. "So, at noon today, I will announce we are closing the Ob/Gyn Department, effective immediately. On Monday morning it will be replaced by a Marital Life and Love Clinic under the direction of Dr. Hank Seelaus."

Hank Woo gasped. Jim Novoa immediately looked at Woo, then Gillespie for his bearings.

Maggie Kealey looked at the men coolly. "Dr. Seelaus and his team will be in this suite in one hour. Ciancini and his men have until noon to pack up and get out. HR has prepared severance packages. Legal will present them with papers for their private attorneys to review." She paused. "Please know I am not naïve. I have no doubt most of our Ob/Gyn patients will follow them out the door in the short term. But when they see the alternative we will provide, when they hear the testimony of our new NFP patients, I'm confident a good many of them will return, and bring the rest of their families and friends with them."

Maggie looked at Al Novoa and Hank Woo. Each appeared shell shocked. Novoa, visibly distressed, spoke first. "Maggie, what do you want from us?"

"I want your support, Al," she said evenly.

Novoa hung his head. There were 16 doctors in the department of internal medicine. He calculated maybe two of them would be open to the plan on the table. And, if presented as a fait accompli, possibly none. "I don't know, Maggie. I need to talk to our docs. I think there may be some misgivings." He shot a nervous glance at Woo and Gillespie.

Maggie nodded, patiently. "Take the morning, Al. Come see me after lunch. I need to know where you, and your department, stand."

She turned to Hank Woo. "What about the Cardiology Department, Hank? Can I count on your support?"

Woo began making an odd humming sound that Maggie recognized as a trained reflex to tension. She remembered Jim telling her she'd have to push hard for a commitment. "I really hope our cardiologists will join our oncologists," she glanced at Novoa, "and our internists in supporting this initiative, Doctor. The solidarity is essential for the hospital's survival."

She peered intently into the eyes behind the horn rimmed glasses. They were inscrutable. She understood he was counting votes, as was she. With Oncology behind her, and Seelaus prepared to replace Ciancini, she needed one of the two: either cardiology or internal medicine. She could always replace one of the department heads and explain it away as collateral damage. Two, however, would be far more difficult in the court of public opinion, both inside the hospital and beyond. Two would constitute mutiny.

Woo was humming but he wasn't speaking. Jim Gillespie fixed him with a benevolent gaze and said quietly, "Hank, this is for the best. In the long run, it's the only sustainable niche for a small Catholic hospital."

Woo's eyes glistened and Jim thought he might be on the verge of tears. Still, he said nothing.

Jim looked at both men. "You know we say all the time we have to change our payer mix. It's true. But let's be honest. We can't compete in our areas of specialty with Jeff and Penn. We've just don't have the talent and the resources. The market knows this. The suburban women with insurance aren't going to come here for me, or for any of us. But they will come for NFP if we market the program effectively through the parishes and various Pro Life groups. And once they come and see what we have, and experience firsthand the fruits of our new Clinic, who knows, maybe they will come back for the internal medicine and the cardiology and the oncology." He paused and looked at both men, shaking his head emphatically. "We can't kid ourselves, fellows. Doing the right thing is the only option for a small Catholic community hospital like Regina. And, we all know, this is the right thing."

Silence.

Al Novoa broke it with a question that revealed his turn of mind. "What if our docs don't support this, this new 'Department'? Would it actually be a Department?" He looked at Maggie for clarification.

"Yes, Al," she replied, nodding slightly. "It will be a fully constituted Department required to comply with all the hospital's policies and procedures. It will be wholly owned by Regina Hospital, and its staff, including Dr. Seelaus, will all be 'at will' employees, just like the rest of us."

"What happens if my men and women say no?" Novoa asked more directly.

Jim moved quickly to head off impasse. "Why would they do that, Al? Why wouldn't you champion the new initiative, sell it in, ask for their support?"

Novoa fidgeted. "My docs have long standing relationships with Ciancini and his men. This wholesale sacking will, might, make them skittish."

"The whole hospital knows what's been going on in that department for years," Maggie interjected a bit too pointedly. "The only question has been: will anyone stand up and say 'this is wrong and it must stop.' Well, today, at noon, it stops. Period."

Jim Gillespie winced. Much as he loved his woman, her confrontational manner short-circuited her agenda. What especially pained him was his inability to help her understand what the private baggage of old wounds represented in her professional career. "Al," he said quietly. "Why not ask them to give it six months? If they don't like what they see, we'll help them get new positions elsewhere."

Woo, apparently, thought this proposition reasonable. The humming stopped and his head began nodding. There was no change, however, in his expression.

Novoa glanced at Woo nervously, as though he had jumped the fox hole. He looked at Gillespie and said, "Here's the problem I think some in my department may have, Jim. Women make the health care decisions for the family. They want ... reproductive rights. They will have to be 'weaned off' those, ah, services. If we just pull the plug and make them go cold turkey, we're liable to lose them forever."

Gillespie nodded quickly to head off any comment from Maggie. "Possibly, Al."

"So, even if we physicians support the plan, our women patients might go and take their families with them," he said, brightening at the prospect of an escape hatch. "In other words, Maggie," he said turning to her. "It's not about whether the docs will support your new Department, it's whether our patients will."

Maggie eyed him calmly and replied, "Good. Then you'll ask your docs to give it a chance?"

Novoa grew visibly anxious at having boxed himself into a corner. He looked to Gillespie for help. Jim smiled empathetically and said, "You raise a good point, Al. Let's just ask our staffs to give the new Department a chance; to let the patients decide." He paused. "That's only reasonable, right?"

Novoa hung his head. Into his chest, he said quietly, "What if the patients say no, Jim, and we docs get stranded on the SS Titanic? Who will take care of our families while we're trying to put our careers back together?"

It was on the table. Jim looked at Maggie who appeared ready to respond. Suddenly, Hank Woo made a slight movement of his arms, and then pulled his chair back from the table. "I must get back to my office, I'm afraid," he said with grace and civility. "This is all very interesting. I will give it much thought."

"Hank!" Maggie exclaimed with more than a hint of exasperation. "This isn't *interesting.* Nor is it something I'm asking you to think about. It's the way we are going to operate this hospital beginning Monday morning."

Woo looked at her with equanimity. "What is it you are asking, Maggie?"

"I am asking for your personal support, and the support of the entire staff of our Cardiology Department," she answered patiently. "Now, do I have it?"

Woo nodded discreetly and bowed slightly. "I will see if I can obtain that support."

"Hank, I need it by 2:00 p.m. That's when the announcement will be made to our employees."

He nodded. "Yes, I understand." Then Hank Woo stood, turned and left.

Al Novoa looked at Jim. "I take it I also have until 2:00?"

Jim nodded.

"Okay," he said, standing. He turned to Maggie and said, "I will call you at 2:00." He turned and followed Hank Woo out the door.

Maggie looked at Jim, who simply shrugged his shoulders. They sat there in silence, at opposite ends of the table. Finally, Jim looked at her with tenderness and said, "You did the right thing, Maggie. I'm proud of you. And you've now done all you can do. From here on out, it's beyond our control. So, we sit and wait. And we prepare ourselves to accept God's will."

Tears filled her eyes. "Jim, you don't think we're going to get the support, do you?"

He smiled to ease her pain. "You look exceptionally lovely this morning, Mrs. Kealey. Do you have plans for dinner?"

Her taut body relaxed and she smiled, coyly. "As a matter of fact, I do."

"Anyone I know?"

"No, you wouldn't know this man," she replied. "He's a prominent physician and a consummate gentleman."

•  •  •

Jim Gillespie was worried. When he went to Maggie's home to pick her up for dinner, he found the house empty. Over the next three hours, he called and left four voicemail messages on her answering machine. He also left three e-mails, hoping she had her Blackberry with her. He drove back over to the house at 10:00 p.m., and again at midnight. Between those visits, he called his friend, Lower Merwood Police Chief Jim Sharkey, who notified his night crew to be on the lookout for an "attractive executive-type woman in her late 50's" who may or may not be missing.

His concern slowly turned to fear as the night wore on. The phone calls from Woo and Novoa came in, one just after the other, shortly before 2:00 p.m. Each was a Scud missile which had penetrated her heart. Woo said the Cardiology Department was "up in arms," and were threatening a walk out on Monday morning. Novoa said essentially the same thing. Jim smelled collusion, and if not collusion, at least collaboration. Maggie Kealey had run herself right smack into a power play. It was now simply a matter of who would blink first. He did not think it would be the love of his life.

At about 2:00 in the morning, laying on his back and fingering his rosary, he was jolted upright by an inspiration. He rose immediately, dressed quickly and got in the car. It was a moonless, chilly October night. He drove the four minutes to the church in two, and parked in John Sweeney's rectory driveway, trusting the good pastor was soundly sleeping. He entered the side door of the church with the aid of a personal key and made his way quietly upstairs to the main church. There on the altar was a prostrate figure who appeared to be sleeping.

He removed his shoes and crept quietly to the altar in his stocking feet. There, at the foot of the altar, lay Maggie Kealey, still in her work clothes. She was on her stomach, fast asleep. Jim knelt and gently rubbed the back of her neck. She didn't move. He grew alarmed. He shook her shoulder with a bit of force. She stirred. He was startled at the depth of her slumber. As she stirred, taking first note of her surroundings, the realization of where she was began to seep into her consciousness. Suddenly, she jerked herself upright into a sitting position and turned to face Jim. He hugged her. She smiled but said nothing. Slowly he got to his feet and bent down to lift her with great gentleness. He was shocked at how light she was. She was unsteady on her feet and still not fully awake. He wrapped his arm around her waist and ever so deliberately led her out of the church.

The bracing night air awakened her senses. By the time he got her to the car in John Sweeney's driveway she was weeping. He set her in the Porsche's passenger side seat and buckled it. He drove the four blocks to her home, slowly, not wanting to arrest the attention of the borough's only night policeman on duty. When he arrived at her home, he parked in front of the steps and quickly made his way around the car to the passenger side. He unbuckled the seat and lifted her carefully to her feet. He felt her shiver and wrapped his arms around her back and chest to shield her from a wind which was just picking up and rustling leaves around their feet.

He half lifted, half carried her up the two steps to the front door. She was leaning on him heavily and he was beginning to tire. He wrested a hand free from her waist and opened the door. He lightly kicked it open with his right foot and led her inside, kicking it closed with his left. The warmth of the home was welcoming. He debated what to do next. She was fully awake but trembling. He removed her coat and tossed it on the back of a couch in her living room. He guided her to the steps. He counted 12 steps to the landing and stifled a groan. With great difficulty he arrived, occupant in arm, and led her to the master bedroom. She began calling his name. He hugged her tightly. At the foot of the bed, he turned her slowly and gently laid her down on her back.

As she lay there, he looked at her and quivered. Her loveliness simply overwhelmed him. He fought off a biological urge of such intensity he wondered if it would abate. He teetered there, between grace and temptation for a long moment.

He reached down to gently brush a wisp of hair from her forehead. She clutched his wrist with both hands. The resolve he felt in her hands shocked him. She pulled him down to her bed. He fell in sections, as if in slow motion. He ended up half on, half off the bed. Soberly, he slid back off the bed onto his knees and reached for her. He held her head in his hands, kissed her with deep feeling, and said, "I love you, Maggie."

Her eyes filled with tears. "I love you too, Jim. I need you, Jim. Please, please, don't ever leave me."

He gently brushed her tears away with his fingers. "I won't, sweetheart. I'll stand by you forever."

"Please don't leave me, Jim. I can't go on without you."

"I won't, Maggie. I won't. I'll stay by your side. I won't let anyone harm you, ever. I promise."

She looked at him and her expression softened. "Jim, I don't mean at the hospital. I mean, I don't want to ever be apart from you. I want to live with you. I want to spend the rest of my life with you. I love you, Jim."

His chest was aflame. His temples were pounding, his palms suddenly clammy. "Maggie, I love you. I live now only for you." He buried his head in his arms lest she see his tears. He had waited nearly 20 years to hear what he was now hearing from this woman, and in this moment he truly believed for the first time in his life that all things were indeed possible.

She clasped his face and pulled it closer and kissed him again and again. She caught his tears on her fingers. He placed his hands around hers. He was half mad with desire. He begged for grace. Her head fell back onto her pillow and she gradually relaxed her grip on his face and neck. "Jim," she whispered. "I'm going to go see Father John today. I'm going to ask him to get the paperwork started on my annulment."

It was at that moment Jim Gillespie began to cry as he had never cried in his life. His whole body shook and the muffled sounds that arose came from a place so deep within him that it mystified even as it overwhelmed him. It was the sound of an unfathomable, seemingly unattainable, joy burrowing into the core of his being, taking possession of his soul, then taking wings and lifting the whole of him to undreamt of heights. From somewhere beyond himself he saw the two of them in the bedroom. Then he saw them on an altar with Father John Sweeney, as in his dream.

It was the first time in his life, he was to say later, that he felt the unconditional, purifying love of God the Father. He felt bathed in it, baptized in the ineffable mercy of it. And in that instant, he came to know his Divine Lord in a way he never knew him. He understood him as a holistic and eternal dimension of this new inexpressible love coursing through his being. And, in a blinding flash, he came to the realization that his conscious awareness of this experience was itself a gift of the life-begetting offspring of that love, the very Spirit of love shared by Father and Son.

He rose transformed. He stooped to kiss her one last time. She moaned softly and reached for him. He clasped her hands in his and said, "Rest, sweetheart. I'll come back for you at noon. We'll go see Father John together." Then he turned and started for the door.

At the doorway he heard her voice. "Jim?"

"Yes, Maggie."

"It really is true, isn't it?"

"What's true, Sweetheart?"

Suddenly, she lifted herself into a sitting position. Her eyes were shimmering like the surface of the sea at dawn. "God really does know how to bring good out of evil."

Jim Gillespie smiled and replied, "He does indeed, my love." He turned and made his way down the steps and out into the early morning frost. Dawn was just breaking.

# 43

---

The huge, ornate Lincoln Ballroom on the second floor of Philadelphia's historic Union League was, at most, half filled. Michael Burns regarded the indignity as a final professional humiliation. He had argued for the Michael Burns Tribute to be held in one of the more modestly-sized reception rooms on the first floor. Ultra Com, specifically its charismatic CEO Hanley Siliezar, had rejected that suggestion out of hand. The Sendoff was to be big or it was not to be.

Hanley Siliezar did not attend.

The governor of the great state of Pennsylvania did. Michael wished he hadn't. He went on and on about all the things Michael had done for the Commonwealth over the course of his "long and distinguished career." Of course, the great bulk of the good works cited were in support of this particular governor's own programs. The fact that this governor was a democrat and that one of the programs cited was the State's financial support of Proper Parenthood through its local step child, Women's Right, was not lost on Michael

Burns' family and friends. Nor was it lost on Cardinal O'Hallaran and his two auxiliary bishops, who were also in attendance.

Sitting in the audience, Fr. John Sweeney winced and wondered if the politically savvy governor was intentionally embarrassing the guest of honor. He glanced quickly at Carol Burns sitting at the head table next to Michael with the rest of their family. Her face was stoic in the extreme. He looked at the two sons. The eyes of both had fallen. Michael Burns himself had a small frozen smile on his Celtic face. John Sweeney couldn't ever remember his friend looking so tortured.

The Mayor of Philadelphia was up next. He talked about the model Michael had been for so many young businessmen in the city. He himself, or so he claimed, had been inspired to enter public life by Michael J. Burns' commitment to the city and its civic institutions. He compared Michael to Jimmy Stewart's character in *It's a Wonderful Life.* John saw Carol turn to her husband and smile warmly. He knew they rented that movie and watched it together every Christmas Eve.

Cliff Ackerman represented Ultra Com. He was stiff and wooden and spoke in clichés. It was apparent he either didn't know Michael Burns very well, or he did and didn't like him very much. John thought his friend's face, which was becoming more florid with age, turned at least two shades redder during Ackerman's remarks. Ultra Com's chief operating officer portrayed Burns as a "visionary" and a "man of purpose and action," but then chose not to link either tribute to any concrete vision, purpose or action.

Aaron McKenna rose to speak on behalf of the 220 employees of Burns Advertising. Michael's eyes followed him to the podium. *Lord, now I know how you felt when Peter denied you in the Garden.* McKenna avoided eye contact. He looked out and over the room and let his eyes rest on Ed Mobley. He winked. Michael caught it and felt a blast furnace in his stomach belch gas and fire. For an instant, he actually thought of storming the podium and thrashing his former protégé in plain view of all. At that moment his wife's hand gripped his and calmed his ire.

He looked at her and saw her in partial silhouette against the garish ballroom lighting. She was still, even at 60, uncommonly beautiful. When she smiled she could light up a room like no one he knew. And now, late on a Friday afternoon in mid autumn, she was smiling, at him. Her love for him had never wavered and it seemed to actually grow stronger in particularly difficult moments like the present. They had shared a long, eventful roller coaster ride together, and the bond between them had been forged time and again through the fire of adversity.

Michael's mind flashed back to the early problems in their marriage when they were forced to make the adjustments all couples must make to move through the Romance and Disillusionment phases of a life together, in order to enter the graced and enduring phase of Joy. He remembered the signature dispositional tensions: they were both moody, the early money problems, her physical sufferings, his career derailings, the children's physical and emotional traumas, and great fissures within their own families. It was a life, or perhaps more descriptively, a post modern life in America, and through it all they had stood shoulder to shoulder and survived. Indeed, after 40 blessed years, they were more in love than they had ever been.

Michael Burns did not know what he would do with the rest of his life, but he gave thanks to God that he would have Carol Burns at his side when he embarked on that great and uncertain adventure.

Aaron McKenna chose to begin with a small joke. "I'm here today to speak on behalf of 220 men and women who love Michael Burns. And we all just want Michael to know," he paused and glanced in Michael's direction, careful to avoid eye contact, "we're all billing clients while we're here."

Nervous laughter. Michael felt the eyes of the room settling on his to note any embarrassment. He tensed and froze a small smile. He felt Carol clasp and unclasp his hand.

Now relaxed, McKenna launched into a rambling tribute. "I owe my career to this man," he began soberly. "He has been, *not like* a father, but in every professional sense *an actual* father to me. He has counseled and guided me, and protected and advanced me, and now he has picked me to succeed him in running the city's largest advertising firm." He paused for effect. "Well, let me tell you, I'm under no illusions. No one— I repeat *no one*— could ever replace Michael J. Burns."

A ripple of applause swept through the room, but it never caught, and by the time the sound of its echo returned to the front of the room it sounded thin and remote.

"Any success I have as the new CEO of Burns Advertising, I will owe to that extraordinary man right there," he pointed, without looking at the head table. Another smattering of applause, sporadic and self conscious. "I'd also like to thank another man who isn't here today. His name is Hanley Siliezar. As some of you know, but most do not, he is the chairman of Ultra Com, the world's largest advertising firm. Hanley, as I say, couldn't be here today, but I wish you all could meet him. He is one of the most important men in the world. You will all hear his name, and read of his exploits, in the years ahead. He is working very hard to make the world a better place. He is guiding some of the most important projects ever undertaken. He is doing all of this in the name of the world's poor and suffering. All I can say is that I couldn't be more delighted to have the opportunity to work so closely with the great man himself."

In his seat, Michael Burns began to die to self. His ferocious pride, wounded to its core, rose in his breast and lodged before ebbing. The pain of his humiliation was fresh and intense. He wanted to get up and run from the room. He scanned the room for friendly faces. All were focused on the tall, slim, elegant man behind the podium. Michael thought of his former protégé's remarkable resemblance to Phil Hankinson, HM Healthcare's CEO, and wondered if the two of them would ever meet and collaborate. He believed they would find in each other kindred spirits, ambitious young men who would eat their own to advance their careers. It is just such men who give free enterprise a bad name, he thought, conceding his was a minority voice with an axe to grind.

McKenna then launched into his plans for the agency. Again, Michael searched the crowd for sympathy. Surely some would recognize this horrific breach of etiquette. Instead, the room seemed transfixed. He had learned long ago, a great part of humanity believes advertising is, at root, pure sorcery, and find behind the scenes peeks at what actually takes place endlessly fascinating. By the time he finished, McKenna had created the impression, no doubt intentionally, that Burns Advertising was badly in need of a makeover, and that Aaron McKenna was just the man to make it over. A second implication settled over the room. The great man himself, Hanley Siliezar, had recognized the structural problems in the diminishing asset he had purchased, and had acted just in the nick of time to abort serious hemorrhaging.

Michael understood McKenna had to justify his treasonous actions to the employees of Burns Advertising, and had decided his Farewell would be the occasion, Michael Burns' family and friends notwithstanding. For Michael, his humiliation and degradation was now complete. His life's work had been unmasked as morally compromised and badly flawed in front of the people who mattered most to him. He squirmed uncomfortably in his seat. His mind was racing: searching for escape routes, sorting options, envisioning scenarios.

Suddenly, he rose. He didn't know where he was going, but he simply could not sit and absorb any more humiliation. He was aware that the eyes of the room were now upon him. At the podium, McKenna sensed something was going on in another part of the room. He followed the eyes to Michael and grew slack when he saw him standing and glaring at him. Next to him, Carol was tugging on his coat sleeve. "Please Michael, sit down! Sit down, please! Patrick is up next."

Michael looked across the table to his son. Patrick was studying his handwritten notes, visibly nervous. He looked up and their eyes met. It was clear to Michael, his son did not know what his father was going to do. The significance of that uncertainty unsettled Michael. A son must always know his father will do the right thing. Michael understood the moment as metaphor. His heart filled, and burst. He fought off tears. He sat down. His wife grabbed his hands with both of hers and whispered, "Thank you, Michael. It will all soon be over."

McKenna glanced nervously at his former mentor and recognized in the eyes that stared back a signal to wrap up, and he did. He ended his tribute with flowery impromptu words of praise for the guest of honor, and waited a bit uncertainly for applause so he could flee the podium. Reluctantly, ever so sporadically, it came. It was clear the crowd was not at all certain just what, let alone who, it was applauding. McKenna took the opportunity to escape, rendering the podium momentarily unattended. No one moved for what seemed like an eternity. Then, a stirring. Michael Burns' son, Patrick, rose and moved slowly from the head table to the podium. His head was down and he was nervously checking his notes. When he arrived at the podium, however, both the nerves and the notes were gone. He commanded the podium and an appealing serenity graced his youthful face. He was a strapping lad just shy of six feet with a sturdy build and a strong jaw. He made his living with his hands, and those hands clenched and unclenched the podium, and a vein in his thick neck bulged ominously.

"My father is the greatest man I know," he began, searching out Aaron McKenna now seated in the back of the room. "He is the best husband I know. He is the best father I know. And," he paused, "he is the best businessman I know." There was a smattering of applause, but it died un-ignited. "He has made a gift of his whole life to others. I wish all of you could see all the things he does for people that no one ever hears about. He never says no to anyone who asks him for anything."

The young man paused to gather himself. "When we were growing up people would call, some even came to the door, to ask for help. That usually meant money. My dad would go into the study and return with his check book. And he would tell the person, 'Now, someday somebody will come to you and ask for help. Can I count on you to say yes?' The person would always nod his head and say 'yes.'" The young man paused and looked down at the podium. "I think the best thing my dad is ... is a teacher. He's always teaching other people how to solve their own problems. Even when he writes a check and gives it to them, he always, first, helps the person to find a way out of the fix he's in, and convinces him he can do it. And he always offers help, whenever the man needs it."

Patrick Burns paused as if trying to remember what else he had written in his notes. He suddenly began nodding in recollection. "A big part of my dad's life has always been his faith. He taught us all how important it is. And we watched him live it, through good times and bad. He always told us, 'Nothing so purifies a man's soul as suffering.'"

Small smile. "Of course, my dad didn't always like suffering for himself." Laughter erupted in a corner of the large room and spread quickly, engulfing the crowd. "We used to run for the hills when that famous temper erupted." More laughter. "One time one of us brought home an F on a report card," slight pause, "well, actually, that happened a lot." Loud guffaws. "Anyway, I'm certainly not going to name names here, I mean I'd never rat my brother Mike out in front of strangers, right?" Borderline hysteria. "So, Mom sees the report card and tells Mike to hide it. Mike hides it under something hanging on the refrigerator door. I think it was a picture of Dad with a 200-pound Marlin." The thought of it caused Patrick to shake with laughter. "So my dad comes home and goes right to the refrigerator for a beer. He opens the door and grabs one and kicks the door shut with his foot. The whole refrigerator starts shaking, and I'm thinking, uh oh." Laughter erupts again. "Well, all of a sudden all the stuff on the refrigerator door falls to the floor. My dad curses ..." Patrick Burns looked at his dad and smiled apologetically. "Yeah, well he does that sometimes." The tables filled with the employees at Burns Advertising started hooting. "So, he bends down and starts picking the stuff off the ground. Then, he sees it: Mike's report card. The whole family ... we're holding our breath. All of a sudden he stands up and just hauls off and punches the refrigerator." Explosive laughter spreads throughout the large room. "I mean he hit that thing so hard, he put a dent in it the size of a softball. You shoulda seen it. It was incredible."

At the head table Michael Burns laughed for the first time. His own son had rescued the event. His heart filled with pride. He may have made some rather implausible blunders in his life, but raising this young man was not among them.

"So, he's not perfect." Laughter. "Who is?" Silence. Head nodding. "But he's an honest man and he taught *us* to always be honest. I remember one time a guy came to the house. He had a beef with Dad. He had one take on a business deal; Dad had another. I'll never forget hearing my dad say, "Listen, I don't remember agreeing to that, but if you heard it I will honor it. My business is communications and if I can't, or don't, communicate clearly, the fault rests with me." The son again glanced at his father and smiled approvingly. "Thanks for teaching us that, Dad." Somewhere in the back of the room applause started. It rushed like a wave to the front of the room where it broke over the Burns' table. Carol reached into her purse for a tissue. The eyes of the three daughters filled, glistened, leaked. Michael Burns Jr. pointed to his brother at the podium and gave him a strong, loud chest pump.

Patrick Burns was now fully relaxed. The room was his. "I can't speak for the company he started, but I have to believe, things can't be all that bad, right?" Burns Advertising employees rose as one and applauded. The last to stand, Michael noted, were Ed Mobley and Aaron McKenna. Each was looking at the other and applauding indifferently. Patrick Burns waited for the staff to sit and the tables to settle. "I mean, the company went from, what, zero to over $200 million in billings in 20 years." He paused. "I mean, I don't know your business, but that's pretty good, right?" The room erupted in applause again.

At his table, Michael Burns was busy taking stock. He had worked hard to create a material legacy. He took great, perhaps even undue, pride in having done so. In a stinging rebuke he had heard his private vineyard revealed, publicly, to be poorly tended. Now he was being reminded that he had another life. He was husband and father. And he was suddenly aware only one of those legacies would endure.

In the public witness of a child telling others how he had been raised, Michael felt a lance split his heart. He had grown unworthy of his son's testimony. His son did not know the compromises he had made to secure the other legacy. Or perhaps he did, having heard the governor, and simply trusted there had to be an explanation. The father who had raised him would never take money to help women kill children. Patrick Burns would never accept that. He would deny it, Michael knew, even in the face of conclusive evidence to the contrary.

This is what thrust the final dagger into Michael's open heart. It produced a pain far greater than the others. The revelation of his compromise, the critique of his company, the uncertainty of his future— and the very public nature of it all— had opened large and painful wounds in a proud warrior. It was the simple childlike trust of a son, however, the innocent belief in his father's goodness, that created pain that paralyzed. It also induced fear. He saw in a flash he had substituted gods for God. He saw, too, there was need of a reconciliation. He began to pray quietly. *Lord, I've made compromises I never should have made. I let my heart be seduced by things I had no right coveting. I fell, Lord. I'm sorry. Forgive me. Create in me a clean heart, O Lord. Look not upon my sin but on my desire to please you, Lord. Help me find my way back to you, Lord.*

His eyes filled with tears. Carol sensed a shift in his emotional equilibrium and laid her head on his powerful shoulder. She clasped his left hand tightly in hers. He returned the squeeze. He felt the other children looking at them. They were smiling. The room began to blur. Michael's heart took flight. It soared above the tables to the ceiling some 35 feet above. He was filled with a clarity he had exchanged long ago for something else. This clarity, he realized, was the rarest of earthly treasures. It was grace itself. The very life of the Trinity poured out, freely, on fallen man. Nothing asked in return, pure gift. There for the ... accepting.

Michael accepted, submitting mind and heart, intellect and will. He immediately felt enveloped in a warm and ethereal peace. He felt flush, slightly dizzy, awash in a Father's love for a prodigal son. And, as he looked toward the podium, he felt the love of a son for a prodigal father. Tears, sudden and sodden, appeared and found their way down his cheeks and onto his suit jacket and sleeves. He made no attempt to hide them.

When his son finished, the crowd stood as one and applauded. Their eyes settled on Michael. He reached for his wife's hand and raised it high over her head, as in the manner of a victorious boxer. He pointed to her. In the deflection of unwarranted praise, he was surprised to discover another layer of peace. He noted it and stored it for further reflection.

Then he gathered his family and left. He had no wish to say anything in public.

At least not yet.

# 44

It was 10:10 p.m. when Joe Delgado finally entered his home. He immediately went room to room on the first floor, turning out all the lights his wife and daughter had failed to shut off, despite his insistent requests. They were no doubt sleeping, he assumed, even as the utility meter in the basement was whirring delightedly and inhaling his cash.

It had been a long day. Ordinarily, he spent Tuesday through Thursday evenings alone in his apartment in Manhattan. This Tuesday evening, after a full day in the office, he came home because he had an important doctor's appointment in the morning. He was holding a return ticket on a metro liner for 2:08 p.m. Wednesday afternoon.

The doctor, Ted Sluman, both friend and golfing partner, had begun offering a new sleep apnea procedure, which reportedly offered long suffering CPAP machine prisoners an 80% chance of escape. The procedure, called Pillar after its inventor, implanted a stent in the soft tissue in the back of the throat, enabling it to permit the passage of heretofore obstructed air. The examination was to determine if Joe qualified for the procedure. He hoped, in fact prayed, he did. He always told friends his CPAP machine, which he had to lug on every overnight across state, country and continent, would be the death of him. About a third of the nights he awoke on his back, throat parched and sucking air. It always seemed to happen in the middle of a recurring nightmare. Someone was chasing him and he was running out of places to hide.

He wandered into the kitchen, the only room without a light on. He flicked a switch on a wall near the entrance, and watched the room, bathed in earth tones, add light to its warmth. He detected the nascent aroma of pasta, and moved to the oven to see if it grew stronger. It did. He opened the refrigerator in search of a plate wrapped in tin foil. He immediately saw just such a plate on the top shelf and removed the foil in great expectation. He discovered sautéed chicken and broiled shrimp and sliced mushrooms imbedded in angel hair pasta. It was swimming in something. He put his index finger in a corner of the dish, removed it and put it to his lips to taste what it had absorbed. The dish was drenched in Vodka sauce, his absolute favorite. He could not believe his good fortune. He felt giddy. He moved to the microwave on tired but now happy feet and set the timer. Tonight he would eat like an actual head of household. He made a mental note to leave a hand written thank you for his daughter, Terry.

He departed the kitchen in search of his diary. He entered the library and headed straight for the bookshelves lining the back wall. The library, he told his wife after the home had been constructed, was the only room that was right sized, that is to say, not over-sized. She didn't much care to hear his opinion and said as much, graciously of course. He fingered two volumes on the upper shelf. One was a collection of GK Chesterton's prose; the other a George Bernard Shaw anthology. They maintained sentry duty for a slim, leather bound volume lying behind them. His fingers did not find the object of their search. His heart quickened. He moved to the right, his arm now extended well above his head. He removed a third volume, bound Shakespearean Classics. Nothing. His heart was racing now. He tried a fourth, a volume of John Cardinal Newman's exposition on the state of post enlightenment man at the dawn of the 20th century. Still nothing. His heart plummeted. Every dark thought now entered his mind. None made their way to the exit.

He re-entered the kitchen in a panic. To lose a diary twice in the same month was not possible. It took two weeks for him to accept he would never again see the first edition. It had been stolen, literally, right out from under him, taken from its hiding place beneath a pillow in his room at the King David Hotel in Jerusalem. He had taken great pains to reconstruct its contents in a second diary and update it with hard data and reflections on the eventful trip to Israel. This one he had buried himself late one night, *at home*, when all was quiet and dark. The irrational now had free reign, his mind dazed and disoriented. He firmly believed whoever had stolen the first version of his diary had stolen its replacement. He began checking the phones for bugs. He checked every phone on the first floor and found nothing. He grabbed a wing chair in the library and stood on it, and examined the two vents in his library. He expected to find a micro camera. He did not. He jumped down and collapsed into the chair behind his cherry desk. He was sick with anxiety.

He heard the microwave ding completion of its task. He sat devastated, unable to rise even for warm pasta doused in Vodka sauce. He sat there in the dark for a very long time, fighting off the temptation to go into the kitchen and remove the plate from the microwave and, at the very least, drink the Vodka sauce. *Lord, this would be as good a night as any to fall off the wagon. Any chance you might lead me to where my wife hides her liquor?* He actually waited for inspiration. None arrived. *Well ... okay. I didn't really think you would.*

He looked at his watch. It was 11:13 p.m. It was time for bed. He gathered himself and made his way to the circular staircase. He looked up at the 14 steps and resisted the seduction of the couch in the library. At the landing he thought he heard a noise in his wife's bedroom, but dismissed it as unlikely. He put his ear to his daughter's room. Nothing. He removed his shoes and crept oh so carefully toward the room of a known al Qaeda cell, lest he inadvertently set off an IED. The enemy was sleeping. *There is a God.*

He opened the door to his own room and stared at his bed. His heart quickened. His diary was lying in the middle of the bed with an envelope propped up against it. He shut the door and moved quickly to the bed. Heart pounding, he picked up the diary first and leafed through it. A wave of blessed relief washed away the tension. Its contents were undisturbed. He sat down on the edge of the bed and picked up the envelope. He opened it. It was a handwritten note. It read:

*Joe:*

*Please forgive me. I have been so worried about you. You look so different since you came back from the mid-east. I saw you working away at this diary night after night and, I'm so sorry, I just wondered if you were planning on leaving me. I DON'T WANT THAT, JOE! I really don't.*

*I can't believe what I read! Joe, are you safe!? Are bad people trying to kill you? Will they come after us? This is horrible. I am so worried, Joe. I can't sleep at night anymore. I'm afraid. What if they kidnap Terry and the boys? I never know when you leave on Tuesday mornings if I'll ever see you again. God help us!*

*Joe, I am so sorry for everything I have done to hurt you. You have always been a good and faithful husband and a great father to the girls. I'm afraid I've made a mess of things. Can you find it in your heart to forgive me? If you can, I promise I will stop drinking and mend my ways and be a good wife to you. Please, please Joe. Give me another chance! Maybe we could just start over and forget all the pain and sorrow. Is it possible? Please say yes, Joe.*

*Whenever you read this, just know I am awake. I'm in my room waiting just in case you decide to forgive me tonight. We can talk, Joe. All night or even just for a few minutes, whatever you want. Please come see me. I miss you and I love you. I'm waiting for you even as you read this letter.*

*Come to me tonight Joe. Please …*

*Fran*

*P.S. I'm wearing the camisole you bought me for our 10th wedding anniversary. The pink one. Do you remember? It's a little snug but I managed to get myself into it. Now I need you to get me out!*

Joe put the letter down. He was flooded with mixed emotions and he knew it would take him a long while to sort through them. It was his nature to proceed through life cautiously, even without a field of land mines in front of him. On the one hand, he felt outrage that his privacy had been breached, yet again. This time in his own home. He could understand her knowing he was keeping a diary, but how had she known where to look for it? What had she absorbed about the particulars of what he had written? Had she shared any of it with her friends? Would he walk into his Country Club and find people avoiding him? Would his own daughter take her children and move out of their home? *Well, maybe there is an upside to this thing after all ...*

He felt himself growing extremely angry. He envisioned himself tearing into her room and throwing her out of bed and onto the ground; he saw himself standing over her and screaming into her face that she was a worthless wretch, the worst mistake he ever made, and not to ever expect forgiveness from him ... because what she had done was unpardonable.

Her fear, however, tapped into the protective nature of his paternity. She was the mother of his children. She was all but paralyzed with fear. This was unacceptable. She would wear that fear everywhere she went. This meant Terry would smell her mother's fear and both adopt and adapt it to her own maternity. This, too, angered him. He wanted to confront his enemies, physically. He wanted to batter them, dominate them, choke the very life out of them. But who were they? Where could he go to confront them? Were they headquartered in Israel? Or, perhaps, were they headquartered here in the U.S. and giving orders to people in Israel?

He felt his mind settling in an unexpected place. He was husband and father. This was his core identity. He was, at root, a protector, like his namesake. He was born to protect so he would protect. He would protect his wife. He would protect his children. He would protect his children's children.

But he would not compromise truth. He had done that once before and he had died a death of a thousand small cuts. Never again, he had promised himself then. Never again, he reminded himself now.

He got up and walked to his wife's room in his stocking feet. Tonight was a night for, if not reconciliation, at least a promise. A promise that he would honor his vows. That he would put her safety ahead of his own and keep her safe from harm. As he approached the door he wondered what would happen when he opened it. What would he see in her eyes? Would he see fear? Would he see longing? Would he see disorientation from a recurring bout with the bottle? More importantly, he asked himself, how would he respond to what he saw in her eyes? Would her fear induce a tight protective hug to wring from her all apprehension? Would her longing stir him and direct him to her bed?

He got to her door at the far end of the corridor and leaned his head against it. He heard a sound. It was the gentle resonant sound of a woman snoring. His wife was asleep.

Joe Delgado turned and went back to his room. He, too, needed sleep.

• • •

It was a little after 3:50 p.m. when he arrived at his mid town office building. The train ride to New York was uneventful, which permitted him to reflect on the evening before. He was up early for Mass at St. Martha's, so he missed his wife. He left a note for Terry thanking her for the cooked pasta and asking her to hold it for another 48 hours. He started a note to his wife but abandoned it half way through. He just wasn't quite certain about what to say; and it was his nature to say nothing until he was quite certain.

He had slept fitfully. At dawn, while lying awake staring at the ceiling in his room, he felt an inspiration to dress and go to Mass. He arrived early, hoping Father John would hear his confession. He had been away from the sacraments for too long and felt an urge to reconnect with the deepest comfort he had ever known. He caught the pastor as he entered the sacristy. John Sweeney greeted him with a warm smile and a tight, expansive bear hug. Joe's confession took but minutes and he felt lighter, freer immediately. He told Father John he had something important he wanted to discuss with him on the weekend, and had given him some idea of the subject matter. The priest's face registered surprise and, Joe thought, a hint of apprehension. They agreed to meet for coffee after the 8:00 a.m. Mass on Saturday.

As he entered the executive suite he heard voices in Chad Henley's office on the other side of the common area, and decided to swing by for a peak. He ducked his head in the door, a barb on the tip of his tongue, and froze. He was stunned by what he saw. More precisely, he was stunned by *who* he saw.

Henley was standing behind his desk, right shoulder facing Joe. Seated in front of him were Geoff Benton and Hanley Siliezar. At the sight of him, all discussion ceased. Henley, clearly nervous, diverted whatever the topic of conversation had been to Joe's late morning examination in Philadelphia. "Joe, didn't expect you back in the office today," he said glancing quickly at Benton and Siliezar. "How'd the exam go? Did you qualify for that procedure?"

Joe was still in shock. He had never seen Benton in the HM Healthcare building in New York, and he couldn't wait to hear what had drawn his presence. As for Siliezar, he was the man the world's press referred to as the Silver Phantom. His movements and whereabouts were all but state secrets. The odds of finding the two of them in the same place at the same time, regardless of where that place was, were, in Joe's view, extremely remote. The odds of them both sitting, at the same time, in an office across from his, were beyond remote.

"I did," he replied abruptly. "Thank you for asking."

He stood waiting for acknowledgement from the others. It

was not forthcoming. Neither of the two men seated even so much as glanced in his direction. Somewhere in the pit of his stomach an alarm went off. Henley sensed it and sought to shut it down. "Joe, I'm just finishing up here with these fellows. How about I catch up with you in an hour or so?"

Joe nodded. He felt a familiar cold dread working its way through his central nervous system. He turned to leave. He heard Henley calling after him. "Joe, are you free for dinner?"

For some reason his mind immediately produced an image of a plate of pasta sitting in a microwave in his kitchen at home. He felt hunger. "Yes," he said, simply.

"Good. I'll drop by in a bit."

He crossed the common area and entered his office. The lights were off. He flicked them on and dropped his attaché on his desk chair. His eyes scanned the room, taking inventory. Nothing appeared to be amiss, but he knew such appearances could prove quite deceiving. Nevertheless he decided against a more painstaking effort. What was to be gained at this point? His diary, version 2.0, was now back in seclusion. This time in his *own* bedroom, between his box spring and his mattress.

He turned his computer on and saw he had 114 messages. He knew from experience only six to eight would be of consequence. He checked his watch and decided he had sufficient time to sort for the consequential, and delete or respond perfunctorily to the inconsequential. It took him the better part of an hour to complete the task. He printed out four attachments for bedtime reading, two of which were pro formas for new compounds. He reached into the Inbox sitting on the right corner of his desk and began a similar sort. He quickly tossed low interest items in the wastebasket he kept under the desk. Items of high interest, along with a portion of his personal correspondence, joined the printed attachments in his take home file. He glanced at his watch. He was surprised to see it was now 5:12. He was not surprised Henley had not yet arrived to darken his door. Clearly whatever they were discussing, no doubt something to do with The Project, was absorbing their full energies. He did, however, want to see Henley at his door soon. He was extremely tired and he did not want another late night. At 61, he was learning he did not travel as he did when he was 31, or even 41. Tonight he would need sleep.

Henley arrived at 5:47. He offered no explanation for the delay, let alone the earlier presence in his office of two august members of Revolution 4's esteemed triumvirate. "Ready when you are, Joe," he said brightly.

"Oh, I'm ready, Chad. Been ready," he replied with a small sting.

Henley ignored the jab and said, "How about a steak house over on the west side?"

Joe immediately affirmed the choice. "Works for me."

"Meet you at the elevator in five?" Henley asked.

"Yep."

Joe began to collect his things. He felt a tug to call his wife. He picked up the phone only to set it down again. Not being able to see her eyes and assess her mood he was reluctant to commit himself. He crossed the room to grab a book off the credenza. It was A.J. Liebling's storied treatise on the Sweet Science. A friend had given it to him, and he was anxious to dive into the heart and soul of it. He stuffed it into his attaché along with the other files and zipped the bag closed. He glanced around the office and noted a picture of Terry and the boys. They were smiling. He remembered the photo shoot. It had taken 20 minutes to dress each of them, less than two minutes for each of them to undress themselves, and another 20 minutes to subdue them so they could once again appear fully clothed. He wondered what would become of the irresistible rascals. He hoped he lived long enough to find out.

He met Henley at the elevator and they rode to the lobby in silence. Once outside, Henley re-emerged as Henley again. He began chatting Joe up about everything, save business. Suddenly, he was a New York Giants football fan. He took to trash-talking Joe about his Eagles. Joe thought the conversation odd, Henley certainly didn't understand professional football. But then, in his mind, that didn't differentiate him from other Giants fans he knew.

They arrived at a small storefront on 48th , just off 10th Avenue. They climbed out of the cab and walked down a half flight of steps and into the restaurant. The maitre 'd greeted Henley warmly. "Hey, Brit. We redid the menu. All the entrees are now in pounds sterling."

Henley smiled good-naturedly. "Fine by me, as long as I continue to get paid in U.S. dollars."

The dinner itself was uneventful. Like all New York steak houses, and most of its other restaurants for that matter, Manhattan restaurant food was uniformly excellent. Service was almost never an issue and a patron could get in and out in under an hour if he wished. On this night, that was indeed Joe Delgado's wish. The dinner conversation, guided by Henley, also avoided any mention of business. Having heard far less than enough, Joe decided to address the issue directly. "What's going on, Henley?" he asked pointedly.

"What do you mean?"

Joe simply stared, unblinking.

"Really, Joe. I'm not sure what you're driving at."

Joe probed the man's eyes. He concluded Chad Henley was a most experienced and convincing prevaricator. "Why were Benton and Siliezar in your office? Why did they fail to acknowledge my presence? Why have we talked about anything and everything this evening ... *except business*?" He paused. "*That's* what I mean, Chad."

Henley didn't blink. It was clear he anticipated the question. "Look, Joe, there are some things about 4 that are discussed only on a need-to-know basis. There's nothing sinister going on. We just don't think you, and the others, need to know certain details about certain aspects of The Project."

Two words impaled themselves in Joe's heart. He regarded each as a lapse on Henley's part. His use of the word sinister was calculated, and revealed, confirmed, what Joe knew they thought of him and the reservations he had voiced about "aspects" of The Project, both in the U.S. and in Israel. This alarmed him.

The other word was more problematic. Benton and Siliezar were not men who concerned themselves with details. Joe knew Henley had an inclination to use words judiciously. The word details had not been cast merely as a diversion. Joe knew from experience it meant Benton and Siliezar were involved in at least some of the details for at least some aspect of The Project. This left him feeling uneasy, but he did not know where to go with his anxiety. He knew Henley would quickly seal off any further discussion on that point, so he tried another tack. "Chad, why did Benton and Siliezar avoid looking at me?"

"I can't answer that, Joe. You'd have to ask them," was the immediate and summary reply. Too much of each, Joe decided.

"Think they have a problem with me, Chad?"

Henley squirmed. Joe regarded it as an important signal. "Look, Joe, you've certainly, ah, given voice to some of your deep reservations about the, ah, work. Surely you don't expect those comments to go, what, unexamined?"

"Of course not," Joe replied too quickly. He paused to gather himself. "But under HM's constructive devil's advocacy imperative neither do I expect them to make me persona non grata in my own office suite."

Ever so slightly, Henley nodded. He said, however, nothing.

"Let me ask you this, Chad." Joe leaned across the table and looked directly into Henley's eyes. "I think my diary was stolen by someone working for the company. What do you think?"

The question caught Henley off guard. His physical response, his body language, provided the answer Joe had long suspected. He didn't bother listening to the evasive, discursive words which followed. Joe now understood all. Suspecting he was keeping written notes, HM Inc had ordered his room ransacked and the confiscation of his personal diary. The three men in Henley's office this afternoon had all read his entries. They were discussing the details of what to do about what he had written, when he happened upon them unexpectedly. They had simply concluded their discussion after he left.

Joe pulled his elbows off the table and sat erect. He saw his immediate future. This was his last supper. Tomorrow morning, Chad Henley would call him into his office and tell him he was fired. A familiar anger welled up within him. He looked around the restaurant to see if he knew anyone. A somewhat unconventional thought lodged itself in his subconscious and hurdled the barriers to his conscious. He would pick Chad Henley up by his lapels and crash a vicious right into his solar plexus, collapsing it and sending the man into a paroxysm of pain accompanied by massive internal bleeding, perhaps even death. It would all happen so quickly that none of the restaurant's other patrons would observe the whole of it and would, therefore, be unable to render an accurate account of just what had transpired.

"Well, I really have to get moving here, Joe." Henley was interrupting his own death scene. Joe wondered if perhaps he ought to let the man in on it. Perhaps, he thought, let him choose his own end, like an interactive video game. "Got to catch the 8:00 train to Greenwich. My wife's expecting me. Her mother arrived this afternoon from the continent. About now, Helen is into her third martini and taking my name in vain," he laughed the laugh of the man without a care in the world.

Joe simply stared back. He teetered between homicide and helplessness. Henley paid the check and stood. Joe let his body relax. Helplessness it would be. "Okay, thanks for dinner, Chad. See you tomorrow?" Joe peered intently into the other man's eyes for any stray signal. None sent.

"Yes, you will. I'll be at my desk at 7:00. I know you'll beat me in. You always do," Henley replied. He turned without waiting for Joe and made his way hastily to the door in search of a cab to Grand Central Station.

Joe turned to go to the men's room. When he came out their table had been cleared and a man and woman were seated. Life does indeed go on, he mused.

He left the restaurant and walked into a cold, clear mid-November evening. The city was alive, pulsing with bustling humanity moving frenetically to and from offices and apartments, cafes and theatres. It was a night for walking the 12 short blocks north and two blocks east to his apartment just off the southwestern corner of Central Park. Joe cut over to Eighth Avenue at 50th to savor the theatre crowd, disproportionately represented on this night by blue-haired women from, he guessed, Northern Jersey. He crossed 58th Street and entered the Park just west of the Plaza. He followed a trail leading to an exit just below twin 56-story apartment towers. His was the second of the two buildings. His apartment was on the 48th floor and overlooked the park.

As he approached the building, he smiled at the new doorman, forgetting his name. He was a tall black man from Jamaica, and Joe always made him laugh by pantomiming the archer posture made famous by his countryman: the great Olympic sprint champion, Usain Bolt. He was about to ease into his pose when something caught his eye. A man who looked all too familiar was exiting the building hurriedly through the front doors. He was wearing a light trench coat and a gray fedora that sat on his huge head at an odd angle. He was so massively wide he appeared to have no neck. His eyes were cold and feral. He walked lightly on the balls of his feet like a wrestler, or perhaps a Judo champion. Joe made eye contact from 15 feet. The man immediately averted his eyes and changed direction. Joe knew him from somewhere. He was sure of it. He simply couldn't place him.

He gave the doorman a light pat on the arm and entered the building. He gave a distracted wave to the uniformed man behind the desk, who did not return it. He headed to his elevator bank deep in thought. He was now greatly agitated that he couldn't summon the occasion of his acquaintance with the hulking man he had just encountered. He arrived at his apartment and fumbled in his wallet for a key. He let himself in and immediately flicked the light on in the small entranceway. He moved through the living room, kitchen and bedroom doing the same. He saw nothing amiss. He returned to the hallway and removed his coat, hanging it on a wood hanger in the closet. He tossed his plaid Jeff cap onto a shelf above his head. He picked up his attaché and dropped it onto his easy chair in the living room. He went into the kitchen and opened the refrigerator and removed a can of Diet Coke. He took off his suit jacket and his tie with his right hand, opened his bedroom door, and tossed them on his bed. He returned to his chair, removed his attaché, and fell into it exhausted. He drained half the can of Diet Coke. He opened his attaché and removed his folders. He looked at them for a brief moment and stuffed them back in his bag. He reached for the A.J. Liebling classic on boxing. He thumbed through it and marked the chapter on the first Marciano-Walcott fight in South Philadelphia, September 23rd, 1952. He decided he would read himself to sleep in bed.

He finished off the Diet Coke and dropped it into a waste container in the kitchen. He turned the lights out in the hallway and living room, but left the one in the kitchen on. He moved into his bedroom and hung up his suit jacket, removed his trousers and hung them on a separate hanger. He removed his dress shirt and tossed it in his laundry bag, replacing it with a University of Pennsylvania tee shirt from his bureau. He climbed into bed, only to climb back out and hit his knees. *Lord, I do believe I am in some sort of trouble. I turn to you, now, for protection. I think I'm going to be fired tomorrow. Please give me the courage to go through with what I have promised you I would do. You are all I have, Lord. I am all alone now. And if anything happens to me, please, Lord, please protect my family.* He said a Hail Mary, blessed himself and got back into bed.

Joe Delgado read for maybe 15 minutes before he fell asleep. He awoke after several minutes with a start, aware he was snoring loudly. He reached for the mask on top of his CPAP machine and placed it on his face and turned the machine on. It did not start. He depressed the start button again. Still nothing. He sat up, highly agitated, and removed his mask. He moved the night table and discovered the plug was lying on the floor. He plugged the machine back into the wall socket and pushed the start button. Still nothing. He was now in a state of quiet panic. He was exhausted. He desperately needed a good night's sleep. His only hope was this balky machine to which he was figuratively chained. He picked it up and saw the bottom was missing. He had never seen the inside of the machine before and wondered why he was seeing it now. His curiosity, however, would have to await renewed energy. All Joe Delgado wanted to do in this instant was to get the damn machine working and turn out the lights, both literally and metaphorically.

It was then that he saw the problem. The other end of the plug had been removed from the back of the machine. Probably the cleaning service, he assured himself. He inserted the plug and immediately heard the quiet, reassuring whirring sound that signaled the machine was functioning. Joe smiled. *Thank you, Lord.* He placed the mask on his face again and tightened it. He turned off the lamp on the night stand and, with great relief, laid his head on his pillow.

It took Joe Delgado only four minutes to fall soundly asleep.

It took him only an additional four minutes to die from the effects of a carbon monoxide capsule crudely installed in the interior of his CPAP machine's humidifier.

# 45

Maggie Kealey awakened in stages to the smell of morning coffee. She heard steps on the stairs and panicked. She did not want this morning. She did not want this man on this morning. She did not want this moment with this man on this morning.

The night had been torturous. Again and again she lay helpless as at least four different D-Day scenarios played themselves out in her mind. In one, she arrived at the hospital and discovered there were no doctors and nurses, instead there were 300 staffers waiting outside her door for an explanation; in a second, she arrived to discover nothing had changed, as though Friday's High Noon showdown with her Physician Board had never taken place; in a third, she was met in the parking lot by security and escorted off the premises before she could even set foot in the hospital to find out what, if anything, had happened; in a fourth scenario, she entered the hospital and discovered her entire Ob/Gyn department cleared out just as she had ordered, and been replaced by Hank Seelaus and his new Women's Clinic.

As the night wore on, she found herself spending less and less time in this fourth scenario.

The bedroom door opened. "Hello, Sweetheart. Just wanted to drop by and let you know you don't have to go in today. The world ended this morning at 4:00 a.m. eastern standard time."

Maggie laughed despite herself. She sat up and reached for her coffee. "I'm sorry, Jim. You must think I'm such a wimp."

He nodded. "I do indeed. Just another one of your irresistible charms."

"Did Father John say the 6:30 Mass?"

Jim Gillespie nodded again. "Yes, and in his ever so brief homily he asked why I allowed you to sleep in this morning." He shrugged. "So I explained."

"Jim, he didn't! *You didn't*! Please, tell me you're joking."

He was more surprised by the fear in her eyes than her naiveté. He sat on the edge of the bed and waited for her to withdraw the cup of hot coffee from her lips. As soon as she did he moved to hug her. She pulled back abruptly. "Jim! Are you forgetting or just ignoring what Father John said? I'm still a married woman. We can't do that again."

"What? I can't even hug you when you're frightened?"

"Not while I'm in bed. Please, Jim, you shouldn't even be in here."

He chafed at the lecture and fell silent.

"I'm sorry. I didn't mean that the way it sounded," she said softly.

"Well," he replied. "I suppose I'll wait for you downstairs. That is, assuming you intend to go to the hospital this morning."

She held his gaze. She fought off a strong impulse to set her coffee on the nightstand and pull him toward her, and hug him tightly and not let go. "Jim, think we'll make it until the annulment comes through?"

He looked at her with surprise. "Do I think *we* will make it?" he repeated. "I know *I* will make it; *you*? I'm not so sure."

She laughed and the pure joy in the sound lifted the room temperature.

"Of course," he added, "you have the far greater temptation, resisting me. Besides, you women always have only one thing on your minds."

She laughed so hard the bed shook. Jim, delicately, lifted the cup from her hands so she would not spill its contents on her gown or bedspread. When she composed herself she reached for his hand in silence. He extended his left hand, holding her coffee in his right. She looked at him longingly. "Jim, I love you," she said softly, in a half moan.

"I love you too, Maggie."

"No matter what happens today, it won't ..." she stopped and looked down, afraid to hold his gaze.

"Do you mean, if you punch out Sister Kathleen will I call off our engagement before we announce it?"

She began to giggle, eyeing him intently. "Jim," she said gently. "Please, please don't leave me. I don't think I could live through another disappointment."

The weight of her wounds fell upon him like a roof in spring unburdening itself of winter snow. "Maggie, I *will* disappoint you. That's what we men do. We disappoint women we love. But, I can promise you, it *won't* be because I stop loving you. I've loved you from the first moment I saw you in the cancer ward, 20 years ago. And," his voice caught, "I will love you until the day one of us dies."

She began to cry. He set the cup of coffee on the night stand and moved closer on the bed until his body was only inches from hers. He put his arms around her shoulders and buried his head in her disheveled hair, and he, too, began to cry. They sat as one, suspended in time and hope, for several minutes. Finally he pulled away, not wanting to cross a line he knew would only bring regret. She looked up at him and smiled through her tears. "Wait for me downstairs," she said with quiet resolve. "We're going to face the future together, Dr. Gillespie. Starting this morning."

. . .

The 30-minute drive into South Philadelphia took almost 50 minutes on this wintry gray morning. An accident on the Expressway shut it down, and traffic into town was re-routed onto its major arteries, adding distance and stress to the normally difficult Monday morning commute.

There was little conversation in the light blue Porsche carrying the CEO of Regina Hospital and the head of its Oncology Department and Women's Clinic. Jim had Stephen Sondheim's *A Little Night Music* playing to elevate the mood, and he was trying to hold hands with his boss, but the constant lurching in heavy traffic caused him to ultimately abandon that effort, triggering her laughter.

When they arrived, each was relieved to see the parking lot nearly full, though neither commented on it. From all appearances, Maggie assured herself, it was just another Monday morning. She looked at her watch. It was 8:23 a.m. How ironic, she mused, if she were late for work for the first time in her entire career on her last day. She banished the thought from her mind.

Jim shut the engine down, turned toward Maggie and reached for her hands. "Maggie," he said quietly, "whatever happens, remember we have each other."

Pain immediately creased her eyes. "You don't think," she stopped abruptly and fought back tears.

He looked around to make sure no one was looking. He pulled her hands to his chest. "I don't know, I truly don't, Sweetheart," he replied. "All I'm saying is it doesn't matter. It really doesn't." Suddenly his eyes were filled with light. "We're in love, Maggie! We're in love! And we are going to spend the rest of our lives together!" He tried to close the distance between them but the gear box did not entirely cooperate. "What's better than that?" he asked, his face now less than a foot from hers. "Maggie, what more could we possibly want than each other?"

She kissed his hands and nodded silently. She was now filled with dread. The moment she had spent the entire evening with was now upon her. She had granted it permission to deny her sleep, to deny her peace, even to deny her the consolation of the sacred body and blood, soul and divinity of her Lord and savior in the morning Eucharist. She grew angry with herself. She lacked trust. And in failing trust she failed the first principle of the spiritual life: living in the present moment. That, she knew, was the precursor to all manner of confusion and anxiety. She had created space for the demonic. And true to form, he had entered her thought life and rearranged the furniture.

She patted Jim gently on the cheek and said, "Okay, Doctor Gillespie. Let's go see if we still have a hospital to run." They got out of the car and felt the unexpected bite of winter in a stiff breeze blowing west from the Delaware River several blocks away. They hurried to the back entrance of the hospital and were ushered inside by Henry White, a large maintenance man in his 70's who had celebrated his 50th anniversary with the hospital during the past summer. "Take your time, Mrs. Kealey. Can't have you trippin' now. We need you upstairs in that corner office."

Maggie smiled. "Thank you, Henry. We need you just as much as me. So *you* be careful today, and every day from here on out, okay? Will you promise me that?"

"Yes ma'am, I will," he nodded in earnest reply.

When they were safely out of earshot, Jim mimicked, "Now you, on the other hand, Gillespie. You can fall down dead pretty much anywhere in here. Just don't make a mess for me, okay? By the way, where'd you get the white coat?"

Maggie ignored him. She was busy setting her game face. Scenes from her childhood flashed in and out of her mind. She saw herself in a small desk on her first day of school, at her family's dining room table on a Sunday night, on a narrow wooden bench during her first piano recital, on a step ladder crowning the Virgin

Mary in eighth grade, and in the principal's office on her last day
of grade school listening to Sister Camilla tell her she might have
a religious vocation.

She entered the elevator with Jim. She immediately shut her
eyes and prayed. *Thank you, Lord for the blessings of a good childhood.*
*Thank you for allowing me to be raised and taught and supported by good*
*parents and good teachers and a good community of families. And thank*
*you for this good, strong man at my side. Without them, I could not face this*
*moment. I don't know what I am walking into, my Lord. But whatever it is,*
*I know you are walking into it with me. And that is all that matters to me.*

The elevator opened at the fourth floor, and Jim held the door
for Maggie's exit. Together they entered the executive suite. As they
entered the common area, Maggie stopped and turned and said,
"Thank you, Jim. I'm alright now. You can go down to the floor."

He smiled and clasped her hand. "No thank you, Mrs. Kealey.
I'm all in. Where you go this morning, I go."

Maggie squeezed his hand and released her grip. She made her
way to the corner office, Jim trailing two steps behind. She was
relieved to see Lori Needham was late again. She was surprised,
however, to see her office door slightly ajar. She was always careful
to close and lock it each evening, particularly on a Friday evening.
There were far too many sensitive files in her credenza.

As she approached she sensed a physical presence in the office,
though the lights were off. She stopped before entering and turned
to Jim and shrugged, palms up. She entered and froze. There seated
behind her desk was Sister Kathleen Sullivan. Their eyes met. In
that instant, Maggie understood all.

"Good morning, Maggie," she said evenly. Then, seeing Jim
enter behind Maggie, she added, "Oh, Doctor Gillespie. What a
surprise."

"Well, make yourself at home, Sister. Oh, I see you already
have," Gillespie returned volley.

Maggie didn't know what to do. She resisted sitting in one of
the two chairs on the opposite side of her own desk. And she felt
uncomfortable standing in her own office waiting for instructions

from an unwelcome visitor. In an effort to regain control, she held the nun's gaze and said, "How about we conduct this meeting in the executive conference room?"

Sister Kathleen stood immediately and followed in silence.

They arrived at the small conference room in the rear of the executive suite and entered one by one in awkward silence. Jim flicked on the lights and held the back of chair closest to the door for Maggie. She ignored the gesture and went immediately to the head of the small rectangular table and took her seat. Sister Kathleen ducked her head and flashed a small smile at her CEO's statement. She sat in the chair Jim was holding, forcing him to the other side of the table.

"I chose your office for our discussion for a reason," Sister Kathleen opened.

"And what might that reason be, Sister?" Maggie replied matter of factly.

"Privacy," the nun answered tersely, adding, "Yours …"

"Well, that's very considerate of you, Sister. To what do I owe this pleasure?"

The nun looked at her with the barest hint of disdain. "Maggie, the Order has decided to replace you as CEO."

Maggie froze. Her heart stopped. She felt as though she had just been shot at point blank range. She resisted the impulse to look at her chest to check for blood. She was suddenly aware her hands were shaking, as were her knees. She became acutely conscious of her bladder. She lowered her hands, placing them on her lap and out of range of sight. "May I ask why?" she heard herself ask in a voice that surprised her in its strength.

The nun fixed her with a stare that signaled impatience. "Well, Maggie, we concluded it's better to run a hospital *with* doctors and nurses."

Maggie's eyes widened but she said nothing.

"Excuse me, Sister," Jim said with exquisite deference. "I'm a doctor and I work here and I don't intend on going anywhere."

Sister Kathleen turned her attention to the only physician in the room. "Yes, Jim, and the Order is grateful for your many years of service. Unfortunately," she paused and shifted uneasily in her seat "too many of the other doctors have decided they do *not* want to work here if Maggie Kealey remains as our CEO."

Jim Gillespie fairly leapt from his seat. "Who?" he bellowed.

The nun, surprised at his uncharacteristic outburst, looked at both of them before answering. Jim was offended that she milked the moment at Maggie's expense and would forever resent her for it. "Well, let me recollect," she paused one very theatrical beat. "All of the Ob/Gyn's, of course." She looked at Maggie and paused again before resuming. "And all our Cardiologists and Internists ..." She paused a third time and glanced at both of them. "Oh, and all but two of our surgeons. Hayes and Lincecum were apparently together on a hunting trip in upstate New York over the weekend, and none of the other doctors were able to get in touch with them." She stopped and began picking imaginary lint from the lap of her skirt.

Jim and Maggie watched her in silence. When she looked up, the tension in the room was palpable. Maggie broke it with a simple question. "And you, Kathleen Sullivan, are prepared to give an accounting before Almighty God for the choice you have made?"

The other woman's face froze. It was several moments before she trusted herself to speak. "Well, as you know," she began as though addressing a multitude. "In these matters the Order," she paused to emphasize her hiding place, "tends to make its prudential judgments very carefully."

"In this case, within 24 hours," Jim Gillespie interrupted, politely.

The nun ignored him. She had been scripted and she was on message. "We balance all considerations against the needs of the community we serve. For five generations we have been a healing presence among those abandoned by the system."

"What system?" Gillespie interrupted again, not so politely. "The system that is solvent as opposed to ours, which is insolvent and will remain so unless we attract more of *their* patients, which indeed is our mandate from the Order?"

She ignored him again and continued. "In the final analysis, the families who rely on us do not have alternatives. Without us, their parents would die prematurely and their children would not have a place to be born."

Maggie Kealey felt her flesh contract in pure revulsion. She struggled to control herself. She opened her mouth to speak only to close it. Then: a damn burst. "You are a disgrace to religious life!" she began in the interest of clarity. "The Order is corrupt and will have to be disbanded." She paused only to escalate the decibel level. "The Lord Himself set before you life or death. You chose death. He will hold *you* accountable, Sullivan, along with those other frauds."

Kathleen Sullivan smiled. She expected a verbal assault and was delighted to receive it graciously. It confirmed what she had told her superiors prior to Maggie's appointment. Nurse Kealey was an unbalanced zealot who would self destruct within one year of her tenure as CEO. Kathleen Sullivan took great pride in the prophetic accuracy of her caution and believed it would earn her a promotion in due time.

Jim Gillespie stirred uneasily. He did not want to see the woman he loved come unhinged. He sought to intervene. "Sister, I do believe you are making a mistake."

She turned to him, eyes wide in surprise. She heard rationality in his voice and for that she was less prepared.

"Sister, if we continue dispensing contraceptives and referring couples to grossly ineffective fertility clinics and sperm and egg banks, we will hollow out our market in a single generation. There simply won't be enough children having enough children to keep our doors open." He paused for effect. "Sister, we're sacrificing tomorrow for today. With all due respect, the Order has never, ever, operated this way. It has always reflected Holy Mother Church herself in taking the long term view of its healing mission to the poor."

When it was clear to her he had concluded she looked down at her lap and resumed picking lint.

Maggie had heard enough. "You are a scandal," she all but spat.

This drew a sharp and surprising response. "Oh, I wouldn't go there Mrs. Kealey."

Confusion streaked across Maggie's eyes. Jim understood immediately. "Why shouldn't she go there, Sister?" he asked in his best bedside manner.

Kathleen Sullivan squirmed in discomfort. Turning to Maggie, she tried to change the subject. "All the terms of your contract, as regards severance, will be honored of course. The HR department ..."

"Answer Doctor Gillespie's question, Sister!" Maggie demanded.

The nun looked like she wished she was cloistered. "Well, scandal is a very loaded term, Mrs. Kealey ..."

"Yes, I know. I loaded it."

The nun appeared to have found a modicum of resolve she did not know she had and used it to hold her ground. "There has been talk ... about you and Dr. Gillespie."

Jim Gillespie exhaled loudly.

Maggie erupted. "What kind of talk?" she bellowed.

The nun folded her hands, placed them on her lap, and let her eyes follow them down. Jim understood she was signaling she had said all she was going to say.

"What are you accusing us of?" Maggie was standing now, hands on hips. "Are you accusing Doctor Gillespie and I of having an affair?"

The nun's eyes remained downcast.

Maggie was very nearly apoplectic. "I'm a practicing Catholic! I've been chaste since the day my husband abandoned us 23 years ago. Who do you think you're slandering, Sullivan?" She was standing next to the nun and towering over her. Looking at her, Jim thought her to be in full Irish dudgeon. He found it enormously attractive.

He stood and walked around the other side of the table.

Maggie saw him coming and her eyes reflected her anger and confusion. He walked up to her and grabbed her left hand. Turning to the seated nun, he said, "Sister, the talk, as you refer to it, is baseless and unworthy of repetition. This woman is incorruptible." He leaned down and winked. "Believe me, I've tried." Maggie started to interrupt and he squeezed her hand tightly to head her off. "The Order has just lost the best thing to come down the pike in the two generations I've been here. This decision will cost many, many jobs. Please God yours will be among the first."

He led Maggie to the door. She followed light to the touch. He turned at the doorway and said, "Oh, I almost forgot. Sister Kathleen, you'll have to also find a new Head of Oncology. I resign. As I said before, human cancer I can handle. Institutional cancer, I can't."

With that, Doctor Jim Gillespie and Maggie Kealey went in search of Hank Seelaus. They had an idea they wanted to discuss with him.

# 46

John Sweeney was exhausted. He entered the sanctuary at midnight with anger he found difficult to excise through prayer. He awoke at dawn, prostrate before the tabernacle, still angry. He gathered himself, said one last Memorare, and left with what he concluded was a righteous anger.

Now, standing in the doorway between the sanctuary and the vestibule, watching virtually all of Narbrook file into St. Martha's for Joe Delgado's funeral rites, he was still struggling to douse the embers. It was his task to eulogize a dear friend. He did not yet know what he would say. He continued to pray that it would be worthy of the man and the life he lived.

The crowd filing in was uniquely Irish in its grave solemnity and irrepressible spontaneity. Somber faces soon yielded right of way to unburdened hearts; unburdened hearts sought clandestine refuge behind somber eyes. Taking it all in, John Sweeney marveled anew at the Irish view of life from within what his dear mother liked to call 'this vale of tears,' and was reminded, yet again, that Narbrook manifestly understood how to bury its dead.

After a slow, somewhat halting procession from the back of the church and a solemn reading of the introductory rites, John took his place on the altar surrounded by his seminary classmates. Their presence lent a heightened gravitas to the sacramental embrace of a dearly departed soul. Indeed, these men were his closest friends, hearts forever quickened in solidarity with each other's solitary ministry.

As he listened to the readings, John was mesmerized by Fran Delgado's grief. She was a woman broken by calamity; she bore the insufferable pain of those who understand for perhaps the first time what has been irretrievably lost. She sat bent, sobbing into her eldest daughter's chest. Terry Delgado's face was set in a mask of horror and resolve. There had been no goodbyes, John suddenly realized. The family was suffering the excruciating pain of the lost goodbye. His anger returned: whiter, hotter.

He was surprised by the sound of the congregation getting to its feet for the Gospel. A wave of fatigue washed over him and for an instant he doubted whether he was up to the demands of the moment. With more determination than he would have liked to concede was required, he stood and walked on wooden legs to the marble lectern. He read the Gospel acclamation, thumbing the traditional anointing of forehead, lips and heart. He announced chapter and verse: Matthew 2:13, and read of Joseph's flight into Egypt with virgin mother and child. He finished and the throng, now spilling out into the steps and street below, sat in anticipation. John Sweeney knew his people, knew that they had come to hear righteous anger; he was determined they would not be disappointed.

"The culture of death claimed another victim last week; this time it was one of our own," and thus began a eulogy that would be remembered by all who heard it, and all who would claim they had heard it.

"Let's be clear from the outset. Joe Delgado was by no means an innocent bystander in America's culture wars. He was a marked man." He paused and swept the congregation.

"New York's Mayor and Police Chief lied. Joe Delgado was

*not* a victim of mistaken identity. He was *not* in the wrong place at the wrong time. The carbon monoxide capsule inserted into his CPAP machine last Wednesday evening in his Manhattan apartment was *not* intended for the leader of a Mexican drug cartel.

"It was intended for him.

"Joe Delgado was murdered," he thundered. "He was murdered because he saw what evil was planning, and decided to alert his fellow man so it could be stopped dead in its tracks." He paused and gripped and re-gripped the lectern. He looked at Fran and Terry Delgado. "Joe Delgado died a hero. A man who dared speak truth to unspeakably evil power."

He became aware of fidgeting in pockets of the congregation. *Too strident? Good. Let me ratchet it up a notch.* "It was Jesus, your Lord and Savior," he said, pointing randomly to sections of the seated congregation, "who called Satan a cosmic liar. Not me! It was Jesus, not Father Sweeney." He paused breathing heavily. "Let me ask a question. Show of hands. How many don't believe Satan exists?"

The congregation sat in silence for a long moment until several uncertain hands were raised, triggering the raising of a handful of others, then finally a reluctant critical mass. It was clear. Satan was a no show in the garden. Far from discouraging John Sweeney, this only served to fuel his white hot anger at evil's greatest achievement in the post modern moment. "He exists!" he thundered. "And he who says he doesn't calls *Christ* a liar!"

He let the weight of that indictment settle uncomfortably while he composed himself. "We know this about the murder in Manhattan," he said in a more modulated voice. "It was conceived. It was proposed. It was approved. It was sponsored. It was planned. It was executed. It was vacuumed. And, when the evil deed was done, it was bathed in lies."

He paused and looked at the crowd which had formed on the steps outside in an effort to hear him. "But evil leaves a stench that even industrial grade disinfectant— make that corporate grade disinfectant— can't fully dissipate. It is the tell tale sign of demonic presence, Satan's personal calling card."

He raised his forefinger and bellowed, "in our generation, it is the same stench we find in America's abortuaries, in her IVF clinics with their infamous Petrie dishes, in her sperm and egg banks, in her plants where hormonal contraceptives are manufactured, in her biotechnology labs where embryos are stripped of their humanity and their parts used to feed the engines of commercial research.

"In an earlier generation, it was the stench of the wanton massacre, the stench of the mass grave, the stench of the concentration camp."

He paused and lowered his voice. "In both, it is the demonic stench of death, the demonic stench of a culture of death, the demonic stench of the rotting corpse of a decomposing society."

He paused and thundered. "This is the power of the lie. The power to kill what lives. The power to hate what loves. It is a power that is once and forever the most seminal force in the arsenal of the world's most evil men."

He looked down at the lectern and thought of Joe Delgado's final moments. He felt a blast furnace swing open in the pit of his stomach. "This truth about the lie forces a demand upon the rest of us – we who would claim to be the People of God. And this demand is nothing less than the central challenge of our time: we have a Divine Mandate to expose the lie for what it is, death's first and final blow."

He paused and lowered his voice. "Because it is always the lie that precedes the death of the innocent child, that *will* precede the planned death of the elderly, that *is* preceding the carefully engineered death of the Christian way of life in our time."

He paused and leaned into the mic and spoke softly. "Just as it was the lie that preceded, and succeeded, the death of a good and faithful husband and father, and a very dear friend to many of us, in Manhattan last week."

The fidgeting stopped. He was now staring into hundreds

of pairs of eyes wide with astonishment. This, he saw, was a John Sweeney his own people did not know.

"Joe Delgado got a good look at this lie. He and I had one conversation about it and agreed to have another the day he was murdered." He permitted himself a small smile. "I assure you I am not breaking the seal of confession. Our discussion was informal and, as I recall, we each had a Michelob in our hands." The laughter was spontaneous and it relieved a suffocating tension which was building quickly.

"Joe worked for a corporation that has chosen to play a decisive role in what is being called man's final revolution, The Life Sciences Revolution. From his position on the inside, Joe came to understand that the goal of the people behind the revolution is first and foremost ideological. They intend to create life in *their* own image and likeness." He paused briefly for effect. "Please see this for what it is. In Genesis I, God creates man in his image and likeness. In Genesis II, man in his hubris, 6000 years later, sets out to create *himself* in *his* own image and likeness.

"My dear friends, this is nothing less than a new Tower of Babel. And heaven's response to *this* provocation will be no different."

He paused. "Make no mistake. This is the work of the devil. His life force is only to nullify in hate what God creates in love. Joe Delgado had a deep understanding of this evil, and he was prepared to risk all to expose it. On the day he died, he showed up in the vestibule before the 6:30 Mass. I was surprised to see him. He attended Mass and received Holy Communion." He chose not to mention his parishioner's request for sacramental reconciliation, lest those listening think he was indiscrete. "After Mass, he asked me if we could have a follow up conversation about his work and certain matters of conscience. He seemed deeply troubled. We agreed to have breakfast Saturday morning after the 8:00 Mass."

He looked down at the lectern and hesitated. He wanted full control of his voice. "Thirteen hours later he was dead."

When he looked up, he was staring into the eyes of Michael

Burns. They locked and held. Burns was pitched forward, fore-arms on knees, rocking intently. John read the signal. He had seen it many times. Michael Burns was in the booster phase. Soon, he would be a heat seeking missile. John saw his sons to his right and Carol on his left. The contrast was stark. Michael Burns, he knew, would own whatever John Sweeney held bound from this pulpit.

"In the second chapter of Matthew," he continued in yet another gear, "we see an angel appearing to Joseph in a dream. He tells him to rise and take the child and his mother and flee to Egypt, and to stay there until he is told it is safe to return. The angel tells him Herod was going to begin searching for the child to destroy him. Sacred Scripture tells us Joseph rose immediately and did as he was told."

He straightened up to his full height. He was suddenly aware of his classmates on the altar behind him. "Joseph Delgado died doing what he was told to do. He died in obedience to what he was taught right here in this very parish, right here in this very school, right here in this very church."

He felt his voice catch. He stopped abruptly. He looked at his friend's widow, and his favorite child, at the other daughters with their husbands. He felt the warmth of tears which stung his eyes. "Joe, like all of us, was taught to confront evil. To call it what it is. To do everything in his power to defeat it."

He suddenly felt the inspiration he had awaited since he mounted the lectern. "Joseph Delgado was taught something else. He was taught that in the work of confronting evil, he would for-ever have an indispensable Ally. An Ally that was fully accessible through the sacraments, through prayer, through recourse to a vir-gin mother. An Ally who also died that truth would prevail in the ultimate confrontation between good and evil. Perhaps this is why on the very day he died, the Holy Spirit moved him to encounter his Divine Ally in the form of ordinary bread and wine."

John stopped to let the prophetic nature of that extraordinary truth settle in the minds and hearts assembled. He resumed in escalating decibel. "Joseph Delgado was taught this. And because he was taught this truth in this very church, he believed it. And because he believed it he was willing to die for it."

He paused and swept the church and lifted his voice another level for the benefit of those outside. "In his death, Joseph Delgado gave life to what our beloved John Paul II wrote in Veritatis Splendor. That once we discover truth, and the transcendent Love who makes of it a gift to mankind, we have an obligation to that truth even to the shedding of blood, if necessary."

He stopped. The church was utterly quiet and there was no discernible movement. "So let us, each of us, ask ourselves this morning, 'Am I prepared to do what Joseph Delgado did? Am I prepared to give my life, if required, to expose the evil of the lie that destroys life in our time?'"

He paused and concluded. "Because, my dear friends in Christ, I *guarantee* you, if we are not willing to confront the evil of the Big Lie *now*, the shedding of our blood will most assuredly be required of us in the days to come."

He turned and walked down from the lectern and up to his seat behind the altar. He sat, head bowed, deep in prayer for several minutes. *Lord, we have failed love. And in failing love we have failed truth. And in failing truth, we have failed your mystical body. Please look with tender mercy upon those of us whom you entrusted with the keys to the kingdom in this age. We are weak and pitiable men, none more so than me. If we are not willing to rouse ourselves, then please send the Holy Spirit to rouse the spirit of your people. Please give them the courage to expose the lie, to defend life, to bear witness to the truth. And, Lord, please have tender mercy on the immortal soul of our own Joseph. Please welcome Joe Delgado into the community of saints. For Lord, if he cannot be counted among them, what hope is there for the rest of us?*

Father John Sweeney stood. The congregation stood. Together they prayed.

# 47

Michael Burns' heart and head were pounding and his palms and arm pits were moist. A small oriental woman of uncertain age and lineage was smoothing the imperfections from her work on his forehead and cheeks. She dabbed a small sponge in a jar of foundation, and ever so carefully accentuated the area around his eyes. Michael moaned softly, "Father, save me. Am I in purgatory?"

"It's starting to feel too close to hell to me, Michael," John Sweeney replied. He was sitting less than eight feet from his friend in the makeup room of the Fox News Channel studio in mid-town Manhattan. In less than 20 minutes, Michael Burns would go live with Grant Strid on his popular prime time access news show that reached over three million viewers nightly. Though it was sleeting outside on 6th Avenue below 48th street, it was exceedingly warm under the hot lights in the small, cramped room.

The journey to this moment had been quite a rollercoaster ride for both men. Fran Delgado had given John Sweeney her husband's diary at the funeral. He in turn had given it to Michael

Burns at the cemetery. A week later Burns showed up at the rectory and announced that Fox News was interested in airing a segment on the mysterious murder of Joseph Delgado and the rumors, now being carried by several overseas media outlets, that he had kept a diary which, reportedly, included an entry about the "high probability" of his murder.

Michael Burns had met twice with the show's Executive Producer, Theresa Ibanez, to answer questions about the diary and his relationship with Joe Delgado. On three different occasions during the past month, he had been given dates to appear for a taping, once at midnight. Each time the taping was cancelled. No explanations were ever given. Michael told John Sweeney he was convinced Fox News was under enormous pressure to drop the story.

The call earlier in the day to go live at 5:00 p.m. caught Michael by surprise. It came in a little after 1:00 p.m., just as he was lying down for a short nap. Within an hour he and his pastor were in a town car heading to New York. They prayed all four sets of mysteries of the rosary on the way up, concluding with the Luminous mysteries, petitioning the Virgin Mother that "all would be revealed" in accordance with God's will.

Theresa Ibanez knocked once and ducked her head into the makeup room. "Almost done, Michael?"

"Stick a fork in me," he moaned.

Ibanez was an attractive woman in her early 40's. She smiled and looked at her unhappy guest and said, "You'll be happy when you see yourself on TV. I'm sure your wife is taping it."

"My wife knows as much about the DVR as I do," Michael replied humorously. "We have to wait until the children drop by to play a movie".

She threw her head back and laughed. At that moment the petite cosmetician thumped Michael lightly on the chest and hooked her thumb in the international gesture for dismissal. The wordless incongruity of the scene made John Sweeney laugh.

"Well, this is familiar territory for me," Michael Burns

lamented. "The butt end of all jokes." He turned to Ibanez and said, "Thank you folks for making me feel like I'm at home."

She chortled and said, "Okay, Burns. Time to meet the executioner."

"What, no last meal?" he asked, feigning offense.

She led both men to a small set in the middle of a large studio. Standing behind the anchor desk stood the host, Grant Strid, talking to a sound technician. Seeing Michael step onto the set, he broke away and moved to embrace his guest. "Michael Burns, man you've got some very, very large cohunes!"

Burns smiled and replied, "So do you, my friend. I had all but abandoned hope this day would ever come."

Strid's face transformed in an instant, and he leaned into Michael's left ear and whispered, "Someday, you and I will go someplace where there are no people, and no phones, and I will tell you a story that will make your hair curl."

Burns looked at him and saw that there was a hint of fear around the edge of his eyes. "Well, let's see if we both make it out of here alive tonight, huh?"

Strid laughed and clapped him on the shoulder. "C'mon up on the riser with me. Let's get you mic'd up."

In minutes Grant Strid was reading his intro for the show in a teleprompter. For an instant, the thought of appearing before a national viewing audience caused Michael to feel faint. He was immediately filled with doubt and dread. He chastised himself severely and set his mind on the resolve button. He heard his name and suddenly he was aware that both of the live cameras in the studio had panned to him. Atop each camera was a red button. Each red button, Michael could see, was on. He looked at the host and smiled and heard himself say, "It's good to be here, Grant."

It seemed to suffice. The host provided another lengthy context for the story about the mysterious death of a New York businessman in his own bedroom over a month ago, and what he believed was a botched New York City Police investigation of it. Then he hunched over his desk and looked at Michael and asked a question for which Michael was unprepared. "Michael," the host began, "was your friend, Joe Delgado, ultimately murdered at the direction of Stef Boros, Henley Siliezar and Geoff Benton?"

Michael's heart felt like it had just exploded. He struggled to compose himself. He looked at the host and said as calmly as he could, "The short answer, Grant, is I don't know. I've asked both the governor of Pennsylvania and the mayor of Philadelphia to request a full investigation by the FBI. That was three weeks ago. We haven't heard anything yet."

"So, you're not buying the official line from the mayor of New York and his police chief?"

"No," Michael replied, suddenly feeling relaxed. He had taken a good lick early, and now the game was on.

"So this was *not* a case of mistaken identity?" Strid probed. "The hit was *not* intended for a drug kingpin from a cartel in Mexico?"

"No," Michael repeated, shaking his head. "Joe Delgado was murdered by people who knew him, who feared him, and who wanted him dead."

"And who might those people be, Michael?" the host circled back.

Michael fixed him with a stare. "Grant, I don't know. That's why the governor and mayor have asked the FBI to get involved. Right now, no one knows, except the people who planned the execution and the man who carried it out."

Strid, chastised, moved on seamlessly. "Michael, let's back up. Tell our national audience about your relationship with Joe Delgado."

"We were friends," Joe said quietly. "We were good friends for over 30 years."

Sensing something moving below the surface, Strid set off a detonator. "Were you good friends at the time of his death, Michael?" he inquired softly.

Michael was taken aback. He looked at the host as though he

knew something he couldn't have known and replied evenly, "No. We had a falling out several months before."

"Over what, if I may ask?"

"Over the contents of his diary and what he proposed to do with it. He wanted to go public with what we both knew, immediately. I wanted to wait."

"And what did you *both* know, Michael?"

"We both attended a plenary session in Manhattan last summer of, ah, people involved in the planning of the Life Sciences Revolution. From his work at HM Healthcare, Joe became aware that a global black market was being set up to traffic in human embryos. This is the prelude to a godless end game where citizens will be, ah, encouraged to wear something the planners are calling *"The Golden Lock"* under their skin above the wrist." He paused. "Once that's in place, it'll set off a global effort to create what they're calling the post human. In fact, Joe Delgado had firsthand knowledge that work has already started in a laboratory overseas." He paused again and added, "It was what he intended to do with this knowledge that got him murdered."

Strid was breathless. He looked into the camera and deadpanned, "Okay, anyone want to take a bathroom break about now?"

He turned back to Michael and said, "Okay, let's unpack that if we can. Tell us about the trafficking in human embryos. Who and what and how and why?"

Michael nodded and answered. "As the developed world ages, having failed to replace itself, it will become prohibitively expensive to provide health care to everyone. The productive sector, the people who are actually working, will have access to new drugs and procedures that will extend their lives, and their productivity. In many cases those new drugs and procedures will come from the tissue of human embryos. Today, the demand for those embryos is being created by venture capitalists around the world tied to biotechnology firms who are working in alliance with government policy apparatchiks."

He paused briefly. "There is a global footrace for what are regarded as premium embryos: from people of notable accomplishment and from graduate students at elite universities. This is driving the price of even the component parts – the eggs and sperm in banks around the world – to undreamt of levels." He paused and added ominously, "It's also doing something else. It's driving demand through the roof. So we have corporations, universities, biotechnology firms, even whole countries, who have entered the race and are demanding more relaxation of government restrictions, so many more human embryos can be created for scientific use. These groups are also in an intense competition to arrange dedicated sourcing of embryo supply in countries like Russia, China and India."

Strid paused and asked. "Michael, you mentioned the *productive sector.* What happens to those of us who are viewed as *un*productive?"

"We'll be weaned off the system, gradually," Michael replied evenly.

"*No* access to health care?"

"Oh, we'll have access. But it won't be the kind we're used to. It'll be the kind of access people in developing countries now have. The services will be quite limited, the waits will be disastrously long, and the cost will be quite high."

"And you say, in the end we'll see something called 'post humans?' What are 'post humans?'"

"Nanotechnology will permit scientists to reconstitute matter at a sub atomic level. This means they will be creating new matter, something that never previously existed from sources never previously discovered. This positions them to play God in their own minds. So they are already at work creating, actually re-creating … us!" He paused and smiled. "The new man— the *post human* man, or the *hybrid* man— will be part computer, part alpha animal species, and part alpha human species. In their vision, he will live for 1000 years, like Scripture says our earliest ancestors did, have replaceable parts, and most importantly, he will be programmable. That's shorthand for no wars."

Strid stared into the camera, but said nothing. Then he turned back to Michael and asked, "What's this *Lock* you mentioned? What's its purpose, and how close are we to seeing it?"

"The Lock is what *they* call it. What it will ultimately be called, I don't know. It will be a micro chip inserted just beneath the skin above the wrist. We'll all have one. We'll have to. It'll carry all our medical records and provide touch access to web-based travel and trade links …"

"What's that mean exactly, Michael?"

Michael backed and filled. "No need for visas or passports for international travel. No need for security screening at airports. Universal web access at home or overseas. Direct transaction capability over the internet, catalogue companies and retail stores. Entrée into selected commercial trading circles around the world." He paused. "Beginning to get the picture?"

Strid nodded. "No chippy, no shirtee?"

Michael laughed. He liked Strid. He was clever *and* authentic. Michael hadn't met too many men like that in the advertising business.

Strid asked, "This is all part of, what are you calling it, a Life Sciences Revolution?"

Michael nodded. "There have been three great revolutions in the last two centuries. The Industrial Revolution, which moved men off the homestead and into the factory. The Cultural Revolution, which moved women out of the home and into the workplace. And the Technological Revolution, which accelerated the pace of life for both men and women in the developed world and made the workplace ubiquitous. All of this paved the way for this Fourth Revolution. The men planning it regard it as the Final Solution, though they are careful to avoid that terminology even among themselves when they gather. But, and I think it's important for your viewers to understand, *this* Revolution is, at root, no less demonic than Hitler's Final Solution." Michael paused and debated how far to go. *Why not?* "This is the ultimate nullification of the Creator. These men have decided they can, and therefore will, improve on God's greatest creative act: His creation of man in His own image and likeness. These men have determined they will create a new and improved version of man, in *their* image and likeness." Michael paused and resisted looking again directly into the camera. "Pretty dangerous stuff, huh?"

Strid exploded in laughter. "What are these people thinking?" he yelled at the top of his lungs. "Are they deranged?"

Michael laughed. "Deranged, no. Deluded, yes."

Strid bore in. "So, this 'Fourth Revolution' … when will it all unfold?"

Michael felt his pulse quicken. "It's already started. We have hospitals, even Catholic hospitals, referring patients and profiting at least indirectly from In Vitro Fertilization clinics, various egg and sperm banks, even cryogenic freezers where about a half a million human embryos are currently being stored."

The host shuddered and paused. "Michael, are we talking conspiracy here?"

"No," he answered quickly. He was warned to avoid the 'c-word' like a plague. He knew from firsthand experience in the advertising business it had a unique power to marginalize even empirical truth. "It's a spirit loosed in our time. It has infected a number of very bright people who see the world the same way, and who think this is their moment to seize it and shape their own vision of what society ought to be."

"Who are these people? Where are they working now?"

Michael was prepared for this question. "They work in senior policy positions in governments around the world, and NGO's like the United Nations, the World Court, the International Monetary Fund. They work at the most senior levels in multinational corporations that believe they have outgrown their host countries and are now citizens of the world. They work in prestigious think tanks and they travel freely throughout the developed world conversing with, and greatly influencing, men of great wealth who desperately want to exchange a portion of their wealth for even greater influence in the affairs of man."

"Michael, bottom line: what is it these people want?" Grant Strid asked in a plaintive tone.

Michael didn't flinch. "They want Gulliver cut down. They want America's dominant role in the world ended. She alone is the last remaining barrier to their plans. When she goes, they will take out Israel and they will abolish the 'myth' from the memory of man."

"What myth?"

"The myth of man as a created being."

"Do they honestly think they can erase what is in our hearts?"

"Yes," Michael replied matter of factly. "They will press for a uniform elementary and secondary school curriculum in developed and undeveloped nations to consolidate their educational gains, as they regard them. They are at work as we speak hyper inflating our economy through fiscal policy, with the Federal Reserve's connivance, so they can devalue the dollar and cut her peg to global currency. They are planning energy standards that will be impossible for America to meet, which will allow them to begin the greatest transfer of wealth among nations in the history of man, through the World Court and the IMF."

Grant Strid was apoplectic. He began to become unhinged. "How in God's name can they get away with this?" he stammered. "They can't steal our country in broad daylight!"

Michael nodded and said, "They believe they can, and will. In fact, there is a movement in the works to develop a shadow Constitution, and have it ready for a new generation of American voters by 2020."

"Shadow Constitution? What's that?"

"A new American Constitution with an entirely different philosophical platform and social objectives," Michael replied. "This Constitution will turn our existing Constitution upside down. The focus will be not on what the government *can't* do for 'we the people', but what it *can, and should*, do."

"Who's financing this crap?" Strid demanded to know.

"Boros," Michael replied without blinking.

Grant Strid looked at Michael with awe. "Michael Burns you are a very brave man."

Michael shrugged it off. "No, I'm not brave," he said softly. "Joe was brave." Then he lifted his voice and looked directly into the camera. "Joe Delgado was the bravest man I've ever known. He died as he lived, speaking truth to power, regardless of personal cost. To me, *that's* a hero."

"Michael," Strid probed gently, "does Joe Delgado's diary confirm all this?"

"Yes," Michael answered without hesitation.

"And where is that diary today?"

Michael was aware his hands were off camera. He wrapped them around the slender, leather bound volume and replied, "In a safe place where no one will pry it away from the people in whose possession it now rests."

"Michael, do you think the government is pressuring the FBI to back off the case?"

Michael hesitated for the first time. He knew a tape of this interview would be playing in a number of corner offices around the world tomorrow morning. Some of those offices would belong to senior government officials who were invested in The Project. "I sincerely hope not, Grant. If Americans can't trust their own government to permit the FBI to investigate the mysterious murder of an American citizen on American soil, then we're even worse off than some people think we are."

Grant Strid used Michael Burns' conclusion as a bridge to his sign off. He praised Michael's courage and patriotism and invited viewers to comment on the show by either calling a number which was appearing on the screen, or e-mailing the address on screen. Then he said good night and asked his viewers to pray for the United States of America.

He and Michael stood and pulled the small black wires out of the inside of their shirts at the same time. Unbound, Strid immediately moved to embrace Michael. "Michael, that was incredible! Just incredible! Theresa, have we ever done anything, anything, even remotely close to that?"

From the shadow, came a woman's voice. "No, never."

Strid looked at Michael with undisguised admiration. "I'll say it again, Burns. You are a brave man." Then he smiled at his executive producer and said, "And, by the way, he ain't too bad in front of a camera either, am I right?"

Theresa Ibanez moved out of the shadows and into the light. "You're a natural, Michael. Very much at ease and very convincing."

"What do *you* think, Padre? Michael asked John Sweeney, who was approaching with a big grin on his face.

"I think you crushed it," he said as he embraced his friend. "I don't think they're ever gonna find that ball."

Michael had heard what he most wanted to hear. His pastor's approbation relaxed him. He felt a tremendous weight fall from his neck and shoulders. An enveloping peace descended from above and entered his heart. It both transcended and transformed the moment. He felt a tinge of ecstasy. In his borderline euphoria he was reminded of what lay ahead and the scriptural verse which best summarized it: 'fools are borne aloft by dreams.' He composed himself and said with studied sobriety, "What happens next, Grant?"

Strid shrugged. "It's up to the viewers. If they demand more, we give 'em more." He paused and added, "I'm expecting a huge response. If that happens, it'll make this thing a major news story. Then the main stream media won't be able to ignore it."

Grant Strid knew his audience. What he didn't know was the power of Henley Siliezar and Geoff Benton, and the new young head of the FCC, Graham Forrester, to persuade the major networks that carrying some major news stories could be inadvisable, particularly with hundreds of billions of dollars in advertising revenue at risk, and certain unspecified licensing issues in play.

A story later circulated, never corroborated, that Henley Siliezar himself drafted a single, four word talking point for senior producers and editors at the elite media outlets in New York, Washington, Los Angeles, London, Paris, Rome, Moscow, Beijing, Hong Kong and Singapore. Reportedly it read, "Right wing conspiracy nuts."

# 48

Jim Gillespie and Maggie Kealey sat in adjacent chairs at a small table in Maggie Kealey's kitchen. They were planning a future.

It was a little after 8:00 a.m. and a light snow was falling. They had been to the 7:00 Mass and were surprised to see Michael Burns there. After Mass they learned of his appearance on national television the prior evening. Father John asked for prayers. Maggie suggested a rosary. Not wanting to arouse curiosity, John Sweeney suggested they retire to the rectory parlor to pray five decades of the joyful mysteries, which they promptly did. After a single cup of coffee while standing in the rectory kitchen, they disbanded: Michael Burns to his home for a long winter's nap, Father Sweeney to his office to prepare the Christmas Mass schedule.

Maggie Kealey had finally begun to make peace with her firing. On this gray wintry morning she was upbeat and Jim thought he knew why. "Your eyes have cleared, Sweetheart. The sparkle is back. You're starting to look yourself again."

Maggie blushed. "Well, you *do* have that effect on women, Doctor."

"You're beginning to feel liberated, aren't you?"

Maggie looked at him with surprise. "I guess I am. I hadn't thought of it that way."

"That was a tremendous burden, Precious," he said while tucking a stray wisp of hair behind her ear. "I don't know anyone who could have carried it as long and as well as you did. I know I couldn't have done it."

"If I did carry it as well as you say, Jim, it was only because you helped me carry it." She looked in his eyes and felt a sudden powerful urge to cup his face in her hands and smother it with kisses. "I will never forget what you did for me."

"*With* you, Maggie. *With* you."

They reached for each other's hands and fell silent. After a long moment, Maggie uncoupled their hands and began rubbing his hands with both of hers, massaging, caressing, stroking.

"You better stop now, honey, or I'm going to have to go to confession," Jim deadpanned.

She dropped his hands immediately as if scalded.

He laughed and said, "I suppose making out on the kitchen floor is out of the question?"

She blanched and said, "You know this is every bit as hard for me as it is for you, Jim."

"It most certainly is *not*," he said with conviction.

She grabbed his forearm and hugged it. "How can you say that?" she asked. "Can't you see I'm madly in love with you?"

"You'd have to be mad to be in love with an unemployed oncologist! Hell, there's never been such a thing. Leave it to me."

"Not for long," Maggie chirped. "I'm a true believer. I believe in happy endings, Jim. I do."

Despite his best efforts, he looked at her with a measure of cynicism.

"Jim, it's all changing. Everything. You'll see."

"What will I see, Maggie?" he asked gently, with a forced smile.

"For one thing, Father John will let us lease the old school and will help us promote our new Natural Family Planning clinic."

"Maggie, we don't even know NFP."

"We'll learn!"

"Where are we going to come up with the money for training and equipment and staff, not to mention rent and utilities?"

"Father John will give us the entire building rent-free for the first year."

He laughed. "Have you asked him?"

She looked up at him coyly. "No. I thought you'd want to do that."

He smiled and leaned over and pecked her on the cheek. "Your faith will be rewarded. I know it will, Maggie."

"*Our* faith, Jim. We *both* have to trust if we want God's blessing on our work."

They fell silent. Jim broke it and said, "What about our *life*?"

She looked at him quizzically.

"Our *life*, Maggie. *Our life together.* How do we secure God's blessing on that?"

"We ask him, Jim. And we behave ourselves," she replied with a smile.

His head dropped to his chest. She reached again for his hands. "It will go quickly, Jim. We can do it. The Immaculate will help us."

Jim lifted his head. She peered into his eyes and saw the pain behind the tears. It aroused a powerful maternal instinct within her to minister to him in every way that a woman who loves a man would minister to him. She fought off the ferocious temptation with a fervent petition to the Virgin Mother of God.

It subsided.

The phone rang. It startled them. Neither of them moved until the fourth ring. Finally, Maggie jumped up and took three quick steps and lifted the receiver off the hook. She caught the call just in time. She heard her name being repeated. She answered and fell silent.

Jim watched her from his chair. He suddenly experienced an eerie intuition tragedy was paying another visit to its favorite address. When he saw her body go limp, he jumped out of his chair and grabbed her before she hit the floor; the phone fell from her hand and bounced once on the linoleum tiles. Jim was alarmed that she was already a dead weight. He immediately feared the worst: that one of her children had been in a terrible accident. He picked up the phone with his left hand and stuffed it in his back pocket. Ever so carefully he laid Maggie on her back on the kitchen floor. He went to the sink and dampened a rag with cold water; he returned, crouched, and applied it to the back of her neck which he held in his left hand.

He grabbed his coat off the back of his chair, folded it and made a head rest of it. He started to pray. He was startled to hear a woman's voice coming from the phone in his back pocket, but made no attempt to reach for it. He heard a click and the line went dead.

It was several minutes before Maggie Kealey began to stir. When she did, Jim Gillespie was staring into the face of an angel, her beauty metaphysical. He loved her beyond his own ability to comprehend or, he feared, endure.

Her eyes opened. She tried to sit up but Jim firmly held her in place. Her eyes were pleading. "Don't talk, Sweetheart. Don't talk," he admonished.

She ignored him. "Jim, I love you."

"I love you too, Honey."

"Jim, that was Jane Sammons."

"Who?"

"Jane Sammons, Bill's wife."

Jim froze. His life seemed suspended between the natural order and the mystical order. He could not bring himself to speak. His heart began to quicken. He immediately realized something decisive had just happened.

"She said Bill was killed in a car accident on Route 95 at 2:00 this morning."

Jim Gillespie felt his spirit leave his body.

"She also said there was a 26-year-old woman in the car. Police said they had both been drinking."

Jim Gillespie's mind began to sort out what he was hearing. He probed her eyes, terrified at what they might reveal. But he did not see what he was afraid he would see. Instead, he saw something he never saw before. Her sparkling blue eyes, always the transcendent accent on her great beauty, radiated a joy that made her look in this moment like a young woman again. He was immediately overcome with emotion and began to cry. She reached for him and pulled him down next to her and kissed him tenderly. He put his arms around her neck and shoulders and held her tight. For several minutes they neither moved nor spoke.

Maggie Kealey suddenly sat up. She reached down and shook Jim by the shoulders, her eyes dancing, and said, "Jim! Let's go see Father John and see how fast he can marry us!"

Jim Gillespie started to laugh. He laughed until he cried again. Then he laughed some more. When he stopped, he jumped to his feet and helped Maggie Kealey to her feet. He embraced her and kissed her passionately. He pulled back and looked at her like a child beholding a gift he dared not dream would ever arrive. She was, he thought, more beautiful in that instant than at any other time in his memory.

True joy, he decided, was the difference. He had never before seen her in a state of pure joy.

Silently, he gave thanks to God.

Then he picked up the phone and called the rectory.

# EPILOGUE

---

M ichael Burns held the broadsheet high over his head as flash bulbs and champagne corks popped. He stood in a large open pressroom on the eighth floor of a center city turn of the century art deco building. The room was filled with family and friends and new employees. They had come to celebrate his new venture, a daily newspaper called *The Thorn*.

Beaming from behind a makeshift podium, Michael Burns kissed Carol and hugged her. He raised a glass of champagne and toasted his wife. "This was Carol's idea," he said with a sheepish grin. "She told Father John, 'For better or worse, okay. But *not* for lunch!'"

The crowd erupted. Father John Sweeney, standing in the back, nodded in confirmation as a number of heads turned in his direction.

"My business friends tell me I've lost my mind. Newspaper stocks are in the dumpster, they say. Papers are folding every day in every city in the country. Why start a newspaper? Go open a restaurant." He paused and leaned into the small mic and intoned.

"I tell them," he paused for effect, "because Carol is a better editor than she is cook!"

Again, the crowd erupted. Someone in the back shouted, "Yeah, but Michael, are you a better newsboy than busboy?"

Another eruption.

Michael sensed the time had come to publicly petition the Lord's blessing. "Father John, would you please come up and lead us in a prayer?"

As John Sweeney walked from the back of the room to the front, Michael said, "My friends, this man is simply the most wonderful human being I've ever known. He stands with his people in good times and bad, and I've had my share of both." The sound of isolated laughter echoed throughout the room. "He trusts his people with the truth. He challenges us to live as we ought and when we sometimes fail, some of us more than others, he consoles us and affirms us and guides us back on the narrow path. He is a great light in the life of my family. And we all just love him."

The room broke into warm, sustained applause for the priest who was visibly surprised, and moved, by the sudden outpouring of affection. John Sweeney arrived at the podium and embraced Michael and Carol. He bowed his head, closed his eyes and waited for the room to settle. Then, without lifting his head, he began to pray, "Lord, we praise you and give you thanks for who you are and all that you continue to do for your creation. We ask your blessing on Michael and Carol Burns and their family. We ask your blessing on this new venture. We ask your blessing on all who will cooperate and collaborate with them in this venture to bring truth to the People of God in our time."

He paused and shifted his weight. "Lord, as you know better than any of us, never before in man's history has truth been under such a relentless and vicious attack. We know at its core, this attack is demonic. We ask your protection for this work and all who undertake it. Protect their families, Lord. Protect their spirits, Lord. Protect their immortal souls, Lord."

He lifted his head and concluded in a voice filled with fervor and resolve, "Lord, let this medium of social communications be a worthy instrument in your hands." He paused for an instant. "Lord, let it be a living memorial to the man whose heroic death inspired it." He paused one final time. "And Lord, please permit this newspaper to be, once and forever, a massive and intractable *thorn* in the backsides of the men whose godless plans for *your* creation summoned it."

A raucous mix of laughter and applause greeted the conclusion of John Sweeney's prayer. Michael immediately hugged him, then grabbed him by the arm and walked him over to an elderly gentleman standing unobtrusively on the edge of the crowd. He introduced the two men without disclosing the other man's name. He referred to him simply as "an angel." The three chatted amiably for several minutes.

When they parted, John asked Michael about the man. "How did you two connect?"

"He called me after he saw me on the Grant Strid show," Michael replied. "We met for dinner in Pittsburg. He told me he'd underwrite the start-up costs for a daily newspaper that exposed the agenda of the men I talked about on the show. He pledged up to $10 million. I checked him out. He's the real deal. Made his money in metals. Doesn't want any notoriety. Just wants to hang in the shadows. He hasn't said one word about editorial. If I didn't know better I'd swear he's an angel incarnate."

"God is good to you, Michael," John suggested.

"He is that, Father. I'm unfairly blessed."

John nodded and smiled, "Now, Michael, think you can keep yourself out of trouble for awhile?"

Michael Burns surveyed the joyous scene and looked intently at the crowd of happy faces which included those of his children and grandchildren. He turned to his pastor and replied, "What's 'awhile,' Father?"

Father John Sweeney laughed and shook his head. It was time to get back to the rectory. He had a 40 hours devotion starting at 7:00 p.m.

. . .

What he once dreamt he now saw.

Jim Gillespie was enveloped in a sense of déjà vu. He stood on the altar, in white tux and tie, transfixed by what awaited him. Suddenly she was moving. In a reversal of stunning proportions, after 20 years, Margaret Ann Kealey was coming to Doctor James Arthur Gillespie.

He beheld her dark hair swirled high like a lush honeycomb crown, her exquisitely bejeweled white satin gown, the thin lace veil unable to contain the unspeakable beauty of the sapphire eyes radiating from within. His heart quickened, then soared.

As she grew closer, the redolence of her skin made him feel light headed. His palms began to moisten in anticipation of her touch.

Suddenly, she was there, standing next to him, extending her arm in his and laying her lovely head on his shoulder. In that instant, Jim Gillespie believed he had entered paradise. His God had delivered into his arms the greatest yearning of his heart, the greatest love of his life. A sense of purifying energy coursed through his body and he felt himself captive to the unfamiliar sensation of pure joy.

Together, they made their way up the steps toward a white marble altar, that seemed in late evening almost enshrouded in mist. On the top step, waiting for them, in brilliant white vestments with a royal blue border, was Father John Sweeney. He wore the luminescent face of a cherub, eyes dancing, arms extended wide in welcome. As they approached, he rushed down to embrace them and his tears fell upon their cheeks and necks. They heard him groan in long awaited consolation and thank God for the wildly improbable summoning of two long-suffering spirits to blessed covenantal union.

Maggie started to cry. She buried her head in Jim's left

shoulder, squeezing his arm tightly. He could feel the tension drain from her body as it nestled against his. She lifted her head from his shoulder and kissed him on the cheek. The smell of her warm, sweet breath enchanted him and caused him to sway gently. John Sweeney reached out to steady him.

There was no music, no photographer, no altar flowers. There was no best man, no bride's maid, no wedding party.

There were no guests.

No one was in the church, save the betrothed, their ordained witness, and a snow plow contractor and his son, whose truck got stuck in a drift and were now standing in the back of the church: wet and cold, hats in hand, pressed into service as required lay witnesses.

It was midnight. On New Year's Eve. It was, officially, the feast of the Solemnity of Mary, Mother of God.

Outside, heaven was raining snow. According to news reports, 28 inches had already fallen in Philadelphia's western suburbs. Another 12 inches were on their way. It was a moment of surreal, pure, quiet, motionless, immaculate whiteness.

The selected readings, the recital of vows, the blessing and exchange of rings, the sacramental rituals of Holy Matrimony and Holy Communion, and the final prayers and blessing all proceeded as though time had stopped, suspended by the power and grace of hope tested and affirmed.

When the sacramental moment ended, Jim Gillespie and his bride walked to the back of the church and thanked the snow plow contractors for serving as witnesses. They opened the front door to the church and looked out at the sea of snow, then turned to each other and laughed. Jim turned to John Sweeney and embraced him. Maggie hugged him too. She wanted to say something but there were no words to convey all that this priest had meant to her over the past 30 years. Instead, she kissed him on the cheek and squeezed him tightly and looked deeply into his eyes in quiet gratitude.

Then Mr. and Mrs. James Gillespie put on their coats and hats and leggings and boots and ventured out into the first moments of the New Year.

The short walk to Maggie's home normally took eight minutes. On this night it would take 24 minutes, counting three deep trips into the drifts by Dr. Gillespie and his bride, only the first of which was unintentional.

They arrived home a little after 1:00 a.m.

Jim made a fire. Maggie got the quilts and pillows.

At dawn, it was still snowing. The Gillespies were awake to welcome it.

• • •

John Sweeney bounded out of the house two steps ahead of Joe McManus and promptly fell laughing into the sand dune. McManus tried to run past him, tripped on a clump of dune grass, and instead fell on top of him. From the second story deck of their new ocean front summer home in Sea Isle, Jim and Maggie Gillespie watched, morning coffee in hand.

"No wonder the Church is in trouble," Jim yelled down, shaking his head in feigned disdain. "It's crawl, walk, run. How many times do I have to tell you two?"

"I would have beaten him to the water, I would have," Joe McManus protested.

"Father John was just trying to let you win, Bishop McManus," Maggie Kealey said in defense of her fallen pastor.

The two men gathered themselves and headed to the ocean, which lay vast and glimmering in the morning sun. It was early June and the water, though cold, was sufficiently bearable for the two friends to walk along its edge.

"Let's head up to the inlet," John suggested as their feet confronted the dying remnants of a small wave. Joe McManus nodded.

They walked in silence for several minutes before John decided to take his friend's temperature. "So, Joe, tell me all about the Church of Cincinnati?"

His friend moaned. "Oh, John, I'm in over my head."

John was ever mindful of his friend's faithful counsel and exhortation during what he regarded as his years in exile. He intended to repay his friend's great kindness by listening and praying, which he immediately commenced to do.

"Tell me about it, Joe," he said softly.

"I'm caught in the middle of the last battle of a generational war, John. I can't win. If I discipline a priest for liturgical abuse or doctrinal error, one side declares victory, the other regroups and either attacks me or goes passive aggressive on me, sometimes both.

"If I try to gently encourage traditional Catholics to tone down their rhetoric on the Life issues, in the interests of church unity, they pounce on me and call me soft on magisterial truth.

"I simply can't win. There's no middle ground anymore," he lamented.

"My mandate to lead the renewal of the Church of Cincinnati is dead in the water. I can't raise money. I can't close and open schools. I can't recruit seminarians. It hasn't even been two years, and I'm already a lame duck. There's open speculation … *even in my own diocesan newspaper* … that I'm in line for a promotion to a larger diocese, or to a big assignment in the Vatican." He paused and bitterly lamented, "They think I'm so obtuse, I can't discern wishful thinking!

"When my head hits the pillow at night, I pray for death. I do, John. I really do. This is a cross of intolerable proportions. I wish to God I never studied in Rome. That put me on the fast track. When I came back I got all caught up in the ecclesial struggle between the moral truth faction and the peace and social justice faction. I tried to chart a course right down the middle. I failed. I know I did. I started playing the game. I watched what our sitting bishops were saying and doing, and more importantly *what they were not saying and doing*, and decided I would follow their lead. I began to position myself for the mitre. I started to play the game. I did, John. I have to be honest. I never told you this but I began to compete, not so openly, with another priest downtown who had similar ambitions. Pretty soon factions formed around our respective candidacies. It became contentious and, in the end, quite divisive to the Church of Philadelphia"

John held his tongue. He was hearing nothing new. The other priest, a man John knew only by reputation, had also received the mitre. He was installed as Bishop of a small diocese in the South, two months after McManus' installation in Cincinnati. John had heard this man was also struggling mightily in his new assignment.

"I think about resigning, John. I do. I have no prayer life. I have no peace. I feel I'm in danger of losing my own faith. I'm starting to question things I never questioned before: fundamental tenets of our faith." He paused and looked at his friend who was quietly keeping pace beside him. "I'm afraid, John. I am. I'm afraid my immortal soul is in jeopardy."

John reached out and grabbed his friend by the shoulders. "Joe, you and I are going to pray you through this. Do you hear me?" He looked deeply into the back of his friend's eyes. "Just as you helped pray me through my Dark Night, I am going to help pray you through yours. This is a moment of purification, Joe. Nothing more, nothing less. Our Divine Lord is preparing you for His work. He wants your heart, all of it. This is the way He works when He wants to accelerate the process. It *is* about the cross. That's the intrinsic message and promise of the mitre. You weren't prepared to carry this cross. So now, for the sake of the faithful in Cincinnati, he's going to prepare you."

Joe McManus lifted his head and let out a cry of gratitude. He turned and embraced his friend. "John, your words went right through me. I actually had chills come over me as I was hearing them. They touched my soul in a place I thought was dead. Praise God! Come Lord Jesus! Create a clean heart in me, O Lord."

With his friend vibrating new life, however temporarily, John resumed walking along the edge of the water. The other man caught up and kept pace. After several minutes of silence, he half turned and said to John, "John, I have to tell you. I am so proud of the priest you've become. I remember well what you went through. I praise God for the work of the Spirit in your life and the full flowering of your priestly ministry." He paused and studied his friend for a long moment."You seem so … content now, John. Are you?"

John nodded. "I am, Joe. I am at peace."

They continued on in silence. The inlet was now in view. They could see pleasure boats of all sizes leaving the back bay and heading out to sea for a morning run. "John, may I ask you a question?" Joe McManus inquired softly, reluctant to intrude on what now felt like a blessed moment.

John turned, his eyes refracting the choppy blue waters, and nodded, "Of course, Joe."

"Outside of prayer, where do you find your peace and your joy?"

"In the privilege of accompaniment, Joe," he replied without hesitation. "In being permitted to walk the walk with the People of God. In helping to facilitate their sacramental encounter with Christ. In watching as he reveals Himself to them, and them to themselves."

He laughed. "Then, following them into the stratosphere of achievement or, more often, the abyss of failure. Being there for them. Being alter Christus *to* them. Earning their trust by challenging them to live as they know they ought. Exhorting them to give themselves away, to accept suffering, to seek the will of God in their lives and to find *their* peace … *their* joy… in *their* crosses."

The bishop affirmed the simple wisdom borne of complex suffering. "God's spirit is alive in you, John."

John laughed. "He's more alive than ever before in humankind. I'm convinced of it, Joe." He stopped and turned to his friend and said, "You know, more and more I'm finding my greatest joy in the joy I see in others who have encountered the person of Christ and want to share Him with all the others in their life. The newness of that never gets old. It is vintage wine forever new and fresh."

McManus nodded gravely as he walked and listened. "And how do you keep your own priestly ministry new and fresh, John?"

"The rosary," John Sweeney replied matter of factly. "I petition grace all day, every day. It doesn't matter what I'm doing. At the start of it, in the middle of it, by the end of it: I'm begging the Immaculate for the grace to do whatever it is I'm doing as well as I can, and I'm offering it to her, regardless of how poorly I may have done it, as gift."

McManus laughed. "I take it she's been accepting your gifts, John?"

John stopped again. He looked at his friend with great kindness. He thought of many things to say. But he chose to only say one of them. "Joe, she's never refused me anything, even my worthless gifts."

McManus nodded and smiled coyly. "So, it is the Immaculate who is your greatest joy, John!"

John Sweeney looked at his friend, the bishop, and said, "Oh, no, Joe. She's my greatest *love*."

They reached the inlet and spent several moments alone with their thoughts as they gazed upon the boats carrying happy families to and from their destinations. Then, together, without a word having been said, they turned and headed back.

# BIBLIOGRAPHY

---

Ratzinger, Joseph Cardinal. *Faith and the Future*. Ignatius Press, 2006.

> This seminal book was first published in German in 1970. Several years ago Ignatius Press received the rights to translate and reissue it. It is everything you would expect from arguably the most brilliant churchman of our time. It examines the state of the Faith in the aftermath of the Council and proposes a philosophical and theological basis for the author's belief that the Church of the new millennium will be "smaller and holier." Some 40 years later, it is stunningly fresh in its observation, its candor, and in its prophetic witness. It is a must-read for every Catholic.

Schoeman, Roy. *Salvation is from the Jews: The Role of Judaism in Salvation History from Abraham to The Second Coming*. Ignatius Press, 2003.

> This is one of the most profound books of our time. The author, a converted Jew, takes the most prophetic elements of the biblical narrative, the theological, the historical,

and the political and wraps them all in the metaphysical, adding an existential bow. *Salvation* not only explains the signature events of the 20th century; it foretells what history will record as the decisive events of the 21st century. Schoeman's signature contribution, however, is his reminder that although the Catholic Church is One, Holy, and Catholic, it is also Apostolic -- and it is precisely that dimension that binds the others. Necessarily, he argues, that Gospel imperative extends particularly to our elder brothers and sisters in the Faith.

Bransfield, Father J. Brian. *The Human Person According to John Paul II*. Pauline Books, 2010.

An incomparable distillation of the thought of the 20th century's most gifted mystic and author, evangelist and statesman. The author, the assistant general secretary for the United States Conference of Catholic Bishops, writes from the perspective of an astute moral theologian and breaks new ground in his analysis of JPII's synthesis of how the Holy Spirit works in a soul through the gifts of the Holy Spirit, the living of the Beatitudes, and practice of the virtues. He also positions the beloved Pope's seminal work, *Theology of the Body*, as an eminently reasonable if deeply philosophical response to mankind's three great revolutions of the 19th and 20th centuries.

Brown, Michael H. *Tower of Light*. Spirit Daily Publishing, 2007. A stunning analysis of recent events in light of the Catholic Church's apocalyptic tradition: The author's proposition that we are living in the back end of "end times" is clear, balanced and profoundly insightful. This work is regarded as his most important work on prophecy since his acclaimed best seller, The Final Hour.

Behe, Dr. Michael J. *The Edge of Evolution: The Search for the Limits of Darwinism.* Free Press, 2007.

> This is the breakthrough work that once and forever revealed the myth that random mutation and natural selection are plausible molecular catalysts for the Darwinian theory of evolution. The author is a professor of molecular biology at Lehigh University and is widely acknowledged to be the father of the Intelligent Design movement.

Phillips, Kevin. *Bad Money; Reckless Finance, Failed Politics, and the Global Crisis of American Capitalism.* Viking Press, 2008.

> A deeply insightful and disturbing analysis of the implosive economic decline of the American Empire: The author, a high profile commentator on U.S. economic and political matters, traces the trajectory of America's three great trading predecessors - Hapsburg Spain, the Dutch Netherlands, and the Colonial British Empire - and chronicles their decline to the inversion of the manufacturing and financial services sectors claim on GDP. This, he argues, is the inerrant signal of end of empire.

Senor, Dan and Singer, Saul. *Start-Up Nation; The Story of Israel's Economic Miracle.* Twelve (a division of Hachette Book Group), 2009.

> The remarkable story of a remarkably entrepreneurial people. The authors, distinguished Israeli and American journalists, plumb the depths of modern Israeli history and culture to explain how a tiny race of people can have such disproportionate impact on the world's economy. The universal military requirement, the primacy of technological education, the resourcefulness of its federal government – are all driving forces behind an Israeli economy that has created one start-up company for every 2000 citizens – a record unrivalled in all the world. But,

as the authors make clear, it is the Chosen People themselves – preternaturally gifted and resourceful and curious and industrious and persevering – that are the principal catalyst for modern Israel's astounding miracle.

Talbott, Strobe. *The Grand Experiment*. Simon & Shuster, 2008. An eye-opening account of the progressive movement's relentless crusade to a "unipolar" government. The author, a former Assistant Secretary of State and *Time* magazine managing editor, begins his account with the "People of the Book" in Genesis and ends with the second administration of George W. Bush. On the whole he's more favorably inclined to the governing principles of the former than the latter. His central thesis is that man, from the very beginning, has yearned for peace and stability. War-like nation states throughout history have continually frustrated that quest. Ultimately, he posits, the only guarantor of enduring peace is the submission of these predatory nation states to a central governing authority.

Haas, Dr. John, publisher, *National Catholic Bioethics Quarterly*. The National Bioethics Center, 2003-2009. America's pre-eminent scholarly forum for the lively exchange of Catholic thought on the bio-ethical issues challenging the nation's 60 million catholics. The editorial board boasts a cross-section of renowned professors of law and medicine at America's finest universities; moral theologians and medical ethicists; bio-ethicists and geneticists. The thought of Dr. Haas, Edmund Pellegrino, William Hurlbut, Robert Sokolowski, Elizabeth Fox-Genovese, Luke Gormally, Marilyn Coors, Susan Schmerler, Mark Johnson, David Mortimer, James Walter, and Tonti-Fillippini were indispensible background reading for the contextual development of several chapters in *Motherless*.

Crichton, Michael. *Speech: Environmentalism as Religion.* Commonwealth Club of San Francisco, California, 2003.

> An extraordinarily prescient address from the acclaimed author of *Jurassic Park*, *State of Fear* and *The Andromeda Strain.* Seven years later, his remarks have proven eerily prophetic. The author argues that the greatest challenge now facing mankind is distinguishing "reality from fantasy."

Soros, George. Speech: "Open Society." Central European University, 2009.

> Mr. Soros advances his polemic for restricting free political discourse, particularly commercial advertising, because it manipulates man's capacity to reason and encourages him to make poor electoral choices.

Scanlon, Father Regis. "America can still be saved." *Homiletic and Pastoral Review*, March, 2009.

> A profound article proposing the Church now faces the prospect of a whole generation of unchatechized Catholics who are "invincibly ignorant" of her moral tenets and are therefore receiving Holy Eucharist unworthily, weakening the communal fabric of the Mystical Body of Christ.

CRS Report for Congress." Stem Cell Research: Ethical Issues." Congressional Research Service, August, 2008.

> A veritable gold mine of information on the landmark debate leading to George W. Bush's decision to resist the voices of "free inquiry" and restrict the commercial use of embryonic stem cells to existing lines.

CRS Report for Congress. "Legal Issues Related to Stem Cell Research." Congressional Research Service, February, 2009.

> A revealing behind-the-scenes account of the impact of

a presidential election on America's legal framework for deciding issues regarding human life.

"The UK Stem Cell Initiative: Report and Recommendations," 2005.

A monumental "white paper" which calls for the accelerated mobilization of the UK's human and financial resources to meet the challenges of the coming Life Sciences Revolution, the report includes a review of "the competitive landscape" to include activity and investment in Australia, Canada, China, Czech Republic, Denmark, France, Germany, India, Israel, Japan, Korea, Singapore, Sweden, Switzerland, and the United States. It calls for a greatly escalated government financial commitment for a scientific endeavor it regards as "decisive" to the future of the United Kingdom.

# ACKNOWLEDGMENTS

I am deeply indebted to my collaborators whose inspiration, talents and insights made this work, modest as it is, far better than it would otherwise have been:

- To my beloved brother Knights of the Immaculate – Sean, Bud, John, Brian and Barry.
- To my gifted designers – Mike Fontecchio and Devin Schadt.
- To my generous and esteemed subject matter experts – Bob Morrison, Dr. Les Ruppersberger, and Joe Tevington
- To my dear friends Dan and Jenn Giroux and Jenn's assistant, Megan Morris. Without their continual encouragement and extraordinary support, I simply would not have even attempted to write this book.

Brian J. Gail is a former college and semi-pro athlete, Madison Avenue ad-man, Fortune 500 senior executive, entrepreneur, and CEO. He is currently an educator and author. Mr. Gail has served on numerous civic boards in his hometown of Philadelphia, including The World Affairs Conference, the National Adoption Center, the William Booth Society, St. Charles Borromeo Seminary, and the Regina Academies. He is a husband, father of seven, and grandfather of five. He and his wife of 40 years, Joan M. Gail, live in Villanova, Pennsylvania.

*Fatherless* was the first of a three volume narrative entitled *The American Tragedy in Trilogy.* Now in its third year of print, it has been translated into several languages and is now selling in Europe and Australia. *Motherless* is the second volume in the series. *Childless*, the third volume, is scheduled for release in the Fall of 2011.